Foreword

Since it first appeared, *Blackstone's Senior Investigating Officers' Handbook* has quickly established itself as a key reference document for those involved in homicide and major incident investigation. It provides a valuable supplement to official manuals that detail the techniques and processes of investigation, but which do not always provide practitioners with an insight into how they are applied in individual cases. Investigations carried out at this level are always challenging and there is often huge pressure both from outside and within the police organization to quickly bring offenders to justice. Media coverage can also be intense, and is usually unforgiving of perceived mistakes in the investigation or a failure to make progress.

The authors have drawn on their considerable experience of leading such investigations to provide authoritative advice and guidance to both existing Senior Investigating Officers and those undergoing training. They present tried and tested ways of applying investigative techniques and of making sense of the complex information that is generated. There will never be any substitute for experience in preparing Senior Investigating Officers for their role, but this book ensures that the lessons that the authors have learned from their many investigations are available to others and I highly recommend it.

Dr Peter Stelfox
Head of Investigative Practice
National Policing Improvement Agency

Sophie's

Blackstone's

Senior Investigating Officers' Handbook

Second edition

Blackstone's

Senior Investigating Officers' Handbook

Second edition

Tony Cook

Andy Tattersall

OXFORD

UNIVERSITY PRESS

OXFORD
UNIVERSITY PRESS

Great Clarendon Street, Oxford OX2 6DP

Oxford University Press is a department of the University of Oxford.
It furthers the University's objective of excellence in research, scholarship,
and education by publishing worldwide in

Oxford New York

Auckland Cape Town Dar es Salaam Hong Kong Karachi
Kuala Lumpur Madrid Melbourne Mexico City Nairobi
New Delhi Shanghai Taipei Toronto

With offices in

Argentina Austria Brazil Chile Czech Republic France Greece
Guatemala Hungary Italy Japan Poland Portugal Singapore
South Korea Switzerland Thailand Turkey Ukraine Vietnam

Oxford is a registered trade mark of Oxford University Press
in the UK and in certain other countries

Published in the United States
by Oxford University Press Inc., New York

First published 2008
Second edition published 2010

British Library Cataloguing in Publication Data
Data available

Library of Congress Cataloging-in-Publication Data
Data available

Typeset by Glyph International, Bangalore, India
Printed in Italy
on acid-free paper by
L.E.G.O. S.p.A.

ISBN 978-0-19-958657-8

10 9 8 7 6 5 4 3 2 1

Contents

APPENDICES

About this Book

This handbook has been designed and produced around our intention to reduce fundamental SIO investigative tasks, processes, procedures, and information into one practical and convenient guide. The challenge was to make accurate and readily accessible reference material available to all those who do, will, or may have to undertake the SIO role whatever their level of experience or rank.

There may not always be sufficient time to locate and research text books, guides, manuals, course notes, handouts, CDs, websites, etc. for that much needed advice. For some, this material may not be available at all and our aim was to produce vital information and knowledge via one handy sized book.

The contents focus upon what an SIO needs to know and do, providing not only guidance and explanatory detail but also genuine case studies to help contextualize the contents and add realism. A 'no-nonsense' approach has been deliberate together with widespread use of simplified bulleted lists and keypoints. Appendices have also been included for ease of reference, such as the SIOs' aide-memoire that quickly summarizes key considerations. In this edition, a further chapter has been added on child death investigation due to the complex and sometimes daunting nature of the subject.

We were delighted at the response to the first edition in terms of feedback and sales, which removed any tide of uncertainty and provided the motivation to produce this updated and improved second version. We are immensely grateful for the wisdom and support of many people who have assisted, and to those who have positively commented on the content and style of the book. Our gratitude must also go to our friends and colleagues at the NPIA such as Peter Stelfox, Michelle Wright, Gary Shaw, Duncan McGarry, Mark Harrison, Sonya Baylis, Sue Yates and Alan Theobald. For assistance with the contents of chapter 14 we are also greatly indebted to three very wise men, namely Russell Wate, John Fox, and Dave Marshall.

Finally, we sincerely hope this handbook proves to be a great source of help and inspiration, particularly to those who are in the highly privileged position of performing the SIO role. Our admiration, respect, and best wishes go to them all.

Tony Cook
Andy Tattersall
Sept. 2010

Glossary of Terms, Abbreviations, and Acronyms

3 Ps Principle	positive, positive, positive
5 × WH + H	Who, What, When, Where, Why, and How
A	Action
A&E	Accident and emergency
ABC	Assume nothing, Believe nothing, Challenge/check everything
ABE	Achieving Best Evidence
ACPO	Association of Chief Police Officers
AKA	Also known as
AM	Action manager
ANPR	Automatic Number Plate Recognition
AO	Authorizing officer
AQVF	Alibi Questionnaire Verification Form
ARV	Armed response vehicle
ASAP	As soon as possible
AYR	Are you ready?
BCU	Basic command unit
BIA	Behavioural investigative advisor
BST	British Standard Time
BTP	British Transport Police
CAP	Common approach path
CASWEB	Casualty bureau weblink
CATCHEM	Centralized Analytical Team Collating Homicide Expertise and Management
CCRC	Criminal Cases Review Commission
CCTV	Closed circuit television
CDI	Communications data investigator
CDOP	Child death overview process
CHIS	Covert human intelligence source (eg informants)
CJA	Coroners and Justice Act 2009
CJS	Criminal Justice System
CIA	Community impact assessment
CLO	Communications liaison officer
COD	Cause of death
CoP	Code of Practice

CPA	Crime pattern analysis
CPIA	Criminal Procedure and Investigations Act 1996
CPS	Crown Prosecution Service
CSC	Crime scene co-ordinator
CSI	Crime scene investigator
CSM	Crime scene manager
CSP	Communication service provider
CT scan	Computed tomography scan
DC	Detective constable
DCI	Detective chief inspector
DI	Detective inspector
DNA	Deoxyribonucleic acid
DO	Disclosure officer
DOA	Dead on arrival
DR	Document reader
DS	Detective sergeant
DSIO	Deputy senior investigating officer
DVCV	Domestic Violence, Crime and Victims Act 2004
ECHR	European Convention for the Protection of Human Rights
ENQS	Enquiries
EO	Exhibits officer
FCP	Forward command post
FIB	Force Intelligence Bureau/Unit
FLC	Family liaison co-ordinator
FLO	Family liaison officer(s)
FME	Force medical officer
FPO	File preparation officer
FSS	Forensic Science Service
GP	General practitioner
GSB	Gold, Silver, Bronze
H-2-HC	House-to-house Co-ordinator
H-2-H	House-to-house enquiries
HMC	Her Majesty's Coroner
HMIC	Her Majesty's Inspectorate of Constabulary
HOLMES 2	Home Office Large Major Enquiry System (version 2)
HOSDB	Home Office Scientific Development Branch
HP	High priority
HRA	Human Rights Act 1998
HSE	Health and Safety Executive
HTA	Human Tissue Act
HVM	High volume messaging

HWG	Homicide Working Group
I	Indexer
IAG	Independent advisory group
IED	Improvised Explosives Device
IIMARCH	Information, Intention, Method, Administration, Risk assessment, Communications, Health & safety
INI	Impact Nominal Index
IO	Investigating officer
IP	Internet protocol
IPCC	Independent Police Complaints Commission
ISP	Internet service provider
IT	Information technology
JDLR	Just Doesn't Look Right
LCN	Low copy number
LCU	Logistics Coordination Unit
LEA	Law enforcement agency
LKP	Last known position
LP	Low priority
LSCB	Local Safeguarding Children Board
M	Message
MACP	Military aid to civil power
MAPPA	Multi-Agency Public Protection Arrangements
MBWA	Management By Walkabout
MI	Major Incident
MIM	*Murder Investigation Manual*
MIR	Major incident room
MIRSAP	Major Incident Room Standardized Administrative Procedures
MIRWEB	Major incident room weblink
MIT	Major investigation team
MLAT	Mutual Legal Assistance Treaty
MLO	Media Liaison Officer
MLOE	Main lines of enquiry
MO	Modus operandi
MOD	Manner of death
MOU	Memorandum of Understanding
MP	Medium priority
MPS	Metropolitan police
MRI scan	Magnetic resonance imaging scan
mtDNA	Mitochondrial DNA
N	Nominal
NABIS	National Ballistics Intelligence Service

NCPE	National Centre for Policing Excellence
NCTT	National Community Tension Team
NFLMS	National Firearms Licensing Management System
NHS	National Health Service
NID	National Injuries Database
NIIS	National Investigative Interviewing Strategy
NIM	National Intelligence Model
NMAT	National Mutual Aid Telephony
NOS	National Occupational Standards
NPIA	National Policing Improvement Agency
NPT	Neighbourhood policing team
OBT	Obtain
OCU	Operational command unit
OIC	Officer in charge
OIOC	Officer in overall command
OM	Office manager
OP(s)	Operations
PACE	Police and Criminal Evidence Act 1984
PAS	Police Advisers Section
PCC	Press Complaints Commission
PCSO	Police community support officer
PDF	Personal Descriptive Form
PEACE	P—Preparation and planning E—Engage and explain A—Account clarification and challenge C—Closure E—Evaluation
PII	Public interest immunity
PIO	Police incident officer
PIP	Professionalising Investigations Programme
PLS	Place last seen
PM	Post mortem
PNC	Police National Computer
PolSA	Police search adviser
PPE	Personal protective equipment
PPU	Police Public Protection Referral Unit
PST	Police Search Team
R	Receiver
RA	Raise action
RADI	Rotation, acceleration, deceleration, impact
RARA	Remove, avoid, reduce, accept
RAT	Routine Activity Theory

RI	Re-interview
RIPA	Regulation of Investigatory Powers Act 2000
RRAA	Race Relations Amendment Act 2000
RVP	Rendezvous point
SA	Specialist adviser
SAD CHALETS	Survey, Assess, Disseminate, Casualties, Hazards, Access, Location, Emergency services, Type of incident, Safety
SAG	Specialist advisory group
SAM	Scent article method (police dogs)
SCAS	Serious Crime Analysis Section
SCD	Serious Crime Division
SGM+	Older type of DNA analysis
SIDS	Sudden infant death syndrome
SIM	Senior Identification manager
SIO	Senior investigating officer
SIODP	SIO development programme
SMARTER	(Actions/tasks) Specific, Meaningful, Achievable, Realistic, Time-Specific, Ethical, Recorded
SMT	Senior management team
SOC	Specialist operations centre (NPIA)
SOCA	Serious Organised Crime Agency
SOCAP	Serious Organised Crime and Police Act 2005
SOCO	Scenes of crime officer
SOE	Sequence of events
SOP	Standard Operating Procedure
SPoC	Single point of contact
SUDC	Sudden unexpected death in children
SUDI	Sudden unexpected death in infancy
SUDICA	Sudden unexpected death in infants, children and adolescents
SW	Significant witness
TB	Tuberculosis
TFST	Take further statement
TI	Trace/interview
TIE	Trace/interview/eliminate
TRIAD	Triad of Injuries
TST	Take statement
UF	Unknown female
UKBA	United Kingdom Border Agency
UM	Unknown male
UU	Unknown unidentified
UV	Unidentified vehicle

ViSOR	Violent and Sex Offender Register
VODS	Vehicle online descriptive search
VOIP	Voice over internet protocol
WCU	Witness Care Unit
YJCE	Youth Justice and Criminal Evidence Act 1999

Medical Glossary: Useful Medical Terminology

Abrasion An injury caused by blunt force rubbing off the epidermis, which is the most superficial layer of the skin. In everyday language, an abrasion would be called a graze.

Acute Appearing rapidly (eg acute inflammation), but not necessarily severe as in common usage (contrast with chronic).

Aetiology Cause of a disease.

Agonal Terminal event, immediately prior to death.

Allele A viable DNA coding that occupies a given *locus* or position on a chromosome.

Allele frequency A measure of the relative frequency of an allele showing the genetic diversity of a population or the richness of its gene pool.

Amnesia Loss of memory.

Anaemia Abnormally low blood haemoglobin concentration.

Angina Spasmodic pain.

Ante mortem Before death.

Anterior The front.

Anoxia Lack of oxygen.

Ascites Abnormal accumulation of fluid in the peritoneal cavity.

Asphyxia Consequence of suffocation or mechanically impaired respiration.

Atheroma Furring up of the arteries by fatty deposits.

Atherosclerosis Atheroma causing hardening of the arteries.

Atrophy Pathological or physiological cellular or organ shrinkage.

Autoeroticism Arousal and satisfaction of sexual emotion within or by oneself through fantasy and/or genital stimulation.

Autopsy Synonymous with necropsy or post-mortem examination (autopsy = 'to see for oneself' rather than relying on signs and symptoms).

Bacteraemia Presence of bacteria in the blood.

Biopsy The process of removing tissue for diagnosis, or a piece of tissue removed during life for diagnostic purposes.

Bruises An injury caused by blood leaking out of damaged blood vessels beneath the skin. Fresh bruises are usually red, blue, purple, or black, depending on their depth beneath the skin. Though they may enlarge or become more prominent at a variable rate after infliction, this does not help to age a bruise. Later, the bruise may turn brown, yellow, green, or orange due to release of pigments from the breakdown of red blood cells. The earliest change is said to be yellow discolouration, which does not usually occur until approximately 18 hours after the bruising began. However, such changes are quite variable, and may be subjected to observer variation. The rate of healing in a bruise is very variable, but it is not unusual for a bruise to be visible several weeks after it was inflicted. Consequently, it is not possible to be accurate about the ageing of bruises.

Cancer A general term, in the public domain, implying any malignant tumour.

Carbon monoxide A colourless, odourless, very toxic gas, formed by burning carbon or organic fuels.

Carcinoma A malignant tumour.

Cardio Denoting relationship to the heart.

Cardiovascular Pertaining to the heart and blood vessels.

Carotid Arteries of the neck.

Cellulitis Diffuse acute inflammation of the skin caused by bacterial infection.

Cerebral Pertaining to the cerebrum which is the main portion of the brain occupying the upper part of the cranium.

Cervical Pertaining to the neck, or cervix—neck of womb.

Chronic Persisting for a long time (eg chronic inflammation) (contrast with acute).

Cirrhosis (liver) Irreversible architectural disturbance characterized by nodules of liver cells with intervening scarring, a consequence of many forms of chronic liver injury, especially alcohol abuse.

Clot (blood) Coagulated blood outside the cardiovascular system (contrast with thrombus).

Coagulate Become clotted.

COP Codes of Practice

Comatose Unconscious and unresponsive to stimuli (note that a comatose person is not dead).

Comminuted (fracture) Bone broken into fragments at fracture site.

Complications Events secondary to the primary disorder (eg complicated fracture involves adjacent nerves and/or vessels; cerebral haemorrhage is a complication of hypertension).

Congenital Condition attributable to events prior to birth, not necessarily genetic or inherited.

Congestion Engorgement with blood.

Consolidation Solidification of lung tissue, usually by an inflammatory exudation; a feature of pneumonia.

Contusion Bruise that results from rupture of the blood vessels.

Coronary Pertaining to the heart.

Cranium The skull or brainpan.

Cyanosis Blueness of the skin, often due to cardiac malformation resulting in insufficient oxygenation to the blood.

Degeneration Disorder characterized by loss of structural and functional integrity of an organ or tissue.

Diffuse Affecting the tissue in a continuous or widespread distribution.

Disease Abnormal state causing or capable of causing ill health.

Dorsal Pertaining to the back.

Duodenum First portion of the small intestine.

Ecchymoses Any bruise or haemorrhagic spot, larger than petechiae, on the skin (may be spontaneous in the elderly, usually due more to vascular fragility than to coagulation defects).

Ectopic Tissue or substance in or from an inappropriate site (but not by metastasis).

Effusion Abnormal collection of fluid in a body cavity (eg pleura, peritoneum, synovial joint).

Embolus Fluid (eg gas, fat) or solid (eg thrombus) mass mobile within a blood vessel and capable of blocking its lumen.

Emphysema Characterized by the formation of abnormal thin-walled gas-filled cavities; pulmonary emphysema—in lungs; 'surgical' emphysema—in connective tissues.

Erosion Loss of superficial layer (not full thickness) of a surface (eg gastric erosion).

Erythema Abnormal redness of skin due to increased blood flow.

Fibrillation Fluttering of the heart not controlled by motor nerves.

Focal Localized abnormality (contrast with diffuse).

Gangrene Bulk necrosis of tissues; 'dry' gangrene—sterile; 'wet' gangrene—with bacterial putrefaction.
Haematoma Local swelling filled with effused blood, generally the result of a haemorrhage or internal bleeding.
Haemorrhage Heavy bleeding.
Histology The study of the form of structures seen under the microscope. Also called microscopic anatomy, as opposed to gross anatomy, which involves structures that can be observed with the naked eye.
Hypostasis The settling of blood in the lower half of an organ or the body as a result of decreased blood flow, or poor or stagnant circulation in a dependent part of the body or an organ.
Hypoxia Reduction in available oxygen.
Hyoid bone Small U-shaped bone at base of tongue.
Hypertension High blood pressure.
Iatrogenic Caused by medical intervention (eg adverse effect of a prescribed drug).
Idiopathic Unknown cause; synonymous with primary, essential, and cryptogenic.
Incision A wound inflicted by an instrument with a sharp cutting edge.
Infarction Death of tissue (an infarct) due to insufficient blood supply.
Ischaemia An inadequate supply of blood to an organ or part of it.
Intestine The membranous tube that extends from the stomach to the anus.
Intra Prefix meaning within.
Lacerations An injury caused by blunt force splitting and/or tearing the full thickness of the skin.
Lesion Any abnormality associated with injury or disease.
Lividity Post-mortem discoloration due to the gravitation of blood.
Malformation Congenital structural abnormality of the body.
Malignant Condition characterized by relatively high risk of morbidity and mortality (eg malignant hypertension—high blood pressure leading to severe tissue damage; malignant neoplasm—invasive neoplasm with risk of metastasis) (contrast with benign—relatively harmless).
MBWA Management by walkabout
Membrane A thin layer of tissue which covers a surface or divides a space or organ.
Meninges Thin membranous covering of the brain.

Mitochondrial DNA Mitochondrial DNA is inherited from the mother and offers reduced discriminating factors.

Myocardium The heart muscle.

Parallel intradermal bruising A specific pattern of injury caused when a linear object strikes the body, leaving parallel tracks of bruising in the skin either side of the impacting surface.

Petechial haemorrhages Minute (pin-like) haemorrhages that occur at points beneath the skin. Classic signs of asphyxia usually found in skin and eyes, the conjunctivae, sclera, face, lips, and behind the ears—due to raised venous pressure.

Phalanx Any bone of a finger or toe.

Posterior The rear, behind.

Post mortem After death.

Prognosis Probable length of survival of injury or disease.

Pulmonary Pertaining to the lungs.

Putrefaction Decomposition of soft tissues by bacteria and enzymes.

Rancid Having a musty, rank taste or smell.

Rigor mortis A rigidity or stiffening of the muscular tissue and joints of the body after death.

Sclerosis Induration or hardening.

Septic Infected.

Septicaemia Chronic blood disease characterized by blood poisoning.

Sharp force injury Sharp force injuries are traditionally divided into incised wounds and stab wounds. In an incised wound, the length of the wound on the skin surface is longer than the depth of the wound, which implies that the wound was inflicted with a slashing or cutting motion. Incised wounds may be made by a variety of weapons, including broken glass and sharp plastic, as well as the more obvious bladed weapons.

In a stab wound, the length of the wound on the skin surface is shorter than the depth of the wound, which implies that the wound was inflicted with a stabbing or thrusting motion.

Shock State of cardiovascular collapse characterized by low blood pressure (eg due to severe haemorrhage).

Signs Observable manifestations of disease (eg swelling, fever, abnormal heart sounds).

Steatosis Fatty change, especially in the liver.

Stroke Sudden or severe attack, with rupture of the blood vessel.

Suppuration Formation of pus; a feature of acute inflammation.

Tamponade (cardiac) Compression of the heart, and therefore restriction of its movement, by excess pericardial fluid (eg haemorrhage, effusion).

Thorax Chest.

Thrombo Denoting relationship to a clot.

Thrombophlebitis Venous inflammation associated with a thrombus.

Thrombus Solid mass of coagulated blood within cardio-vascular system.

Toxaemia Presence of a toxin in the blood.

Toxicologist An expert in the knowledge and detection of poisons.

Toxin Substance having harmful effects, usually of bacterial origin by common usage.

Trachea The windpipe.

Trauma Wound or injury.

Vascular Pertaining to or full of blood vessels.

Vein A vessel which conveys the blood to or towards the heart.

Venereal Transmitted by sexual intercourse or intimate foreplay.

Ventricle One of the two lower cavities of the heart.

Viraemia Presence of a virus in the blood.

Vulva The external genital organs in the woman.

Note: Bruising, abrasion, and laceration may all occur in the same injury. Both abrasions and lacerations heal initially by formation of a scab over the injury. The scab is made from blood and tissue fluid which forms an early protective layer, then new skin grows over the damaged area. The new growth of skin may heap up as the healing progresses, forming scar tissue. Both abrasions and lacerations can form scar tissue, but in general the more severe the injury, the more likely it is to scar. Therefore since lacerations are by definition deeper than abrasions, they tend to scar more and take longer to heal. Early scar tissue is red and shiny. It becomes silvery within a week or so, then gradually shrinks, becoming firm and white within a few weeks to months. The rate of scar tissue formation and resolution is very variable—some scars may be invisible within weeks, while others may persist for years.

Chapter 1
Role of the SIO

No greater honour will ever be bestowed upon an officer or a more profound duty imposed on them than when entrusted with the investigation into the death of a human being. It is their duty to find the facts, regardless of colour or creed, without prejudice, and let no power on earth deter them from presenting these facts to the court without regard to personality.

AE Westveer, 'Managing Death Investigation', US Dept of Justice, Federal Bureau of Investigation, (1997)

1.1 Introduction

Few things catch the public imagination quite like murder, rape, armed robbery, violent assault, or kidnap. They are the staple diet of news reporting and documentary or investigative journalism. This has led to a huge range of representations and perceptions of the senior investigating officer (SIO), circulated not only through news media but also television drama, films, and books. Paradoxically, in a society that is apparently fearful and horrified about the levels and extent of serious crime, it also provides fascination and entertainment. The classic murder mystery 'whodunit' conjures up images of Sherlock Holmes or Agatha Christie's Poirot or Miss Marple; more recently ITV's SIO Detective Superintendent Jane Tennison (*Prime Suspect* series). In fictional drama the SIO is often depicted as a shrewd and calculating individual who outwits their adversaries almost single-handedly. This 'sexing up' and fictional portrayal of the role does not always depict the gritty realism and true representation of the complexities of major crime investigations and the change in the make-up of societies though fortunately similar successes are achieved (there is a national annual detection rate of around 80 per cent for detecting homicide, source: Home Office, 2008).

The Senior Investigating Officer (SIO) is the detective in overall charge of a dedicated team of specialist officers and staff who are tasked with the investigation of a serious crime. The profile of an SIO has, however, seen some fundamental changes over the past few decades. Professionalism, dedication, and total commitment are the underpinning principles of the role with the pursuit of objectivity and transparency—a 'search for the truth' not 'search for the proof' (A Sanders and R Young, 'From suspect to trial', in M Maguire, R Morgan, and R Reiner (eds), *The Oxford Handbook of Criminology*, 4th edn (Oxford: Oxford University Press, 2007), 953–89.

The SIO now has to contend with a lot more issues that extend far beyond just catching the offender. One commentator said, 'crime investigation has become extremely professional and is now a high grade intellectual pursuit' (Sir Brian Cubbon (1981) during the review into the 13 murders committed by the notorious 'Yorkshire Ripper').

Major investigations, however, can and do place huge demands on any individual tasked with the role of leading them. There are procedural pressures, internal and external politics, psychological and physical challenges, information overload, uncertainty, an expectation to work long hours, emotional pressures (of the crime itself and those of the victim's families and public expectations), high levels of accountability, and sometimes intense media spotlight. SIOs remain wholly accountable for their actions and decisions made during an investigation. Not only families of victims, their relatives, and friends, not to mention communities, place an enormous amount of moral obligation, hope, and trust in their performance of the role. The judicial process plus internal and external review mechanisms all add to this extreme amount of accountability. The SIO is also held answerable to agencies such as the Independent Police Complaints Commission (IPCC), the Criminal Cases Review Commission (CCRC), the Coroner, the media, and not least, their own organization and team.

While being an SIO is not the easiest of career moves in the police service, it certainly is by far the most rewarding. This first chapter will now go on to outline the various requirements and elements that make up the role, the key skills required, and some other useful pointers and topics to consider against the contents of other chapters in the handbook.

KEY POINT

The police, through the SIO, accept responsibility for the investigation of serious crime on behalf of society and in particular victims and their family and friends.

1.2 Challenge of Homicide and Major Incident Investigation

The investigative task has almost certainly become more challenging. Criminals are far more sophisticated, and media reporting, programmes, documentaries, and shared information on social networking sites render the public far more aware of what goes on behind the scenes. It is also not uncommon for misinformation to be deliberately fed into an enquiry by top-tier criminals to deliberately mislead an enquiry team (eg through informant/CHIS networks), or for people to deliberately shield offenders or destroy, falsify, or conceal evidence, and some even admit to crimes they haven't committed, for example to take the blame for someone they know.

Modern-day barriers have to be overcome, such as the reluctance for the public to 'get involved' or 'grass people up'. Criminal, human rights, and health and safety legislation has made detective work more thorough and professional in meeting stringent requirements and conditions. Conversely, new legislation also provides fresh powers and options for securing evidence as an investigative tool. SIOs must fully exploit these and they must remain part of the toolkit of an effective detective. The Regulation of Investigatory Powers Act (RIPA) 2000 is a good example of how the government provided clarity for law enforcement agencies mounting covert operations, previously authorized by High Court judges.

The role of the SIO is to make sure the investigation is professionally planned, managed, and structured and that all information is carefully analysed and investigated. The SIO must ensure urgent enquiries are conducted, and if it is a murder case, establish the identity of the victim and arrange next-of-kin notification and support. They must piece together and make sense of everything around them and become the main collection point for a mass of information which must be scrutinized, interpreted, and prioritized often very quickly. Solvability factors must be determined and false trails avoided. There must be an ability to absorb details, interpret the crime scene(s), and analyse every available facet and piece of intelligence in order to make sound decisions. The investigational lead must demonstrate flair and be decisive, thorough, and impartial while avoiding tunnel vision, personal bias, or single mindedness.

KEY POINT

Some cases can pose more of a challenge than others, eg:

- lack of victim/offender close contact (eg firearms involvement);
- badly contaminated or disturbed crime scenes;
- unidentified/badly decomposed or skeltonized victims (including 'no body' cases);
- high risk victims;
- multiple victims and series crimes;
- cases that attract widespread public/media attention;
- drug- or gang-related murders (including so-called 'bad on bad' cases);
- absence of criminal pointers (eg poisoning cases);
- low or high information investigations;
- critical incidents.

1.2.1 Responsibilities for the modern-day SIO

SIOs are now more likely to face new challenges rather than the more traditional types of enquiries. Although there are often specialist units and individuals trained and experienced to deal with some matters that feature in the list, it is nonetheless worth considering that the modern-day SIO has to be prepared to be called upon to deal with a whole new range and variety of incidents and major crime investigation. The following list outlines some examples of the modern-day challenges that an SIO might be expected to manage:

- deaths in health-care settings;
- so-called 'honour killings';
- serious case reviews (eg homicide of parent with child survivors);
- complex SUDC/SUDI deaths (sudden unexpected deaths of children and infants);
- IPCC tandem enquiries (eg police complaints);
- Article 2 deaths and corporate manslaughter (eg HSE investigations);
- prison deaths;

- drug-related deaths;
- gang-related firearms/drugs criminality;
- rise in threat from terrorism;
- mass fatality atrocities, accidents, and disasters;
- mental health related enquiries;
- road traffic collisions involving dangerous driving or manslaughter;
- stringent time scales for preparing case papers for trial (eg pathology reports and delayed tests, telecommunication enquiries, CCTV capture and viewing, forensic results;
- crimes involving trans-European or international victims and offenders;
- rise in kidnapping, blackmail, and extortion type offences, child sexual exploitation, abduction, human and drug trafficking;
- increase in use of social networking sites, global communication, travel networks, and 'virtual' communities to facilitate criminality.

1.2.2 Consequences of unsolved major crime

The SIO role becomes even more important when considering the consequences of not solving major crimes such as homicide. Such unsolved crimes, for example, hamper the healing process for the family and friends of victims and have a significant effect on communities and all aspects of confidence in the criminal justice system.

The increased fear factor and loss of public trust and confidence may in turn lead to a reluctance in people coming forward and assisting investigations. This fear can be heightened in communities that are blighted by gangs (eg drugs, guns, and 'turf-war' type criminality) where unsolved cases can create a self-fulfilling prophecy because of the lack of confidence or reliability in the police response and investigation process. Major crime investigations such as homicide are also very costly in terms of public finance and police resources when cases drag on due to being unsolved. Of course, the most important consequence of an unsolved homicide is that dangerous criminals and killers remain free to commit additional offences or become victims themselves in retaliation attacks.

Every case begins with a different level of solvability and probability of arrests. Some cases are easier to solve (eg those in which the offender is still at the crime scene when officers arrive), while others are more difficult or seemingly impossible to solve (such as those where there are no witnesses, no intelligence, nor forensic evidence, and no suspects can be identified). Nevertheless, if the SIO and their enquiry team perform to a high standard and ensure correct procedures are followed the likelihood of solving a case always significantly increases.

1.2.3 High-profile cases

Occasionally incidents occur that become very high profile. They are almost certainly in a league of their own due to the added publicity, scrutiny, and accountability. Notable cases, such as the Soham murders of Holly Wells and Jessica Chapman (Operation Fincham), Damilola Taylor, Stephen Lawrence, James Bulger, the 5 × Ipswich serial murders committed by Steve Wright (Operation Sumac), and even the Madeline McCann missing child investigation in Portugal all became very high profile and of huge public and media interest. Such cases are an extreme test of any police force and SIO. Retaining a very tight focus and dealing with potentially vast amounts of good or bad information, managing major media intrusion, and maybe even unwelcome political influences and interference are some of the added challenges that have to be dealt with.

KEY POINT

Multiple and serial or mass murders are fortunately quite rare. They can occur in one incident, for example when Thomas Hamilton entered a classroom in Dunblane in 1996 and shot dead 16 children, a schoolteacher, then himself. There was also Michael Ryan, who killed 15 people in Hungerford in 1987.

Sadly most multiple killings actually take place within families—often a parent killing a spouse and children and then committing suicide. Serial killings, however, tend to take place over a period of time, eg Harold Shipman and Peter Sutcliffe. Some may even act in pairs, such as Ian Brady and Myra Hindley, or Fred and Rosemary West.

1.2.4 Official categories of murder

These are included here for referral purposes and useful to know when official categories of murder, as defined by the Association of Chief Police Officers (ACPO), can become labels themselves, although they tend to relate more to resourcing than decision making. They are outlined in the table below.

Category A+	A Cat A homicide or other major investigation where public concern and the associated response to media intervention are such that 'normal' staffing levels are not adequate to keep pace with the investigation.
Category A	A homicide or other major investigation which is of grave concern or where vulnerable members of the public are at risk; where the identity of the offender/s is/are not apparent, or the investigation and the securing of evidence requires significant resource allocation.
Category B	A homicide or other major investigation where the identity of the offender(s) is not apparent, the continued risk to the public is low, and the investigation or securing of evidence can be achieved within normal resourcing arrangements.
Category C	A homicide or other major investigation where the identity of the offender(s) is apparent from the outset and the investigation and/or securing of evidence can easily be achieved.

There are also 'major incidents' and 'critical incidents' to consider. An SIO has to decide whether the circumstances should be categorized as such at a very early stage in the proceedings. If this is so then other people such as gold commanders (see below) may also become involved and are highly influential in decisions that affect the investigation. This is because these are the types of enquiry that lead to public inquiries and mistakes can affect the reputation of the organization.

1.2.5 Major incidents

The term 'major incident' is one that has been used for many years by all the emergency services and is well understood in terms of the nature of the response required to manage it. Early diagnosis of this category of incident will help facilitate the deployment of sufficient resources to deal with it effectively. Typically this category refers to major disasters, mass casualties, or fatalities and matters of very large proportions. A major incident may be declared by any of the emergency services that consider the criteria to have been satisfied, and there will often be large-scale and combined resources mobilized. This may be on a standby basis or otherwise.

Major incidents are about consequences such as the requirement to provide additional resources or special arrangements to deal with it. It is the impact and effects of an incident and how it affects an organization that will trigger the decision. Declaring a major incident will:

- initiate plans;
- mobilize and alert support organizations and other emergency services;
- release resources;
- focus attention;
- drive the operational response;
- combine the multi-agency response;
- define a command and control structure.

It is a useful term to understand because once an incident is declared a 'major incident' all those initially responding to the incident should apply the same emergency management principles. This means in theory there should be a consistent approach to the initial response from not just all the emergency services, eg fire and ambulance services, but any other police forces in England, Wales, and Northern Ireland that may become involved. This means scene management layout and terminology is agreed to ensure there is a clear methodology and approach to every incident so categorized.

The initial period of any major incident will inevitably be chaotic as the situation unfolds, but in practice the police and other emergency services should quickly begin to meet to discuss immediate priorities and implement an appropriate management or command structure as required for the incident. It is vitally important the SIO becomes involved in any such meetings, discussions, and decision-making processes to ensure the needs of the investigation are always considered, so that all evidence recovery opportunities remain of utmost importance.

> The ACPO definition of a major incident is:
>
> 'Any emergency that requires the implementation of special arrangements by one or all of the emergency services and including local authorities, for any large-scale incident involving a large number of people and/or casualties, enquiries (media), resources, etc.'

KEY POINT

An SIO is likely to be appointed in a major incident for the overall management of the investigation where there is potentially any criminal liability associated with the circumstances. Where fatalities occur in circumstances other than wholly natural situations the SIO will act on behalf of the coroner to inquire into circumstances of the death(s). As a result of that investigation prosecutions may follow. These duties may also be in order to support other agencies such as the Health & safety Executive (HSE), Department of Transport, Civil Aviation Authority etc. In such cases the SIO must always be included in major incident management decisions from the very outset.

1.2.6 Critical incidents

This term is used to describe any incident where police action may have an impact on the confidence of the victim, their relatives or their wider community. There are very few murders or serious crimes that will not fall within the category of a 'critical incident'. Nevertheless early recognition and declaration as such will ensure that the correct command and control procedures are quickly put into place to assist the SIO to deal with the incident effectively. The term 'critical' may apply to a local area and/or the whole force.

Critical incidents cover a wide range of possibilities and are, however, not just restricted to murders. Other incidents, such as the arrest of a group of asylum seekers, or an assault of a member of the public by a police officer captured on CCTV, may be included.

Critical incidents can often be the consequences of major incidents. The event itself would be dealt with operationally, using the policy, procedures, and tactics laid down for each type of incident. A critical incident response incorporates this but also enables an SIO to deal with all the other aspects of the incident and the context in which it occurs. Critical incident tactical options help to decide upon and address broader family and community issues, deal with long-term consequences, and make clear who is responsible for what. Clear lines of control and accountability are inherent in critical incident response.

The decision to declare a critical incident can take place at any time during the various phases of the investigation being dealt with by the SIO. This identification may occur as early as the first telephone contact received by a call taker. It may also be applicable and appropriate when the incident is being attended either by the initial officer or later by an SIO. It is a means of focusing on all the 'critical' aspects of an incident and consequent decision making, for example how family liaison support or community impact are to be addressed and managed effectively.

> The ACPO definition of a 'critical incident' is:
>
> 'Any incident where the effectiveness of the police response is likely to have a significant impact on the confidence of the victim, their family, and/or the community.'

Deeming an incident 'critical' requires a large application of common sense and sound professional judgement. If it is decided that this term should apply, then the circumstances should be given special priority and consideration as to how they are then managed and subsequently controlled.

It is useful to clarify the specific terms contained within the definition. 'Effectiveness' in this context means the measure of the professionalism, competence, and integrity of the initial response—for example if a victim's family are aggrieved at the level of family liaison support they have received. The term 'significant impact' can be felt by individuals, the family, and/or community and the SIO must make a decision as to whether to declare a 'critical incident' on this basis. 'Confidence' refers to any long-term effects on police relations that may have resulted from the incident.

It may be that as an investigation develops and more information becomes available, the decision to deem the incident 'critical' will need to be reviewed and monitored continually. An example is when community confidence in the police response or the incident itself drops and becomes critical as the investigation develops. As a general rule certain circumstances can become a critical incident at any time, ie in the present, future, or even something from the past.

1.2.7 Ethical standards and integrity

Recent developments within the police service have given new prominence to issues of ethical policing. Notably, a number of high-profile cases of serious corruption and miscarriages of justice have placed questions of ethics and integrity in the spotlight. While such high-profile cases undoubtedly have the potential to damage the reputation of the police, less serious, but more common, breakdowns in integrity also impact negatively on service delivery and public perceptions.

The SIO has the ultimate responsibility for ensuring that an investigation is conducted to the highest degree of moral and ethical standards. A lack of professional behaviour may adversely affect the reputation of the police in a big way; high-profile miscarriages of justice have resulted in far-reaching consequences. Public confidence in the police depends on vast amounts of honesty, transparency, and integrity. Statutory regulation such as the Human Rights Act 1998 and the Police and Criminal Evidence Act 1984 (PACE), and new bodies such as the Independent Police Complaints Commission (IPCC), have provided the public with new ways of challenging police activities and actions.

A concept known as 'tunnel vision' or 'closed mind syndrome' must be avoided at all costs. This refers to the theme of the SIO focusing on an individual (or individuals) and excluding other possibilities that are excluded from their thoughts. Such a narrow-minded approach does not bode well for the integrity of an investigation and will always attract criticism. The effects can also produce miscarriages of justice, corruption, incompetence, and expensive court and human costs. This is why any investigation must begin and end with an independent search for the truth and attempts to verify what is to be relied upon as evidence.

KEY POINT

An SIO must never allow themselves or their team to become overly obsessive about a particular line of enquiry or individual(s) leading to a lack of objectiveness, tunnel vision, and biased thinking. This happened in the West Yorkshire Police 'Ripper' enquiry when the SIO became fixated on letters and recorded messages from a person claiming to be the killer (a.k.a. 'Wearside Jack'). Placing too much reliance on this individual led the SIO and his team on a wild goose chase; meanwhile the real killer Peter Sutcliffe continued to slaughter more female victims. In March 2006, some 28 years later after he had penned his first letter, hoaxer John Humble was convicted of perverting the course of justice and sentenced to eight years in prison.

Potential leaks of information can also be a problem for major enquiries, particularly when there is heavy media attention. This must be stopped or prevented as it can lead to serious complications at a later stage and potentially compromise aspects of an enquiry, especially sensitive ones. Close monitoring must be applied, with strong words of advice, guidance, and support from the management team to all those who are necessarily exposed to, perceived 'at risk' with, or in receipt or possession of information that must be treated with the strictest confidentiality. Swift intervention must be made if and when leaks are discovered or guilty parties identified.

Any misguided concepts based around 'noble cause corruption' must remain in a bygone age. There simply cannot be any attempt at cutting corners and it is ultimately the SIO who will be held accountable in a court of law or public inquiry. While creativity and innovation among entrepreneurial detectives should be encouraged, the SIO must not support deception of any kind that breaches the law. This is different from finding legal solutions to legal problems, which is a core skill of an SIO.

During a serious crime, investigation officers should be under much closer supervision through regular briefings and a highly controlled and regulated administrative system (ie HOLMES2). All activity should be allocated, monitored, reviewed, and supervised with a far greater degree of scrutiny. This should produce a robust and almost inquisitorial system. These integrated administrative controls are there to ensure compliance with legislation and correct guidelines and procedures.

An investigation must at all times stand the test of high integrity and ethical standards. What the SIO must aim for is the right result with the right processes. The consequences of not adhering to rules and being caught out are far reaching. If uncorrected, poor procedures can and do become acceptable. Being exposed by the media, which have their own creative ways of investigating public bodies, is the newest threat. A TV documentary in 2003 entitled 'Secret Policeman', in which a BBC undercover journalist named Mark Daly infiltrated the police as a recruit to expose and covertly record racist behaviour, is one such example.

1.2.8 Managing expectations

High expectations can become burdensome and difficult to manage. Communities and relatives and friends of victims can and do place extra demands and high hopes on the SIO and their team. Pressures from within a force hierarchy can also mount up, depending on the political issues at stake. Morale and motivation levels can become dislodged by under-delivering against expected, anticipated, or promised results.

Strategically, of course, an SIO may decide to hold back success stories or news. This could be to prevent alerting suspect(s) that vital evidence has been obtained, or to avoid building false hopes, or creating 'closed minds' from vital sources of information and/or communities. If this is the case, these details should be fully recorded in the policy file so they can be justified later.

Generally it is far easier to under-promise and over-deliver. Only when absolutely certain and positive about a fact, or piece of information, or update should it be publicized. Predictions, estimates, and speculative promises are to be avoided at all costs, and events or information should not be allowed to assume a greater importance than they are worth. Good results can be spoilt when they fall short of what has been a suggested higher outcome. In the long run, failing to meet expectations will almost certainly undermine an SIO's authority and reputation through loss of confidence and trust.

It is worth remembering what one of the objectives of an investigation is: to conduct a thorough investigation (see paragraph 2.2). Sometimes the result of an investigation may not be the outcome that people hoped for or expected, ie a person believed to be responsible is proved not to have been. Yet investigations must be completed with total professionalism, so that any positive outcomes can also include conclusions that will help make sense of and understand events and circumstances. In some cases this can even lead to a finding that no criminal offences have occurred. Resisting the temptation to take the easy option and being thorough will give an SIO the peace of mind that in the future their conclusions or decisions will not come back to haunt them. Any one of several notorious miscarriages of justice prove the point.

Case Study—Leslie Molseed murder

Lesley Molseed was an 11 year old girl from Rochdale, Lancashire who was murdered on 5 October 1975 on Rishworth Moor, between Rochdale and Ripponden in West Yorkshire. She had gone to the local shop to buy a loaf of bread and her body was found three days later. She had been stabbed 12 times and the killer had ejaculated on her. Stefan Ivan Kiszko (1952–93) a British tax clerk of Ukranian parents served 16 years in prison after he was wrongly convicted of the sexual assault and murder in an infamous miscarriage of justice. He died shortly after being released on appeal. Ronald Castree was eventually found guilty of the crime through DNA evidence on 12 November 2007.

1.3 Definitions of SIO Role and Key Skill Areas

The *Murder Investigation Manual*, or 'MIM' (NCPE (2006), 25–6), states:

> An SIO is the lead investigator in cases of homicide, stranger rape, kidnap or other investigations.
>
> This requires the SIO to:
>
> - Perform the role of officer in charge of an investigation as described in the Code of Practice under Part II of the Criminal Procedure and Investigations Act 1996.
> - Develop and implement the investigative strategy.
> - Develop the information management and decision-making systems for the investigation.
> - Manage the resources allocated to the investigation.
> - Be accountable to chief officers for the conduct of the investigation.
>
> The role of the SIO in a homicide investigation is potentially one of the most complex and challenging positions within the police service. It combines two elements—the role of investigator and the role of manager, each of which must be performed to the highest standards.

As indicated in this definition, SIOs are appointed to deal with all manner of criminality, not just homicide. Incidents such as 'fail to stop' road traffic collisions are often SIO led, requiring essentially the same skills plus extra specialist knowledge. Any crime that involves a degree of complexity may attract the appointment of an SIO. The list is not exhaustive and could include murder and attempted murder, child abuse, arson, corporate manslaughter (eg the Hillsborough football stadium disaster in South Yorkshire in 1989), terrorism, missing person enquiries, kidnap, abduction, blackmail, serious and organized crime, robbery, aggravated burglary, high-value thefts, Health and Safety Executive investigations, mass public disorder, linked serious crimes, hate crime, drugs and people trafficking, critical incidents, or anything that might attract a high level of media attention.

The SIO role is not restricted to the police service and can be used by other bodies such as the Independent Police Complaints Commission, the Serious Fraud Office, the Department of Trade and Industry, or the Serious and Organized Crime Agency.

1.3.1 Role under the Criminal Procedure and Investigations Act

There are added responsibilities contained within the Criminal Procedure and Investigations Act 1996 (CPIA) which deal with criminal investigations. The Act sets out duties for the SIO (and police in general) not simply in relation to disclosure but also in respect of the investigation itself. Section 23 refers to the treatment and retention of material and information generated during such an investigation, and sub-s 23(1)(a) contains a requirement for the police to carry out an investigation. It states:

> . . . that where a criminal investigation is conducted all reasonable steps are taken for the purposes of the investigation, and in particular all reasonable lines of enquiry are pursued.

Part II of the CPIA Code of Practice defines the officer in charge of an investigation and what their role is within the Act:

> Is the police officer responsible for directing a criminal investigation. He is also responsible for ensuring that proper procedures are in place for recording information and retaining records of information and other material in the investigation.

1.3.2 Making use of specialists, experts, advisers, and agencies

The omni-competent murder investigator of yesteryear has now been replaced by someone who can call upon and utilize the services of a wide range of specialists and experts. They are also supported by tactical advisers, colleagues, and outside experts performing diverse roles and functions. It is generally accepted that one person alone cannot solve complex cases by themselves. Thus the skill of the SIO is not only to draw upon their own experience, knowledge, and intuition but also to work closely with specialists and experts and form a strong team, not only to carry out important activities and progress workload but also to assist with and produce useful suggestions and solutions. For example, a forensic pathologist can provide an enormous contribution to scene interpretation and establishing cause of death, while experienced crime scene managers/investigators can advise on scene preservation and forensic evidence recovery. There are others who can be called upon such as ballistics experts, fire investigators, PolSA (police search advisors), geographic and behavioural investigative profilers and advisers, trained analysts, media liaison officers, crime scene managers and coordinators, forensic specialist adviseors, interview advisers and co-ordinators, community awareness and family liaison specialists, palynologists, entomologists, gastroenterologists, forensic anthropologists, and so on.[1]

There are also various units and departments within each force or agency, such as specialist firearms units or covert operations teams, which can provide advice and guidance on a variety of techniques and tactical options. All these, at some stage, may form part of the SIO's team, and it is worth remembering a golden rule of not stepping outside the boundaries of one's own training and expertise.

Nationally there are the National Police Improvement Agency (NPIA), Homicide Working Group, databases such as CATCHEM (Centralized Analytical Team Collating Homicide Expertise and Management), and SCAS (Serious Crime Analysis Section). Other peers and SIOs can also be called upon to discuss issues, make suggestions, test theories, examine work, review assumptions, etc. Peer group reviews (which can be themed at particular topics) are extremely useful and allow a group of experienced and knowledgeable people to gather and contribute fresh perspectives and second opinions. The sharing of ideas with others not assigned to the case provides useful independent objectivity. Formal reviews may also be carried out by an appointed team.

1.3.3 SIO skills and National Occupational Standards (NOS)

According to a police research paper (M Smith and C Flanagan (2000), 'The Effective Detective: Identifying the skills of an effective SIO' (Home Office Police Research Series, Paper 122), the SIO requires a combination of three different categories of skills. These come under the headings of (1) investigative ability, (2) management skills, and (3) knowledge levels. They can be sub-divided as follows.

[1] An SIO can access 24-hour advice on 'experts' through the NPIA Specialist Operations Centre who can be contacted on 0845 000 5463 or <http://www.soc@npia.pnn.police.uk>.

1. Investigative ability

- Investigative competence (eg formulating lines of enquiry).
- Appraisal of information (eg interpreting and assimilating information, challenging assumptions, checking relevance).
- Adaptation (ie being flexible to changing circumstances).
- Being strategically aware (understanding the consequences of actions).
- Innovation (being creative to achieve aims).
- Possessing strong problem-solving and decision-making skills.

2. Management skills

- People management (eg team building, staff support and development, interpersonal skills, ability to manage conflict, and valuing diversity).
- General management (leadership, motivation and morale, communication and interpersonal skills, personnel matters, discipline, resource management, administrative competence, dealing with welfare matters, development of staff, budgets, eg forensic and overtime, monitoring health and safety compliance and equal opportunities policy, multi-agency partnership development).
- Investigative management (planning, decision making, consultation, delegation, quality assurance function, chairing meetings, attending public forums, briefing senior commanders, providing team (de)briefings, etc).

3. Knowledge levels

- Maintaining an awareness of covert and pro-active tactical options.
- Maintaining theoretical knowledge. An SIO must keep up to date with their own continuous professional development and conscientiously seek out and soak up any new knowledge and information that is applicable and useful to the role (eg changes in legislation, legal procedures and definitions, national guidelines and doctrines, crime types, police powers, new forensic procedures, investigative and technological advances, nationally disseminated good practice and learning points, strategic debrief reports, definitions of offences, points to prove, potential defences, new case law, rules of evidence, public and community awareness, national and local force policies, priorities and performance targets, National Intelligence Model, Management of Police Information guidelines etc).

- Adopting a 'learning culture'—continually expanding mental ability of self and others and challenging existing knowledge by replacing it with better and improved information. Creative thinking is important and helps the SIO try to look at things from a different perspective and produce alternative methods and possibilities to achieve results. This is an area that requires an SIO to liaise, collaborate, and share information with other SIOs and peers alike.

KEY POINTS

- Examples of legal frameworks that apply to most investigations and must become well understood by an SIO are: Police and Criminal Evidence Act 1984 (PACE), Human Rights Act 1998 (HRA), Regulation of Investigatory Powers Act 2000 (RIPA), Criminal Procedure and Investigations Act 1996 (CPIA), Youth Justice and Criminal Evidence Act 1999, and Coroners and Justice Act 2009. There are others such as the rules relating time-scales for providing evidence for court cases and sentencing guidelines which the SIO may have to explain to families of victims.
- 'Creative thinking' requires an investigator to look at problems from another perspective and question any assumptions and to query the validity of theories and information. Investigators must continually question whether there might need to be another possible explanation for material gathered (*Practical Advice on Core Investigative Doctrine*, (ACPO Centrex, 2005), 23).
- Essential areas of knowledge would include: knowledge on making policy decisions, major incident room (HOLMES2) procedures, in particular the handling, prioritizing, and filing of messages, actions, TIE subjects (Trace, Interview, Eliminate—discussed in chapter 6), significant witnesses, an awareness of forensic examination techniques in relation to crime-scene examination, body recovery issues, suspect handling, and all procedures relating to exhibit recovery, packaging, storage, examination, and review, including 'fast-track' forensic tests; an awareness of setting strategies for main lines of enquiry, such as telecommunications data, interviewing witnesses and suspects, passive data collection and analysis (eg CCTV footage); disclosure requirements, etc.
- Adherence to procedural requirements and justification of policy decisions are usually what an SIO gets cross-examined on in court proceedings (ie also known as 'trial by policy decision'); whereas historically cross-examination used to focus upon the honesty and integrity of detectives' activities and behaviour.
- There are always unpredictables in a major investigation and an SIO has the overall discretion to allow and cater for variations and flexible decision making.

1.3.4 MIRSAP requirements

The Major Incident Room Standardized Administrative Procedures, or MIRSAP, manual (NCPE (2005), 18–20) outlines roles and responsibilities of the SIO relating to the functions of the Major Incident Room (MIR). These have been standardized to ensure that in linked or series cases there are standard practices across forces. These include the following.

Checklist—MIRSAP requirements

- Responsibility for the investigation of the crime, which includes ensuring, in liaison with other senior officers as necessary, that an incident room with appropriate resources is set up.
- Regular assessment of work levels to maintain appropriate staffing to process documentation at all stages of the enquiry.
- In consultation with the management team, agreeing time scales for review and progress of actions and documents (ie priorities, allocation, and referral). Actions should be reviewed at regular intervals together with the office manager and action manager to decide whether they should remain as referred, or be allocated or filed.
- Logging all decisions in a policy file against signature.
- Reading and making decisions as to the filing of all documents.
- Determining and communicating current lines of enquiry, TIE parameters, SOE (sequence of events) parameters, scene(s) parameters, house-to-house (H-2-H) parameters, personal descriptive form (PDF) completion parameters, unidentified nominal and unidentified vehicle policy, other relevant investigative strategies, eg forensic, media.
- Briefing and debriefing of all staff (including hot-debriefs within first 24 hours of the investigation).
- Ensuring early engagement of the Crown Prosecution Service (CPS) and counsel where necessary.
- In line with the National Intelligence Model (NIM), ensure there is an ongoing process to review accrued covert material with a view to further dissemination and sanitization. This information is to be placed in force intelligence systems in a timely manner.

1.3.5 Becoming a successful and accredited SIO

In his book *Mapping Murder* (2005) a UK leading criminal psychologist named David Canter writes:[2]

> I would suggest that the most successful detectives are those who adjust their strategy to the style and patterns of movements of their prey. This can range from a broadband sweep to a narrow concentration of the most likely option. The successful ones, though, seem to me to be those that choose a strategy that reflects the criminal psychological and geographical journey. The success of the detective depends on how well s/he shapes a mental map and hunting strategy to match that of their prey, the criminal. The search for clues, and routes to the culprit, are built upon their experiences and idiosyncratic mental maps of the sorts of murders that can occur. The strategy that is put in place to solve the murder draws on the recognition by the detective of what sort of murder s/he is dealing with. The 'map' that SIOs have in their heads of the sort of murders that are possible is what distinguishes them from the inexperienced detectives.

Building on the words of David Canter, any newly appointed or aspiring SIO must therefore acquire a broad base of knowledge and experience to equip them for this challenge.

1.3.6 Training and PIP accreditation

The National Policing Improvement Agency (see <http://www.npia.police.uk>) currently designs and develops national investigative training and development programmes, assessment strategies, and registration protocols. These all form part of the Professionalising Investigations Programme (PIP) and are what create the career pathway for SIOs based upon the National Occupational Standards (see <http://www.skillsforjustice.com>).

Core and specialist programmes are part of the essential and desirable criteria, full details of which are available on the aforementioned NPIA website and contain the following.

Core programmes

- Initial Police Learning and Development Programme (IPLDP)—PIP level 1

---

[2] D Canter, *Mapping Murder: Walking in a Killer's Footsteps* (Virgin Books, 2005).

- Initial Crime Investigators Development Programme (ICIDP)—PIP level 2
- Initial Management of Serious Crime Course (IMSC)—PIP level 2
- Detective Inspectors Development Programme (DIDP)—PIP level 2
- Senior Investigating Officer Development Programme (SIODP)—PIP level 3.

Specialist training programmes

- Management of Linked Serious Crime (MLSC)
- Serious Crime Intelligence Management of Information Technology and Resources (SCIMITAR)
- Specialist Child Abuse Investigator Development Programme—PIP level 2
- Investigative interviewing
- Family liaison
- Sexual offences investigation
- Child death investigation
- Counter terrorism SIO.

There may also be further programmes and courses which the individual feels could be useful as part of their ongoing personal development for the role (eg exhibits training, forensic crime-scene examination, etc). Some form of academic study may also be useful to improve research skills and gain an appreciation of useful scientific methods and theoretical expertise.

The Senior Investigating Officer Development Programme (SIODP) is aimed at level 3 accreditation. However, the clear aspiration for SIOs is to gain a good grounding at levels 1 and 2 of the PIP programme and work up to becoming experienced and trained for major enquiries at level 3. A programme of continuous professional development for maintenance of training and skill levels is then required once this has been attained and is necessary to remain a fully accredited SIO.

On-the-job experience alongside an established SIO is perhaps an obvious learning opportunity that should not be overlooked. This is complementary to the specialist knowledge that is essential for the role.

KEY POINT

Lord Byford, in his report on the famous 'Yorkshire Ripper' case stated that the skill base of SIOs must be kept at a high level. Lord Byford stated that the 'career development, training and selection of senior detectives needs to be improved so that they have the management skills to meet the demands of an enquiry on the Ripper scale' (Sir L Byford, *Report into the Yorkshire Ripper Enquiry* (Home Office, 1981).

1.4 Performing the Role

1.4.1 Preparation

There is nothing quite like a a mobile phone ringing at the bedside in the early hours of the morning, or while on call to get the pulse racing and adrenalin flowing. An on-call SIO has to be extremely well prepared for any incident they may have to go and take charge of or respond to, and be capable of springing into action immediately and hitting the ground running. An acronym to remember is AYR:

A Are
Y You
R Ready?

Once in charge an SIO may be engaged on an enquiry for a considerable length of time, putting in continued and prolonged hours, particularly in the early stages of an investigation. Going long periods without proper rest and food, together with pressure and time constraints, are not going to help when making critical decisions. An SIO therefore has to be well prepared and ready for the challenge that lies ahead and able to manage themselves very effectively in order to perform the role.

Checklist—Basic kit for on-call SIOs

- A fresh 'daybook' open at the first page, with a pen ready to record all information, details, and decisions immediately right from the initial contact.
- A fresh policy book (and spare).
- A 'grab' or 'go' bag containing all the essential items.
- Essential documents such as the makings of a paper management system (which would include such things as list of actions raised, paper actions themselves, and major incident (MI) write-up sheets and message forms).

- Mobile phone and charger (and/or spare battery).
- List of important contact numbers (eg CSI, pathologist, FLO, etc).
- Police airwaves radio, spare battery, and list of channels.
- Suitable and/or practical clothing (including change of top).
- Freshly prepared food/sandwiches (in the fridge) ready to go.
- Drink (eg cold drink or thermos flask).
- Street map (eg A–Z or satellite navigation system).
- Torch/batteries.
- Outdoor warm and waterproof clothing.
- Clipboard or similar armed with plenty of writing/drawing implements.
- Forensic suit/mask/gloves/overshoes.
- Vehicle full of fuel and ignition keys at the ready (or other suitable transport, or driver).
- Identification badge and/or ID card (name, rank, and role should be easily recognizable), plus spare ID card for prominent display in the SIO's own vehicle if it is going to be left at or near a crime scene).
- Money/change for emergencies.
- The SIOs' handbook in readily accessible place.

KEY POINT

Some clothing or dress may be suitable for a cold outdoor scene in the early hours of the morning, but might not be ideal for facing cameras or briefing a large team of officers who have just come on duty later in the day. It is sensible to have something to change into if an SIO does not know how long they are to be engaged, which is normally the case.

1.4.2 Stress, resilience, and time management

There is little doubt that performing the role of SIO requires lots of energy and stamina because it is extremely demanding work. In some circumstances it may be necessary to be at an incident room long before others arrive and then still be there when they have all gone home. It is therefore essential, no matter how experienced or professional a person is, to be able to manage physically and mentally under extreme pressure, sometimes fatigue, and probably stressful circumstances. A good manager and leader is someone who can plan to avoid these things and recognize when the symptoms of not coping creep in.

Stress of course is counterproductive. It should be distinguished from enthusiasm and energy, which an SIO does need. Stress is a personal thing which manifests itself in different people in different ways, eg loss of patience, arguing, inappropriate behaviour. It is useful to recognize when this occurs in order to find out what is causing the problem, and deal with it.

Tiredness and taking on too much personal responsibility is one cause of stress. Having a strategy for resilience is a means of managing it, eg the early appointment of a deputy and/or someone to hand over to in order to take some rest. A good analogy for the SIO's office in the early stages of a major investigation is the resemblance to a doctor's surgery, ie lots of people queuing and waiting to speak urgently one-to-one with the SIO and which must be managed effectively. An open-door policy is fine, but sometimes it needs to be kept shut in order to get on with some work or hold a meeting in private. There must be some control over who comes into the office and how long they stay, ensuring other supervisors down the chain are not being by-passed.

Having a reliable and trustworthy deputy increases resilience, as does a good 'loggist' and/or 'staff officer' such as an experienced detective sergeant (who should also monitor the SIO's welfare), and also the delegation of key tasks to relieve the pressure—nominees can arrange searches and team tasks, conduct cascade briefings, manage duties and vehicles, etc. The SIO cannot perform all tasks and speak to everyone, nonetheless they should ensure that whoever has delegated responsibilities reports back at regular intervals. This can be at stipulated times, such as formal or informal briefings.

Time management is critical. The SIO must be ruthlessly efficient at getting the most out of their available and valuable time. Some matters and certain individuals can conspire to commandeer an SIO's time. The SIO should be prepared to be firm and polite to people, pointing out that some things are more pressing and urgent and others may have to wait until later on. Investigative strategy meetings (eg forensic, telecoms, media, etc) need to be carefully managed and controlled to ensure an agenda is properly prepared and rigidly adhered to. Planning a day properly is important, whilst appreciating that things can and do change at a moment's notice. Being unable to complete all necessary and urgent tasks may lead to stress and increased pressure levels. The SIO does not always need to be present at everything—a decision about who should attend a post mortem, for instance, needs to be balanced against other critical responsibilities.

KEY POINT

Creating time to sit quietly and enjoy personal space to gather thoughts without interruption is good practice. Hamsters on a wheel are sensible enough to stop when they get tired, and they go and lie down. The SIO should sometimes think likewise and put something back into their immune system, occasionally resting, even if only for a short space of time.

It is equally important to have a means of mentally 'switching off'. Sometimes it may be difficult to concentrate on anything else while heading up a fascinating and challenging enquiry. Creating time to focus on unrelated matters and pursue other interests at a suitable point can significantly help reduce mental anxiety and stress. It refreshes the mind and clears the head ready to refocus and can be a useful coping mechanism.

Personal health management is fundamentally important, being mindful of energy and stamina levels and workloads. It is a bad idea to go without proper food and nourishment for long periods—if so energy levels can and will inevitably drop. All human beings have physiological needs and SIOs are no different (see Maslow's 'hierarchy of needs' cited in chapter 3). Being on duty for hours on end with a short turn-around time, no matter how keen and committed a person is, will not help when having to make rational decisions. This may be something highlighted later by a review team or external enquiry, particularly if things go wrong. It also applies to other staff, who must be considered in terms of their working time directives. The SIO does not want added fatalities from, say, road traffic collisions on the way home after long shifts due to fatigue and tiredness. This includes specialists such as crime scene investigators, who often spend a lot of time at scenes, maybe battling against the elements and under difficult conditions.

1.4.3 Diversity

SIOs must ensure that investigations take full account of issues relating to race, gender, ethnic origin, religion, culture, age, disability, sexual orientation, nationality, or place of abode. There can be no place for personal prejudices, discriminatory behaviour, or stereotyping of any sort whatsoever. It is particularly important that assumptions are not made which prejudice the facts and narrow the scope of the investigation at the outset. Full account must be taken of vulnerable persons, whether that vulnerability is the result of learning difficulties, trauma, or any other circumstances.

Breakdowns in community relations can occur if there are perceptions of alienation, distrust, negativity, and loss of confidence in the police. This will ultimately lead to a loss of public assistance and non-receptiveness. The SIO must be alive to these issues and deal with them in a Community Impact Assessment document and/or policy file. There must be a clear strategy for how to communicate with hard-to-reach groups in order to maintain public confidence and build a relationship with the enquiry team. Community focus and the benefits of equality and diversity in operational delivery are major components of most policing strategies and is important to community and race relations (see ACPO, 'Equality, Diversity and Human Rights Strategy for the Police Service' (Home Office, 2009)).

The Race Relations Act 1976 (as amended by the Race Relations Amendment Act 2000) defines direct and indirect discrimination and victimization. The Act places general duties on public authorities to take the lead in promoting race equality and preventing unlawful discrimination. The SIO in the leadership role must remain committed to diversity and ensure it is demonstrably part of an enquiry's culture and philosophy. Positive action must be taken against such issues as inappropriate language or behaviour at all times, with adequate mechanisms in place to monitor compliance with the Act.

> Institutional racism as defined by the Stephen Lawrence Inquiry Report, 6.34:
>
> 'The collective failure of an organisation to provide an appropriate and professional service to people because of their colour, culture or ethnic origin. It can be seen or detected in processes, attitudes and behaviour which amount to discrimination through unwitting prejudice, ignorance, thoughtlessness and racist stereotyping which disadvantage minority ethnic people.'

1.4.4 Human Rights Act 1998

The HRA was introduced to safeguard citizens from intrusions by the state into their privacy and rights. There are, of course, legal powers that allow law enforcement agencies and some other public bodies to breach these rights under certain provisions. There are important fundamental rules that must be clearly understood and followed to ensure that investigations, particularly when covert methods are used, are conducted without unnecessary or unfair intrusiveness.

The most relevant articles are:

Article 2: *Right to life*
Article 5: *Right to liberty and security*
Article 6: *Right to a fair trial* (often cited by defence lawyers during court trials)
Article 8: *Right to respect for private and family life*
Article 14: *Prohibition of discrimination.*

Human rights principles that must be incumbent on all investigations are outlined in the table below.

Justification (legality)	There is a justifiable interference with an individual's Article 8 rights only if it is necessary and proportionate for some activities to take place. If this is for any covert breach of human rights then it must be necessary in the circumstances of the particular case for one or more of the statutory grounds in s 28(3) of the RIPA 2000, eg to prevent or detect serious crime.
Necessity	Means that the breach is the only or most suitable way to achieve the objective and that other alternatives have been considered.
Proportionality	If the breach is necessary, the activities must be proportionate to what is sought to be achieved by carrying them out. This involves balancing the intrusiveness of the activity on the subject and others who might be affected by it against the need for the activity in operational terms. The activity will not be proportionate if it is excessive in the circumstances of the case or if the information which is sought could reasonably be obtained by other, less intrusive, means. All such activity should be carefully managed to meet the objective in question and must not be arbitrary or unfair. This is a matter that must remain under scrutiny and constant review to comply with the principles of the Act.

Collateral intrusion	This refers to the risk of intrusion into the privacy of persons other than those who are directly the subjects of the investigation or operation (third-party damage). Measures to reduce or eliminate unnecessary intrusion into the lives of those not directly connected with the investigation or operation should be included and dynamically monitored. This may include certain sensitivities in a particular area, location, or community.

Source: Codes of Practice pursuant to s 71 of the Regulation of Investigatory Powers Act 2000 (RIPA).

1.4.5 Health and safety risk assessments

In accordance with the Health and Safety at Work Act 1974 and Police (Health and Safety) Act 1997, due regard must be paid to the nature of activities and undertakings in order, so far as is reasonably practicable, to provide a safe and healthy working environment. The aim must be to prevent injuries and danger to personnel and to any members of the community. Therefore it is vital that health and safety implications of all work activities are properly assessed for risk and that appropriate arrangements to manage those risks are in place.

Managers of major investigations must ensure that safety systems are in place, such as establishing that protective clothing and equipment are provided and are being properly used, and that adequate welfare facilities are available. It is vital that all work activities posing significant risks to health and safety are identified and suitable recorded risk assessments undertaken.

There is a general requirement to carry out risk assessments under the Management of Health and Safety at Work Regulations 1999. The purpose of this assessment is to identify measures necessary to comply with relevant statutory duties, and introduce control measures to manage risk. Risk assessments are generally rated as being low, medium, or high, and may be either:

1. **Generic**—produced for a variety of activities, eg executing a search warrant. Identification of significant hazards that may be encountered and introduction of suitable control measures aimed at reducing them, but they must be regularly reviewed.
2. **Specific**—a systematic and detailed examination of the particular activity concerned (eg despatching officers to trace

and interview a person who has PNC warning markers and intelligence relating to firearms and violence).

3. **Dynamic**—operational risk assessments may sometimes have to change at a moment's notice due to developments in diverse activities. The staff involved will need to make a decision about their health and safety and that of other people who may be affected. Significant hazards and subsequent control measures will have been identified within either a generic or specific risk assessment. Control measures will assist the member of staff to make an informed decision about the incident and how best to deal with it, and prior training such as officer safety training should help provide dynamic contingencies.

KEY POINTS

- A risk assessment may identify control measures that involve a combination of all three types of risk, ie generic, specific, and dynamic.
- Control measures are introduced in order to lower and counterbalance the degree of risk. For example, if it is a 'high risk' to allow non-uniform staff to enter an area which is notorious for gang activity, drug dealing, and the use of firearms, then a specific control measure stipulating that they must work in pairs, wear body armour, carry a personal radio, inform the control room when and where they are going into that location, take a uniform presence if visiting addresses, etc may be introduced. This should lower the risk from 'high' to 'medium'.
- Assessments will probably depend on thorough research and intelligence. It is important to preserve an audit trail of all enquiries made or material relied upon, and highly advisable to obtain hard copies of rated intelligence and/or clear reference material. This is preferable to any reliance upon verbal briefings regarding background information on individuals, premises, locations, etc that tend to be unspecific and sometimes inaccurate. If, however, verbal information is utilized for assessment purposes, then a fully recorded version should follow as soon as is practicable to act as a permanent record of the informed decision-making process.

1.4.6 Risk and control strategy models

Once a risk has been identified a control strategy must be devised. There are models that exist to facilitate this, such as the risk assessment scoring matrix that measures probability versus impact.

This uses the principle that the greatest risk is caused by a situation produced when the probability and impact scores are high. It follows that risks that are both low in impact and low in probability are not worthy of great concern to the SIO. There are four strategies that can be adopted in relation to risks that need controlling, which are contained within the acronym RARA:

R Remove
A Avoid
R Reduce?
A Accept

Changing tactics to achieve the same objectives will afford a means of removing, avoiding, or reducing risks. Alternatively the risks can be deemed to be so negligible that they can be accepted.

1.4.7 Risk assessment scoring matrix

The matrix below shows how the top column (impact) can be multiplied by the left-hand column (probability) to produce a risk assessment score factor. For example, if it is 'highly probable' (5) that when officers go to arrest a suspect there will be strong resistance and violence used against them to obstruct or effect an escape; and if this occurs the impact will be very serious (4). The assessment score can then be calculated as 20 (ie 5 × 4). However, this score can be reduced by introducing effective control measures, such as using a team of specially trained officers to conduct the arrest who carry protective equipment and staging the operation in the early hours of the morning by an unannounced forced entry to the premises where the suspect is believed to be, to add an element of surprise. The risk assessment score can then be re-calculated because it is now unlikely (2) the arrest will be resisted which produces a far more acceptable score of 8 (ie. 2 × 4).

Impact / Probability	Catastrophic (5)	Very Serious (4)	Serious (3)	Moderate (2)	Minimal (1)
Highly Probable (5)	High (25)	High (20)	High (15)	Moderate (10)	Low (5)
Probable (4)	High (20)	High (16)	High (12)	Moderate (8)	Low (4)

Probability \ Impact	Catastrophic (5)	Very Serious (4)	Serious (3)	Moderate (2)	Minimal (1)
Possible (3)	High (15)	High (12)	Moderate (9)	Moderate (6)	Low (3)
Unlikely (2)	Moderate (10)	Moderate (8)	Moderate (6)	Low (4)	Low (2)
Very Unlikely (1)	Low (5)	Low (4)	Low (3)	Low (2)	Negligible (1)

1.5 **Conclusion**

The SIO role is one that is extremely challenging and demanding with extraodinarily high levels of risk and accountability. There is a lot of expectation and pressure to cope with the various demands and deliver a successful outcome. The role is one that like most other elements of policing has had to move with the times and there are different and varied challenges to contend with. Risk assessments, human rights, diverse communities, media intrusiveness, masses of extra legislation and procedural changes, high levels of accountability, expectations from communities and victim's relatives, and IPCC tandem investigations to name but a few. None of this should be discouraging as most serious and major crimes, particularly murder, are often detected quite quickly. Thankfully series and linked murders ('in extremis') are also few and far between.

While the role can be one of the most complex and challenging, the rewards and job satisfaction more than compensate. Being responsible for playing a pivotal role in solving serious crimes, and ensuring investigations are conducted in a thorough and professional manner, are hugely gratifying. There is no finer job satisfaction than being able to influence an outcome that may significantly help victims and communities recover from terrible atrocities and life-changing experiences, often suffered at the hands of very dangerous members of society. It is hoped that this first chapter will now effectively 'set the scene' for the others that are to follow.

Chapter 2
Investigative Decision Making

Experience creates and sharpens the capacity to assess and act in a situation where assessment or action is required.

SS Kind, *The Scientific Investigation of Crime*, Harrogate: Forensic Science Services Ltd, (1987)

2.1 Introduction

Making sound judgements is a core role and top attribute of any successful investigator, particularly an SIO. Decision making was identified as an essential skill required of SIOs by Smith and Flanagan (2000) see chapter 1 (para 1.3.3). Effective decision making, particularly in the 'golden hour(s)' will ensure opportunities are not missed and potential lines of enquiry are identified and pursued. Fear of failure in this task must not cause the SIO to dither rather it should make them work harder at becoming more confident and competent at making good decisions even when under pressure or time constraints.

Research indicates in the very initial stages of an incident or enquiry when there may be very little information available, initial hypotheses about what has happened and what type of crime has been committed will tend to be based upon knowledge and experience of previous cases:

> In certain types of investigations such as those where there is a lack of information available, detectives will rely more heavily upon their experience and knowledge, thereby engaging in more intuitive decision making processes . . . the ability to draw inferences and make decisions from basic information during the crucial 'golden hour' is an extremely important skill for detectives to develop (M Wright, *Detective Intuition: The role of homicide schemas* (University of Liverpool, 2008), 292).

In reality, responding officers and/or detectives do often have to cope with a lack of sufficient information to begin with and some important decisions may need to be made quickly and intuitively and/or may already have been made even before the SIO takes charge (in which case they will need to be reviewed at the earliest opportunity applying the A B C principle). A key skill involves the tenacity of being able to recognize when there is insufficient time to gather further information and prompt action is required. Intuition, however, derives from knowledge and experience and can be prone to bias therefore decisions made by SIOs should always be based on reasoning and analysis to avoid subjectivity.

Nothing therefore should prevent an SIO from being able to put order into chaos by slowing things down and creating some degree of what is often described as 'slow time'. This is a technique that will most certainly provide a distinct advantage when making key decisions because it allows further information to be sought and an opportunity to think things through more fully. High pressure situations should not be allowed to cloud judgement and it is important for the SIO to remain cool, calm, and detached.

This chapter outlines some useful methods and techniques that will assist an SIO when making key decisions.

Case study—Trace, Interview, Eliminate

A man was picked up and interviewed near to a murder scene and soon released. Upon re-examination of the decision he was quickly re-designated an important TIE subject by the SIO. A decision was made to find him, search his flat, and seize all his clothing. This later proved vital, as a pair of jeans he had been wearing were evidentially linked to the crime scene through forensic botanical evidence. Had the decision not been made to swiftly capitalize on this opportunity, the offender would almost certainly have escaped conviction.

KEY POINTS

- A policy file entry should be made to record why any decisions had to be made quickly, together with an explanation of what the consequences might have been had prompt action not been taken.
- Improving knowledge levels and investigative skills through training and experience will increase confidence and the ability to make important decisions.

2.2 Objectives of an Investigation

Decision making is always directed at reaching goals or objectives. In order to ensure that good decisions are made towards achieving particular aims, it should at some point be determined what the primary investigative objectives are. A generic example of how these may look is as follows:

- Establish that an offence has been committed/not committed.
- Gather all available information, material, and evidence and adhere to CPIA rules.
- Act in the interests of justice.
- Pursue all reasonable lines of enquiry.
- Conduct a thorough investigation.
- Identify, arrest, and charge the offenders.
- Present the evidence to the Crown Prosecution Service (CPS).

KEY POINT

It is good practice to enter the primary investigative objectives into the policy file in the early stages and have them readily available for staff to refer to.

During the process of investigation the SIO will be using their skills to analyse, review, and assess all the information and material that is available. This is an extremely important process as the accuracy, reliability, and relevance of material being obtained will influence decision making. The golden rule is to apply what is known as the 'ABC' principle (also cited in ACPO, *Practice Advice on Core Investigative Doctrine* (Centrex 2005), 62):

A Assume nothing
B Believe nothing
C Challenge (and check) everything

Nothing should be taken for granted and it cannot be assumed that things are what they seem or that processes have been performed correctly. Looking for corroboration, rechecking, reviewing, and confirming are therefore very important activities before a decision can be based on the facts or information available. It is also a useful trait to apply a certain degree of scepticism before placing too much reliance or emphasis on any information that has been collected.

An example would relate to uncorroborated witness accounts that have not been obtained in writing or in the prescribed investigative interviewing process. Another might be when sensitive intelligence (eg from a CHIS) is received that has not been graded or evaluated properly and is received in verbal format. In such cases the SIO might be wise to carefully consider the accuracy of the information that is relayed to them and in the case of the intelligence should check the provenance and reliability of the source prior to deciding whether to act upon the information.

The SIO will also have to make decisions based on what some of their team members tell them and the reported results of certain important tasks. Once more, it is vitally important to challenge and check any outcomes and conclusions to ensure that tasks have been performed to the required standard.

Case study—Operation Pepin

A victim was involved in the movement and supply of large quantities of illegal drugs throughout the country. He disappeared after being picked up by two associates from his home address and taken to a meeting 10 miles out of the city. He failed to return home and three days later was reported missing. From the outset intelligence indicated he had been murdered and a full major incident room investigation commenced.

Widespread searches were made, and the two main associates he had been in company with were questioned but stated he had been left alone after their meeting, intending to return home. Despite extensive enquiries, little progress was made.

After about eight weeks the investigation went cold and was about to be closed. A new SIO then reviewed all the allocated 'Actions' relating to the examination of potential linked incidents reported during the period of the victim's disappearance. This task had been originally submitted as a negative result. In applying the ABC principle, further checks were requested which led to the identification of a report by a member of the public regarding a male being forcibly removed from his vehicle, bundled into the back of a car, and driven away. The officers who originally attended the incident recovered a discarded cigarette nearby but soon closed the incident with no further clues or lines of enquiry.

Upon forensic examination the cigarette was found to contain DNA matching the missing person. A further police log was then discovered relating to the reported finding of a firearm near to a remote fishing pond in a semi-rural area. Initially this was treated as having little or no significance and no link was made.

Over the ensuing months, extensive telephone cell-site analysis, intelligence assessment, and searches were undertaken. Eight months after his disappearance, the skeletal remains of the victim were forensically excavated from a landfill site, on a remote farm near to where the firearm had been found.

Forensic evidence gleaned from the recovered items and the body led to three men being arrested and charged with murder. Following a lengthy trial at Crown Court, all were convicted and given minimum sentences ranging from 25 to 32 years. The trial judge passed comment on the thorough, exceptional, and persistent police work and re-checking of vital information that led to the body being found and the offenders convicted.

2.3 Problem-Solving and the 5 × WH + H Method

Decision making includes an element of 'problem solving'. A logical approach to making decisions often follows a model that contains some important and sequential elements which are as follows (cited in J Adair, *The best of Adair on Leadership and Management* (Thorogood, 2008):

(1) define the objective;
(2) collect as much information as possible (and check accuracy/validity);
(3) develop various options and alternatives;
(4) evaluate and decide which is the most compelling;
(5) make and implement the decision;
(6) monitor and evaluate the consequences.

This model works on the basis that it is preferable to choose a particular course of action out of a range of possible 'options'. The basic point here is that an SIO should not assume there is only one option available. Information lies at the heart of any investigation and gathering sufficient information helps populate the number of options which can then be worked through and a decision made as to which option(s) is/are the most compelling or that no action is required at all (ie the 'do nothing' option).

In order to gather and collect information to satisfy the requirement as at (2) in the problem solving list, a set of interrogative pronouns known as the '5 × WH + H' method—Who, What, When, Where, Why + How can be put to good use. This formula helps to organize the enquiry information and identify where there are knowledge gaps. For a murder case this may look as follows:

- Who was killed? —Victim details (and why this victim?)
- What happened? —Precise details of incident
- When did it happen? —Temporal issues (ie relevant and significant times)
- Where did it happen? —Geographic considerations (location)
- Why did the crime occur in this way? —Motive for the crime
- How did it happen? —Precise modus operandi details

This information can then be developed into a useful matrix, which will help identify the gaps in information by setting out all the relevant details in a logical sequence which is easy to read and understand. The matrix can then be populated as the enquiry progresses and used as a source of reference for the basis of applying the problem-solving model and any associated decision making that is required. The matrix can be cross-referenced to decisions as and when they are made and will serve to illustrate just what was known or not known at the time any particular decision was made—a very important point for justifying why a particular course of action was taken (or not taken).

Using a case study the matrix may look something like the example below.

Question	What do we know?	What else do we need to know?	Where can we get it from?
Who was killed?	31-year-old lone white female (victim named). Single, but has child from previous relationship. Well known in local area, liked and respected. Still resides with parents. Possibly had/having affairs with married men. Always carries two mobile phones. Works at local convenience store.	Detailed victimology. Any previous attacks against this victim? Was she the intended victim? Are other attacks likely to occur? Full details of previous relationships.	Family and friends, work colleagues, local community, intelligence checks. Victim profile and lifestyle analysis. Crime recording checks. Insurance claims checks. Comparative case analysis (consider use of SCAS database) and crime pattern analysis. Full intelligence checks (incl. corporate databases). Risk analysis for further victims.
Who is/ are the suspect(s)?	Victim in stormy relationship with boyfriend—possible suspect? Recently threatened in her place of work by 2 unknown males.	Is she having any other affairs? Full details of incident and of persons involved.	Identify and declare suspect(s) and TIE categories. Victimology. Subject profile(s). TI work colleagues. Telecoms data analysis. Intelligence assessment.
Who witnessed it?	Male walking dog found body at 06.30.	Identify all potential significant witnesses.	Media appeals and H-2-H enqs. Priority TI actions.

What happened?	Battered and strangled. Found in woods near to home address. Semi-naked, trousers pulled down around ankles. Contents of handbag emptied onto ground.	Was anything stolen from victim? Any defensive marks on the body? Does manner of death give indication as to age/sex/physical capability of offender? Weapon—present/missing? Brought to scene by the offender, victim, or improvised?	Conduct inventory of personal belongings. Re-examine body for further bruises. Check clothing for damage, rips, and tears. Consult National Injuries Database.
What occurred prior to murder?	Victim in public house with friends. Then spent time alone with her boyfriend. Walked home alone, having left boyfriend's flat after argument.	Sequence of events for movements of victim. Est. if any forensic evidence in boyfriend's flat. Did victim have any significant arguments or activities in hours before last known sighting?	Crime scene—examination of flat. Telecoms data analysis. TIE all persons in vicinity of scene and at public house (time parameters?). Search for CCTV in area.
		After leaving boyfriend's flat did victim meet anyone by prior arrangement or by chance?	Analysis of witness statements.

Question	What do we know?	What else do we need to know?	Where can we get it from?
What other significant events took place?	Raised voices of couple possibly arguing at approx. 01.15 hrs.	If linked to murder incident.	HP action—TI/TST witness(es). Consider media appeal and conduct H-2-H enqs in vicinity.
When did it happen?	Bet. 12.30 am and 06.30 Sat. (date).	More precise time of death.	Witnesses, 'back record conversion' of alcohol/blood levels, pathologist, entomologist. Gastroenterology (stomach contents exam), CCTV, assessment of physical evidence in conjunction with other events—eg weather—victim's clothing on ground and clothing wet after the rain. Is ground under clothing wet—yes/no? What time did rain start/end?
Where did it happen?	(named location)	Was this where it occurred or is it deposition site? Risk analysis for further attacks. How did victim/offender get to this location?	Full scene interpretation. Forensic analysis of body plus palynological survey. Crime pattern analysis. Social and demographic information. Geographical profiling.

Why did it happen?		Est. motive. Victim knew offender? Stranger/sexual attack? Robbery/ theft? Anger/jealousy?	Check mobile calls made by victim. Forensic and pathological interpretation of scene. Use of offender profiler.
How did death occur?	Post mortem revealed cause of death to be asphyxiation.	Re-examine to see if further bruising/marks on body are now visible. Full medical history of victim and antecedents. Toxicology results for alcohol levels and drug traces.	Forensic pathologist. Victim's GP and hospital records. Forensic science service results.
How was this location chosen?		Was it on or near victim's route home? Scene interpretation. Has victim been there previously? Is it linked to any suspect or TIE?	Victimology. CPA data analysis. Subject profile analysis. Possible media reconstruction. High-profile enquiries in location.
How did offender get to and from the scene?		Is there an easy escape route? Was offender on foot? Any vehicle used? Local transport?	Scene examination. Enqs with local taxis and bus companies. CCTV trawl and speed cameras. Intelligence checks on suspect/TIEs. Use of scene 'tracker' expert.

The matrix is useful for identifying gaps in what is known about the offence and making decisions on determining main lines of enquiry; it also assists the SIO to prioritize. Once created the matrix should be viewed as a 'living document' that is amended or extended as the enquiry progresses. A trained analyst can assist in helping to analyse, identify, and fill gaps using standard analytical techniques. This process will generate key information that will significantly aid decision making in the investigation.

KEY POINTS

1. Any source material for this sort of matrix must be kept under dynamic review. The SIO must frequently re-examine and confirm its validity, accuracy, and relevance, all of which may change over time. Investigative decision-making processes, strategies, and main lines of enquiry that rely upon this process should be constantly scrutinized and evaluated to determine:
   (a) The reliability of the information.
   (b) Whether there is any conflicting or contradicting material known to the enquiry.
   (c) Whether there is a pattern or consistency emerging.
   (d) Relevance of material to the enquiry (eg if it supports a particular hypothesis).
   (e) Whether there is sufficient material or evidence on which to raise the status of any subject in the enquiry, ie to suspect.
   (f) Whether any evidence would be admissible in judicial proceedings.
   (g) Whether the material is 'relevant' under CPIA requirements.
2. Confusion can be caused by information overload or conflicting information. This again underlines the importance of prioritizing and determining the accuracy and reliability of information.

Note: Under point 1(g) above, requirements under the CPIA are highly relevant and place additional legal responsibilities on the SIO, their enquiry team, and the Crown Prosecution Service. Section 5.1 of the Codes of Practice (CoP) under the Act states:

> The investigator must retain material obtained in a criminal investigation which may be relevant to the investigation. This includes not only material coming into the possession of the investigator . . . but also material generated by him/her (such as interview records).

Section 2.1 of the same CoP provides a definition of 'relevant material':

material may be relevant to an investigation if it appears to an investigator, or to the officer in charge of an investigation, or to the disclosure officer, that it has some bearing on any offence under investigation or any person being investigated, or on the surrounding circumstances of the case, unless it is incapable of having any impact on the case.

In some forces this method may also be adopted under a formalized organizational process in which, at regular intervals, the enquiry (and SIO) is/are reviewed to establish what progress is being made, whether additional resources are required, time scales, etc. A full audit trail should be kept of this procedure and noted in the SIO policy files.

The 5 × WH + H structure can also be useful when being briefed or updated about an incident or circumstances. Questions can be posed using the 5 × WH + H headings in order to establish sufficient detail about what may already be known. The method can be used to ensure clear and concise information is supplied in a systematic rather than random approach. Any additional detail can be captured at the end by adding a further question as to what else is known that has not been covered.

2.4 Developing Hypotheses and Theories

Decisions may have to be based on or guided by an hypothesis. An hypothesis is defined as 'a proposition made as a basis for reasoning without the assumption of its truth'; or 'a supposition made as a starting point for further investigation from known facts' (*Oxford English Reference Dictionary*, 2nd edn, OUP).

Developing and using hypotheses is a widely used technique that can be used to try to establish the most logical or likely explanation, theory, or inference for what may have occurred. Adhami and Browne, 'Major Crime Enquiries: Improving Expert Support for Detectives' Police Research Group Special Interest Series, Paper 9 (London: Home Office, 1996) referred to the inferential processes of detectives as a series of 'if-then' rules (involving a sentence that begins 'If . . .' closely followed by: 'then . . . '). Ideally there should be sufficient reliable material available on which to base the hypotheses such as the sex and age of the victim, likely type of offender, modus operandi, location, type of attack, time of day, motive, crime scene interpretation etc. Knowledge and experience of previous cases will also assist in generating hypotheses. Generating and building hypotheses is an obvious and natural activity for an SIO, particularly during the initial stages of an investigation which is likely to commence once notified of the incident. SIOs need to begin to quickly assess information received about a crime in order to be able to generate possible theories and inferences about what they will be or are dealing with. This is a process that forms the basis of early decision making and provides options that can be considered when applying the aforementioned problem-solving skills. As the enquiry progresses the technique can be tailored to approach a particular theme or part of an investigation where it is good practice to set out a declared objective—for instance, establishing how an offender may have come into contact with the victim. The SIO can involve members of their enquiry team in the process to assist with this task and any other useful expert advisers such as scientists, pathologists, geographic profilers, behavioural investigative advisers, etc. This is also an important task for an analyst to assist with and can link into what they may be preparing on inference development and the identification of intelligence gaps that will help test the validity of the hypotheses and inferences (see *Major Incident Analysis Manual* (NCPE, 2005), 100–2 and *Practice Advice on Analysis* (ACPO NPIA, 2008), 79–83).

Clearly if there is sufficient information or evidence already available then there will be no need to use the hypothesis method. When limited information is available a problem-solving approach to decision making will be key, although the risks of making decisions in the absence of information should be recognized.

KEY POINT

Initial information from the first response can help create tentative hypotheses and provide initial investigative direction when there is little information to go on. The term 'keeping an open mind' should be remembered together with the rule that it is better to gather as much information as possible before placing too much reliance on any one particular speculative theory. 'It is a capital mistake to theorise before one has data. Insensibly one begins to twist facts to suit theories, instead of theories to suit facts' (A Conan Doyle, *The Celebrated Cases of Sherlock Holmes* (Octopus, 1981)).

The *Practice Advice on Core Investigative Doctrine* (NCPE, 2005), 73) sets out a checklist of considerations that have to be met when building hypotheses, which have been added to the list below:

Checklist—Hypotheses building

- Beware of placing too much reliance on one or a limited number of hypotheses when there is insufficient information available.
- Remember the maxim of 'keeping an open mind'.
- Ensure a thorough understanding of the relevance and reliability of any material relied upon.
- Ensure that hypotheses are kept under constant review and remain dynamic—remembering that any hypothesis is only provisional at best.
- Define a clear objective for the hypothesis.
- Only develop hypotheses that 'best fit' with the known information/material.
- Consult with colleagues and experts to discuss and formulate hypotheses.
- Ensure sufficient resources are available to develop or test the hypotheses.

The following hypotheses were initially considered:

Case study

The totally naked body of a female aged 17 was discovered in the rear alleyway of an area frequented by prostitutes and clients. Two local petty thieves found the body and reported it to the police. The victim was well known to the local police and often used drugs. There were no visible signs of injury other than what appeared to be needle marks on her arms and some small circular marks on her face. The body was lying on the ground in a supine position in some dirt and there were no traces of her clothing. A post-mortem examination revealed she had been strangled by unknown means and died of asphyxiation. There was no evidence of a sexual attack. It was unknown as to how the victim had ended up at the location or what exactly had happened, and unclear why she had no clothing on.

Local sex workers supplied information stating they never completely undressed for clients as it was too dangerous and limited means of quick escape. The pathologist was of the opinion that there were very few or no defensive marks on the body. The crime scene examiners and forensic scientists were initially unsure about where the murder took place.

1. If their initial accounts prove to be inconsistent or unreliable then the two local thieves who found the body may have committed the murder.
2. If the murder had taken place in nearby flats habitually used by drug abusers and prostitutes then the offender or someone else who found the body may have panicked and deposited it in the adjacent alleyway.
3. The victim may have been murdered at the location where the body was found.
4. If the murder took place elsewhere then this could have been a deposition site.
5. If she had been murdered by a client who was having sex with her at the same location then he/she may have removed and took the clothing to destroy trace evidence, or retained it as a 'trophy'.
6. If a vehicle was involved and the victim was engaging in a sexual encounter as a prostitute with a client then the murder may have occurred after she had voluntarily or forcibly been made to remove her clothing and the murderer made off leaving her body at the side of the alleyway where it had been parked taking her clothes with him to dispose of incriminating evidence.
7. The victim may have been murdered by a friend, boyfriend, or relative for reasons unknown.
8. If the death was unintentional then it may have occurred during some sexual act such as autoeroticism and her partner panicked leaving her body in the alleyway
9. If there was no vehicle involved then she had been in the alleyway voluntarily on foot with a client before she was killed.

Any one or a combination of these hypotheses was initially considered feasible by the SIO. Producing a list as comprehensive as this actually demonstrated the SIO was keeping an open mind and not concentrating too heavily on one or two possible theories. As the enquiry progressed and more material and information became available, a number of the hypotheses could be ruled out.

The outcome was that tyre impressions were later discovered at the scene and it transpired that a vehicle had been used by the offender. The victim had been strangled after sexual intercourse with a client in his car. The actual motive for the murder was never clear but the victim was known to be naive enough to be coerced into taking all her clothes off. The body had been dragged out of the car and left in the alleyway, and clothing was later deposited in a skip away from the scene, which was later found on CCTV footage. Through a process of interviewing previous clients and victim associates, a possible offender was eventually traced and arrested. The tyres of his vehicle matched those at the scene and some fibres from the victim's clothing were found in the boot of his car. After a reconstruction the car was matched with the grainy image captured on CCTV, with a figure putting what looked like clothing into a waste disposal skip. After a full trial he was convicted and sentenced to life imprisonment.

Note: The circular marks on the victim's face were heroin abuse scabs, and not rodent or insect bite marks or cigarette burns, as first suggested by some experts.

2.5 Adequacy and Assertion in Decision Making

There is an important difference between adequacy and assertion and this affects how they relate to decision making. This is because assertions do not carry the same weight as 'adequate arguments'. Assertions are statements or declarations that do not necessarily have to contain essential supporting evidence, explanation, or reasoning. SIOs should always try to construct and rely upon adequate arguments rather than merely assertions, although the latter may be useful sometimes provided they are treated for what they are.

This is important when understanding the construction and recording of decisions made. Adequate decision making should ideally be based upon sound reasoning with supportive argument based upon the information gathered. The SIO must not only identify but also support and evaluate different arguments and theories. The golden rule is that good arguments are backed by evidence, supporting material, and logical reasoning. It is also worth remembering the legal evidential test which in all criminal cases is 'beyond reasonable doubt'. The SIO should pose the question: 'Has the theory or hypothesis been adequately established and logically reasoned, and can it be maintained with confidence?'

In other words, it is necessary to test the adequacy of the material and reasoning that supports any theory or decision that is chosen and to make an appropriate record of the process.

2.6 Categorizing Incidents

Decisions made by the SIO will be influenced by an assessment of the type of incident being dealt with. This assists in making interpretations based on previous knowledge and experience and also adds meaning to the circumstances in establishing what may have occurred. The different types of incident can be categorized as follows:

- Domestic-related (eg current/former spouse, parent/child, child/parent, sexual rival, extended family members)
- Criminal enterprise (eg during course of robbery, burglary, etc)
- Gang-related
- Child victims
- Racially motivated
- Sexually motivated
- Stranger attacks
- Serial offences
- Argument-motivated
- Terrorism-related
- Other (eg religious/sectarian, mass homicide, etc).

Categorizing incidents helps make sense of the individual circumstances. It will also aid the determination of important lines of enquiry and investigative strategies, levels of resources, producing hypotheses, etc. It is vital that the categorization of an incident is supported by adequate material and rationale because incorrectly determining the nature of the incident may take an enquiry off into the wrong direction.

2.6.1 Motives (the 'why?' question)

Working out what cause or reason induced an offender to commit a crime, whether it be homicide or otherwise, is usually a primary line of enquiry. Establishing a motive can link in with decisions about categorization of an incident as defined above, helping SIOs make decisions about prioritizing lines of enquiry, and in turn finding the person(s) responsible. It may also assist in linking incidents and matching modus operandi. Some cases can prove very difficult to solve when the motive is unclear, eg the 'Jack the Ripper' murders in the 1880s in the East End of London.

However, the warning given before is equally applicable, particularly if the media want to emphasize a particular motive or even speculate about it. Mistaken or ill-advised comments or opinions about causes of serious crimes can create unnecessary problems. For example, if the motive is wrongly diagnosed and reported as being 'gang-related', this may instantly demonize the victim and/or the community with which they are associated. This, in turn, may alienate the investigation team from important sources of information or discourage people from assisting the enquiry. A list of motives worth considering are:

- Gain (financial or otherwise)
- Criminal enterprise
- Personal cause
- Jealousy
- Revenge attack
- Gang-related (eg drugs, territory, or power)
- Racism, homophobia (or other prejudice or hatred)
- Anger or loss of control (rejection, argument etc)
- Crime concealment or witness elimination purposes (eg a court witness)
- Sexual gratification, lust, desire, sadism
- Power, control
- Thrill and excitement
- Mental illness/personality disorders (eg, psychopath, narcissism, paranoid, schizoid)
- Political/religious/ritualistic causes
- Terrorism related
- To cover up or in the process of another crime (eg arson, burglary).

Motives can link in with possible contributory causes of crime, such as drugs and alcohol. There is considerable evidence to suggest that violent offenders have often taken/consumed either of these prior to committing a violent act and this may feature as a line of defence (which may require evidence to rebut. It is possible, of course, that victims may have taken them too, which may provide an indication as to what sort of activity they were involved in prior to any attack or even why they were targeted. This can be useful information for building up an accurate picture on which to base a motive and understand the personality and habits of a victim or profile an offender. Violent offences such as murder may also involve an element of victim precipitation whereby the victim is the first to initiate violence towards the offender.

2.6.2 Geography and the 'where?' question

Where an offender commits a crime can reveal a lot of information about them and their relationship with the victim. The Routine Activity Theory (RAT) developed by Lawrence Cohen and Marcus Felson (LE Cohen and M Felson, 'Social Change and Crime Rate Trends: A Routine Activity Approach', (1979) 44 *American Sociological Review,* 588–608) is based on the premise that offenders tend to commit crimes in areas they are familiar with and they have had the opportunity to do so without someone or something being able to prevent them.

The 'where' question will assist the SIO in making key decisions and inferences about the crime under investigation and will impact on processes and procedures at the scene, particularly if it is in a wooded or rural area. The characteristics of the environment such as the local neighbourhood in which a crime has occurred will give an SIO a good 'feel' for the incident under investigation and is one of the reasons why personally visiting the crime scene as soon as possible is so important. (There will be reference to this and other 'wh' questions in other chapters.)

Note: Geographical profiling is a recognized method of using techniques which focus on the likely spatial behavior of offenders within the context of locations and the spatial relationships between various crime sites. It will also help determine the most probable location of an offender's anchor point (eg their place of residence or other base such as their place of work). It is a proven method and forms part of the guidelines for SIOs in the MIM. Advice on geographic profiling can be obtained from the NPIA at <http:www.npia.police.uk/soc>.

2.6.3 Gold, Silver, and Bronze (GSB)

When major or critical incidents are declared, a gold, silver, and bronze (GSB) command and control structure is frequently implemented. These terms are generally accepted nationally across all the emergency services. GSB can also be utilized for any complicated or complex enquiries and tactical operations and the system provides a flexible management structure which separates management activity in order to make the decision making process clear and unambiguous.

In some forces and agencies there may be a computerized system (eg intranet-based) for recording all strategies, tactics, policy decisions, and updates in the GSB format. This is to facilitate contemporaneous recording and ease widespread sharing, dissemination, and accessibility of information. The three levels of operational management are as follows:

- gold (strategic—'what to do');
- silver (tactical—'how to do it');
- bronze (operational—'doing it').

These levels do not have to be rank-specific. They are relevant to decision-making levels and to the experience and expertise of the role holder.

This model of command and control is not designed to work just within 'police only' operations, but enables individuals at all three levels to interact effectively with their counterparts in other services and organizations—an important aspect of critical incident response.

2.6.4 Gold command

The gold strategy is the overall intention to combine resources towards managing and resolving an incident or operation. This may lead to the implementation of a gold group, headed by a 'commander', whose members will meet at regular intervals to discuss the way a critical incident is progressing and being managed, and ensure that all courses of action are being undertaken in a timely and efficient manner (often referred to as an 'organizational review'). In the police service the role of gold commander is often taken by a person of Assistant Chief Constable (ie ACPO) rank or someone of equivalent status.

An ACPO lead normally performs the role of Officer in Overall Command (OIOC) and is responsible for setting strategy, directing activity, and coordinating resources and partnership support for the most high-risk and complex investigations. The strategic functions performed by the gold commander are critical components of an effective policing response and investigation.

Early effective command and control has been shown to be the key determinant of success in major and critical enquiries. These principles are described further in ACPO (2009) 'Guidance on Command & Control' and ACPO (2007) 'Practice Advice on Critical Incident Management'. It was also a notable contributor to the success during Operation Paris: the investigation conducted by West Yorkshire Police into the disappearance of Shannon Mathews (see NPIA (2009) Strategic debrief—Operation Paris).

A gold commander should be viewed as a useful asset to the SIO. One of their tasks is to ensure the police investigation does not undermine public trust and confidence, essential ingredients that can determine the success or otherwise of an investigation. Gold Commanders have the wider strategic perspective to consider and must ensure, for example, that activities such as house searches and TIEs are managed in such a way that the relationship with local communities is not adversely affected. They will also have the responsibility for managing and mitigating any risk to the reputation of the police force concerned in considering the repercussions of what are to the SIO probably standard investigative procedures. It is always in the best interests of the enquiry that the SIO manages their relationship with the gold commander very carefully. Handled professionally they should be able to take some considerable pressure off them.

A gold commander will probably set up a 'gold strategy group' and the SIO will be expected to be a member of it. Other members may include a local operational commander, the Head of Media Branch (or Corporate Communications), a member of the Local Authority or an Independent Advisory Group member and anyone else deemed necessary. If there are sensitive tactics or operational considerations the SIO does not want to mention to the entire group during these meetings this needs to be mentioned to the gold commander beforehand to avoid compromise.

Checklist—Gold function

- Has overall responsibility and accountability for providing resources and finances towards a strategic objective.
- Manages any business continuity issues when other areas of policing might be affected (particularly for prolonged enquiries).
- Most probably the person who selects and appoints the SIO and any other silver commanders who may be required (eg silver commander for community impact or a firearms silver commander).
- Sets, reviews, and updates the terms of reference for the gold group and any strategies, which may include setting or agreeing tactical parameters.
- Initiates, arranges, and chairs all meetings of the strategic gold group and acts as co-ordinator if there is a multi-agency/ disciplinary response.
- Consults with partners when determining strategy.
- Considers the wider strategic repercussions of standard investigative procedures and in particular the effect the investigation will have on public trust and confidence (ie consequence management).
- Is involved in agreeing initial media strategies.
- Is in overall command and has full governance and overall responsibility for the incident under investigation, and any other associated matters.
- Ensures that the gold strategy is fully recorded in order to provide a clear audit trail, including any changes to the strategy.
- Responsible for ensuring the resilience of the command structure and the effectiveness of silver.
- Risk manages the reputation of the police force concerned and any other pertinent issues such as family liaison.

2.6.5 Silver command

In major investigations, particularly when there is more than one incident being investigated, an SIO will probably feature in a command and control structure at a 'silver' level. There may also be the appointment of other (multiple) silvers whom the SIO may have to work alongside such as a Police Incident

Officer (PIO—otherwise known as scene silver commander), or a firearms tactical silver commander when engaged on pro-active and pre-planned operations to make arrests; or a 'public order' silver commander during protests, marches, or at major events, or even a Senior Identification Manager (SIM) if there are mass fatalities.

Checklist—Silver function

- Is responsible for developing and co-ordinating the tactical plan in order to achieve the strategy set by gold.
- Determines the way that resources are used to achieve the strategic intentions within a range of approved tactical options.
- Must ensure that all officers/staff are properly briefed and debriefed.
- Must be located so as to be able to maintain tactical command of the operation.
- Must ensure all decisions are documented within a policy log.
- Provides the pivotal link between managers and staff, ensuring that all are apprised of developments.
- Reviews, updates, and communicates changes in the tactical plan.
- Ensures that tactics employed by bronze meet the strategic intention and the tactical plan.

2.6.6 **Bronze command**

This role carries a responsibility for the operational implementation of strategic and tactical decisions. Examples of bronze 'commanders' in a murder investigation might be media liaison, family liaison, or at the incident scene there may be a cordon bronze commander and/or traffic bronze.

When there is a pro-active operation which has a pre-planned element, bronze roles may be allocated roles such as a surveillance unit (eg Bronze 1), Road Policing Unit supervisor (Bronze 2), community liaison (Bronze 3), intelligence cell (Bronze 4), and so on. This clearly assigns ownership and specific responsibility.

Checklist—Bronze function

- Should have knowledge and clear understanding of silver's tactical plan and their role within it.
- Organizes the group of resources to carry out the tactical plan.
- Should be available to those under their command.
- Must ensure staff within their area of responsibility are fully briefed.
- Keeps silver updated on current developments, including any variation to agreed tactics.
- Must be located to maintain effective control.
- Must ensure that all decisions are documented within a policy log.

KEY POINT

Gold, silver, and bronze roles should not lead to blurred lines of responsibility or over-complicate the chain of command. A record should always be made of what each role is responsible for and either entered into the SIO's policy book or recorded separately, signed off after agreement by each role holder, and eventually registered onto the HOLMES2 database as an official document.

2.7 Conclusion

Investigative decision making is a core skill requirement of an SIO's role. This chapter has covered a variety of useful methods and topics all of which can have a bearing and impact on making sound judgements. These have ranged from setting objectives, using problem-solving methods, and developing hypotheses, categorizing incidents, establishing motive, and considering the geographical location in which the incident occurred and GSB decision-making structures. These methods and concepts provide a useful foundation for the following chapters.

Chapter 3
Leadership, Teambuilding, Innovation, Creativity, and Welfare

'It is almost true to say that leaders are made rather than born'.

Field Marshall Viscount Montgomery

3.1 Leadership

Leadership tends to be an 'umbrella' term and includes elements of management and supervision. Strong leadership is widely recognized as important because it is the key to driving performance and achieving success. It is one of the key assets a successful SIO must possess. It involves inspiring and influencing human behaviour towards the completion of goals. This can sometimes be a difficult skill to master and an area where it is easy to come unstuck. It is also not just about achieving results—there is a moral element involved, as the *means* of achieving results is very important.

There are a variety of models and theories which an SIO can draw upon, and 'influencing' seems to best describe the all-encompassing skill which the effective leader requires. This is not a passive function but a pro-active one. Good attributes of leadership can be effectively summed up in the following word repertoire: commitment, enthusiasm, motivation, passion, approachable, decisive, assertive, courageous, inspiring, adaptable, high physical stamina and vitality levels, skill in dealing with people, honest and trustworthy, dedicated, and above all being positive, confident, and determined. Success will depend on an ability to demonstrate these core pillars of leadership and convey them as strong beliefs and traits to others.

A good SIO will ensure that everyone agrees on thoroughness and attention to detail (hence the maxim, 'the devil/god is in the detail'). They must be authoritative but yet very approachable and quickly able to spot those caught up in a 'time warp' who still resort to the 'Ways and Means Act'; counteract pessimism, cynicism, and negativity, and challenge poor values, standards, or behaviour. It is not always possible to try to get everyone to like the leader, and some tough decisions may not necessarily suit everyone, but good leadership involves acceptance of responsibility. Taking firm action for poor behaviour or negligence is neither a motivator nor a developer, but in most circumstances will provide for the maintenance of good standards.

KEY POINTS—What is meant by leadership?

- To lead involves influencing others.
- Where there are leaders there are followers.
- Leaders seem to come to the fore when tough decisions and decisive action is required.
- Leaders remain visible and are respected by their team.
- Leaders are people who have a clear idea of what they want to achieve, how, and why.

(Dr C Rogers, *Leadership Skills in Policing* (Blackstones OUP, 2008)

3.2 Choosing a Leadership Style

Leadership and management styles vary significantly. What works for one may not always work for another. Some believe that good leaders have a 'presence' or gravitas. Being charismatic is another trait often considered significant. It really is a case of whatever is comfortable and achievable for the individual. Feedback from others on an informal or formal basis will give an indication as to whether the chosen style is appropriate or effective.

Generally speaking, leaders adapt to and create their own style. There are no universal characteristics. One may choose a traditional hierarchical, autocratic 'top-down', directive method; a more 'levelled-out' delegation style (ie autocratic/democratic); or even a laissez-faire, laid-back attitude. This may depend on the leader's personality or the task at hand. Giving direct orders and instructions may be wholly appropriate in certain circumstances, whereas an entirely different approach may be required when dealing with matters such as managerial and/or personnel issues. The team being led may respond better to one than the other and the SIO has to decide which style to use. Good leadership needs to be moving, fluid, and dynamic.

Remaining flexible is one solution. In any event, management styles and techniques are not magic mantras but simply tools to be used at the right time for the right occasion. Hovering closely when necessary can be better than remaining at a distance, dependent on the situation. Sometimes an unapologetic directive is preferable to a prolonged participatory discussion, and this is for the SIO to decide.

Taking charge and being in command does not have to involve a reluctance to assume control for fear of resentment from the team. In fact, the opposite is the case. Teams that have good, strong leaders perform better because they have someone at the helm.

3.2.1 Displaying confidence and being inspirational

Good leaders have to control their emotions while under pressure. Panic is not acceptable. Often SIOs attend incidents where people are running around causing chaos. The SIO cannot let themselves become paralysed in any situation and must remain calm, composed, and in control. Displaying a strong mental attitude and self-assurance in high-pressure situations is a key skill and reassures those who are looking for someone to be in command and take charge.

Doing simple things such as going out to lead 'from the front' goes down well. For example, if a pre-planned or spontaneous operation to arrest offenders in 'strike' situations requires an SIO lead, it is wise to be in a command position that is located near to where the activity is taking place. This demonstrates a confident style and provides a good position for decision making which may have to adapt to changing circumstances observed first-hand as opposed to being updated in an office. Displaying such confidence carries an important message to those being led, and is more genuine, authentic, and sincere.

Being inspirational also involves a strong personal element. It's easy to become bogged down in day-to-day routine tasks, forgetting to try to view things from different perspectives. It must be remembered that the SIO needs to be a creative, innovative, cutting-edge type of leader and manager. This will help stimulate and encourage fresh ideas and new suggestions from within the team to solve problems.

KEY POINTS

1. Some ideas are so simple they are brilliant. For example, in a large major enquiry that involved utilizing resources from other forces, a decision was made for any exhibits to be accompanied by an evidential statement from people recovering them. Thus, when months later a file of evidence was required, there was no need to trace people who had long since returned to their forces and units, because the statements relating to all exhibited items had already been obtained.
2. Inspiration can come at unusual and inconvenient times. It is a good idea to keep a pen and paper handy to make a note of them so they aren't lost or forgotten, eg at the bedside for jotting down ideas that are immensely difficult to recall the morning after.

3.2.2 Winning respect

A good SIO and leader should win the respect and trust of their team and it is easier for staff to give their loyalty and have confidence in those they do respect. The list below contains several areas that should enhance respect in an SIO's leadership qualities:

- Encouraging staff to contribute. Encourage staff to speak freely and frankly, and not just to comply and conform out of loyalty or fear. Independent ideas and contributions are always useful.
- Keeping up to date. An SIO should never show that they have a distinct lack of knowledge of information, facts, actions, events, activities, key names, workstreams etc.
- Being consistent. Inconsistent decision making causes confusion amongst staff as does moody or changing attitudes and behaviour. An SIO should try not to be cheerful one minute then moody or depressed the next—staff will not know where they stand or what to expect from their leader.
- Displaying high levels of personal integrity. Good leaders demonstrate good self-control and apply professional ethical and moral standards; being wholly dependable, not displaying inappropriate behavior or abusing levels of authority.

- Being professional. Relay a belief in others that the role and responsibility is being taken very seriously and that decisions can and will be made when and where necessary.
- Showing concern. Sympathize and empathize when necessary.
- Working hard. Staff want their leader to put in as much if not more effort than they are, and this includes being available, approachable, and demonstrating a firm commitment to the enquiry.

3.2.3 Teambuilding

A key leadership function is for an SIO to build their team into an efficient and effective working group. Professor John Adair is internationally acknowledged in the field of management and leadership development and sets the scene by describing how teambuilding consists of three overlapping needs:

1. Task need
2. Team maintenance needs
3. Individual needs

Individual tasks must be completed and will involve frustration and low morale if those who have the task to complete are prevented from or unable to complete it. Team maintenance needs are also important because group cohesiveness is essential under the 'united we stand, divided we fall' principle. Individual needs are also key and include psychological and physical needs such as reward and recognition, a sense of doing something worthwhile, job satisfaction, and status. The three overlapping elements can be represented as shown in figure 3.1:

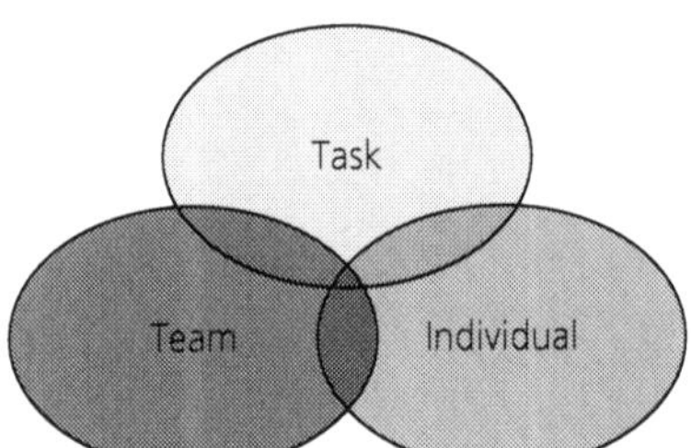

Figure 3.1 Team-building elements

The overlap is present to indicate how all three elements are mutually interdependent, ie achieving the task builds the team and satisfies individuals; if team maintenance fails because the team lacks cohesiveness, performance on the task will be impaired and individual satisfaction is reduced; finally, if individual needs are not met, the team will lack cohesiveness and performance of the task will be affected (J Adair, *The Best of Adair on Leadership and Management* (Thorogood, 2008).

The effectiveness of a team needs to be constantly monitored and this can be done through essential management functions such as evaluating the standard of work being returned, speaking to individuals and listening to feedback, checking at briefings to ensure that every individual knows and understands what their role is, what is expected of them, and what the SIO's objectives for the investigation are. It is important to remember the core role that briefings and de-briefings play in the management of an investigation, where communicating (ie speaking and listening) is crucial to get right and should cover the three main issues of task, team, and individual needs (see also Chapter 7).

3.3 Motivation

A key element for holding any team together is motivation. In simple terms it is the amount of effort staff are willing to put into their work, and motivated staff are always more productive—fact. The inverse also holds true.

Increasing demands are often required on finite resources. Therefore the SIO must get their team to perform to a higher standard than available resources would normally allow. They have to generate a strong sense of enthusiasm and energy for the important task ahead and sometimes make the most of what is available by maximizing the potential of all available resources.

3.3.1 Trust and mutual respect

One way to motivate is for the SIO and management team to demonstrate openness (unless the issues are too sensitive—if so, record in a separate and secure policy file). Explaining policy, objectives, ideas, and thinking is preferable to 'management behind closed doors', which creates mistrust and discontent. Gone are the days of blind obedience; whereas a more inclusive approach will engender a stronger team spirit. The SIO and their management team should strive to create an atmosphere of trust, mutual respect (ie between the SIO, management and their team), and commitment.

Allowing people to encounter new challenges is a useful stimulant and raises self-esteem. Enabling staff to demonstrate their qualities and skills is what makes an enquiry attractive, interesting, and fulfilling. It is important to facilitate development by providing opportunities and responsibilities for tackling new challenges, remembering that it is important to keep an eye on what they are doing.

3.3.2 Interaction

Plenty of interaction between those who are going to carry out activities and their leaders and managers is also important. A good leader keeps abreast of everything that is happening in order to find out quickly when doubts are growing. Building strong relationships with team members through good communication is a key element. Explaining the 'why' as well as the 'what' is more acceptable, as are regular briefings and meetings with all team members; noticing those who aren't providing updates or contributing, and establishing why; picking up on subtle shifts in the behaviour of team members.

3.3.3 Supervision and support

An ability to supervise discreetly can sometimes be a great asset, provided swift action is taken when things are done incorrectly. This sends out the right message regarding (non-) acceptable professional standards. Being able to pick up, read, and interpret signals is important—for example quickly noticing and acting when morale is dropping or complacency and lethargy are creeping in. This includes managing and dealing with tensions and inappropriate behaviour as and when they arise.

The SIO must know or find out what problems the team are facing and must never assume they know what it is like for their staff. Teams will respect a leader who is willing to leave their comfort zone and put themselves out to see what working lives are like first-hand (often referred to as 'management by walkabout' or through the acronym 'MBWA'). This is not 'intrusive management' but seeing the world through their eyes—for instance understanding why members of the public will not cooperate (eg cultural barriers, fear, or mistrust of the police, abusive and difficult people). Often the only way to understand is to go out there and find out.

Support must be provided to those who, for one reason or another, have suffered or had a difficult time during the enquiry. This gives reassurance so that staff understand they will not be abandoned by their leaders when the going gets tough, and it generates more loyalty, which is a better culture to work with. This extends to ensuring tasks are not overly hazardous and are properly risk-assessed by limiting or controlling any potential dangers.

Tasks that are repetitious and tedious can produce temptation and/or boredom. Some types of enquiry, such as tracing a large number of owners of a particular brand and size of training shoe, or sitting in a car taking vehicle registration numbers in the red light district (which Greater Manchester Police and West Yorkshire Police officers did during the Yorkshire Ripper investigation in 1977/8), can be tedious and soul-destroying, yet still very important. The SIO must take steps to keep their teams motivated by regularly emphasizing and reminding staff of the importance of the task and swap duties around or provide breaks from monotonous or repetitive tasks.

Staying positive is also essential to maintaining morale. Using simple terms and language which emphasize what can be done rather than expressing and discussing things negatively, is preferable than dwelling on difficulties. It is always easier to detract than to construct and some team members may prefer to take the easier option of being destructive rather than constructive, if so this type of unhelpful attitude has to be deterred. Above all, it should be abundantly obvious that the SIO has strong professional pride and commitment for the very important and highly challenging yet rewarding task ahead. The truth remains that a good leader can and will make a difference to the motivational levels of their team simply by their own positive attitude and behaviour.

3.3.4 Mutual accountability

The challenge is to create a sense of agreed mutual accountability, with everyone pulling in the same direction. An enquiry team should have a shared sense of direction and goals, deep commitment towards success, and a supportive rather than critical working environment. Everyone is accountable, working down through the chain of command, although the principle starts with the SIO.

3.3.5 Maximizing potential

It is useful to have a good mix and spread of talents and attributes. Some, for example, may have a relaxed, easy communication style, readily adaptable to fit most circumstances, and like to be seen and heard. They are most likely to be extrovert personalities. Quieter, more introverted types may just get on with allocated tasks in a less obvious fashion and prefer to be left alone. Some thought has to go into understanding individuals and how best to motivate them. The skilful SIO will analyse the strengths and weaknesses of all their team and allocate tasks according to their attributes. For example, trying to encourage and support potential witnesses to give evidence or information may be more suitable to some than others. Watching hours and hours of CCTV footage or ferreting out intelligence, although arguably core detective skills, may be better suited to particular types of individual.

SIOs should also be aware of their own strengths and weaknesses in order to build a team around them. This helps to identify gaps where an SIO's needs are greatest. Taking responsibility for self-development, setting high personal standards, and 'leading by example' are important. This involves accepting liability when things go wrong or when others cannot handle situations. Giving credit, praise, and recognition for any effort, struggle, and determination is enormously beneficial to building team spirit.

Hard-to-solve cases require tenacity and the SIO must involve all the experience, empirical knowledge, and creative thinking from within their team. Dispelling a ridicule culture for any suggestions, however 'off the wall', is therefore vital. The best policy is to create an environment which rewards and supports the contribution of ideas so that stronger members do not dominate at the expense of others.

KEY POINT

Communication skills: good relationships and contacts need fostering. People like to be able to put a 'face to a name' when they are being called upon to provide assistance. This is the same with experts or anyone who can provide help to an enquiry. Staff (and when appropriate the SIO) should be encouraged to try and meet with and speak face-to-face with people or agencies who may have other competing demands, in order to seek their commitment and willing co-operation. The personal touch can sometimes achieve a lot more. In an era of modern communications such as email and mobile phones, this can sometimes get overlooked.

3.3.6 Empowering staff to use their skills and experience

It is essential in all investigations that investigative action is coordinated through the Major Incident Room (MIR) because failure to do so can lead to loss of focus, duplication of effort, and important information being overlooked. But this level of command and control should not seek to stifle an investigator's natural desire to use their skills and experience to full advantage. Good SIOs empower their staff to apply their skills and experience within the SIO's investigative strategy and the framework of action management imposed by the MIR. This will allow the team to realize their full potential and not only maintain a high standard of morale but also perform at the highest level.

3.3.7 Positive thinking (the 3P principle)

Positive thinking is always the best way to approach problems and maintain or build morale. Being negative and pessimistic is not going to influence others to do their best and work hard, whereas an optimistic and enthusiastic attitude from the SIO and their management will almost certainly have a significant and positive effect on the team. Positive attitudes provide for tasks to be approached with vigour, energy, and vitality, focusing on what can be achieved rather than what cannot. Those members of the team who focus on and constantly display negativity traits should be asked to balance these views with positive ones. It is not good for the team to get constantly bogged down discussing hurdles and obstacles; focusing on solutions is always preferable. In such circumstances the SIO should regularly remind their staff to remember the 3P principle, which can be summed up in three very important words:

POSITIVE
POSITIVE
POSITIVE

3.3.8 Maslow's hierarchy of needs

This is a theory in psychology proposed by Abraham Maslow in his 1943 paper *A Theory of Human Motivation*. Although it may seem a bit academic the principles of this are so very basic and realistic it is worthy of inclusion and useful to remember when considering needs and their link to motivation. It must be remembered, however, that staff members are all individuals who have their own unique needs and differences, also that the items in the list can become relevant at different stages and times.

Maslow identified five motivating factors in his hierarchy of needs:

1. Physiological needs (including hunger, thirst, and rest)
2. Safety needs (security and protection from danger)
3. Social needs (belonging, acceptance, social life, friendship)
4. Self-esteem (self-respect, achievement, status, recognition)
5. Self-actualization (growth, accomplishment, personal development).

Figure 3.2 is an interpretation of Maslow's hierarchy of needs represented as a pyramid with the more basic needs shown at the bottom.

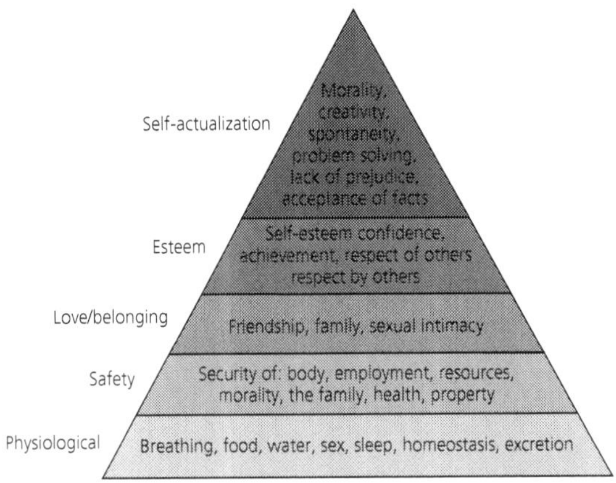

Figure 3.2 Maslow's Hierarchy of Needs

Checklist—Motivation

- The SIO and their management team need to show they are highly motivated.
- Job satisfaction is very important.
- Motivation not only comes from individuals but also the environment they operate in.

- Treat staff well. The SIO should try to be personable as well as maintaining a level of distance so people still look up to them.
- Checking on well-being and remembering personal details are small gestures that build good relationships between the SIO and their team.
- Physiological needs such as adequate food and drink are important.
- The SIO should always be positive, and encourage and remind their team to think likewise.
- Realists and pessimists are fine, but too much can damage morale. There is more to be gained from enthusiasm and optimism.
- Understanding individual temperaments can help in formulating ways to approach and treat individuals.
- Be observant and sensitive to people's individual needs and temperaments.
- Set realistic and challenging tasks—too high-level a task creates feelings of non-achievement. More low-level, realistic tasks should be balanced against slightly higher targets to provide new challenges. Small task additions enrich job satisfaction.
- Consider job rotation for boring and repetitive tasks.
- Non-monetary rewards such as a thank-you note or words of praise can provide simple job enrichment.
- Remember empowerment—give responsibility to motivate.
- Penalizing individuals can demotivate a team. Control and management is preferable to imposing sanctions but the SIO must act swiftly when the need arises and not be seen as a 'soft touch'.
- Try to understand when team members face difficult barriers and problems and get involved in finding ways of alleviating them.

3.4 Innovation and Creativity

Good leaders and managers must be capable of having or recognizing good ideas and using them to make things happen. Innovation, meaning 'to bring in or introduce new methods and ideas' (*Oxford English Dictionary*, 2nd edn, OUP) draws together new ideas and their implementation. Good team leadership should create a consistent ethos and culture of finding solutions and new ideas to problems and avoiding negativity. Inventive ideas that enliven and arouse the spirit of teams should be the aim, and the SIO should be pro-active in taking the lead in making creative and stimulating suggestions for others to follow. Assumptions based on traditional beliefs and prehistoric knowledge should be challenged in favour of finding new ways of doing things, with new tactics and technology. This does not mean traditional methods do not work when they are clearly tried and tested, but that being more radical is sometimes necessary to succeed.

Checklist—Innovation and creativity

Innovation and creativity are going to be better in enquiry teams where:

- participation is encouraged;
- facts and information are readily available;
- change is seen as a positive activity and is managed accordingly;
- staff are encouraged to use their skills and experience to the benefit of the enquiry;
- internal communications between the management team and their staff are good;
- there is mutual respect amongst all staff;
- the SIO and their management team are creative and highly motivated;
- the generation of new ideas is pro-actively encouraged.

Case study—Operation Eagle

An inner-city area had a reputation for brutal gang violence whose perpetrators were managing to stay ahead of the law. Despite suspicions that gang members were involved in a number of serious offences including murder, trying to secure convictions proved difficult. Culprits were forensically aware and knew how to dispose of firearms residue. They would burn clothes and there would be nothing to link them to any victim. Despite an excellent witness protection scheme, people were unwilling to give evidence for fear of reprisals.

A radical and revolutionary approach was required and Operation Eagle was born. An investigative team set out with a new strategy to uncover any evidence of gun- and gang-related activity, including links between shootings and suspects and/or weapons, proving gang existence and membership, and the impact on the local community.

> The team turned to officers as opposed to members of the public to provide the necessary evidence. Officers came forward with information about stopping gang members and recording them wearing body armour. One officer was able to provide evidence that gang members were in the habit of pointing their fingers in the shape of a gun at passing patrol cars. A gun component previously recovered was linked to a suspect, previous instances of firearms residue found on clothing, spent cartridge cases found in a house search, and a housing officer who provided evidence on gang-related graffiti all proved valuable evidence.
>
> This was putting together a jigsaw of evidence, each piece of which on its own would have been insufficient. Rather than prosecute offenders for murder, they were charged with conspiracy offences. Seven males, some of whom had become almost serial killers, were each convicted and sentenced to nine years' imprisonment. The result led to a significant lull in the amount of gun- and gang-related criminality, and the creative blueprint for the strategy was successfully used again on similar operations.

3.5 **Managing Welfare**

Major crime enquiry teams can and do become adversely affected by the nature of their work. They may be coping under intense pressure and/or engaging in emotionally charged dialogue with victims, witnesses, or members of the community. The SIO and their management team have an important responsibility for dealing with and minimizing the consequences and subsequently controlling adverse effects, as far as possible.

There is a statutory duty for employers under the Management of Health and Safety at Work Regulations 1999 to assess the risk of stress-related ill health arising from work activities, and under the Health and Safety at Work Act 1974 to take measures to control it. This means there have to be risk assessments carried out for potential stress-related problems and adequate control measures implemented. In addition to legal requirements, stress can adversely affect the performance of individuals and there are strong ethical reasons for treating staff properly and providing support when it is needed.

People use a variety of coping mechanisms to deal with stress and pressure. The SIO must notice the warning signs, remembering there is always a cause for irrational behaviour. Dealing with death and brutality is a horrible business, often taken for granted as 'part of the job'. Experiencing the trauma of a young child's death or a maggot-infested, mutilated, decomposing corpse is never just 'another day at the office'. There are the emotions, antics, and sometimes verbal and physical abuse from extremely unpleasant and vicious people to cope with. People have to put their feelings aside during the working shift, deal with any potential negative psychological effects, then try to be ordinary people at home, yet actually suffer from post-traumatic symptoms.

It is important to spot the link between welfare, morale, and stress. The SIO must not overlook or neglect this area because s/he is too busy with task management. Welfare should never be treated as an afterthought.

Checklist—Practical approaches to addressing welfare

- Identify stress hazards and indicators, eg long hours, demanding workloads, poor working relationships, sick leave, poor morale, and try and introduce measures to keep them under control.
- The SIO should be sensible enough to recognize when their own stress levels are too high and have adequate coping mechanisms ready.
- Send home people who have worked long hours and/or arrange for them to be relieved—task someone to do this and monitor working hours.
- Informal debriefs at the end of a working day are a useful means of winding down before everyone goes home.
- Discuss stress issues and welfare during team briefings.
- Appropriate humour is a good antidote and can reduce tensions and keep morale high.
- Keep staff properly nourished, eg if no canteen facilities send out for a food buffet for everyone to share.
- Choose words carefully when debriefing things that have gone wrong. People naturally become defensive if told they have done 'wrong'. Use positive words and phrases, and discuss how things could have been done differently, which is easier to tolerate and accept.
- Arrange social functions where everyone is encouraged to attend. Alleviate travel problems and excuses by arranging or subsidizing transport.
- 'Away days' are useful and provide an opportunity for a change of venue and environment, and can be concluded by a social get-together.

- Establish confidential access to welfare support or counselling (formal or informal—a friend or colleague may be just as good as a professional). Ensure confidentiality is maintained if necessary and appropriate. Counselling can also be conducted in groups.
- Enforce time off and leave.
- Establish workload variance (eg redistributing hard-to-do or tedious tasks—without losing continuity in a line of enquiry).
- Periodic welfare and basic health checks are important.
- Encourage people to stay fit and healthy. Nothing happens without energy, which may have to be considerable during prolonged working conditions.
- Proper food and drink are a necessity—keep up blood/sugar levels.
- Make the best use of 'down time'—use it to fully recharge the batteries ready for the next challenge.
- Constantly monitor and review effectiveness of any remedies.
- Communicate with staff regularly.
- Encourage early admission of errors, oversights, or mistakes for prompt remedial action.
- Make a record of any problems identified and how they have been addressed.

3.6 **Conclusion**

This chapter has covered a key skill area that has to be worked hard on to perfect. Leadership is not an easy concept and becoming an effective leader as well as a good investigator can pose a significant challenge. However the more time and effort an SIO can put into studying the various principles outlined in this chapter the more they will find that becoming a leader and good manager will come naturally.

Through developing a talent for leadership the SIO will increase their chances of a successful and rewarding career, not to mention produce good results. The chapter has provided what has been intended to be a mixture of practical advice and some essential academic principles. It is hoped these will provide sufficient guidance and inspiration when it is most needed. The idea is to keep working at these principles and a good SIO will always take something away and learn something new from every enquiry they are involved with to increase their skills and knowledge. The lessons learnt can sometimes be harsh but such is the nature of this contentious and challenging responsibility. Self-development in this area cannot be ignored and time must be taken to reflect on personal style to grow into the type of leader that matches an SIO's vision of what a good leader should look like.

Chapter 4
Initial Response

4.1 Introduction

The key to any major crime investigation is the early gathering and recording of accurate and detailed information and securing evidence. This process starts from the very first moment the initial call or report is received and continues with subsequent attendance and management of the scene and the investigation. The SIO needs to be aware of which initial actions should have been completed. These should form part of the early considerations before and after the SIO has attended the incident.

It is essential that all those involved in initial procedures adopt the right approach. If there is any doubt whatsoever about what they are dealing with, the incident should always be treated with respect as to what it may be (or perceived to be), particularly with regard to offences such as homicide. This is because the initial assessment is fed back to the control room and supervisors who ultimately determine how it is categorized and dealt with in terms of seriousness, priority, and appropriate resources. This is in a period often referred to as the 'golden hour(s)'.

While this chapter contains useful checklists that attempt to serve as practical guides, aide memoires, or prompts, it must be remembered that sometimes over-reliance on fixed routines can be detrimental to the essential principle of 'keeping an open mind'. Each case will always be unique in some way and may require a tailored approach in one aspect or another.

At some point the SIO will take charge and direct and control the investigation. However, it is the actions taken and tradecraft used during the initial stages, ie the call or report to a passing patrol and first response, that are so critical to success. Unfortunately these preliminary stages are usually outside the control of the SIO; it is therefore essential that any actions taken are soon afterwards analysed and reviewed. This is one point of focus in this chapter—the importance of the SIO finding out what has been done, by whom, and to what standard, in order to put things right if they have already gone wrong. This cannot be done without having an appreciation of what others should have done or should be doing.

Most investigations begin with the first report and then attendance at the crime scene(s). Both can yield an abundance of information and evidence as a starting point for the enquiry. The initial information, together with a successful and professional response in smartly securing physical or trace evidence from a scene(s), gets things off to a promising start. No two circumstances are identical and the adoption of the fundamental principles can be easily adapted to suit most requirements of any particular case.

One consideration that may not be so obvious when dealing with the circumstances and nature of any incident, but nevertheless of prime importance, is the training of personnel. No opportunity should be lost in operating a methodical and professional approach in any suitable cases, even if they turn out to be of lesser importance. This will afford key staff an opportunity of becoming familiar with correct procedures and good practice.

4.2 The 'What?' Question

The object of any initial response and assessment is to try and accurately determine what has happened and ascertain the precise nature and type of incident to be dealt with. For example, if a death is involved and the deceased's doctor has issued a medical certificate as to the cause of death, there are not usually grounds

Figure 4.1 Considering the 'What?'

to suspect there is a potential homicide (the infamous Dr Harold Shipman case being an obvious exception). On the other hand, a deceased person may be laid on the floor in their own home with head injuries and signs of a struggle having taken place. Some circumstances will not always appear unequivocal, making it very difficult to rule criminality in or out straightaway. These cases are often the most challenging to deal with because of their uncertain and unpredictable nature. It may also be appropriate that a variety of less obvious offences have to be considered, including neglect or breach of care issues relating to, say, corporate manslaughter from deaths in health-care settings, prison deaths, or industrial accidents.

Therefore, as a general rule, initial responders should exercise extreme care and keep an open mind, making good use of their investigative skills to obtain as much information from the scene and any witnesses as possible (using the 5 × WH + H model). They should always take care to question and clarify any facts presented (applying the A B C principle), and record and note everything. Where there is any doubt whatsoever, the case should be handed over to a senior detective and/or SIO and other specialists to supervise and/or assume command and control of the initial assessment and any subsequent investigation.

It is a fact that some assessments and enquiries prove resource-intensive and prolonged, particularly if a major investigation is launched and a final conclusion eliminates any criminal involvement. Some serious assault victims may even make a full recovery and then refuse to assist or support the enquiry team. However, any temptation to bypass time-consuming correct procedures or to 'cut corners', make wild guesses and take unprofessional risks in order to save time and effort should always be avoided. This approach tends to prove very costly when trying to 'back track' at some later stage; whereas thoroughness is far less risk-oriented.

In most cases clues are present and just need finding. Once again, good use of the 5 × WH + H questions holds the key. The following case study shows how this method can be applied.

Case Study

Paramedics attend at an address and pronounce a young male deceased in the lounge of an apartment. There is heavy blood staining evident on the body and no obvious signs as to how he died. The police are summoned and begin seeking information (as per the problem-solving method discussed in Chapter 3—the 5 × Wh + H questions). The following questions are posed: Who is the deceased? Who raised the alarm and/or found the body? What can the paramedics tell us (eg condition of the body, any idea where the blood came from, any injuries under his clothing, did they have to force entry to get in)? What does the evidence at the scene tell us (eg any signs of a struggle)? How secure was the front door to the apartment? How was it locked (eg from the inside)? How else may entry have been gained (eg window)? What secure access or control to the communal door to the apartments is there (eg any CCTV or security staff/warden)? Were there any signs of a struggle? Who else occupies or visits the premises? What do the neighbours know? Where are his wallet, keys, and other personal belongings? What state of dress/undress was he in? When was he last seen alive, who by, and where? What was he doing/what were his movements prior to his death? What is the likely time of death/time since death (latest date on newspapers, documents, or letters inside the apartment)? What is the deceased's medical history and social/criminal background? Who and where are his close family, friends, and associates? What other potentially linked incidents have happened at this address or neighbourhood recently? What are the possible motives and hypotheses? Etc.

These are essential investigative skills for those faced with making an initial assessment and establishing what may have happened. In this scenario it could have been either a natural death due to a medical condition (causing internal bleeding) or an attack leading to the male's death, ie murder, suicide, or even an accident. A forensic post-mortem would be required to establish the cause of death and the scene should be secured awaiting the outcome, thus preserving any potential trace evidence. If these procedures and decision-making approach is not being adopted by those initially in charge an SIO must intervene and ensure that it is.

KEY POINT

A determination as to what has happened must be based on the total information available. In the early stages of a preliminary investigation it is very unlikely there will be sufficient information on which to reach a conclusion, particularly as in most cases of uncertified deaths a post-mortem will be required before a cause of death can be ascertained.

Note: See also 'Developing Hypotheses and Theories' in Chapter 2 above.

Case Study—The importance of the 'what?' question

During the early hours of the morning, a report was received of a road traffic collision involving one vehicle, which had careered off the carriageway on a remote moorland road. Police and paramedics rushed to the scene to find a BMW motor vehicle had come to a stop on the grassed verge and was positioned with the front of the car on the wrong side of the road. The vehicle had minor damage and its air bags had not been activated. A male (an off-duty police officer) was stood out of the vehicle with minor injuries, however his female partner was found in the driver's seat slumped across the front passenger seat. She had massive head injuries and the interior of the vehicle was covered in blood. His initial account was that his partner had been driving the car at about 50 to 60 mph when she was looking for a CD and had hit something in the road. The car then swerved and drove off the road colliding with a fence. She had not been wearing her seat belt. The female was taken to hospital but later died of her injuries. She had at least five fractures to her skull. Collision Reconstruction Unit officers who attended the scene noted the very minor damage and the position of the vehicle and quickly formed a view that the account given by the male did not match the physical evidence at the scene.

Quick thinking officers immediately went and attended the couple's home some eight miles away and found a blood trail in the downstairs rooms leading from an upstairs front bedroom of the property. The address was declared a crime scene and a full forensic examination conducted. A further crime scene was also established when a pool of blood was discovered on the driveway of an isolated house some 200 metres from the collision site. Further forensic examination revealed numerous blood spots extending down the driveway consistent with someone who was bleeding heavily close to the floor. Tests later proved that this blood was that of the victim.

The off-duty officer was arrested and later charged with the murder of his girlfriend. He admitted during an argument he had hit her with a hammer, then panicked, later putting her in the driver's seat and staging an accident. He subsequently appeared at Crown Court where he pleaded guilty to murder. When asked to account for the blood on the driveway he stated that he stopped the vehicle at the house in an attempt to get help, however he realized she was too badly injured to survive and struck her again with the hammer to 'put her out of her pain'. He was sentenced to life imprisonment.

4.3 Special Procedure

Some reported incidents are bound to require more in-depth investigation than others, for example deaths, in order to rule out the possibility of criminal involvement. In some forces these are known as 'special procedure' enquiries and force policy will dictate that they require a higher degree of investigation, led or supervised by a senior detective/SIO. The types of special procedure deaths would include:

- Death of any person under the age of 18 (eg SUDI or SUDC deaths—see also Chapter 14).
- Illicit drug-related deaths.
- Suicides.
- Death resulting from accidents, not being road collisions.

Note: There may also be other serious crimes that may require special and enhanced levels of initial response and investigation, such as armed robbery, sexual crimes (eg rape), or terrorist acts.

KEY POINTS

1. All deaths are investigated on behalf of the coroner and investigations must be conducted to their satisfaction, whether criminality involved or otherwise. Necessary enquiries should be duly completed along with any potential evidence gathered in order to assist the coroner to confirm the identity of the deceased and make a verdict on the cause and manner of death.
2. It may be that during an assessment of the scene a brief examination of the body of a deceased person cannot be avoided, if the cause of death is not obvious. While checking for any wounds, injuries, or recent trauma on exposed areas of the body, *protective clothing and/or gloves* should be worn and the minimum of disruption observed wherever possible and the SIO must be notified about what has been disturbed. Consideration must also be given to some religions that do not like the body being touched at all.

4.4 The JDLR Principle

There will always be a use for practical common sense and shrewdness that can't be taught on training courses or listed on checklists. SIOs should expect that officers entrusted with attending any report of serious crime will be able to spot or notice things that appear unusual or out of place (such as a 'staged crime', for instance) and put all their intuition and policing skills and knowledge to good use. It must be stressed that they are the ones who do not always have the luxury of slow-time, or a textbook, or aide-memoire to hand, nor indeed are they likely to have the benefit of all the essential facts and information that becomes available later on. This is why an on-call SIO who takes command of an investigation *must* thoroughly check and review what initial actions have been taken and any decisions, assumptions, and conclusions that have been made.

Clearly attending and dealing with reports of sudden deaths, suicides, or reports of missing persons requires a lot of tenacity. The latter category in particular is a challenge for any experienced investigator. For example, a man who reports his female partner missing and has in fact murdered her, may leave some important clues around. Initiative should be applied to find and note things that look out of place, such as missing or broken items of furniture or ornaments (indicating an argument has taken place), signs of recent cleaning such as the smell of disinfectant, or a small bonfire in the garden, or a missing shower curtain (to wrap up a body perhaps), heavily mud stained shoes, outer clothing or a muddy vehicle (from digging or body concealment) are such examples.

KEY POINT—The Jdlr Principle

A very simple principle for officers to follow when responding to reported incidents and making initial enquiries, is to use their instincts and to look for anything that 'JUST DOESN'T LOOK RIGHT' (JDLR).

Taking the initiative and responding to 'gut instinct' or being bold and sensible enough to listen to what instincts are suggesting can, in some circumstances, lead to the early detection of major crime.

> **Case study—The Yorkshire Ripper**
>
> At 10.50 pm on Friday 2 January 1981 Sgt Robert Ring and PC Robert Hydes were on patrol off Melbourne Avenue in Sheffield when they saw a V8 Rover 3500 parked up with male and female occupants on board. His name was Peter William Sutcliffe from 6 Garden Lane, Heaton, Bradford, and she was Olivia Reivers. When Sutcliffe got out of the car, which was bearing false number plates, he went to use the toilet behind a nearby stone porch and an oil storage tank. He was later arrested on suspicion of theft of the car number plates. However, the sergeant later made the most crucial decision of his career when he instinctively went back and searched the area around the storage tank. He shone his torch on the ground and lying by the wall was a ball-pein hammer and a knife. When Sutcliffe was later confronted with this evidence he confessed to being the man dubbed the 'Yorkshire Ripper' and having been responsible for murdering 13 women and attempting to murder seven others, for which he was later tried, convicted, and sentenced. These offences spanned a period of six long years.
>
> Largely through the instinctive actions of the two patrolling officers, Sutcliffe was caught and entered the history books as one of the UK's most notorious serial killers.

4.5 Good Teamwork

The SIO takes responsibility for investigations into crimes that are of utmost gravity and likely to contain many complex and connected actions, challenges, and procedures. It is likely that a sizeable number of these will present themselves in the initial stages and an essential ingredient for success is *teamwork*. This involves a combined effort between a group of dedicated professionals who join forces to produce an efficient and effective response. Each person and stage of the process connects to become part of a chain that is only as strong as its weakest link. Even if the SIO does not become involved immediately, they must set the tone for a teamwork approach as soon as possible by leading, managing, and co-ordinating all work and activity for various roles and responsibilities involved in the enquiry, which may include such roles as:

- call handler/taker/radio operator and despatcher
- duty officer/incident manager (supervisor)

- counter clerk/patrol officer
- first response officer(s)
- patrol supervisory staff
- any designated bronze or silver commanders
- detective officers (and senior/supervisory detectives)
- FLOs
- crime scene investigators/managers/coordinators
- other experts (pathologist, forensic scientists, etc).

4.6 Dealing with Emergencies at the Scene

Officers may have to deal with pressing emergencies at crime scenes and must be able to spot dangers, think quickly, and adopt a dynamic approach. They may be faced with very challenging circumstances and, in extreme cases, may have to instinctively abandon crime scenes, remove or avoid danger, and seize vital exhibits such as weapons, or leave a crime scene because of the severity of the danger or risks involved. Potential threats to members of the public and/or police officers in some circumstances may present no alternative. Safety considerations and the preservation of life are priorities that will always override the needs of an investigation.

Inner-city areas where there is distrust of the police, bitter gang feuds, and regular firearms usage, or hostile families and friends of victims, are classic examples. These are of course the exception rather than the rule, but worthy of mention because they can present added complications. In such cases the SIO may have to look at alternative ways of recreating scenes by use of, for example, CCTV, media footage, witness accounts, or photographs, because of the problems in containing contaminated or dangerous areas.

Safety of the public and the personnel sent to deal with emergencies and serious crimes is at all times of paramount importance and non-negotiable. If there is a conflict of interest between public safety and the investigation, the former always takes precedence.

4.7 The 'Golden Hour(s)' Principle

The 'golden hour(s)' concept is one largely used by the medical profession and relates to a basic rule that, in cases of severe trauma, medical complications can occur if a patient is not managed appropriately and expeditiously. The same principle can be applied to the first actions taken and response to a reported serious crime. The benefits associated with getting the most out of initial evidence-gathering opportunities and fast-tracking urgent enquiries are similar to those in medical settings—except there are threats not only to life but also to the potential loss of evidence that can never be recouped. Early decisions and actions have far-reaching consequences, and that is what the golden hour principle refers to.

The rule is applicable after the moment of very first contact, made either to call management centres, public service desks, enquiry counters, or via reports made to police officers and staff. The correct identification of an incident at this point, be it serious crime and/or homicide, is vital in order to orchestrate a thorough and dynamic response. Many homicides and other serious crimes are detected as a direct consequence of prompt and decisive actions such as locating and arresting offenders, obtaining witness details, seizing valuable CCTV footage, preserving forensic evidence, etc.

The golden hour(s) is a time when forensic evidence is most fresh and easiest to detect (eg blood is still wet), memories are still sharp, witnesses are likely to be at their most co-operative, offenders are nervous and unguarded, and lies and alibis are at their most vulnerable.

4.8 Initial Actions—Roles and Responsibilities

The following sections deal with the roles and responsibilities of those who are most likely to form part of the initial response. The SIO must fully understand and appreciate what these vital roles entail in order to conduct a review process and confirm they have performed them correctly.

Once more the importance of the A B C principle is applicable (Assume nothing, Believe nothing, Challenge/check everything). Mistakes and errors can and do happen and it is absolutely essential any mistakes or omissions are discovered and recovered quickly. There must, of course, be a clear audit trail of any remedial action taken, thereby demonstrating transparency and total honesty of purpose.

When debriefing those involved in initial actions the SIO must recognize it is *essential* to encourage people to be open and honest about what they did or did not do in order to rectify any mistakes. Mistakes cannot be put right if they are withheld or concealed in order to keep someone out of trouble. Openness and honesty must be encouraged in order for all staff to feel comfortable and not too intimidated so they communicate honestly about what actions they took. Inevitably some will not do so, which is why it is important to *check*, *check*, and *check* again.

KEY POINT—The 'Five Building Block Principles'

The Murder Investigation Manual uses an analogy and well-known term known as the *Five Building Block Principles*. These are used to describe the main principles which underpin the intial response by officers and staff who become involved in the initial stages of a major crime investigation. The headings contained within the 'blocks' will be discussed at length in this handbook and are visualiy represented here to consider alongside all the procedures that will be discussed:

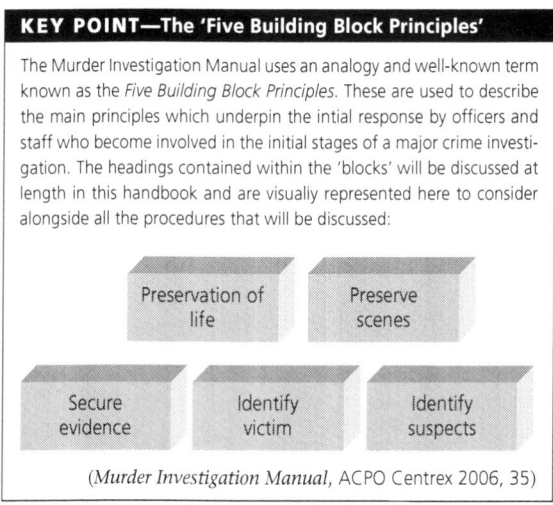

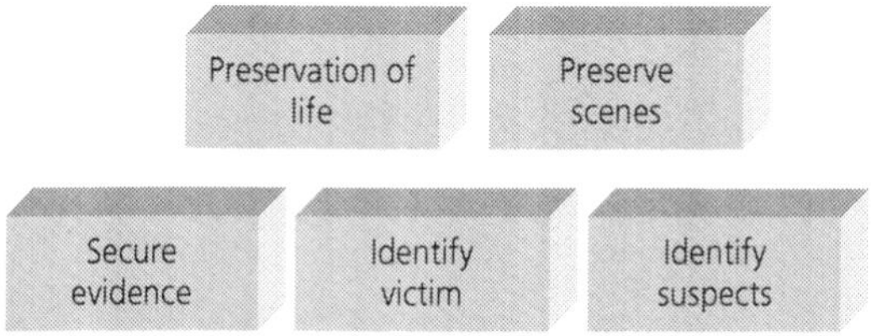

(*Murder Investigation Manual*, ACPO Centrex 2006, 35)

4.8.1 Role of call takers/call handlers/resource despatchers

Historically the role of call taker was viewed as administrative in nature, but in recent years the importance of the information gathered and subsequent action at this initial stage has been well recognized. The role has changed to one that is more pro-active and investigative in nature. However, there are practical difficulties in that most call takers are inundated with a vast number of calls of a routine nature, work in a high pressure environment, yet still need to be able to distinguish those of a more urgent type.

The call handler is the first point of contact for the maker of an emergency call and as such their priority must always be the preservation of life; and first aid advice may be required. They must also gather evidence and intelligence, adopting the mindset of an investigator, thinking of the WHO, WHAT, WHERE, WHEN, WHY and HOW principles. This call may be the only opportunity to elicit crucial information from the caller, who could also be the victim, offender, or a significant witness.

It is acknowledged that serious crime can be very distressing and affect people in different ways. Some may be angry, confused, shocked, or even hysterical, and before information can be elicited they may need a lot of reassurance from the person receiving the report. The caller may have a wealth of information and might need to be asked direct questions in order to obtain the necessary information. This is after they have been calmed, reassured, and dealt with supportively and professionally. Nonetheless, there is always the potential to secure valuable evidence at this stage by giving clear instructions to the caller and those being despatched.

It may be that the first call or report is to ask for assistance for an injured person, or report 'shots fired', screams heard, or major public disorder, etc. The initial report may not always provide sufficient information to enable the true nature or full extent of the incident to be assessed. This is where the skill of the call taker comes in.

KEY POINT

The exact words spoken by the person who first reports the incident, be they a suspect or witness, may be crucial to the investigation. There must be careful probing and eliciting of information from the person making the report and accurately recording all the details on a log, without contaminating their personal recollection of events.

The control room incident log and recording of the emergency call becomes the cornerstone of the investigation. All information must be factual, relevant, and accurately recorded. Alongside must be an assessment of the caller's vulnerability, be they a victim, suspect, or witness. Each call must be recognized as unique and reassurance must be given to the caller in every circumstance. It is the role of the call handler to assess the information and determine and quickly arrange an appropriate response, despatching the necessary resources and ensuring sufficient detailed information is provided to those concerned.

A further important element is the provision of advice on basic scene preservation and evidence recovery wherever possible. It may be impossible to totally protect a crime scene at this stage; however, advice from the call taker can reduce the risk of contamination and assist in preserving forensic evidence. For this reason the call handler should be skilled in forensic awareness and witness care, forming part of their ongoing training and development.

Advice from the call handler can reduce risk of contamination by limiting interference at the scene and preserving forensic evidence. It is necessary to make best use of the initial communication with the caller to maximize forensic potential.

KEY POINT

Different forces and agencies may have their own particular methods and structures for dealing with calls or reports regarding incidents of serious crime. The terms used—'call handler', 'call taker', and 'resource despatcher'—are therefore intended to be synonymous. There are other roles that may also be separate or included in this function, such as 'radio operator', referring to the task of despatching and organizing resources and the subsequent police response. Senior control room supervisors may also be labelled differently, such as 'force duty officer' or 'force incident manager'—normally of police inspector rank or equivalent. They are usually informed immediately and should become directly involved with reports of serious crime such as homicide or wherever specialist resources are required. They assume a supervising and controlling role in the first instance.

Checklist—Call handlers/radio operators/resource despatchers/control room supervisor (needs of the SIO)

- Create an 'incident log' on which to record accurate detail of all information received and transmitted.
- Make an early identification of the potential seriousness and nature of the incident.
- If English is not the caller's first language or they cannot be fully understood, consider use of appropriate interpretation facilities.
- Give priority to the preservation of life. Call emergency services if required and/or provide first-aid advice.

- Ascertain whether the caller is injured; if so, do they require medical assistance?
- Obtain factual, accurate, and detailed information.
- Adopt the mindset of an investigator, ie 'Who, What, Where, When, Why and How' principles.
- Be aware the caller may be the victim, offender, or significant witness (so exact words used and information elicited may become crucial and must not be distorted or recorded incorrectly).
- Reassure caller police/help is on the way.
- Give advice to remove caller and/or victim from any immediate danger.
- If suspect still present, consider keeping caller on the line (any background noise should be recorded and could be used as evidence as well as monitoring the incident).
- Deploy resources to key points quickly and confirm their attendance.
- Make patrol supervision and duty patrol inspector aware and request them to attend immediately.
- Request detective(s) to attend.
- On confirmation from supervisory officer at the scene, inform senior detective and/or on-call SIO.
- Keep all logs, tapes, and other documentary evidence relating to handling of the incident.
- Do not give out any details to the media unless authorized to do so by a senior officer and/or the duty SIO.

Information gathering

WHO:

- Who is making the call? (Identify the caller.)
- Identify the caller and/or details of victims if known.
- Establish whether caller is willing and able to remain at the scene.
- Who is involved?
- Who is still at the crime scene?
- Who is the victim and what, if any, relationship are they to the caller?
- Who else knows about it (witness identification)?
- Who is/are the offender(s)? Are they still at the scene or nearby? If not, which direction did they go in? Are they on foot or in a vehicle? Consider search/road checks. Circulate details.

- Who or what has already been despatched (eg confirm ambulance en route if required).

WHAT:

- What has happened or is happening? (Is violence being used or threatened now?)
- What is offence type (eg murder, rape, robbery, etc)?
- What action has caller already taken? (If practicable, request their assistance, ie that nothing be touched or disturbed, and not to allow anyone to enter the crime scene, touch a body, tidy round, drop litter, etc.)
- What is accurate description of offenders, including sex, colour, age, height, build, and clothing?
- What is the individual situation and caller's vulnerability?
- What is going on in the background? (Listen to any background noise for what may be going on or where they might be.)
- What vehicles are involved? (Obtain make, model, colour, and registration number.)
- What weapons have been used or seen? (In the case of a firearms incident or potential shooting, inform a specialist armed response team to attend the scene and render it safe for other, unarmed personnel.)
- What support ('back-up') is required?
- What information needs to be circulated immediately (eg details or descriptions of offenders, vehicles, etc)?

WHERE:

- Where exactly did it happen? (Identify exact location of incident, crime scene(s), or any other location which may be linked, eg vehicles, offender's address.)
- Where is caller now? (Advise they stay at that location and await police response.)
- Where is the rendezvous point (RVP) for staff, emergency services, eg ambulance?

WHEN, HOW, and WHY:

- When exactly did it happen? Obtain precise details of timing of the incident.
- How did it happen?
- How many offenders?
- Why has incident occurred, eg any precursor incidents?

Note: Consideration should be given by resource despatchers to what/where/how resources can best be utilized. For instance, where offenders may have gone, particularly if in a vehicle. Armed robbers, for example, usually have carefully planned escape routes. Also note that use of helicopters over crime scenes may attract curious onlookers and make scenes harder to protect. Specialist resources such as firearms officers or even covert resources may be an important consideration.

4.8.2 Reports to patrolling officers or counter clerks

Occasionally reports are made of an incident to officers on patrol or at a public enquiry desk. These officers and staff are then placed in a position similar to that of a call handler and should adopt the same principles and method of eliciting factual information, carefully noting the time and recording full circumstances. The person making the report should wherever possible be encouraged to remain with the officer and not be allowed to disappear. This is in order to allow sufficient time to determine the full extent of what they have seen or heard and arrange for a fuller interview.

If an individual refuses to provide personal details, the officer should record all they can about them—full description, clothing worn, who they are in the company of, vehicles, etc. This may assist in later trying to establish their full identity and conduct a follow-up interview. It must be stressed that the person could well be involved in the incident or even be the perpetrator. If there are reasonable grounds to suspect their involvement, then consideration should be given to having them arrested. It is not uncommon for offenders to speak to officers or make reports at or near the scenes of crime, trying to look helpful, or return to crime scenes to watch what is going on, or even offer themselves as witnesses. Sometimes they also talk to the media (consider the example of Ian Huntley who had just murdered Holly Wells and Jessica Chapman in the Soham murders case). This is one of the reasons it is so vital to record as much accurate detail as possible.

Case study—Murder and arson at hotel

In the early hours of one morning a fire was started on a guest-room floor at a large hotel situated in a prominent town-centre location. A spare fold-up bed left in a corridor was deliberately ignited. The offender was employed as a night porter at the premises and involved himself in raising the fire alarm and helping people evacuate the premises. Tragically, two elderly guests perished in the fire. The offender initially co-operated fully with the emergency services and police investigation, even providing false evidence at a coroner's hearing. But he was later arrested and charged with two murders in a crime that also caused multi-million-pound damage to the hotel. The initial account of his movements and activities became crucial to the prosecution case as it could be disproved. It helped convict and sentence him to life imprisonment on all counts.

Person finding a victim or witnessing serious crime

For a member of the public or even the police it may be a harrowing experience to come across or be involved in a horrendous and shocking incident. They may themselves be badly affected by the experience and require support and welfare, either immediately or at some later stage. The effects of post-traumatic stress disorder may not be obvious initially and can affect even the most hardened and experienced officers and staff. In this case consideration should be given to arranging suitable support and professional counselling. This should not be forgotten and welfare must always be taken into account and monitored, with appropriate support being supplied if and when necessary.

4.8.3 First response officer(s)

A major crime scene, particularly homicide, is perhaps the most important any officer will ever be required to deal with, and may happen only once or twice during their service. They are, however, the initial investigating officer in control and responsible for making key decisions until further assistance and supervision arrive. This will involve an initial assessment being relayed back to the control room supervisors, upon which the level, nature, and type of response are likely to be determined. A whole host of critical decisions and procedures will then depend entirely upon the effectiveness and professionalism of the first responders. Attending officers must apply their practical and investigative skills and knowledge to gain as much information from the scene as possible. Aspects that seem irrelevant in the initial stages of an investigation often gain more significance later on. It is therefore crucial to record and note everything.

Rarely is the first attending officer ever an actual witness to the incident, instead they have to depend on what they are told, their training, intuition, and good judgement to make sense of what they are dealing with.

Any decisions made and actions taken, of course, will vary significantly depending on the nature of the incident. For example, they may be greeted by a composed individual who can provide a detailed account and retrace their steps to indicate where they have found a body. Alternatively, there could be screaming, hysterical, boisterous alcohol affected males/females in emotionally charged and extremely volatile circumstances, with even an offender(s) present and looking to make an exit. Language and cultural barriers may cause added difficulties.

Whatever the circumstances, responding officers must try to remain calm and begin the preliminary yet vital stages of an investigation. This may be simply to arrive and be satisfied that all is required is immediate preservation and protection, such as shutting front and rear doors to premises, or more complex such as taping off an urban or rural scene comprising of several arterial roads, side streets, or open land. On other occasions instant action may be needed to save life, quell public disorder, attend to a victim, and/or arrest violent offenders.

KEY POINT

Officers should always be aware that the last person to see the victim alive or the person discovering the body has often been found to be the murderer.

4.8.4 Scene safety and preservation of life

The first priority for initial response staff is to make the scene safe and preserve life. A key consideration for making the scene safe is to ensure the incident does not produce any further casualties. Following this the condition of potential victim(s) or any other casualties should be assessed. With a rapid response to any major crime scene comes an overriding priority for the preservation of life and tending to the medical and welfare needs of any member of the public, especially victim(s). If there is any doubt whatsoever as to death or possible signs of life because it is not abundantly clear and obvious, first aid and resuscitation techniques should be attempted and medical assistance summoned immediately. Due to significant advances in medical science and resuscitation techniques, casualties who have suffered serious trauma can often be kept alive for a longer period of time, and as a consequence frequently make a full recovery.

In some instances there are clear and obvious indicators of death, such as decapitation, rigor mortis, decomposition, lividity marks, and so on. It should be noted, however, that police officers are not expected to be medical practitioners. A suitably qualified person has to officially pronounce life extinct and certify fact of death (not cause of death—that is for a pathologist or in some circumstances a doctor who has been treating the deceased before they died), which is normally done by a qualified paramedic, Force Medical Examiner (FME), A&E unit at a hospital, victim's own doctor, or a forensic pathologist. This should be done with the minimum of disturbance to a body (ie crime scene).

While the priority must always be the preservation of life, the following actions can minimize the impact of any scene disturbance:

- If available, visual recording and photography equipment can be used to record the detail of scenes, particularly the location of victims.
- Anything that is moved can be noted as to its original position (the people who are engaged in this activity should also be noted).
- Identifying and managing the route into and out of the scene by medics.
- Making an accurate record of any actions taken and reporting them to the SIO at the earliest opportunity.

Initial assessment

After the primary duty of preservation of life comes the requirement to conduct an initial assessment and relay a situation report to supervisers and/or the control room. This should include observations and any details of information that has been obtained from any victims, relevant locations, and other important information about the incident under investigation. Only when absolutely necessary should this ever have to include an exploratory examination of a body for any wounds, injuries, or signs of recent trauma, and if so must be very minor in nature and limited to exposed parts of the body (ie head, face, neck, and forearms). Protective gloves must be worn to do this and total avoidance of substantial disturbance of any forensic evidence and the SIO must be notified that this has taken place. Normally it is not necessary as the relevant information can be obtained from medical staff who have certified or confirmed death and in doing so will have had chance to look at the body.

Case study—Evidence contamination by FME

A partially clothed female's body was found on a piece of wasteland. It transpired she had been raped and strangled and her body dumped at this location. A force medical examiner (FME) attended the scene and pronounced life extinct. In doing so the doctor turned the body over onto one side, causing blood to stream out of the deceased's nose onto her face and mouth. This effectively contaminated and ruined any later potential DNA examination. Fortunately, some sperm traces were found inside her gums and mouth and in the oesophagus, which could be linked to an offender.

If it can be avoided no attempt should be made to search any victims for identification at this early stage as this action could destroy vital evidence or mislead. For example, a badly beaten and deceased victim found behind their front door had his pockets turned inside out and searched by officers who were looking for evidence of identification. This gave the appearance of a theft/robbery having taken place which remained a strong theory until the officers explained what they had done at the scene.

The initial assessment may also include a flash search of a crime scene or specific location for suspects, weapons, discarded clothing, witnesses etc and any information should be fed back to the control room, supervisors, and other attending officers and resources such as circulating any description of suspects and their potential entry and escape routes, vehicles used etc. Compiling and relaying a situation report can be done by using the 5 × WH + H method.

It may be useful to know that a pneumonic often provided to help conduct an initial assessment at incident scenes is SAD-CHALETS, which stands for:

S Survey (make observations, eg position of a body and any possible injuries)
A Assess (determine what has happened, eg murder or natural death)

D Disseminate (relay information to those who need to know)
C Casualties (determine approximate number and their condition)
H Hazards (eg terrain, public disorder, weather, dangerous buildings etc)
A Access (best routes for emergency vehicles and supporting resources)
L Location (using landmarks, street names, buildings etc)
E Emergency services (present and/or required)
T Type of incident
S Safety (all aspects of health and safety risk assessment)

Worthy of note is that if a victim of an assault is critically ill and the injuries are likely to prove fatal, the investigation should be categorized and treated as a full-scale murder. There should be no reliance on the possibility that the incident may not progress to this level, as valuable time and opportunity may be lost in conducting the necessary procedures and seizing any potential evidence and pursuing all valuable lines of enquiry.

KEY POINT

1. Checking for signs of life and attempting resuscitation are of paramount importance. If there is the slightest doubt whether the victim is deceased, a presumption should always be made in favour of them being alive. Human beings can give the appearance of being dead when they have in fact got vital life signs which may be very slight and hardly noticeable, for example in hypothermia cases.
2. What responding officers see, hear, record, touch, move, and do will unquestionably prove vital to an investigation. That is why it is so important to debrief properly and obtain these details before they go off duty.
3. Initial responders and supervisors should consider what/where/how and when supporting resources can be put to best use—for instance covering possible exit routes instead of all resources going to the scene when suspects are making good their escape elsewhere.
4. Any flash searches should be systematic and methodical in order to make a swift identification of useful evidence, suspects, or witnesses, and recorded to assist fully managed (eg PolSA or forensic) searches later.
5. Public areas and transport links such as taxis and buses can be checked for offenders or witnesses (including local hospitals).
6. Scene preservation is important but so too is tracking offenders and pinpointing their direction of travel. Human scent dogs (SAM—scent article method) are useful for this but need to be used quickly.

4.8.5 Basic crime scene kits

In order to assist the first officer attending a serious crime scene and be equipped to preserve the scene and minimize the chance of contamination, kits should be carried by all operational staff. As a minimum standard these should contain:

- roll of barrier tape;
- 2 × pairs of disposable overshoes;
- 2 × pairs of disposable gloves;
- major incident scene log forms;
- first-aid kit;
- aide-memoire card of checklist actions.

4.8.6 Preserving the scene(s)

This task is in three parts and comprises of:

(1) identify,
(2) secure; and
(3) protect any potential crime scenes.

Precious time may be ticking away for limiting the chances of destruction, loss, or contamination of evidential material so it is clearly important to ensure all areas relating to any scene(s) are cordoned off and scene logs commenced. A duty of the first officer(s) attending is to prevent any disturbance and stop all unauthorized persons entering crime scenes. This includes supervisory and senior officers unless there is an urgent operational need to gain entry. The three procedures are now explained in more detail.

1. Identify

The identification of all scenes is a priority activity. Dependent on the incident there may be more than one scene or the initial response may send officers to what is only part of the scene. It will be necessary to define (or redefine) scene parameters which can be based upon information, observations, air support images, CCTV etc.

2. Protect

In addition to safety issues, officers should try and prevent any disturbance from the public, media, weather, animal etc interference. A common approach path (CAP) should be determined for a single access and exit route.

3. **Secure**

Making good use of cordons, police vehicles, natural boundaries, road closures, stationing officers along perimeters etc will be necessary. The use of a designated supervisor performing a scene bronze commander role will be required for larger more complex scenes (eg outdoor).

Note: Points 1–3 above are covered in more detail in Chapter 5.

KEY POINT

In some cases there may be more than one scene that requires identifying and securing. For example, a sustained violent or sexual attack that takes place in an apartment block may provide multiple scenes, ie one of the apartments, an elevator, a landing, interior stairwell, and/or an adjacent car park. Sufficient staff will therefore be required to assist in securing and protecting those areas as quickly as possible to exclude contamination, eg from bona-fide visitors and residents.

Any item at a scene can be of evidential value, therefore nothing should be touched or moved. If, however, a need arises because something of a physical nature is in immediate danger of being lost, destroyed, or contaminated, steps should be taken to protect or recover the item in order to secure forensic evidence. In such instances, an officer should effect removal with minimum disturbance, carefully recording the exact position and location of the exhibit. Ideally it should also have been photographed in position. Fragile exhibits, ie those that can be easily lost or destroyed may include such things as footprints or tyre impressions in mud or soil that may get washed away in the rain, or blood traces that need covering up to protect them from inclement weather. Sometimes ingenuity and creativity have to be relied upon to cover items with an array of on-hand 'make-do' objects until the correct equipment arrives.

As further information becomes available, various other locations, in addition to the primary scene, may also become crime scenes, requiring immediate protection and preservation. Once preserved and contained, then usually nothing further need be done with a scene until a detective, CSI, and/or an SIO has arrived and takes charge. At this stage the only other pieces of evidence that should be collected are details of possible eyewitness accounts, any information offered and spontaneous statements of suspect(s) caught at the scene.

> **Case study—Bomb threat/blackmail**
>
> A call was made to a shopping centre from a public call box stating a bomb would detonate inside the premises that was packed with shoppers unless money was handed over. The call was traced to a call box which was found to be empty when checked. Officers quickly treated the phone booth as a crime scene and put a secure cordon around it. The store was evacuated and a hoax device safely dealt with by bomb disposal experts. The phone box was forensically examined and the offender's DNA recovered which led to him being arrested and charged with making a false bomb threat and blackmail. The successful identification and arrest was entirely down to the prompt actions taken by the officers who effectively identified and protected an important crime scene from which the crucial evidence was recovered.

Practically speaking, at such an early stage it is next to impossible to know or determine the exact boundaries for crime scene cordons and preservation. If the incident occurred indoors, the task is made that much easier; outdoors there may be additional considerations and complications, such as the weather, crowds, traffic, security, media intrusion, etc. The rule is to make the cordons as wide as possible as they can always be reviewed and brought in later, but this cannot be done the other way around.

4.8.7 Golden hour(s) actions

Here is a list of 10 golden hour actions for the first officer(s) responding, remembering an overriding priority of public and officer safety:

> **First Response officers—10 × 'Golden Hour(s)' Actions**
>
> 1. Make any scenes safe and preserve life. Identify and attend to any victims, casualties, or fatalities, and administer first aid and/or check for signs of life. Summon medical assistance where required. If victim(s) obviously deceased, cause as little disturbance as possible and ensure medically certified dead (and note precise time and by whom).
> 2. Conduct an initial assessment (apply A B C principle) and provide situation report to the control room using 5 × Wh + H method (eg what happened? how? what additional resources required? where? etc).

3. Identify, protect and secure all potential crime scenes and any items of evidential value that may be easily lost, destroyed, or contaminated (eg CCTV, weapons, discarded clothing, blood distribution, footprints, or other potential exhibits).
4. Identify entry/exit to scene with only one point of entry, a designated CAP and RVP for other attending resources. Mark out and protect perimeter, eg using barrier tape and cordons. Prevent unauthorized access and cross-contamination and commence incident scene log(s).
5. Note all actions taken and by whom.
6. Establish any victim's identity and next of kin details without disturbing evidence (descriptions, identifying marks/tattoos/features/clothing/vehicles can also be used). If family, relatives, and friends present, deal sensitively, giving preliminary support and advice.
7. Identify and arrest any suspect(s) and/or their likely escape route/direction and means (eg public transport, vehicle, or on foot). Once arrest made note any replies or significant comments and treat them as a crime scene.
8. Note details of all persons and vehicles at the scene(s).
9. Identify and separate witnesses, record details, and get initial accounts.
10. Identify, obtain, and exploit any information gathering opportunities (apply ABC principle) carefully and note the source and 'fast track' lines of enquiry (eg circulation of vehicles involved or descriptions of suspects etc).

4.8.8 Emergency service responders

Paramedics and fire-crews who attend crime scenes require debriefing as soon as possible as they have a habit of redeploying and leaving to deal with other calls and emergencies. Often they will have arrived at the scene prior to any police involvement, particularly if despatched first, or separately by the public, or their own control room. Emergency service responders create and keep their own records of their involvement and the circumstances including what they find or are told when they arrive, and sometimes even obtain or hear accounts from victims, witnesses, or even suspects. In some instances, consideration may need to be given to treating them as significant witnesses dependent on the extent of what they have seen or heard.

Emergency services personnel are, by and large, not trained investigators and therefore must be properly debriefed for any relevant information useful to the investigation such as how they gained entry to the scene (indoors or outdoors) and where they have been and what they have touched or moved. They should be asked questions such as: Who was present? What did they see? What did the victim say? (The fundamental 5 × WH + H principles.) In some circumstances they may even take photographs, which may contain valuable information about who was around the scene when they were in attendance (eg the fire service may take photographs to assist their own assessment and investigation into a fire, which may contain details of an arsonist, an associate, or a significant witness). Quite a number of emergency service vehicles now carry visual recording equipment to capture images that should be a priority to obtain as exhibits.

KEY POINTS

- As a general rule medical personnel (eg paramedics) have primacy at a scene until the fact of death is confirmed. If the death is believed suspicious then the investigation and preservation of evidence takes precedence and a victim's body should not be transported to hospital or further disturbed until an SIO says so.
- Medical teams who arrive at scenes tend to unavoidably disturb and/or contaminate potential evidence (understandable—their first priority is to save life). This, however, should be borne in mind when interpreting the crime scene. There is every possibility a body will have been moved to administer medical aid. Use of emergency resuscitation devices such as defibrillator pads can cause slight injuries to the body, which together with any discarded medical equipment need to be accounted for.
- Sensible judgement should apply to the recovery of trace evidence from emergency services' personnel, clothing, footwear, or vehicles, eg ambulances. Local agreements between the police and health authorities should provide guidance on what should/should not be retained or impounded for forensic examination. Usually samples can be taken without the need to disrupt the ability of the emergency resources to continue providing a normal service. If ambulances and/or rapid response-type vehicles are within a cordon, a path can be cleared for their release and tyre impressions can be taken or photographed prior to their release or at some later stage for elimination purposes. Normally if victims are placed within ambulances, the only items that should be considered seizing are blankets. It is not a sensible idea to seize equipment needed for other patients such as defibrillators. The SIO may need to refer to the crime scene manager to discuss and agree how best to deal with such circumstances.

4.8.9 Supervisory actions and duties

Responsibility for command and control of a major crime scene normally passes to a sergeant/inspector (or equivalent) once they become involved. They must attend the scene quickly to provide full assistance and support to the intial response staff. Continuous communication should be maintained with a control room supervisor and an assessment as to the nature of the incident made or confirmed as quickly as possible. The main actions of the supervisor can be summarized as follows.

Checklist—Supervisory officer—responsibilities

1. Attend the primary scene, and assume command and control.
2. Debrief those in attendance and determine scale, nature, and category of incident.
3. Provide a situation report to the control room.
4. Decide whether to declare a critical or major incident.
5. Check any victim's welfare and medical needs are being taken care of.
6. Check and review all responsibilities and 'golden hour(s)' actions of first officers attending have been completed correctly.
7. Establish what disturbance, if any, has been made at the crime scene, eg door/windows locked/open, lights on/off, body moved or cut down, fire on/off, etc.
8. Check that all potential crime scenes have been identified, protected, and secured.
9. Check whether essential resources are being or have been contacted, eg senior detective, CSI, and an SIO.
10. Identify any health and safety risks associated with circumstances and location and introduce adequate control measures. Also check/monitor staff welfare.
11. Make an assessment of the number and type of resources required, what equipment, additional specialist resources and contingencies is/are required, eg emergency lighting, scene tent, mobile police station, catering, extra staff, firearms officers, public order response teams/tactical advisers, back-up staff, dog handlers, road policing unit, media liaison officer, crime scene investigator(s), detective officers, local authority departments, etc—and initiate their acquisition, etc.

12. Formulate initial plan for dealing with management of any scene(s) and initiate any fast-track actions, eg arrest of offenders, scent dog searches, road blocks, circulation of persons, descriptions or vehicles, arrest teams, custody arrangements etc.
13. Allocate duties, tasks, responsibilities and prioritize activities. Ensure all persons involved are briefed as to their role and supervised.
14. Liaise with any other emergency services which may be in attendance and co-ordinate the combined response (unless/until a silver commander is nominated).
15. Make assessment and survey of area for correct scene parameters and ensure adequate inner/outer cordons in place that are staffed and secure.
16. Establish and/or review an RV point and/or FCP (forward command post).
17. Review appointment of scene loggist(s), ensure they are positioned at RV point, fully briefed and equipped with appropriate forms and documentation.
18. Review most suitable entry/exit point into scene, ie least likely/likeliest route taken by offender(s).
19. Check whether there are any other crime scenes and ensure adequate supervision.
20. Ensure collection of details of all those who are/were present (if large crowds, consider use of evidence gatherers and/or visual imaging/photography—remembering offender or significant witnesses may still be present).
21. Check to ensure all staff have recorded their actions and involvement.
22. Ensure next of kin and immediate family of victim are aware of their condition/death and are receiving adequate support from the police (if homicide, arrange suitably qualified family liaison officer (FLO) without delay).
23. Ensure unauthorized persons are removed from inside any crime scene cordons.
24. Ensure all potential witnesses are identified and their details obtained.
25. Ensure any exhibits identified are forensically preserved and confirm appropriate continuity relating to finding and location.
26. If victim conveyed to hospital, despatch officer to accompany them to note anything said and ensure evidence recovery (clothing, etc).

27. If suspect(s) in custody, confirm arrangements for custody reception, avoidance of cross-contamination, and collection of clothing and samples.
28. Make arrangements for completion of a community impact assessment.
29. Consider issuing preliminary media release and monitor and control media intrusion and interest, ensure no statements given by staff (utilize media liaison officer at earliest opportunity).
30. Identify all staff who have been involved in the initial response and arrange 'hot debrief' and collection of all notes before they retire from duty.
31. Notify and brief the senior detective and/or SIO as to what actions taken and information/evidential material obtained.
32. Make a comprehensive record of all actions taken and decisions made with accompanying rationale.
33. Consider logistical resilience in all designated roles and tasks.

4.8.10 Detective officer responsibilities

At an early stage a detective(s) should be at the scene to assist with the commencement of the investigation. For serious crime a senior detective should be summoned who will assume the role of SIO and take command until such time as a more senior 'on-call' SIO takes over. This is important, particularly if it is going to be some time before the SIO can arrive at the scene, and it should be made quite clear who is in charge until then.

Usually the hierarchical structure of the police service provides for a systematic command and control chain, with more senior supervisors and detectives attending to take control as the incident develops and becomes more serious in nature. Before an SIO is summoned, a number of assessments and decisions will probably already have been made. The initial detective has to establish what these are in order to provide a helpful briefing for the SIO.

If there is still uncertainty about the nature and type of incident, the detective will usually make an initial assessment and come to a decision about whether to hand over to a more senior detective and/or SIO. Until then it must be clearly understood that it is they who are in charge of the investigation at this point.

It may be that preserved scenes have to be entered to conduct further assessments with perhaps a CSI and, if so, this should be done with the minimum amount of contamination and whilst wearing fully protective clothing.

Detectives usually deal with and/or arrange witness interviews. They should be trained and experienced enough to know the correct procedures for when witnesses need treating as 'significant', 'vulnerable', or 'intimidated'. They should also be in possession of or have access to the appropriate documentation in which to begin a basic enquiry management system, such as message forms, personal descriptive forms, house-to-house questionnaires, exhibit management logs, forensic labels and bags, etc. These processes form the basis of detective training courses, and most should be skilled at implementing standardized administrative procedures. These are outlined in the MIRSAP (Major Incident Room Standardized Administrative Procedures) manual.

A further point is that detectives can usually adopt a different role to that of the uniform staff in attendance. They can take advantage of rummaging and engaging with useful sources of information who may otherwise be reluctant to speak with a uniformed officer. Detectives are adept at eliciting information from onlookers and 'working the crowd' and mingling with bystanders. Sometimes people will tell detectives things they would not tell to uniformed officers. Building rapport with people who may be useful as witnesses, 'confidential sources', or informants (better known under RIPA 2000 as Covert Human Intelligence Sources, or CHIS for short) is a key skill of a detective. They are also adept at using their intuitive insight like a sixth sense, gut feeling, or hunch that tells them something is not right.

Checklist—Detective officer—responsibilities

1. Record exact time of arrival.
2. Establish full circumstances of the incident and details of victim(s) and their family, relatives, and friends.
3. Ensure all possible scenes and evidence properly identified and secured.
4. Ensure any 'fast track' actions have been determined and progressed.
5. Establish whether there are any witnesses and if first account obtained. Arrange 'hot witness interviews' if necessary and assess their correct status (ie 'significant', 'vulnerable' etc).

6. Canvass the area, noting surroundings, and speak to and obtain details of all those around as either possible witnesses or sources of information.
7. Record weather conditions and lighting/visibility conditions.
8. Obtain details of all police staff and others, eg police surgeon, who are or have been present.
9. Obtain a complete description of the scene and surrounding area.
10. If emergency services in attendance, eg paramedics, fire service, establish full details and actions taken for all those who attended the scene.
11. Speak to supervision and/or first officer(s) in attendance to establish sequence of events, full circumstances, actions taken, and current information available.
12. Establish and log what exhibits may have been seized or protected, and determine what type of recovery is required (eg a weapon or item of clothing found nearby that requires careful forensic recovery by a CSI) and/or where they have been removed to as applicable.
13. Arrange and/or commence early intelligence research on victim(s) and possible suspect(s).
14. If suspects/prisoners in custody, ensure correct processes and procedures carried out (eg early examination for injuries and samples taken, collection of clothing, no cross-contamination, separate custody offices, etc). Determine what useful evidence or exhibits they have in their possession.
15. Gather any useful intelligence and information, geographic data, eg local maps, useful community intelligence, and any other possible sources of information.
16. Ensure an exhibits officer is appointed and correct procedures are adopted following the basic MIRSAP model.
17. Check for linked or precursor incidents.
18. Arrange early house-to-house enquiries within vicinity of the scene and formulate initial questionnaire.
19. Arrange early capture of any passive data systems (eg CCTV).
20. Make early contact with, and fully brief the SIO.

4.9 SIO—Initial Actions and Response

The SIO is rarely one of the first officers to attend the crime scene and is normally notified after a host of other staff and supervisors have attended, taken action, and made important decisions. Therefore there is a lot of information an SIO has to catch up on in order to take effective command of the investigation. The first contact will usually be by telephone, so good, clear communications are vital.

If the SIO is contacted in the middle of the night or at some other awkward moment, a good practical tip is to get the caller to ring back. This allows time to gather thoughts, become focused, and/or generally get completely ready to deal with the caller properly. Another useful point is to ensure that the person who contacts is someone who knows the full facts; time and energy are important and should not be wasted by having to repeat the process.

KEY POINT

If there is pandemonium and chaos the SIO must demonstrate professionalism and composure by competently bringing matters under control. This is precisely what SIOs are known and respected for, and good at—using their core skills and attributes by remaining COOL, CALM and DETACHED and sending out a clear statement of intent as to how they are going to lead the investigation.

What must be clearly understood is that as soon as the SIO is notified and called upon to become involved they are already assuming command of the investigation. By reviewing, checking, and giving instructions, the process has already begun of taking ownership of the investigation. This is true even though it may be some time before the SIO can physically attend at the scene, the police station, or an RV point. It is accepted that certain things may happen while en route that may be outside their control because they are happening in 'fast time' and at a distance. Also there may be other (eg silver) commanders who are in charge of other aspects of the incident who are outside the control of the SIO, eg if the fire service is extinguishing a large fire or a police silver commander is dealing with major public disorder or a 'crime in action' type incident. Nonetheless, the SIO must accept responsibility for and take command of the criminal investigation element of the incident or operation at the earliest opportunity and begin controlling that aspect of the incident.

KEY POINTS

1. The SIO, if unable to reach the crime scene immediately, should confirm who at that time is in command and control of the incident (not investigation because that is the SIO's responsibilty). All directions or instructions given should be recorded, making it abundantly clear what is required. Until the SIO attends the scene the senior detective or uniform supervisor will be making fast-time decisions and should always keep the en route SIO informed of any developments as soon as practicable via communications link (eg mobile telephone or radio).
2. Verbal instructions may be more prone to misinterpretation than written ones, particularly in highly pressured working environments. All instructions must be given as clearly as possible and repeated back, with the SIO keeping an accurate record of what they have been told and the actions they have raised, who to and when (ie the makings of an initial 'paper' action management system, see Appendix B).
3. The process of reviewing and updating fast-track actions should commence as soon as possible. These must be well founded, particularly if based upon uncorroborated verbal accounts of witnesses.
4. The SIO is responsible for bringing order to the many activities that have been initiated during the initial response. If not brought under control, these activities run the risk of generating further confusion and important evidence recovery opportunities could be lost.

At the very outset a fresh notebook for keeping notes relating to the enquiry should be commenced, contemporaneously recording:

- date and time notified and by whom;
- means of notification (eg phone or in person);
- full details of incident and the victim(s), using the 5 × WH + H method and details of what action has been taken so far;
- all fast-time instructions and tasks given;
- initial policy decisions.

The same notebook should continue to be used throughout to log all the actions, decisions, and relevant information received. Initially, any policy decisions can be recorded in it, together with times and dates, although these will later need to be formally transferred into an official policy file. The SIO needs to remain calm, confident, and be totally objective. Important instructions must be given to the person who is currently in charge. These must be recorded, timed, and dated in the notebook, together with important contact numbers of those at the scene whom the SIO may need to keep in close contact with.

KEY POINTS

The SIO should:

- begin assuming command as soon as the first notification of an incident is received;
- be fully briefed before arriving at the scene, whilst en route, and again on arrival. It is best to stipulate when and how often they should be contacted and updated. This is often a critical time as there are risks from lack of continuity and even temporary loss of direction and momentum if any handover is not managed properly;
- conduct all briefings out of earshot of witnesses, relatives, and friends of any victims, the public, and the media;
- use good note-taking to slow down and set a calmer tone for subsequent events at and around the crime scene. It ensures that attention is paid to precise details that should be delivered to the SIO in a manner that allows them to be recorded coherently;
- preferably to ask questions using the 5 × WH + H method to elicit relevant information. If the caller is left to deliver facts without selective and structured questioning, the briefing may become disjointed and more difficult to follow; any notes recorded will also be more difficult to make sense of;
- soon begin gathering initial thoughts such as 'what are we dealing with?'. An early assessment will trigger useful thought processes, eg what type or category of crime it is, what the motive is, any early investigative strategies, theories, and managerial considerations.

It is useful to keep a separate list and running log of important contact names and telephone numbers rather than having to thumb through pages of notes to find a valuable number that has been written in amongst something else. A printed table kept on a clipboard and readily available is always useful. It may look as simple as the following table.

Contact numbers

Name	Role	Number
Mark Tracey	Crime Scene Investigator	07562 543121
Ron Deardon	Patrol Inspector	02256 890245
Debbie Garside	Forensic Pathologist	01356 978354

It is sensible and good practice to appoint an early staff officer and/or loggist to assist. These become an invaluable asset to the busy SIO and can relieve a lot of the work and heavy demands, particularly in ensuring all policy decisions and information received plus actions issued are recorded correctly and contemporaneously. Once appointed they should stay by the side of the SIO at all times, and can have other responsibilities such as fielding non-urgent calls and writing out details of initial decisions in the policy log.

Early thoughts should be given to appointing other key people and resources who will be needed fairly quickly, for example a Deputy SIO, Crime Scene Manager, Cordon Supervisor, House-to-House Enquiries Manager, Exhibits Officer, Family Liaison officer(s), incident room accommodation and staff, outside enquiry teams, etc. This is the formation of an initial investigation and management team. Where and how to get these important resources is always going to be challenging, yet extremely important.

See Appendix A for a comprehensive SIO aide-memoir checklist.

4.9.1 Attendance at the scene or police station?

An early decision must be made as to where the SIO is going to attend, which may be at the scene RV point, a nearby police station, or some other suitable place. If the scene is indoors and well protected, there is an opportunity for the SIO to attend at a station which has the advantage of being a better place at which to receive a full and comprehensive briefing, examine any relevant data and maps/plans, and make fuller preparation. It is also an ideal point to meet and brief key people who may accompany the SIO to the scene, such as a pathologist or crime scene manager.

If, however, there is an outdoor scene then the SIO will probably not wish to create any delay in attendance at the RV point to get everything under their full control, such as arranging scene preservation and examination to their satisfaction, etc. If it is a high-profile incident, the SIO must get to the scene and take control as soon as possible, making themselves highly visible so people can clearly see *who* and *where* the SIO is and demonstrating good leadership qualities. This is also one way of applying the ABC principle and ensuring nothing is assumed or taken at face value and that everything is properly checked—for example making sure everyone's details at the scene have been obtained and that all vehicle numbers have been fully recorded. Importantly, the sight of an SIO turning up at the crime scene will boost the morale of staff and make everyone aware of exactly who is in charge.

Note: It may also be worth stipulating in advance who the SIO wishes to see and meet when they arrive (eg a full briefing and walkthrough the scene by the senior officer/detective who has been in charge).

4.10 Health and Safety Considerations

Initial response staff who attend at crime scenes may have to face a range of hazards that, because of their spontaneity, require dynamic risk assessments. Examples of these include:

- dangerous suspects and/or volatile crowds or individuals;
- liquid blood and body fluid samples;
- items stained with blood or other body fluids;
- items infested with parasites;
- drugs and drug paraphernalia, eg syringes;
- hazardous chemicals;
- explosives, improvised explosive devices (IEDs), biological, radiological, and nuclear agents;
- unsafe buildings or materials;
- firearms and ammunition;
- sharp items and weapons;
- difficult terrain or dangerous environment and weather;
- disease and poison risks.

Generic risk assessments should exist for attendance at crime scenes. However, given the above, it is essential wherever possible that appropriate advice is sought and personal protective clothing is worn when required. In addition to protecting the individual this minimizes the possibility of contamination. At a major or serious crime scene, once cordons are in place standard protection consists of a scene suit with hood up, face mask, overshoes, and protective gloves.

4.11 Dealing with Victims, Witnesses, and Suspects

4.11.1 Victims transferred to hospital

When a victim is moved from the scene to the hospital the identity of the ambulance crew and the details of the hospital should be established. Ideally an officer should always travel to hospital with the victim in the rear of the ambulance, making sure they do not interfere with any medical treatment being administered. This is to provide evidence of continuity and to co-ordinate investigative actions at hospital. If this is not possible, an officer or civilian investigator should attend hospital as soon as possible. They should remain with the victim once they have arrived at hospital and be ready to listen and receive any comments or facts they may wish to make about the incident, particularly if it becomes a dying declaration.

An officer should liaise with the hospital staff about the careful removal of any clothing, although local arrangements and agreements may exist to cater for and standardize this process. For instance, any cuts should be careful to avoid bullet holes, or tears, or cuts that may have been caused by other weapons. Pre-transfusion blood samples are also important to the investigation at this stage.

As a general rule, casualty treatment rooms and theatres, etc should not be sealed off as crime scenes unless an incident has taken place within them. As with the rules for dealing with ambulances and emergency vehicles, the only items worth seizing are probably likely to be sheets or blankets used to cover the victim. Bodies can be moved to side rooms to free up treatment rooms and avoid any disruption to other patients. These decisions can form part of the forensic strategy and be entered into the policy file.

Priorities for officers attending the hospital should be:

- establish identity of the victim(s);
- if victim is conscious, try to establish what has happened including details of suspects, witnesses, and others present during the incident;

- obtain medical opinion about the victim's injuries and condition;
- obtain details of family, friends, or associates of the victim;
- arrange forensic seizure of any clothing, possessions, or other potential exhibits.

4.11.2 Victim pronounced DOA (dead on arrival) at hospital

If a victim is pronounced dead on arrival at the hospital, an officer must do the following.

Checklist—Victim—DOA at hospital

- Obtain full details of medical staff involved.
- Confirm precise time that victim was officially pronounced life extinct and who certified fact of death (and collect any accompanying documentation).
- Establish any probable cause of death.
- Check and agree where body will be transferred to and how (eg if being moved from emergency ward or treatment room).
- Declare body a crime scene and commence a scene log.
- Ensure body is protected as a crime scene (keeping it sterile).
- Seize any exhibits such as clothing and personal belongings, and anything removed from the victim, eg bullets or sharp instruments.
- Obtain any pre-transfusion blood sample.
- Beware of possible interference and contamination of body by medical staff and/or relatives, friends, and associates.
- Obtain medical notes and any x-rays in readiness for pathological post mortem.
- Relay details of death to supervision and SIO at earliest opportunity.

4.11.3 Dying declarations

Under common law, on an indictment for either murder or manslaughter, a dying declaration from a victim can be accepted in evidence, provided that the judge is satisfied they were conscious of their dying state at the time it was made.

The general principle for a dying declaration to be admitted in evidence is that there must be a settled hopeless expectation of death in that the victim must have abandoned all hope of living. They do not need to be expecting to die immediately but certainly within a short time. It must be shown that when the declaration was made the victim believed death was impending. Dying declarations are admissible only where the death of that victim is subject of the charge and the cause of death subject of the declaration.

Checklist—Dying declaration

- Can be taken anywhere.
- Can be taken by any person.
- Need not be in writing.
- The accused need not be present.
- The victim need not be on oath, but must be in settled and hopeless expectation of death.
- The contents of the declaration must relate to the cause of death.

4.11.4 Witnesses and/or victims

All attending officers need to ensure that any potential victims and witnesses are quickly identified. There are many considerations with witness interviews that are the subject of Chapter 10. However, details that are recorded during this initial period can prove time-critical and vital to the early stages of an enquiry. It is not uncommon, for instance, for enquiry teams to spend hours and hours of work later down the line in trying to find the origin of comments recorded in officers' notes made at the scene. An example is when details of a potential witness are noted down without any reference to where they came from or who made them, and how they came to have such information (ie provenance). For example, an officer standing near a cordon noting that he had been told the name of the person responsible for the murder, but could not recollect who had told him or how he came by the information (reaffirming the importance of the 5 × WH + H principles!).

An initial account can be crucial and it is poor practice to have different officers repeatedly asking the same witness for their account. If the initial officer obtains a witness's initial account and records it, any subsequent officer can get details from them rather than asking the witness all over again. This may also affect the account given and the integrity of the process.

4.11.5 Identification and arrest of suspects

The arrest of an offender should always be a priority for officers and investigators attending incidents, being ever mindful that the suspect may still be at the scene or may in fact return. In order to reduce the risk of cross-contamination, wherever possible the arrest of a suspect should be made by an officer who has not already attended the crime scene. However, there may be a situation when the first officer responding is forced to make an arrest. In such cases the officer should take steps to reduce contamination and fully report the circumstances to the SIO (see also Chapter 11).

Significant statements and unsolicited comments

If an officer makes an early arrest then as a general rule they should not interrogate the suspect. This is something that will need to be carefully managed under the SIO's supervision later on. If, however, the suspect is talkative and insists on providing a version of events, once the caution has been administered their comments must be recorded properly. The suspect should then be invited to sign the record, and asked to endorse the comments with words similar to 'I certify that this is a true and accurate record of what I said'.

A danger occurs where officers then engage the suspect in conversation asking further questions as a result of these comments, which then effectively becomes an interview.

The treatment and questioning of a suspect are contained in Code C, paragraphs 11.1A, 11.1, 11.4, and 11.4A of the Police and Criminal Evidence Act 1984. The Code ensures that all persons suspected of involvement in a crime are dealt with in a fair and proper manner in accordance with the law:

> 11.1A An interview is the questioning of a person regarding their involvement or suspected involvement in a criminal offence or offences which, under paragraph 10.1, must be carried out under caution. Whenever a person is interviewed they must be informed of the nature of the offence, or further offence, concerned.
>
> 11.1 Following a decision to arrest a suspect, they must not be

interviewed about the relevant offence except at a police station or other authorized place of detention, unless the consequent delay would be likely to:

(a) lead to interference with, or harm to, evidence connected with an offence; interference with, or physical harm to other people; or serious loss of, or damage to, property;
(b) lead to alerting other people suspected of committing an offence but not yet arrested for it; or
(c) hinder the recovery of property obtained in consequence of the commission of an offence.

Interviewing in any of these circumstances shall cease once the relevant risk has been averted or the necessary questions have been put in order to attempt to avert that risk.

11.4 At the beginning of an interview the interviewer, after cautioning the suspect, shall put to them any *significant statement* or silence which occurred in the presence and hearing of a police officer or civilian interviewer before the start of the interview and which has not been put to the suspect in the course of a previous interview. The interviewer shall ask the suspect whether they confirm or deny that earlier statement or silence and whether they want to add anything.

11.4A A *significant statement* is one which appears capable of being used in evidence against the suspect, in particular a direct admission of guilt. A significant silence is a failure or refusal to answer a question or answer satisfactorily when under caution, which might, allowing for the restriction on drawing adverse inferences from silence, give rise to an inference under Part III of the Criminal Justice and Public Order Act 1994.

Identification of suspects by a witness

The principal methods used to identify suspects connected to any criminal investigation and the requirement to keep records are contained under Code D (revised on 1 August 2004), Police and Criminal Evidence Act 1984, ss 60(1)(a), 60A(1) and 66(1) Codes of Practice A–G effective from 1 January 2006.

3.1 A record shall be made of the suspect's description as first given by a potential witness. This record must:

(a) be made and kept in a form which enables details of that description to be accurately produced from it, in a legible form, which can be given to the suspect or the suspect's solicitor in accordance with this code; and
(b) unless otherwise specified be made before the witness takes part in any identification procedures under paragraphs

3.5–3.10, 3.21, or 3.23.

(c) A copy of the record shall where practicable, be given to the suspect or their solicitor before any procedures under paragraphs 3.5–3.10, 3.21, or 3.23 are carried out.

(This is dealt with in more detail in Chapter 10.)

4.11.6 Transporting suspects

There are usually clear guidelines for transporting prisoners to custody offices, but in exceptional cases they may have to travel in the rear of 'ordinary' police vehicles instead of appropriate prisoner vans. This has to be managed carefully to avoid any inferences later of unsolicited comments and admissions made during the journey. Any comments or admissions about the case are best saved for the formal interview process when the suspect's rights under PACE can be assured and proper legal representation arranged.

Care should be taken when managing these arrangements and, if there is more than one prisoner, separate vehicles/vans should be used to transport them. Separate custody offices should also be used wherever possible to avoid cross-contamination or contact between them (see also Chapter 11 about suspect arrest strategies).

4.12 Firearms Incidents

Serious crime sometimes involves the use of firearms and this presents different problems and considerations for attending and dealing with crime scenes and the initial response.

If any incident involves the criminal use of firearms then only armed officers in a protected vehicle should initially attend the scene. This is potentially the time when the public, the police, and other emergency services are at greatest risk from the suspect(s). The advice that should be given to the first officer attending should be to make an immediate assessment of the situation from the information to hand using the aforementioned SAD CHALETS model.

Officers who attend should apply basic firearm tactics, known as the Six Cs.

1. Confirm	as far as possible the location of the suspect and that firearms are involved *without unnecessarily exposing yourself to danger.*
2. Cover	to be taken, if possible, behind substantial material. Brick walls are usually sufficient. Motor vehicle bodies or wooden fences *do not stop bullets.*
3. Contact	your supervisors and convince them of the serious nature of the risk and call for suitable back-up.
4. Civilians	should be directed to a place of safety. *Be positive.*
5. Colleagues	should be prevented from coming into possible danger areas. *Direct them positively.*
6. Contain	the situation as far as practicable. Try to maintain observations on the suspect, but place *emphasis on safety.* See also *Manual of Guidance on Police Use of Firearms* (ACPO, 2006) and *ACPO Emergency Procedures Manual* (ACPO, 2002).

The operational response to the incident may initially be one of neutralizing the scene and ensuring it is safe to deploy other resources, including ambulance personnel. This does not necessarily aid the successful securing of the scene for evidential potential, but may nevertheless be essential for safety reasons. It may still be possible, however, to establish a rendezvous and forward control point provided they are not so close as to be in danger from gunfire. A log should be commenced at this location. Routes to and from the rendezvous point must also be 'safe'.

An inner cordon can be arranged utilizing available unarmed personnel until suitable replacements by armed personnel become available. An outer cordon is also required which provides a buffer zone between the public and the inner cordon. In these circumstances a gold, silver, and bronze command structure should be quickly established, with the SIO adopting the silver commander (investigation) role.

The forensic recovery of firearms and ammunition, and the examination of scenes where firearms have been used, present different requirements and considerations. The important points to stress for the initial considerations have already been covered in this section in terms of scene and exhibit preservation prior to a full and detailed examination and search.

4.13 Conclusion

This chapter has aimed to outline and explain the core functions and responsibilities of all those who may be involved in the initial response to a serious crime, and to explain the roles and responsibilities involved and high standards required. In doing so it is hoped it will provide those tasked carrying out these roles, and more significantly the SIO, with a good appreciation of what is required.

Checklists of duties for various tasks are never going to be exhaustive, nor are they intended to prevent the use of initiative. It must also be remembered and stressed that it is a team effort and the successful response that kick-starts any major investigation will always depend on the dedication, commitment, professionalism, and co-operation of all concerned.

It is intended that the lists provided will be useful for the SIO when they attend at the scene or even when they are first contacted about an incident. The early organization of thoughts around initial duties and responsibilities is a good process to apply the mind to as quickly as possible. Checking and re-checking things that should be done have been done is what the role requires; there is hopefully less chance then of missing something that may be crucial to the investigation. It must be stressed that the final decision about appropriate investigative action and activities must be driven by the circumstances and nature of each individual investigation, and not by mere compliance with a checklist.

Finally, the most important points for the purposes of the SIO from this chapter are not only to demonstrate good leadership skills by taking early control of what could be chaotic and frantic circumstances, but also to check and review what important decisions have been made and activities have already taken place. This is because the initial response comes in the period often referred to as the 'golden hour(s)' and as such will almost certainly have a critical bearing on the success of an investigation.

Chapter 5
Management of Crime Scenes

'The truth is present at every crime scene. It is the job of the SIO to find it.'

5.1 Introduction

The French medico-legal pioneer of the nineteenth century, Edmond Locard, was responsible for the principle 'every contact leaves a trace'. This means that anyone who enters a crime scene both takes something of the scene with them and leaves something behind—known as the Locard Exchange principle (E Locard, 1929). It is important to search for and secure this evidence.

The investigation of a crime usually starts at the point where the offence is committed (or in homicide cases where the body is originally found). In a search context the investigation may begin with the search 'for' rather than the search 'of' a crime scene. This is normally referred to as 'Scene (1)', and any further scenes are sequentially numbered thereafter. The importance of preserving any crime scene and conducting a comprehensive scene assessment cannot be over-emphasized. The evidence that may be available can produce a solid base on which to build or support a case.

It is interesting to note that in a survey of 32 SIOs from the Metropolitan Police, the greatest solvability factor that contributed to the solution of a case identified out of a long list was forensic material (38 per cent).[1]

[1] M Roycroft, 'What Solves Hard to Solve Murders', (2007) 3(1) *Journal of Homicide and Major Incident Investigation* (NPIA).

The types of information from the crime scene can include determining the modus operandi (criminal method or behaviour), linkage of people and objects to/from the scene, or offender/suspect, corroborating/negating witness and suspect accounts, identification of suspects or witnesses, providing investigative leads and any potential other locations where a crime may have taken place. Crime scenes vary considerably in type, ranging from domestic buildings to vehicles. Outdoor crime scenes can include back gardens, beaches and coastal zones, inner city woodland areas and public open spaces, to entire open moorland and remote mountain slopes; although often the most important scenes are in fact the victim and offenders themselves.

A huge variety of forensic trace evidence can come from sources such as vehicles, cigarette ends, clothing, bullets and firearms, fibres, paint, implement/tool marks, bodily materials and fluids (hair, semen, blood, saliva), and impressions (finger/palm prints, tyre and footwear marks), soil, rock fragments and geological raw materials such as brick, glass, plasterboard, tiles, concrete, and cement. Virtually anything can and may provide forensic evidence.

Crime scene evidence and characteristics can and do provide other useful information that may help solve a crime, eg the personality type of the offender will be represented. This is because an organized offender will likely leave behind very little evidence at a crime scene because they have taken time and consideration to plan and prepare for the execution of their crime. By contrast, a disorganized offender will leave behind lots of information and evidence, probably because the offence has occurred during a mad frenzy after a spontaneous reaction. This will also be dependent on an offender's knowledge and experience on what may be detectable.

An advantage of physical evidence is that it cannot be affected by faulty memory, prejudice, bad eyesight, or any preference 'not to get involved'. However, it must be remembered that in order to use it evidentially it must be proved to have been recovered properly. This involves the correct sterile examination, packaging, labelling, proof of continuity, forensic sampling, preparation for analysis, types of analysis, interpretation, and reporting. The 'integrity' of any exhibit needs to be proved beyond any doubt as to preservation, recovery, storage, and avoidance of interference or cross-contamination. The chain of custody of any forensic samples in particular must be given careful consideration. All relevant legislative authorities and powers must also be strictly complied with, and practically speaking if there is any possibility that a search warrant is required then the rule of thumb is always to get a warrant.

Primary crime scenes are normally where the main part of the crime itself actually took place, while secondary scenes are usually associated crime scenes. The potential for the sudden creation of a secondary scene should be included in any pre-planned search strategy, for example searching buildings or land for a suspect or to conduct an arrest. There is usually a need to consider an examination of that scene for blood staining, discarded clothing and footwear, mobile telephones, computer usage, a weapon etc. In such cases any scene preservation and resulting forensic recovery planning should be recorded and treated as any other primary scene examination, ie under the supervision of a CSM and authorized by the SIO.

5.1.1 Crime scene examples

- Location where offence took place.
- Body (or body part) recovery site (the body itself should be treated as a crime scene and a body recovery strategy carefully developed, and an evidence recovery strategy should be determined, samples being taken prior to any removal, wherever possible). (Note: In terrorism cases a body part has been deemed by the coroner to include anything over 5 cm^2.)
- Place where a body has been moved to/from.
- Location where a body or object may be suspected of being located.
- Any victim.
- A witness who has come into contact with a victim, an offender, a crime scene etc.
- A suspect.
- An attack site.
- Anywhere there is trace or physical evidence, eg tyre marks, footprints, location of a weapon, blood distribution, clothing, body concealment tools, eg a spade etc.
- Any articles connected to victim(s), witness(es), or offender(s).
- Vehicles connected to an incident (including those used to transport suspects or victims such as police vehicles and ambulances).
- Premises connected to offender or suspect.
- Access or escape routes to/from primary scene taken by offender(s).

- Casualties or bodies removed to hospitals or mortuaries. (Note: try to prevent hospital staff placing all clothing in one bag to avoid cross-contamination.)
- Location where a crime has been planned or some element of the offence has taken place.

Note: It is important that the first officer(s) attending any 'scene' is(are) aware of the potential for multiple crime scenes and the need to protect and preserve them also.

5.2 Role of the SIO

What constitutes a crime scene is up to the SIO to decide. Prior to the arrival of the SIO, however, certain decisions will probably have already been made. These must be reviewed and further decisions made as to the following:

Checklist—SIO initial decisions at crime scene

- What constitutes the scene(s) and whether there are any others that have not yet been identified or defined.
- Clarify or amend scene parameters and any search or scene boundaries.
- Confirm arrangements for security and protection.
- Ensure adequate resources are in place to protect, supervise, and manage the scene(s).
- Check scene logs are being completed correctly and that staff engaged in compiling them have been properly briefed and are being supervised
- Decide what experts and specialists are required and arrange attendance (eg CSM/CSI, photographers, pathologist, forensic scientists, geo-forensics specialists, ballistic experts, etc—and the sooner they arrive the better for maximizing the recovery of forensic evidence).
- Consider the order upon which experts will need to visit the crime scene to avoid any cross contamination or destruction of potential evidence.
- Establish if an RV Point has been nominated for resources to attend at and what logistical arrangements may need to be made (eg parking facilities).

Before entering any crime scene, the SIO and crime scene manager (CSM) must not only determine its boundaries but also decide how to approach it and determine what fragile evidence may be present that requires special and perhaps immediate attention (eg a body or something such as a footprint out of doors). The scope of the search is usually determined using the 5 × WH + H principles. Any developing hypotheses must remain fluid and the SIO must remember that *initial theories are always provisional and must remain dynamic.* New facts emerging may mean theories may have to be reassessed or modified.

A good SIO is wise to remember that anything and everything may be classed as evidence and become significant later, and must be treated with care until proven otherwise.

KEY POINT

A crime scene always belongs to the SIO and there might only be one opportunity to get it right, so the SIO should ensure that correct procedures and processes are adhered to and they are done thoroughly and professionally.

5.3 Role of Crime Scene Manager and Co-ordinator (CSM/CSC)

Once involved in the investigation of a major enquiry or a large complex case the SIO should ensure there is an appointed crime scene manager and/or co-ordinator if more than one major scene is involved (CSM/CSC). The status or seniority for these roles may vary according to the nature of the investigation. For some investigations, including all homicide cases, they should go to accredited crime scene managers (CSM), although for less serious cases an experienced Crime Scene Investigator (CSI) may be utilized.

The CSM or CSC should form part of the SIO's management team. Their role includes assessing, deploying, and managing staff both from the force crime scene examination unit perspective and also from other agencies. They act as an adviser to the SIO on examination strategies, evidential types, values, and prioritization of exhibits; they also maintain comprehensive notes and contribute to the SIO's forensic strategies. They are effectively the focal point for all forensic-related enquiries, after the scene examination has finished and beyond.

The earlier a CSM/CSC is involved the better managed and more coordinated the investigation will be. For pre-planned crime investigations, involving a CSM at the preparation stage will enable appropriate tactical options to be put into place prior to any searches (eg execution of warrants) and therefore forensic recovery potential will be maximized.

The CSM appointed to the investigation should be the SIO's first point of contact for any deployment of CSI staff. The SIO should not try to deploy a CSI without prior consultation with the CSM, because it is essential for the CSM to be involved in the management and development of all crime scene strategies and processes, etc. The CSM is also the most appropriately qualified person to deploy additional CSI staff as they have an overview of all other aspects of the investigation, and are also able to develop appropriate strategies and advice on the most suitable sampling techniques, best practice, and brief forensic staff on behalf of the SIO.

Note: There are also available specialist forensic advisers that can be supplied by either a reputable forensic provider or from the NPIA (who come free of charge!). These are usually experienced scientists who can perform a co-ordinating and reviewing role and advise the SIO on possible examination options to ensure that all possibilities for achieving results to support the investigation are explored.

Checklist—Role of crime scene co-ordinator (CSC)

- Acts as liaison between the CSM and investigation team.
- Co-ordinates all scenes within the investigation, providing the CSM with necessary resources.
- Advises the investigation team on the viability of forensic evidence.
- Liaises with other relevant agencies.
- Briefs relevant persons on scene examination and scientific support matters.
- Accurately records information as prescribed in national and local procedures.
- Ensures compliance with health and safety legislation.
- Provides quality assurance prior to the release of a scene.
- Attends forensic strategy meetings when required.
- Ensures that all aspects of staff welfare are considered.

Role of crime scene manager (CSM)

- Ensures adequate preservation measures have been taken to protect the scene.
- Esnsures a scene log has been started and that the officer in charge of the log is aware of their responsibilities.
- Decides on the sequence of evidence gathering, requesting other services if required (eg specialist photography, forensic scientists).
- Alleviates resources effectively within the scene.
- Updates the CSC and SIO at regular intervals.
- Liaises with the exhibits officer and offers advice on forensic examination of items.
- Accurately records information as prescribed in national and local procedures.
- Ensures swift submission of items.
- Ensures compliance with health and safety legislation.
- Attends forensic strategy meetings when required

(Source: *National Crime Scene Investigation Manual*, issue 1 (ACPO National Crime Scene Investigation Board, 2007), 46–7.)

5.4 **Role of Exhibits Officers (EO)**

An EO has a pivotal role in any investigation and should be an experienced detective or investigator trained in all aspects of exhibit management, including packaging, storage, documentation, and the HOLMES2 Exhibit Management System, together with an up-to-date knowledge of forensic techniques and their applications.

From the outset of the investigation, the EO should be identified and remain for the duration of the investigation through to the completion of any trial. They should attend all briefings and must establish a close working relationship with the CSM, CSIs, first officers responding, and indeed all the investigators, in order to ensure that all recovered exhibits are properly handled and packaged, together with the necessary signed labels. Extreme care must be exercised to guard against the risk of contamination or cross-contamination throughout the entire exhibit-handling process. The importance of preserving the integrity of an exhibit cannot be overstated. The best prosecution case can fail if there is a breakdown in continuity of a key forensic exhibit and that is a core responsibility of the EO.

The EO should be allocated a dedicated office with appropriate storage, freezer, drying facilities, and a HOLMES2 terminal. Throughout the investigation all exhibits must be kept under close review, particularly those sent for specialist forensic or fingerprint treatment or examination. The management team should hold formal exhibit reviews on a regular basis in order to assess the forensic potential of every exhibit and check on any outstanding examination results that are awaited.

5.5 Processing a Crime Scene

The various phases of managing and processing a crime scene are as follows:

1. First response officer(s) and any other emergency services attend the scene(s) (as dealt with in Chapter 4).
2. Identification, security, and protection of the scene(s) takes place.
3. A crime scene assessment is conducted.
4. Detailed forensic examinations and searching take place.
5. Correct scene documentation and exhibit recovery and management procedures are applied.
6. Any relevant material (ie under CPIA requirements) is correctly recorded and recovered.
7. Health and safety and cross-contamination risks are carefully managed and controlled throughout 1–6 above.

5.6 Scene Security and Preservation

It must be remembered that the actions taken by the first responders at a crime scene have a huge impact on the outcome of an investigation. Destruction, contamination, or loss of evidential material is most likely to occur at this stage or very soon thereafter. When the police are despatched to incidents or reports of suspicious circumstances there may well be other competing demands for their attention as well as the requirement to preserve evidence, eg violent confrontations, public disorder, casualties, distressed victims, families, friends or witnesses, environmental challenges etc. They must nevertheless *ensure* that correct procedures at some point are applied in order to give the recovery of trace evidence every chance of success.

The fundamental principle is that once identified and secured, crime scenes must be preserved and protected from entry by unnecessary and unauthorized persons (including the family, friends, and relatives of victims, offenders, and in particular the media). This is to avoid physical evidence being altered, moved, destroyed, lost, or contaminated. No one should be allowed to enter a designated crime scene except to save life or certify life extinct until the arrival of a senior detective and/or the SIO and crime scene manager/investigators. Any official persons, including supervisory personnel and senior officers, who do not have a specific or valid reason for being inside the crime scene should be regarded as *unauthorized* persons. Only the SIO or the crime scene manager can grant access to a crime scene, and this rule must be firmly communicated to all those involved at the scene(s).

Upon arrival at the scene, the SIO should conduct an immediate assessment of the security arrangements and parameters, position, and adequacy of the cordons. This should take cognizance of the circumstances of the case and any information that is known, such as possible routes the offenders took to and from the scene. The exact parameters, when determined, should be both recorded in writing and indicated clearly and accurately on a sketch, plan and/or map. If any alterations are made to the parameters then these also need accurately recording.

Note: When entry into a scene is authorized by the SIO, say for a medical professional (or an expert) they should, wherever possible, be provided with suitable protective clothing, eg scene suit, overshoes, gloves, mask, and hood. A member of the crime scene investigation team should also accompany them.

Case study—waste bin clue

A drinks can was found in a waste bin situated marginally outside the police crime scene cordon. Because of its position, tape fastened to a nearby lamp-post at a bus stop initially excluded the bin. Fortunately the SIO reviewed and extended the cordon parameters to include the

Case Study—Waste bin clue

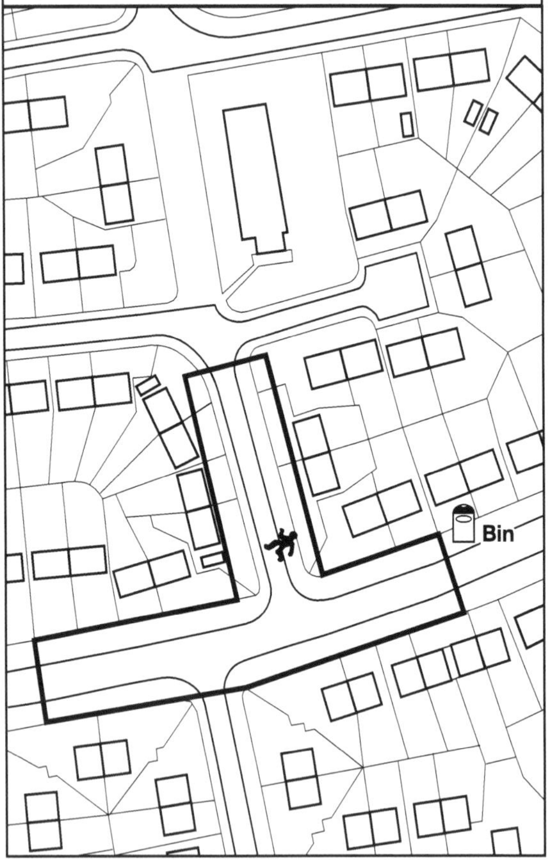

area covered by the bin. A witness subsequently identified the offender as having stood at the bus stop before the murder was committed, drinking from a drinks can, which he was then seen to place in the waste bin. The can was forensically recovered and revealed the DNA profile of the offender.

KEY POINTS

1. The size of a cordon is important to protect and preserve evidence. A cordon that is too big can be reduced whereas a cordon that is too small cannot be enlarged so *the rule is always err on the side of caution and start big.*
2. In firearm discharges stray bullets can and do travel much further than a target or victim's location. Therefore, proposed search areas for bullet heads may need to be significantly extended—a fact worth considering when setting cordon parameters.

5.6.1 Use of scene cordons

Security cordons are vitally important, not only for guarding the scene but also protecting the public, controlling sightseers and the media, preventing unauthorized interference and access (eg by suspects), facilitating the emergency services response, and for preserving evidence and avoiding contamination. An initial response should always involve arranging scene security by putting as quickly as possible effective cordons in place. This can become challenging, particularly if there is a large area to cordon which is outdoors. At a later stage it may have to be proved to the satisfaction of a court that there was no possibility of any interference with or contamination of the crime scene, particularly by the offender if trace evidence links them to the scene.

Cordons can be very resource intensive to maintain their integrity and the SIO will depend heavily on uniform police colleagues to ensure there are sufficient resources made available to make them effective. They become a highly 'visible' part of the investigation and what the public sees if they are at the scene or watching on television news reports. Apart from an essential security and scene sterility function they influence community confidence on how the enquiry is being managed and must look and be extremely professional.

KEY POINTS—Visibility and professionalism

1. Officers tasked with scene security duties should be clearly visible to the public. Cordon control officers are on display and indicative of the level of police professionalism. Shoddy standards from officers looking bored or undisciplined (eg sat in a police vehicle reading a newspaper) send out bad messages and affect public trust and confidence.
2. While on cordon duties officers should be encouraged to talk to anyone around and passers-by who may have vital information to offer which can be fed into the incident room. They must be warned, however, about not giving out details of the investigation without prior permission of the SIO, eg to media reporters or members of a victim's family.
3. Scene preservation and security officers must be properly briefed. A daily briefing sheet could be handed to them, explaining why the scene is being preserved in a form that could be communicated to members of the public. This could include a list of key questions to ask and will enhance their role as members of the enquiry team.

Indoor scenes are usually comparatively easier to secure by the closing of doors and restricting entry into premises, initially by the presence of officers at entrance and exit points. This is because they are self-contained. However, with outdoor scenes there can be additional considerations and complications such as weather, crowds, traffic, security, media intrusion, elevated observation points nearby, etc. In such cases cordons should be made as wide as possible and can always be reduced later. Restricting access to outdoor scenes can be achieved by the use of metal barriers or cordon tape, vehicles to block entrances, officers or PCSOs positioned around the perimeter and entry/exit points, dog handlers, mounted branch (if large rural area for instance) to ensure boundary lines cannot be crossed. Natural boundaries such as hedges and fences can also form part of a cordon, bearing in mind the potential for offenders to have discarded items such as weapons, blood stained clothing, mobile phones, or stolen items over such boundaries. Road blocks may also be necessary dependent on the location. Scene cordons *must* be adequately guarded along their entire perimeter to ensure there is no unauthorized access.

It is good practice to assign ownership for managing scene cordons to a supervisor in a designated 'bronze commander' role, ie as dedicated Cordon Manager. Their task is to ensure adequate resources and arrangements are in place to safeguard the integrity of and eliminate unauthorized access to the crime scene, which includes briefing and continuously supervising all those on cordon security duties. It also includes ensuring that scene logs are completed correctly.

KEY POINT

An SIO should be intrusive by challenging the effectiveness of cordon management and scene security. This can be simply by questioning cordon officers about the duties they have been tasked to perform, who is in charge of them, and checking the content, accuracy, and quality of their scene logs.

5.6.2 Making use of inner and outer cordons

There are usually two types of cordons—inner and outer. In some instances it may be necessary to set up an additional outer cordon, ie a third cordon. This would be a wider cordon covering both the inner and outer cordons. This might occur when there is more than one significant scene within close proximity. An example occurred in Operation Sumac which was a linked series of five homicides in December 2006 near Ipswich in Suffolk. Two of the victims bodies (Annette Nicholls and Paula Clennel) were located very close together adjacent to a busy country road. At these scenes, inner and and outer cordons were created with an additional outer cordon to keep the media and public out of the perimeter. (See (2008) 4(2) *Journal of Homicide and Major Incident Investigation* (NPIA), 94–7.)

Note: The terms 'hot zone', 'warm zone', and 'cold zone' may sometimes be used to manage a scene which involves contamination of any sort, and essentially the zones relate to cordoned areas.

Inner cordon

The inner cordon is a designated area that is closest to where the main examination will take place. This may be where a body lies or the main attack site. The inner cordon usually has quite small parameters and provides a boundary for detailed forensic examinations to be conducted. It must be very tightly controlled. This is where the SIO may wish to consider the use of a large tent or other similar screening equipment in order to safeguard the privacy of the scene, in particular away from distressed on-lookers or long-range media cameras or observation equipment.

Outer cordon

The outer cordon allows for a larger area to be contained and covers the peripheral parts of the inner scene. This provides a secure area not only for examination but also preparatory work to be undertaken and the adequate distancing of members of the public and media. This area may also be subject to forensic examination but is unlikely to be as detailed as the inner cordon.

Each cordon must have adequate 'access control' to ensure only authorized people can gain access. The SIO must set adequate policies and give instructions to cordon officers as to who is to be allowed in, which may differ between inner and outer cordons. The SIO will make this decision probably in consultation with the CSM, and there may well be separate and distinct policies for both. For this reason both cordons will require a separate log to be completed (scene logs are covered later).

Case study—Proving security of a crime scene

A victim had been beaten, raped, and strangled at an outdoor semi-rural location adjoining parkland. The outer cordon required wide boundaries and parameters because of the large number of potential entry and exit routes to/from where the attack took place. Unauthorized access was prevented by use of uniform staff, dog handlers, and the mounted branch. An offender was later found to have trace evidence on his clothing linking him to the primary scene.

At the subsequent trial his defence team claimed he had visited the scene post-murder out of curiosity as he lived close by. The police inspector responsible for scene security (bronze commander) was intensively cross-examined regarding security arrangements. All scene logs were heavily scrutinized, together with briefing notes and hand-over arrangements, proving the offender could not have entered the crime scene. The efficient and professional handling of the scene security withstood inquisitorial attacks and the offender's defence was rejected by the jury, who found him guilty.

5.6.3 Rendezvous points (RVP)

An RVP is usually the best place to site the officer compiling the outer cordon scene log and should provide precisely what the name suggests. A suitable location should be found where all necessary scene resources can go to meet up and discuss examination and search tactics. A signed police vehicle may be used in the first instance that is easily identifiable, and if there are good communication systems on board they can also be put to good use. There may be practical and logistical difficulties to consider (such as parking or briefing facilities) with the sheer volume and type of resources that may be required to attend. The SIO may feel it is easier to control all their required resources if they are directed to attend an RVP located nearby but not directly at the scene cordon. If the SIO is going to require specialist services or agencies that bring large vehicles and equipment (eg an underwater search unit) then an area needs to be identified where these resources can safely assemble, park their vehicles, gain access to catering facilities, change clothing, rest, and recouperate etc and not be impeded by the public or media. In which case the SIO (and in some cases this may be a requirement of a gold or silver commander) should nominate a further supervisor to take control of managing all the necessary arrangements for the resources required at the scene. In some cases this may include traffic management if there are vehicle and public route diversions involved. These roles are usually given to designated bronze commanders. The suitability of RVP points (and secondary RVP points such as a Forward Command Post (FCP)—a term used in some major incident response contingency plans) must be a consideration. Risks and safety also have to be considered when locations are chosen, particularly in terrorist cases where unexploded secondary devices may have been deliberately placed; in which case any potential RVP will have to be searched before it is deemed safe and suitable for use.

5.6.4 Common approach paths (CAP)

A common approach path needs to be designated and marked out at the earliest opportunity. This should be the designated route into and out of the crime scene for all those subsequently attending for examination purposes etc (and removal of victims). It is likely that the most direct route to any victims will have been taken by responding officers and medical teams. Where possible this route should be used to exit from the area, unless it becomes clear the offenders have used that route (eg if eye witnesses say so, or there are footwear marks or other tell-tale signs). Protective stepping plates are usually used to protect the surface underneath and particularly if inside premises where trace evidence on flooring and carpets may need to be preserved.

It is vital that the details of all those initially attending are recorded so that the route taken can be clarified before the CAP is determined. A sketch plan may be useful which can be exhibited and registered on the HOLMES2 database at a later stage. The golden rule is that a CAP should be established on the *least likeliest route taken by the offender(s) or victim(s)*. The CAP may also have to be wide enough to enable CSIs and other experts to carry in equipment and for the removal of any bodies.

KEY POINT

At outdoor scenes an SIO should try to select hard-standing or compact gravel type path areas for the CAP as they are more practical to use, also easier and quicker to search to render them clear than other surfaces such as foliage or grassland.

Checklist—Scene security and preservation

- Both inner and outer cordons are required (and in some circumstances even a third cordon).
- Each cordon will require a separate log.
- Clear the largest area possible. Parameters can always be narrowed later.
- For cordon parameters make a quick and objective evaluation based on:
  1. Location of the incident (or body).
  2. Presence of any physical evidence.
  3. Eyewitness accounts and or information/intelligence.
- For outdoor scenes make good use of natural boundaries (eg trees, streams, gates, fences, lamp-posts, building lines, etc) for use as cordon boundaries.
- Consider the possible entry/exit route used by offender(s) and victim(s)—and *avoid when determining a common approach path* (CAP).
- Consider the possibility of other linked crime scenes (eg abandoned vehicles, attack site) that may also need to be preserved.
- Initial responding officers are to be told not to examine anything at this stage—only to identify the scene(s) then secure and protect them.
- They may recover or protect any physical evidence that is at immediate risk of being lost or destroyed (eg cover any tyre or footwear impressions if inclement weather).
- Cordon areas should be marked out clearly (ie with identifiable crime scene tape).

- There must be restricted access to unauthorized persons and clearly communicated instructions that no one is to enter without express permission of the SIO.
- There should be an avoidance of contact with any suspect(s) or witness(es) and person(s) at the scene(s) to avoid any cross-contamination.
- At outdoor scenes there should be early use of a protective tent and/or high screens regardless of any weather forecast (also protects dignity of victims from public/media).
- Appoint a bronze scene cordon manager to supervise cordon responsibilities.
- Arrange an RVP.

KEY POINT

In terrorist attacks it is not uncommon for secondary devices to be placed for deliberate targeting of responding emergency services and to cause maximum carnage and destruction at places where cordons and RV points are likely to be located. This must be borne in mind at these types of scenes.

5.6.5 Displaced residents and vehicles

Some scenes are located in areas difficult to contain. These may be where residents have possessions or vehicles that get stranded inside a cordon, or even residences or business premises where the placing and security of cordons means that innocent people become effectively displaced and their lives disrupted.

An example is when cordons are placed in streets within residential areas. Residents can become trapped or displaced, together with their vehicles, inside the cordon and sensible solutions are the answer. Freedom of movement can be facilitated by devising and recording (in consultation with the CSM), an appropriate strategy, eg utilizing protective clothing or, in the case of vehicles, having them examined by a CSI, and recording or photographing their position. When satisfied there is no link to the crime, supervised removal can be arranged. Residents can sometimes be permitted to use their rear doors as opposed to front, and if necessary put into protective suits to allow access in and out of the cordon. A protectively suited officer can visit each address to explain to residents the arrangements for their movements and the reasons, with an explanatory note from the SIO and/or local police commander apologizing for the inconvenience. This should be recorded in the 'community impact assessment' (CIA) document.

5.7 Legal Powers—Entering and Securing Crime Scenes

The vast majority of the law-abiding public are quite willing to cooperate with the police and allow access to and examination of scenes of crime. Clearly it is sensible for them to follow police advice which may be supported by other agencies such as the fire and rescue service, health professionals, or local authority representatives. There are also legal powers conferred in ss 8, 18, and 32 of PACE to secure premises for the purpose of a search. However, there may still be some lingering doubts over general crime scenes, particularly those on private property.

In the case of *DPP v Morrison* QBD, 4.4.03; (*Telegraph*, 17.4.03; *The Times*, 21.4.03), a decision confirmed that under common law the police do have a power to erect a cordon in order to preserve the scene of a crime. The Divisional Court upheld this rule in this case and, given the importance of this function in investigating serious crime, it would have been highly surprising had it done otherwise. It is probably because of the ruling in this case that no legal power has, to date, been enacted.

The case of *Rice v Connolly* (1966) QB P414 had previously re-affirmed long-established principles that have not been challenged. It was confirmed that the police are entitled to take all reasonable steps to keep the peace, prevent and detect crime, and bring offenders to justice. It is within these principles that the police are entitled to secure scenes of crime for examination by specialists, forensic scientists, etc.

It follows that, if any individual were to frustrate, hinder, or obstruct the securing of a crime scene, that person would commit an offence of obstructing a police officer in the execution of their duty. This would include any civilian police employee such as a crime scene investigator who is regarded as an investigator under the provisions of the Criminal Procedure and Investigations Act 1996 (CPIA).

The *Murder Investigation Manual* also provides some useful advice:

> Where a scene is on private property, SIOs will need to negotiate access with those in control of the premises. Considerable tact and

diplomacy will often be necessary for this, particularly where the scene is occupied or controlled by a suspect's family or associates or where the scene requires to be searched for objects suspected of being buried or concealed. If necessary, alternative arrangements should be made for their accommodation until the scene is released. Where a crime scene is likely to have a significant impact on commerce, SIOs should consult their force legal department for advice about the length of time it can be held. [*Murder Investigation Manual* (ACPO Centrex), 136].

Note: If the incident under investigation is terrorist related the police have powers to impose and enforce cordons under sections 33-36 of the Terrorism Act 2000.

5.8 **Crime Scene Assessments**

It is essential for the SIO and the CSM/CSI and any other experts that have been summoned to work together as a team in order to establish and agree what constitutes the scene parameters, what preservation measures are necessary, and what the scene forensic examination, search, and evidence recovery plan will look like. This includes any plan that may be required to recover a victim's body.

The initial crime scene assessment is usually a precursor to any tactical meeting which may take place at a suitable venue outside the inner cordon (but perhaps within the outer cordon) when the precise methods and plans for the scene are discussed, decided, and agreed. This meeting should be attended by any relevant experts and advisers the SIO calls upon in order to produce the most effective search and evidence recovery plan, and may include a forensic pathologist, biologists, ballistic examiners, and any other of experts or 'ologists' as required. Once agreed, the strategy and tactical plans should be recorded and any resulting document ideally countersigned to the SIO's satisfaction by all parties contributing to it.

A crime scene assessment is therefore effectively the first part of the process and provides not only an opportunity to review and check that important preservation procedures are in place but also is an opportunity for the SIO to get a firsthand 'feel' for the scene and begin the process of initial thoughts and hypothesis building.

The SIO may want those who have already been involved at the scene (such as the senior detective who responded and initially took charge) to 'walk and talk' them through the crime scene, taking care to prevent any risk of contamination or cross-contamination by wearing protective clothing. This will enable the SIO to make an evaluation of the nature and extent of the crime and the subsequent examination and searches required, including the requirement for any specialists or forensic experts. In the case of a body remaining at the scene, any decision making should always include a forensic pathologist. If a murder has occurred this process is vital for determining and agreeing a full forensic body-recovery strategy from within the primary crime scene (also covered in Chapter 12).

KEY POINTS

1. A crime scene assessment can be aided by first accounts from witnesses, paramedics, and first officer(s) attending the scene. It can also be done with the aid of a review of a visual recording made of the crime scene by a specialist photographer, followed by a physical inspection by the SIO and CSM. This may also include any other appropriate forensic experts as determined by the SIO, who must also be provided with relevant information about the case.
2. If there are good reasons for not entering a scene to conduct an assessment, ie due to the high risks and dangers involved such as after a large fire or contamination, some agencies (including fire and ambulance) may have the means of providing live-time imagery via 'reach-back' or microwave/transmitting technology. Specialist equipment can be deployed which communicates with a command and control point and can be useful for assessing, planning, and observing evidence recovery.
3. Scene assessments provide an opportunity to identify evidence that may need recovering quickly, not just forensic items but things such as passive data (eg CCTV or ANPR cameras) that may have recorded something vitally important. Early recovery could enable vital fast-track actions to be instigated.

5.8.1 Potential scene contaminators

It is always worthwhile during a scene assessment and when looking at scene preservation considering potential evidence contaminators or destroyers.

Checklist—Potential scene contaminators

- The weather—particularly if the scene is out of doors. Blood, prints, body fluids, DNA, etc can be ruined by inclement weather such as the rain, frost, snow, wind, direct sunlight, heat, etc.
- Relatives or friends—either of the victim(s) or suspect(s), or members of the public wishing to be helpful.
- Suspects or associates—in attempts to destroy or remove any incriminating evidence, or indeed legitimately put themselves at the crime scene and negate incriminating trace evidence that is subsequently recovered.
- Spectators, onlookers, concerned members of the community or general public (eg ghouls with morbid fascination), displaced residents—people who cannot return to their homes, for instance, or move vehicles because they are within cordons, may pose a serious threat and problem to scene security.
- Officials, experts, or supervisors—people who may think they have a right to enter crime scenes need to be dealt with quickly and the SIO needs to make a decision as to who has or has not got permission to enter. Reasons must be included in a policy file.
- Animals and insects.
- The media—probably the biggest culprits for potentially breaching cordons in order to get pictures and/or interviews (we deal with this in Chapter 13).
- Geological disturbances, particularly if the crime is outdoors, eg flooding, landslides, seeps, springs, subsidence, gas emissions, landfill and waste, areas of ground contamination, pollution, weathering, and erosion.

5.9 Forensic Recovery, Planning, and Prioritization

Any item that is identified as being required for forensic examination should, as a general rule, be left in its original position for a decision on how best to recover it. For general items this decision is normally taken by the CSI in consultation with the CSM, it is then at the SIO's discretion to determine what items are to be made subject of a tactical meeting and generally recorded as a policy entry or in a separate strategy document. Larger or fragile items will come under this category such as vehicles, eg if the victim was murdered in a vehicle or the suspect abandoned one. Some items, such as spent/empty cartridge cases from a firearm or used condoms in an alleyway, may need a policy as to how they are to be recovered, with a consideration of what tests will be required and prioritized (eg DNA or fingerprints). These are decisions to be taken by the CSM and SIO working collaboratively.

This is where an assessment and pre-examination briefing and planning process comes in. The SIO will have an opportunity to discuss recovery of items with their crime scene team, ie CSM and CSI, forensic scientists, forensic pathologist (any other required scientific advisers and experts such as environmental profilers and botanists), anthropologists etc. It will also allow all those concerned to focus on the scene as a whole and not just their own specialist areas before starting to work on the scene. The meeting and subsequent examination and recovery plans should help the SIO and their CSM maintain firm control of the proceedings.

5.10 **Crime Scene Administration and Documentation**

Forms of scene administration and documentation used will vary from force to force in accordance with local procedures. However, it should generally include the following:

- crime scene logs;
- crime scene strategies/tactics and policy file entries;
- lists and details of all exhibits seized;
- correct exhibit recovery methods, packaging, labelling, transportation, and storage procedures;
- exhibits 'books' or computerized exhibit management systems;
- sketches, maps, and plans indicating scene parameters and cordons, location of victims, exhibits etc (including topographic, soils, and geological maps);
- search policies that stipulate precise parameters;
- CSM/CSI/other experts' notes and their exhibit lists;
- any other lists and details of exhibits recovered;
- still and visual imagery (including aerial and satellite imagery);
- any notes or sketches compiled by forensic experts;

- exact scene location on a map or plan (including full description);
- victim descriptives and body maps;
- crime scene reconstruction material;
- where legislative authorities utilized, correct and accurate documentation and appropriate forms that must be completed.

Note: All 'relevant' material must be retained and details submitted to the major incident room for processing under disclosure rules in accordance with CPIA 1996.

5.10.1 Crime scene logs

Scene logs are quite simply an official audit trail and record of everyone who enters a crime scene. They not only deter unauthorized access but also preserve the integrity of the scene. There are specifically designed forms to use for this purpose which, when completed, should include details of the person(s) keeping the log, full details of all persons who enter or leave the scene against signature, the exact date and time in and out, the reason for entry, and whether protective clothing is worn or not. The officer who is maintaining the outer cordon scene log is normally positioned at the RVP to capture all persons attempting to enter the scene.

There are normally clear instructions printed inside the front cover of scene logs. Spare booklets should be stored in a readily accessible place because they are not generally issued to all staff and are only used as and when required, primarily at major crime scenes. There should be a separate log for both inner and outer cordons (and for a third cordon if one is used). All logs, once completed, must be submitted without delay to the major incident room for examination and processing on HOLMES2.

Designated scene 'logists' should record on the log only details of those who actually enter or leave the crime scene (the 'sterile' area). Entries should clearly record reasons for a person entering the scene on the log. The logs need to be detailed, accurate, and comprehensive. If for any reasons the correct log forms are not immediately available, then a pocket book or other note-taking format should be utilized, but the same amount of care must be taken even if it is recorded on plain paper.

There are some common mistakes made with scene logs. Some are as follows:

1. Incorrect forms used or none at all. Using a makeshift piece of paper or officer's pocket book is not very professional. Experience indicates that if official forms are not used then usually the necessary detail is not recorded.
2. Precise and accurate details not recorded. Each and every box and question on the form is there for a specific reason. There should be no gaps, for instance if protective clothing has not been worn the box needs to state this and must not be left blank. If it is a requirement to note the weather conditions at regular intervals, this should be completed correctly.
3. Incorrect detail recorded. Attention to detail is vital, even down to the correct spelling of people's names. Scene logs are entered onto the HOLMES2 database with all the names of persons attending the scene. Any that are not spelt correctly can lead to dual registration and foul up the nominal indices.
4. Entries on forms not being signed. Some officers may feel awkward asking people who are wearing protective suits or whatever to keep signing themselves in and out of scenes. All entries should be made against signature, with no excuses.
5. Briefing and supervision. It can be a tedious and thankless task to perform the role of scene logist or security. Those tasked with this function should be correctly briefed as to the importance of the role, and the logs checked at regular intervals by a supervisor to ensure they are being completed correctly.
6. Hand-over periods. These should be fully recorded as to date, time, and persons involved, and properly managed to ensure consistency and professionalism in approach.

KEY POINT

A sensible approach to log-keeping is sometimes required. For example, when CSIs are returning to and from their vehicles or equipment that are located just outside the outer cordon on a regular basis there is no need for them to be constantly logged in and out as they are effectively still 'in the scene', provided the SIO and CSM are satisfied there is no risk of contamination.

5.10.2 CSM/CSI notes and exhibit lists

Any crime scene exhibit list compiled by the CSM or the CSI during the scene examination (and their notes) must be copied and handed to the SIO via the exhibits officer for eventual processing by the MIR at the earliest opportunity. This may contain details of important items that the SIO may need an immediate awareness of so that important decisions can be made and actions raised. Often it is the case that these important lists get taken away with the CSIs or whoever until such time as a strategy meeting is held, which may be too late to instigate fast-track actions. This rule also applies to any other experts who attend and examine aspects of the scene and may prepare their own exhibit lists, such as forensic scientists.

5.10.3 Maps, plans, satellite images, and aerial photography

Producing a detailed plan drawing or map of the scene is something normally considered useful for the SIO and their investigation teams. The exact position, scale, proximity, and dimensions of locations and objects of interest can prove invaluable. This complements any scene photographs or visual recordings that are good at recording 'close-ups', etc, but a detailed plan produced by an expert or map can be used to show context and precise locations, particularly at complex crime scenes. These may also be used to facilitate the effective communication of information, which may be helpful if several multi-disciplinary specialists are involved with the investigation. Maps may also be used to delineate possible search areas if there is evidence or suspicion that an object, items, or further scene may require to be located, or proven otherwise absent from a particular location.

KEY POINT

Any crime scene plan or map must always have a relevant title, key, date, time (if necessary), and orientation, usually given by the inclusion of a north (N) arrow.

The SIO can also produce their own rough sketches or plans of scenes when they attend to act as a visual aide memoir for considering cordon and search parameters, early hypotheses, conducting briefings, etc. It may of course be some time before they receive an official map or plan from the expert who has been allocated the task. Maps and plans can also be considered not just at major crime scenes where the offence has occurred but also at other possible crime scenes such as during house searches to show the exact location of where exhibits have been found.

Worthy of consideration is a fly-over of an outdoor scene by an aircraft (eg police helicopter). This will help record the exact location of, for example, a body deposition site and may also help make other significant discoveries. The resulting photography will provide a valuable tool for later briefings and decision-making processes. The SIO may also wish to take advantage of some of the satellite imagery that is now available on the internet such as Google earth. These types of satellite images can be invaluable for helping to get a good appreciation of the layout of scenes and their proximity to other significant geographical locations, including buildings and roads, although the date the imagery was taken must always be borne in mind. Maps obtained from the internet should not, however, be used or relied upon for evidential purposes.

5.10.4 Computerised scene reproduction

Depending on the nature of the case there may be opportunities to produce a computerized reproduction and/or a reconstruction of the crime scene to help gain a better understanding of what took place, in what sequence, and how it happened. This will help in:

- the formation of hypotheses;
- testing individual hypotheses by additional analysis;
- producing the most probable reconstruction theory.

Sophisticated computer enhancements, animated reconstructions, 3D models, and 360-degree camera shots can now be used to recreate a crime scene and examine witness accounts, timings, distance, etc. This is a developing area of investigation, which can be used in court to show a jury the exact sequence of events, positions, and importance of exhibits and forensic samples, or how the evidence combines, making a clearer picture of fragmented or complex evidence. It can make a big impact on juries, however a cautionary note is that the process can be very time-consuming to complete which may make the examination process of scenes take a lot longer.

5.10.5 Exhibits management

An SIO should always be mindful that correct procedures for the handling, packaging, transportation, and continuity and integrity of exhibits, must be able to be proved beyond all reasonable doubt in a court of law.

KEY POINT

Processes, procedures, records, and documentation will all come under intense scrutiny from defence legal teams if an exhibit becomes a key piece of evidence in a criminal trial.

Two terms often referred to in the context of crime scene management and evidenced recovery activity are 'continuity' and 'integrity'. They are highly significant to the SIO and the evidential case and are clarified now for avoidance of doubt.

Continuity—A continuous, complete and accurate record of all the movements of any evidential material from identification at the crime scene, subsequent recovery, transportation, examination, storage and any other investigative processes until the ultimate destination—production at court.

Integrity—The handling, packaging, and storage of evidential material that can demonstrate beyond all doubt that there has been no interference, contamination, cross-transfer, tampering, destruction, or loss that could have occurred to the item, either intentionally or accidentally.

Where any evidence of contact is required it is vital that there can be no allegation or suggestion of contamination or cross-transfer from any other person or item. These terms are also clarified as follows:

Contamination—Occurs when something is added to an evidential sample from another, either accidentally or intentionally. An obvious example is when an officer's DNA is allowed to contaminate an evidential item that is to be examined for DNA from the victim or offender.

Cross-transfer—Used to describe the process in which material from one location, person, or item is transferred to another. This can occur in a wide variety of situations, for example when an officer who has been to the crime scene then arrests a suspect and transfers material from the scene onto the suspect.

5.11 Legal Powers to Seize Evidence

Generally speaking, when not under the power of a magistrate's search warrant (s 8 of PACE which allows anything to be seized and retained for which the search is authorized) then s 19 of PACE is relied upon for a power to seize evidential items which are on *premises*. This power states that a constable or civilian is designated an investigating officer (under the Police Reform Act 2002, s 38, Sch 4, Pt 2, para 19(a)) provided:

(a) they are on premises lawfully; and
(b) there are reasonable grounds for believing:
  (i) that the item seized is either (1) a thing which has been obtained in consequence of the commission of an offence (s 19(2): eg stolen items or the proceeds of crime); or (2) that it is evidence in relation to an offence under investigation or any other offence (s 19(3)); and
  (ii) that it is necessary to seize it in order to prevent it being concealed, lost, damaged, altered, or destroyed (s.19(2)(b) and (3)(b)); and
(c) the item is not one for which there are reasonable grounds for believing it to be subject to legal privilege (as defined in s 10 (s 19(6)).

The term 'premises' for the purposes of this power under the PACE is one that may be open to legal interpretation. However, the case of *Ghani v Jones* (1969) provides a ruling on the justification for taking articles where no one has been arrested or charged and is not restricted to being on 'premises'. This power should also extend to civilian investigating officers under Sch 4 to the Police Reform Act 2002. In sum, the ruling states there must be reasonable grounds for believing:

(a) that a serious crime has been committed;
(b) that the article was either the fruit of the crime or the instrument by which it was committed or was material evidence to prove its commission;
(c) that the person in possession of the article had committed the crime or was implicated in it; and
(d) the police must not keep the article or prevent its removal for any longer than is reasonably necessary to complete the investigation or preserve it for evidence; and
(e) the lawfulness of the conduct of the police must be judged at the time and not by what happens afterwards.

There may be occasions when this case ruling may be useful, for example when dealing with persons who are potential 'scenes' but not under arrest or on *premises* and items are required from them for examination such as clothing or personal effects or mobile phones.

5.12 **Crime Scene Searches**

As part of the crime scene forensic examination strategy the SIO must also consider a search strategy. Such searches aim to locate evidential material or items that can then be recovered and examined by CSI personnel. Crime scene searches can take the form of searches of buildings, open areas, water, vehicles, and vessels. Usually these types of search are managed and supervised by a PolSA (police search advisor) using a trained police search team (PST).

There may be conflicting objectives in using search strategies. For example, with a primary crime scene there is always the requirement to conduct a forensic examination and also a physical search of the same area for weapons, discarded clothing, stolen property, etc. The latter may compromise the former and therefore a careful decision will have to be taken by the SIO, almost certainly in consultation with a crime scene investigator/manager and/or forensic scientists. Usually the forensic search takes priority, however in some circumstances a physical search may take primacy, for instance where an immediate search is required for a suspect.

KEY POINTS

1. The role of a search is to locate any items sought, the aim of the CSI is to examine and recover any evidential items found. The ideal model is to move proportionately from non-invasive searching to forensic recovery. A balance should be struck between searching an area to a high level of assurance without negatively impacting on any forensic retrieval of evidential finds.
2. All searches should be intelligence-led and based on facts that enable a hypothesis to be generated.
3. An SOP should be developed for each search.

Any briefing of search teams should be carefully recorded for future reference because failure to communicate important information will impede the effectiveness of the search. This safeguards the integrity of the process by recording the details of what was provided for the benefit of the teams and what they have been tasked to do. There must be no doubt whatsoever what the objectives of the search(es) are, what information was available at the time to base these decisions on, and what information and briefing was provided to the search teams.

Crime-related scene searches can be classified as follows:

- crime scene searches;
- premises searching;
- searches of open areas including water;
- searches of vehicles and vessels;
- searching the ground and underneath it.

KEY POINT

Outdoor searches provide added benefits other than what they are primarily intended for, ie finding evidence. They can provide a visible reassurance for the community and show the victim's family and relatives that work is in progress as they can see it in progress. These images also usually featured on TV news bulletins showing officers conducting fingertip searches, house-to-house calls, the deployment of an underwater search unit, or any other resources that may have an impressive array of specialist vehicles and technical equipment on display. This is a point worth considering for inclusion in a community impact assessment. However, this must also be balanced with the intrusive and distracting nature of media personnel recording search activity and the potential for them to broadcast evidential finds live on TV.

5.12.1 PolSA searches

The SIO is always responsible for making the decision whether to deploy a PolSA-led search. This can be based on advice and guidance given by the PolSA. Once it has been decided to conduct a PolSA-led search, the SIO will:

1. Retain responsibility for deciding which persons, premises, or areas of ground are to be searched, and in consultation with the PolSA will also set the parameters in accordance with the investigative objectives. The policy should be recorded and cross-referenced with an entry in the SIO's policy file.
2. At all times have access to the advice of the PolSA, who may suggest areas of search, methodology, and techniques, search assets, health and safety aspects, logistical and technical constraints, and limitations of the search.
3. Decide at which stage the crime scene examination teams and/or search teams will be deployed.
4. Ensure the PolSA is briefed with the appropriate intelligence and information in relation to each individual search and is fully informed of the purpose of the search and what the objectives are.

5. (Where it is evident that the search will be protracted, complex, or that a large area has to be searched, the SIO and PolSA may) wish to consider a number of other agencies or specialists, eg blood/cadaver dogs, underwater search unit, air support unit, height access or confined spaces teams etc.
6. Possibly also require other types of specialists, such as forensic geologists (including geophysicists, geochemists, hydrogeologists, geomorphologists etc) archaeologists, anthropologists, botanists, palynologists. Searches involving buried and concealed items in land, water, or engineered structures/infrastructure (eg houses, buildings, bridges, dams, roads, motorways, railways, utilities) may require expert advice from the NPIA helpdesk and/or the National Search Adviser (tel 0845 000 5463 or email <soc@npia.pnn.police.uk>).

Role of the PolSA

A PolSA will be responsible for:

- advising the SIO on all aspects of a search;
- planning, directing, managing, implementing, and recording the searches as required by the SIO;
- obtaining technical resources for each search and ensuring a search policy log and comprehensive records of each search are maintained.

PolSA search policy

On requesting a PolSA-led search it is essential that the SIO or delegated person from the management team meets the PolSA and CSM/CSI in order to discuss and agree the search policy and parameters.

The search policy should be recorded and include the following points.

Checklist—PolSA search policy

- Information that is known to date about the incident.
- The objectives of the search (eg what items are being sought and the search strategy, eg 'to search the dwelling, garden and its environs to confirm the presence or absence of any concealed human remains, or associated objects or items').
- Full parameters of the search, both written and marked out on maps/plans of the search area. Maps have at minimum

a clear title, scale, north arrow, legend, date, and initials/name.
- The reason why the area is being searched and under what lawful authority.
- How the search will be conducted, what methodology, instrumentation, resources/assets will be deployed and what will be the expected duration of the search.
- What personal protective equipment (PPE) will be required.
- Whether any aerial, building, or sub-surface utility plans are required.
- What specialist resources will be deployed and their phased order of deployment, eg victim recovery dogs and underwater search units.
- If a ground search is to be conducted what data and information may be required such as historical and current Ordnance Survey maps, geological maps published by the British Geological Survey, archive and current air photos etc.
- If a site reconnaissance visit is required to, for example, identify any logistical or technical constraints (such as points of access, locations overhead, or underground utilities which may exclude the use of certain geophysical instruments etc).
- A standard operating procedure (SOP) which should be produced for the search. This will help to provide a high level of consistency and allow independent peer review.
- How the media and visiting public are to be managed.
- How any evidence found will be forensically preserved upon discovery, recovered and recorded (ie staked, photographed, and/or recovered by a CSI).

KEY POINTS

1. Some PolSAs and CSIs may be trained as forensic trackers and can be used to assist in identifying entry and escape routes to and from a scene, therefore concentrating resources on the best possible opportunity for evidence recovery. An environmental profiler such as a botanist or palynologist can also be used to identify vegetative disturbance.
2. Where the same officers search more than one premises or area there may be potential for cross-contamination. This must be catered for

by recording why there are no cross-contamination concerns or how they are to be controlled or managed, eg search teams having full change of protective clothing prior to attending subsequent scenes. This is a matter the SIO should discuss and agree with the CSM/CSI and PolSA beforehand.

Case study

Following an inner-city fatal stabbing, the main crime scene was forensically managed by the appointed CSM. The scene was clearly identified and marked out. Due to time constraints, public perception, and the sensitive location, the outer areas were searched in tandem under the management of a PolSA using a trained search team.

Commensurate with the intelligence given by the SIO and guidance from the CSM it allowed for two strategies to be adopted: (1) a search team wearing forensic suits and masks in the inner cordon on hands and knees with the expectation of finding small evidential items linking suspects; and (2) a search team at walking pace covering the larger outer cordoned area. This allowed the SIO/CSM to eliminate the larger area quickly.

It also helped the SIO deliver an efficient search by:

- reducing police time on site;
- increasing chances of evidence retrieval by implementing two rapid search techniques simultaneously, and decreasing opportunity for offenders or associates to retrieve possible evidence from around or near to the 'main scene';
- specific tasking, ie search of a nearby bottle bank for weapons and clothing managed by a PolSA.

5.12.2 Premises searching

It is highly likely during the course of an investigation that there will be a requirement to conduct extensive searches of premises that may or may not constitute crime scenes but should be approached as such until proven otherwise. These may be as crime scene searches or as part of an arrest or general search strategy. In most cases premises searches are simpler because they are easier to contain and secure; they may not present the same challenges as some outdoor scenes, eg rural and remote searches.

If an in-depth and thorough search of premises is required then a PolSA-led team should be considered. This will ensure a high assurance search is conducted once the forensic teams have finished. The SIO should also consider involving experienced detectives and maybe even a supervisory detective of sergeant or inspector rank who, although would not physically search, would at least be on hand to advise and guide the search team through their more extensive knowledge of the case. An exhibits officer will also be required.

Even if the search is not forming part of a designated crime scene, a CSI should, whenever possible, be deployed with search teams to accurately record and sometimes photograph the evidence and advise on the appropriate recovery, packaging, transportation, and storage of items.

The type of premises and incident under investigation will determine what the search strategy should entail. For example, bathrooms and kitchens are popular places to wash away forensic traces or dismember bodies. Therefore, baths, sinks, and shower traps should be examined for blood or flesh deposits, together with towels, soap, and shampoo bottles. Checking for any signs of a struggle or disturbance may also be important.

When recovering clothing and items against set criteria there needs to be a clear policy to determine what should/should not be seized. For example, if checking footwear, it is advisable to take photographs or drawings to compare against otherwise seizing too many exhibits may result. Also important is working to a clear examination and retrieval strategy. For instance, when recovering clothing that is to be forensically packaged and sealed, best practice is to have it photographed *in situ* prior to recovery, and then front and back photographs prior to packaging. Although time-consuming, this negates the need to submit numerous items for assessment to the forensic service providers, and allows the SIO to prioritize certain items. This is because items are difficult to see or describe once in bags that should be opened only under laboratory conditions.

KEY POINTS

1. A useful technique to consider is using someone who is familiar with the premises to go through them with the SIO (or nominated person) bit by bit (being careful about any possible contamination issues). They can help identify anything that is out of place, missing, unusual, or suspicious or any factors inconsistent with the lifestyle of the victim.
2. Some areas of premises may require specialist equipment to search below floors or behind walls, eg geophysical instruments.

If searching dwellings where there may be innocent third parties and occupants it may be worth considering a displacement plan. Sometimes people who have nothing to do with criminality get caught up in traumatic events because of their unfortunate association with or in relation to suspects and offenders. It is worthwhile anticipating this in advance and having a plan to minimize the disruptive effects of searches where they impact on others.

Note: This may also provide a suitable opportunity to speak to people who may be able to assist the enquiry.

Checklist—Primary crime scene search of premises (ie scene (1))

(Note: Not all these may be applicable, depending on the requirements of the search, and the list is not exhaustive.)

- Ensure a scene log has been commenced.
- Conduct a review of the security and utilize cordons and/or security measures where necessary.
- Conduct a health and safety risk assessment.
- Determine power of entry, ie warrant/PACE, etc.
- Premises may need to be searched and cleared for suspects prior to searching or examination.
- Look for signs of any forced entry.
- Consider offender's route to and from the premises. Consider use of search trailing dog or trained police tracker.
- Establish a common approach path into and out of the premises.
- Determine personal protective equipment (PPE) policy, ie face mask, oversuit, gloves, overshoes.
- Use stepping plates where applicable (beware of slippery modern flooring).
- Consider utilities, gas, water, electricity; include in safety check.
- Consider additional scene lighting.
- Consider visual/still/aerial/360-degree photography.
- Consider whether a crime scene surveyor is required (to produce detailed plan).
- Decide which forensic experts (eg entomologist) may be required.
- Decide whether a forensic pathologist is required.

- Record whether lights on or off, heating on or off, curtains/blinds open or closed.
- Record door and window positions.
- Consider use of specialist trained detector dogs to search for human blood, human cadavers, drugs, firearms, explosives, or accelerants.
- Check any mail or newspapers, diaries, letters, photographs, newspaper cuttings (eg linked to crime under investigation), computers, personal organizers, mobile phones, etc. Photograph them *in situ*.
- Consider footwear impression examinations.
- Look for signs of any disturbance in all interior places.
- If obvious traces of blood, arrange blood pattern analysis, ie drops, contact marks, cast-off, splatter, or whether any fingerprints or footwear impressions in blood (may need expert scientific blood interpretation).
- If weapons present, consider recovery policy (eg DNA preservation).
- If any firearm present, need to render safe. Then arrange joint examination by CSI and firearms officer and/or ballistics expert.
- Set a fingerprint examination policy.
- Set clothing recovery policy and consider examination and/or photographing prior to being packaged and labelled.
- Determine computer type device and mobile telephone recovery policy (seek advice beforehand from experts).
- Check for vehicles or keys that may belong to associated vehicles (and search *in situ* or transport to undercover examination area). Check for soil deposits in footwells, boot, and wheel arches.
- Check any washing machines and laundry baskets (consider tests on handles and powder boxes, eg for blood traces or soil).
- Examine baths, sinks, shower traps, towels, soap, shampoo bottles for evidence of clean-up activity, plus door handles, mats, and carpets for forensic traces.
- Examine curtains (transfer of samples after opening/closing or for use by offender in cleaning themselves) and bedding for traces (eg sexual partners).
- Recover any cigarette ends or anything else that may contain traces of DNA of visitors.

- Search under floorboards, in loft, behind bath panels, inside water cisterns, and in other likely concealed areas.
- Search all rubbish and dustbins.
- Search the exterior of premises that are connected to it (gardens, outhouses, sheds, garages, roof, guttering, voids, or sub-surface areas, etc)—this may require specialist geophysical equipment (eg metal detectors, magnetometer, electromagnetic surveys, ground penetrating radar, or microgravity).
- Check for indicative or collateral material and lifestyle indicators, eg drugs, sexual fetishes, magazines, or any other significant or unusual artefacts or items.
- Check what possessions are in the premises and who they belong to (may need inventory of all items in premises or certain areas or rooms to link people evidentially to items).
- Look for items that are clearly missing, eg in missing person cases the shower curtain may have been used to wrap up the body; damaged or missing furniture may be indicative of suspicious circumstances, eg severed cables or missing telephones.

Case study—House search evidence

During an enquiry into a missing person who had a criminal background, a house search was conducted at an address linked to a criminal associate. The officers conducting the search were briefed to look for any items that might belong to the missing person, eg mobile phone, jewellery, personal belongings, or any evidence of a struggle or fight. The search team was provided with a full briefing as to the circumstances of the enquiry. During the search, one officer found a length of rope beneath the kitchen sink which he seized as an exhibit. He believed it might have been used for incapacitation, although there had been no specific information to suggest this had occurred.

When the body of the victim was found six weeks later, his hands were tied in front with a short piece of rope. The cut ends were discovered to be an exact microscopic match to those on the rope found during the earlier house search, from which the piece had been cut. This proved a damning piece of evidence against the offender who was convicted after a lengthy Crown Court trial and sentenced to life imprisonment.

5.12.3 Open area and underwater searching

Open area searches encompass a wide range of environments and settings. They can include, for example, public parks and areas of public open space, farm land, woodland, landfill sites, old mining areas, remote moorland and mountainous areas, and town centre precincts. By their nature they tend to be larger search areas than traditional localized urban crime scenes and generally do not have clearly defined boundaries. It is therefore essential that the SIO, CSM, and PolSA visit the proposed search site as part of a reconnaissance site visit and 'walk-over' inspection, to eg:

- define the extent of the search area;
- determine any logistical and technical constraints;
- identify the geology and ground conditions;
- perform a dig-ability survey and instrument tests at an established control site;
- identify factors that may inhibit the use of geophysical instruments (such as over head power lines, underground utilities or metal fences);
- develop a conceptual geological model for the target;
- discuss how it will be cordoned, contained, and searched.

A balance has to be struck between ensuring vital evidence is not left outside the search area and ensuring that, for example in the case of a public park, the entire park is not cordoned off resulting in extensive resource and cost implications for cordon security and many days required searching the entire park. Similarly, to aid such decisions the focus should be on what is being sought and using predictive modelling on where those items may be best located. Again, using a public park as an example, it may be considered proportionate to only search the paths and tracks through the park to locate and recover any evidential items discarded by an offender in their escape from the crime scene. Search fatigue is also a relevant consideration in large area searches and research has shown that searcher focus can rapidly decrease in effectiveness if speculative line searches are conducted over large swathes of open land. Weather conditions and reduced winter daylight hours may also influence the search types and duration.

When considering searches for concealed and buried items then the use of specialist geological advice and equipment must be considered. A forensic geologist will advise on ground conditions (ie soils, rock, groundwater, and any artificial deposits) and what would be the most appropriate, cost-effective geophysical detecting equipment in that environment. Once the choice of equipment has been identified the most effective methods for its deployment must be considered. This will be influenced by the type of instruments chosen, topography (eg is the search area flat or steep, wet or dry).

Search equipment, such as geophysical instruments, are available from many commercial and university sources but most typically from the HOSDB (Home Office Scientific Development Branch), the military and X list contractors. Additionally, police detector dogs could be utilized dependent on what items are being sought (most typically detector dogs are deployed for drugs, firearms, human blood, and remains). Both dogs and geophysical equipment do not replace a police officer searcher but greatly enhance their detecting capability. The aim should be to use a combination of all these resources taking advice on their various benefits and limitations within the specific environment under consideration.

Once the correct choice of search instruments has been decided and the most cost-effective search methodology chosen, the suite of instruments must always be tested at the search site or crime scene. Body disposal and the burial of objects and items usually take place in soil or sediment or softer rocks. The ease by which the soil can be dug (ie its dig-ability) and placed back into the ground (or reinstated) is of importance and this can be assessed at the instrument 'test' or 'control' site. This must be located away from the main cordon/search zone but in an area of similar and, if possible, identical geology. Representative objects should be buried at a similar depth and in the same conditions as the anticipated target. The advantages of the control site are that it: (a) allows detections limits to be identified; (b) provides a means to test the equipment; (c) provides the opportunity for search officers to become familiarized in the use of the equipment before its deployment at the designated search area.

Whatever search strategy is developed, its use of specialist resources should always aim to ensure a minimally invasive search so that any surface or sub-surface evidential find can be examined and recovered by crime scene investigators and, where applicable, assisted by a forensic archaeologist where necessary (eg buried victims). Therefore, it must be recognized that line searching and practices such as widespread strimming and raking should be avoided wherever possible due to the impact they have on vegetation. Police dogs and geophysical detecting equipment are less invasive and any indications by either can be physically confirmed as evidential finds by a police search team officer. Trained forensic geologists may be able to observe and identify any subtle ground disturbances and suggest whether these may have been caused by natural processes or digging and the reinstatement of the displaced soil.

5.12.4 Searches in water

Where an underwater search is considered necessary, advice should be sought from the local police underwater search contractor (many forces have disbanded their police dive teams due to efficiency savings and either call upon nearby regional forces or have standing contracts with private companies). Additionally, further advice and guidance should be sought from geologists, geomorphologists, or marine scientists with regard to water types and quality (eg saline or fresh), flow, discharge and recharge rates, tidal movements, current paths, bathymetry, sedimentation rates and flood plains, etc. Inland and offshore waters of the United Kingdom are covered by many regulatory bodies including the Water Ways Authority and the Environment Agency. One resource increasingly useful to SIOs is the National Oceanography Centre that has historic and current water data and, more importantly, experts who can interpret it (they can be contacted via the NPIA SOC—tel. 0845 000 5463). Underwater searches can present very difficult challenges due to the dynamic nature of the medium as in the case of a body it may have moved from its original entry point and may even have moved since its discovery and prior to recovery, here underwater video and photography can be of use in recording best evidence of the actual state of the submerged body prior to its examination on-shore where often in the process of recovery the body suffers further trauma and disarticulation. There are available a variety of geophysical and other instruments for searching beneath lakes, ponds, rivers, canals, and other water bodies.

5.12.5 Vehicle and vessel searching

In most investigations, vehicles and vessels are involved as either the crime scene itself or in transporting to and from the crime scene. UK police search teams have established methods to search systematically vehicles and vessels, which may be considered to be over and above what would be conventionally conducted by a crime scene examiner. Vehicles and vessels contain many voids which criminals can exploit to conceal evidential material. The search strategy should aim to move proportionality from a non-invasive search, perhaps utilizing specialist detecting instruments (x-ray and police detector dogs like a drugs dog) to a more invasive search of voided areas. Where waterborne vessels are considered for search the UKBA maintain well-resourced and skilled search teams that can assist police investigations if required.

Note: See Appendix D for information on missing person searches.

5.13 National Search Adviser

The National Search Adviser is a service provided by the National Policing Improvement Agency (NPIA), which has a remit to provide operational support to forces in relation to search matters. These include:

- homicides, no-body murders, missing persons, abductions, and mass fatality disasters;
- locating human remains, concealed or otherwise;
- reviewing previous search activity or strategies on critical or cold cases;
- preparing and writing search strategies for SIOs and PolSAs.

The role includes acting as an independent adviser and facilitator to access specialists in relation to searches requiring geological (including geophysical, geochemical, hydrogeological, geomorphological), underwater and canine techniques.

More information about the National Search Adviser can be obtained from the NPIA website (see <http://www.npia.police.uk>).

5.14 Collection of Physical Evidence

There are general rules that apply regarding the collection and seizure of physical evidence from a crime scene (or from any other place not so specifically designated). These are as follows.

- Always make use of a designated exhibits officer who should collect and collate all the items recovered.

- Record precisely where items are found and, where possible, photograph prior to recovery (remembering it may be necessary to link offenders to items nearby the article, eg in a wardrobe).
- Always consider a full forensic recovery of any items avoiding risk of contamination.
- Temporary, fragile, or easily lost evidence should be collected first.
- Consider the storage and transportation of sensitive exhibits that may be susceptible to degradation during transit.
- Evidence should be placed in appropriate containers/bags and packaged/labelled correctly (label to be signed by everyone who has handled the item).
- Each item should be packaged separately.
- Search documentation and witness statements need to be comprehensively completed afterwards.
- Always ensure that the chain of continuity and custody of each item is adhered to.

KEY POINT

Proving continuity, chain of custody, and safeguarding the integrity of all exhibits by clear audit trails is of paramount importance. If useful trace evidence is found and relied upon in evidence, this is an area that will come under close scrutiny in any subsequent proceedings. Each and every item recovered from a crime scene (or elsewhere) must have an exhibit label attached that is clearly marked and signed/dated by all those coming into contact with it.

5.15 **Releasing a Crime Scene**

A crime scene should be retained as long as is necessary to allow for all potential searches and forensic examinations to take place. Any decision to release a scene *must* be very carefully considered. There are undoubtedly important practical and resource implications to consider when deciding how long a crime scene should be retained (particularly if it is a large one outdoors and/or located in a residential or urban area). The SIO and CSM should work closely together to make this decision, taking all relevant circumstances into account. For example, a review of the scene searching and examination strategy should first be made to ensure sufficient time has been given so that nothing can have been missed, both from a prosecution and a defence perspective (ie in compliance with CPIA rules).

The problem with releasing a scene too early is that new information might come to light afterwards that requires different or fresh considerations. A primary crime scene should not be released before the initial high-priority main lines of enquiry have been completed, such as interviewing significant witnesses, viewing vital CCTV, or interviewing a suspect who has been quickly arrested. This is because new information may be forthcoming that has to be contextualized at the crime scene while still in its preserved state.

An SIO must be shrewd enough to plan and prepare for all eventualities. This includes changes in information that can develop in the early stages. For example, new witnesses may come forward who provide information requiring further examination of the scene; or suspects may say things in interviews that require clarification; or forensic experts may want to revisit the scene, etc. Once a scene is released, its sterility and integrity have been lost. Scene examinations need to be conducted painstakingly and thoroughly so the rule needs to be repeated: *never release a scene too early.*

KEY POINTS

1. Some crime scenes may present health and safety hazards for members of the public. If so, they cannot be released until they have been thoroughly cleansed and deemed fit for use.
2. Before any scene is released the SIO and CSM should conduct a 'walk through'. This is a satisfaction check that all investigative opportunities have been considered and the evidence retrieval harvest has been thorough and complete.

Some crime scenes, eg household premises can become a magnet for thieves and vandals once police security has been removed. The owner must therefore be encouraged to acknowledge responsibility for security and may need some appropriate crime prevention advice.

5.16 Health and Safety Considerations

Crime scenes present a range of hazards that require dynamic risk assessment. Examples of these include:

- liquid blood and body fluid samples;
- items stained with blood or other body fluids;
- items infested with parasites;
- drugs and drugs paraphernalia (eg syringes);
- hazardous chemicles;
- explosives, explosive devices (IEDs) etc;
- unsafe buildings;
- firearms and ammunition;
- sharp items;
- difficult terrain or dangerous environments (eg high voltage electricity, dangerous buildings, traffic conditions, etc);
- difficult weather conditions (hot/dry or cold/wet);
- confrontation with difficult or dangerous individuals.

Generic risk assessments may exist for attendance at crime scenes. However, given the above, it is essential wherever possible that appropriate advice is sought and personal protective clothing is worn when required. In addition to protecting the individual this minimizes the possibility of contamination. At a major or serious crime scene standard protection usually consists of a scene suit with hood up, face mask, overshoes, and protective gloves.

When dealing with scenes containing blood staining or known infectious diseases, extra care must be taken to avoid hazards and risk from potential blood borne infections, eg HIV or Hepatitus B. Gloves should always be worn when handling items or persons covered in blood, or other bodily fluids. Dried blood is also a hazard as it can enter the body through mucus membranes. Wearing a disposable mask can reduce the risk of inhaling particles. Footwear or other items of police clothing may also need to be decontaminated to avoid the risk of cross-transfer.

Firearms and explosive devices or dangerous substances quite obviously present extra hazards. Firearms must never be handled until they have been rendered safe by a qualified firearms officer or equivalent expert and explosives need very specialist advice and resources.

Sometimes crime scenes are hazardous places and officers must remain alert to spot any dangers, think quickly, adapt, and take a flexible approach. In exteme cases, staff may have to instinctively abandon crime scenes, pick up exhibits, or leave a deceased in place because of the severity of the danger or risk involved. Potential threats to members of the public and/or officers in some circumstances may present no alternative.

Some priorities may therefore override the needs of the investigation and it may not always be possible to keep a crime scene sterile.

In some inner city areas or amongst unruly communities, for example, there may be a distrust of the police, gang feuds, and regular firearms usage, or hostile or distressed families and friends of victims, which can pose difficult circumstances to work under. Fortunately these are exceptions rather than the rule. In such cases it may be possible to have a small cordoned area (eg immediately around a victim) and extend it when support arrives and crowds disperse. Later there may also be alternative ways of recreating crime scenes by use of, for example, CCTV, media footage, witness accounts, or photographs.

Safety of the public and the personnel who are engaged at the scene is at all times of paramount importance and non-negotiable. If there is a conflict of interest between public safety and the investigation, the former always takes precedence, although it should always be the aim to try to minimize the destruction or loss of evidential material.

Reasons why emergency actions were taken should be recorded and made known to the SIO and CSM/CSI as soon as practicable. Actions that have limited the potential for forensic recovery must be justified at a later stage, and it is wise to record in precise details exactly what and why there was a necessity for not preserving evidence. This demonstrates good standards of integrity and honesty of purpose.

KEY POINTS

1. The SIO and CSM should ensure there are adequate safeguards in place for all the staff engaged at a scene. Members of the examination team may need to spend a lot of time in what might be wet, cold, or unpleasant working conditions and provisions must be made for their welfare and safety. Simple things such as providing warm and dry rest, changing, cleaning, toiletry, and refreshment facilities within easy access will make a great deal of difference to their working environment and ability to maintain high levels of morale.
2. The appropriate level of personal protective equipment (PPE) must always be incorporated into risk assessment control strategies.
3. At major incidents it is the responsibility of the CSM or co-ordinator to liaise with the SIO to ensure that adequate police protection is available for all scene investigation personnel (*National Crime Scene Investigation Manual*, Issue 1 (ACPO National Crime Scene Investigation Board 2007), 50.

5.16.1 Use of a Specialist Advisory Group

In certain cases there may be a need for the SIO to establish a specialist advisory group (SAG) comprising appropriate experts in the various fields when dealing with a risk assessment for entering any dangerous scene, for example in fire/arson deaths, explosions, dangerous premises, mass fatality incidents, or suspected chemical or structural dangers when the SAG may have to include senior representatives from agencies such as:

- ambulance, fire and rescue service;
- media liaison officer(s) to assist with managing the media;
- structural engineers;
- medical advisers (eg Health Protection Agency);
- health and safety advisers;
- local authority (eg emergency planning officers);
- representatives from businesses/premises at/around scene (eg shopping centre manager);
- site clearance managers;
- professional standards branch duty officer (ie if there is a police complaint that they are investigating at the same time as the criminal investigation);
- welfare managers;
- local contingency planning officers.

KEY POINTS

Whenever there is to be a joint enterprise amongst agencies to deal with a delicate, dangerous and/or prolonged crime scene assessment or examination, the communication means must be 'interoperable', ie on-site communications equipment must be compatible to facilitate an effective and successful operation.

5.17 Exhibit and Forensic Submission and Review Process

It is the responsibility of the SIO, exhibits officer, and CSM to keep all seized exhibits under continuous review. This is best achieved by adopting a screening process at regular review meetings whereby each exhibit is rated for both forensic potential and priority. In practice, the exhibits officer usually prints off a list of all exhibits and along with the SIO each one is scored as follows:

F—shows whether the exhibit has forensic potential, then graded with a score of '1–3', 1 being high priority, 2 medium, and 3 low priority.
P—fingerprint examination required.
O/D—other document or exhibit for disclosure only.
O/R—other document or exhibit for research.
O/C—other document or exhibit required for court.

The results of the exhibits review are then entered into HOLMES2 as a registered document. This is a process that requires regular reviews and revisits as the enquiry progresses.

All exhibits graded 'F1' should be discussed at a forensic strategy meeting in order to ensure the appropriate examination is considered. The meeting should be held at an early stage in the investigation and should include the SIO, the management team, the CSM, a representative from the fingerprint unit, the forensic scientists (if applicable), and any forensic submissions officer (if applicable), who often holds the forensic budget. In view of the high costs of forensic examination it is essential that care is taken to prioritize only those items that may provide a result of significant evidential value.

Further review meetings should be held throughout the investigation to ensure all priority exhibits are fully considered for forensic examination. Minutes of all meetings should be recorded on the HOLMES2 database. Reasons why exhibits were sent for examination or why they were not should be noted, along with a full rationale and explanation for all decisions made. Minutes should be cross-referenced in the SIO's policy file and any submission (for examination) form should clearly indicate what the SIO expects the forensic scientist to prove scientifically.

In some cases the early retrieval of evidence from seized exhibits becomes time critical, for example when suspects are in custody pre-charge. In such circumstances it may be of use to consider the use of an exhibits assessment (or review) team, who can be tasked with checking, reviewing, prioritizing, and exploiting evidential opportunities for all items seized (eg identifying fast-track items). This is particularly useful when there are a large number of exhibits such as documents, computers, or mobile phones (and SIM cards) etc and a conventional exhibits strategy meeting would create an unacceptable time delay. The review team may include experts who can examine items such as computers and telephones.

Note: Such a system if utilized should not be allowed to bypass the MIR process and a rigorous method of ensuring all appropriate entries on decisions and movement of exhibits are properly recorded onto HOLMES2.

5.18 Fast-Track Forensic Submissions

It is essential during the early stages of any homicide investigation for the SIO, working alongside the CSM, to identify *fast-track* forensic submissions that may result in the early identification of a suspect and give a speedy arrest. These should be a standard feature and agenda item for discussion at any forensic and/or exhibit strategy review meetings.

Case study—Fast-tracked forensic evidence

A 10-year-old schoolgirl had been playing with some friends during a warm summer evening near to her home. She did not return home and was reported missing. A search of the local area began, involving family, members of the public, and the police. Unfortunately her grandfather found her in the early hours of the following morning in nearby dense woodland. She had been beaten to death and concealed in undergrowth, beneath a pile of leaves.

The scene was cordoned off and a huge murder investigation commenced involving over 400 police staff. A detailed forensic examination of the crime scene was undertaken which covered a large rural area including trees, bushes, and shrubs.

Within a few feet of the body recovery site, forensic scientists found minute airborne droplets of the victim's blood on surrounding leaves and vegetation at various height levels. This was consistent with the actual site and nature of the attack causing the death of the young girl.

During the early hours of the investigation, a 17-year-old youth was identified as being one of the last people to see the victim alive. He was treated as a TIE subject and as part of the elimination process his clothing and footwear were seized for blood and fibre screening. On initial visual examination of his training shoes, small blood spots could be seen.

The youth was arrested and taken into custody for questioning. The usual PACE custody time limits came into operation, whilst in the meantime his training shoes were sent off for fast-track forensic examination. Within three days, inside the custody time limits, the tests were completed. They revealed blood on the suspect's training shoes originated from the victim and was of the exact shape and size as the airborne blood distribution found at the attack site. This result linked him to the victim at the time of her death. The youth was subsequently charged and later convicted of the murder based on the evidence from the blood found on his training shoes.

5.19 Expert Adviser's Database

There are many types of forensic evidence, examination techniques, and experts who may be able to provide assistance in providing useful evidence. Some sciences are constantly evolving and the SIO and their enquiry team should strive to make the best use of what is available to them. It is always useful to keep up to date or find out what scientific methods and techniques there are. The NPIA Specialist Operations Centre (SOC) maintains a database which contains details of a wide spectrum of forensic experts. The SOC identifies areas of expertise and forensic experts who can assist in major crime investigation. There are staff available who can help to identify and are able to supply a list of expert advisers. They can be contacted by email at <soc@npia.pnn.police.uk> or by telephone at 0845 000 5463.

5.20 Conclusion

The extensive procedures and topics covered in this chapter in relation to crime scene management have included explanations of the roles of the SIO, CSM, and exhibits officers. The complex subject of crime scene processing was separated into six stages for ease of reference, followed by sections on forensic exhibit reviews and the all-important fast-track forensic actions. It is hoped the relevant checklists will act as a quick and easy guide and aide memoire for reference purposes and give added benefit to the SIO when considering those vitally important scene and forensic recovery strategies that so often can produce that one piece of irrefutable evidence.

Chapter 6

Setting Up and Managing an Investigation

6.1 Introduction

This chapter outlines roles, responsibilities, strategies, conventions, and standard procedures which the SIO uses to mount an enquiry after the initial response. These ensure professionalism and accountability, augmenting formal prescriptions established in law, eg disclosure principles under CPIA, and serve as foundation blocks for the investigation.

A synthesis of major incident-room standard procedures will be required, plus resources and suitable accommodation and equipment that are fit and adequate for running a major criminal investigation. This chapter will look at what the important roles are, moving on to some invaluable strategies and administrative methods that enable the SIO to launch and manage the investigation successfully.

There are sections on formulating main lines of enquiry and using investigative strategies; how to deal with information; action management, including fast-track actions; TIE, TI, and statement policies. The chapter ends by outlining the important function of accurate record keeping and the SIO's policy files. These are all *must do's* for the SIO.

Other material in the handbook could equally be included in this chapter, such as that relating to suspects and witness strategies. But what is contained here is more of a guide to the major components that will aid the SIO in establishing early, if not almost immediate, *structure and control*. These are vital ingredients and will get a professionally led investigation off to a flying start.

6.2 **Setting Up a Major Incident Room**

An incident room is the 'beating heart' of any investigation. It is the place where the enquiry is managed and controlled, although some investigations set off at such a fast pace that lots of enquiries and information have already been dealt with before it is in place. This is particularly so with a 'crime in action' (eg kidnapping) or terrorism-type incident. This means it is even more important to set up the major incident room (MIR) as quickly as possible in order to stabilize the policies and procedures required.

One function of the MIR can be said to have similarities to that of a medical 'triage' system. In adapting a definition of this term, it acts as a place for the sorting out and classification of information and material to determine priority of need.

Major incident rooms will vary from place to place. Ideally there will be one available that is the right size, has good equipment and facilities, and is ideally located. In the early response phase a makeshift room may have to be utilized until a suitable MIR becomes identified and available. If so, the management of any transfer and administrative movement needs to be carefully managed so as to cause minimum disruption to the enquiry. The early appointment of a 'finance manager' will greatly assist and will take a lot of pressure off the SIO as the early administration and logistical issues can be passed over to them.

KEY POINT

Most forces now choose to run major enquiries on HOLMES2, with specialist incident rooms and trained staff dedicated to major investigation. An early decision may have to be taken as to whether the enquiry should be run on the computerized database known as HOLMES2 or on an equivalent 'paper' version of it (there are effectively 3 levels of HOLMES usage, ie 'full', 'intermediate', and 'minimum'). HOLMES2 provides a massive analytical and research facility, plus action/exhibits management, etc. There are a lot of advantages in putting an enquiry onto HOLMES2.

However, it must be remembered that, whatever management system is chosen, the golden rule is that HOLMES2 must not be allowed to dominate or take over an enquiry. It is there to assist the smooth running and improve effectiveness. At all times the SIO and management team must take a disciplined approach to putting in place monitoring and review mechanisms to check what work the system is producing. But the SIO and investigation team run the enquiry—not HOLMES2!

Therefore, the SIO, once officially appointed to take charge of the case, will need to fill some key roles in the incident room. These may vary depending on the type and nature of the enquiry and with the exception of the SIO (mentioned elsewhere) are outlined as follows.

Roles in an MIR

Role	Primary Responsibilities
Deputy SIO (DSIO)	Has responsibility for conduct of the investigation in absence of SIO, plus any other tasks as nominated by the SIO (eg dealing with all sensitive intelligence). [Normally DCI/DI rank.]
Office manager (OM)	Manages MIR staff, ensures systems, procedures, and effective running of MIR are maintained. Implements SIO instructions and monitors high-priority actions, reads and assesses all documentation, and approves for filing. Keeps awareness of all developments and informs SIO. [Normally D/I rank.]
Finance manager	Co-ordinates all matters of administration and finance, such as accommodation, vehicles, staffing, exhibits storage, duty records, overtime, expenses, etc. [Normally police support staff member with requisite status and experience.]
Receiver (R)	Usually most up to date in respect of current state of enquiry as all material incoming into MIR goes through this person first, who assesses it determines priority and urgency of information, and identifies important developments. [Normally D/I or D/S rank.]
Action manager (AM)	Manages and allocates actions to enquiry team members. Must have current knowledge of all staff workloads, their skills, and experience to inform allocation decisions. Liaises with SIO to examine action allocated and pending lists and recognize priorities. [Normally D/S rank.]
Document reader (DR)	Reads all statements, officers' reports, interviews, and other documents (eg PDFs, H-2-H questionnaires, etc) in great detail. Decides what additional actions need raising from them to progress the investigation. Assesses importance and priority of documents, producing a summary of contents where necessary. [Normally D/C rank.]
Action writer	Raises actions as directed in a document or from specific instructions. Ensures actions are not being duplicated and that the originating authority is clearly outlined. [Normally D/C rank.]

Roles in an MIR

Role	Primary Responsibilities
Indexer (I)	(HOLMES2 database) Indexes all documentation as indicated by R or DR, raising actions as indicated and maintaining designated indexes and categories on the HOLMES2 database. Inputs results and endorses documents. (Note: Indexers often perform role of action writer as well.) [Normally specially trained police support staff.]
Registrar (Reg)	Usually an indexer who is also tasked with registering documents (ie on HOLMES2). Could be separate role if high-volume messaging system utilized (eg in Cat A+ type incident) to ensure documents entered onto database as soon as possible. [Normally trained police support staff.]
Exhibits officer (EO)	Records and safeguards all property recovered and ensures correct packaging and labelling of exhibits. (Note: Should be extremely forensically aware and knowledgeable on correct forensic procedures for packaging and avoiding cross-contamination, therefore must have correct training and experience.) [Normally D/C rank or trained support staff.]
H-2-H co-ordinator (H-2-HC)	Manages all H-2-H enquiries. Checks documentation and ensures completed correctly with any actions raised through the MIR. Agrees content of questionnaire, level required, and parameters of area to be covered with SIO. Supervises and briefs all H-2-H staff. [Normally D/I or D/S rank.]
Disclosure officer (DO)	Appointed at beginning of enquiry. Examines and is responsible for disclosure of all material in enquiry. Prepares all schedules for prosecutor and edits relevant material prior to service on defence. (Must be trained in CPIA 1996 and HOLMES2 if used.) [Normally D/C rank.]
File preparation officer (FPO)	Prepares case papers in consultation with SIO, OM, DR, and EO. Liaises with prosecutions team. Arranges storage of all case papers and associated material. [Normally D/S and/or D/C rank.]
Researcher	Undertakes detailed research of HOLMES2 to seek out important links and information that may be missed by other more specific office roles. Can be specifically tasked by SIO on large enquiries. [Normally D/C rank or police support staff member.]
HOLMES2 account manager	Ensures compliance with rules and conventions plus MIRSAP. Checks indexing and registration categories and documents. [Normally D/S rank.]

Roles in an MIR

Role	Primary Responsibilities
Typist	Types documents from original statements, officers' reports, messages, and other documents as required. [Support staff member.]
Analyst	(See Chapter 8.) [Specialist support staff.]

KEY POINT

There are other roles and positions within an enquiry in addition to these, such as Intelligence Officer, Communications Liaison Officer, or Passive Data (eg CCTV) Co-ordinator. These may be equally important roles to fill quickly as their responsibilities may fall within the SIO's main lines of enquiry. Job descriptions are outlined in the *Guidance on Major Incident Room Standardized Administrative Procedures* (MIRSAP, ACPO Centrex, 2005), 18–42). It suggests how some roles can be combined (often referred to as 'double hatting') when necessary if resources are limited. For example, Deputy SIO may be combined with Office Manager or Action Manager; receiver with document reader; document reader with file prep officer, etc (pp 58–9).

6.3 Resources

Complex major investigations will require the SIO to manage all their resources carefully as a large number of staff, including experts and those brought in from elsewhere to assist, need to be managed and instructed in what is required of them. There will be considerations such as budgetary requirements (and constraints), technical resources, vehicles, overtime costs, and expenses to consider in addition to ensuring the correct amount and type of resources are available.

It is orthodox practice to make substantial resources available in the early stages of a major investigation. This is to ensure that as much evidence and information is captured and secured as possible, before it becomes lost forever or contaminated. Enquiry teams can be reassessed and trimmed at a later stage when resource implications may not be as critical. It is worth keeping a regular check on what resources may be available in advance, particularly if undertaking 'cover rota' duties.

Sometimes, because of competing demands, an essential management skill is getting teams to perform to a higher standard than their numbers would suggest is possible. In reality there are only finite resources available and the SIO should record staffing problems of balancing investigational needs against (non-)available resources. This will help safeguard the SIO if a review of an undetected crime comes later. Nonetheless, provided staff are willing, eager, enthusiastic, and passionate about their tasks, attitudes inherent in good SIOs, success can still be achieved despite staffing limitations. The SIO has to *get the most out of available staff* by setting achievable and realistic priorities.

KEY POINT

1. It is common practice for staff engaged on major enquiries to work in pairs. This, however, halves the quantity of resources available. Unless there is a high-risk task to complete, or corroboration is required, or a complex TIE is to be completed, then it is a suggestion from experience that there is little justification for working in pairs other than for the sake of tradition or maintaining morale. This is a luxury that can no longer be sustained due to resource constraints. If an obstacle to working in pairs is lack of available vehicles, then look into borrowing or leasing some to alleviate the problem.
2. One good piece of advice is to get an early idea as to the nature and scale of an investigation in order to make an informed decision on the quantity and type of resources required, eg what category it is (Cat A, B, etc) and the gravity of the crime, plus likely political, community, and media impact. This will need continuous reassessment. Wherever possible, the SIO should appoint a person to manage and control all the logistical issues, as well as to find the right staff with the requisite skills and abilities (eg trained FLOs, witness interviewers, search experts, etc). Correctly matching tasks to skills and experience and facilitating potential development opportunities need to be borne in mind.
3. If an enquiry is going to be long and protracted, a human resource manager should be tasked with monitoring the development and career aspirations of those engaged on the investigation. Sometimes prolonged attachments can hinder career opportunities if they are not managed properly.

Factors affecting resourcing

In addition to considerations of categorization, there are other factors to consider:

- Volume of work (eg number of victims, suspects, and scenes).
- Solvability factors (forensic, witnesses, suspects, or CCTV potential).

- Complexity (organized crime, specialist area, linked crime, etc).
- Levels of media interest.
- Political (eg status of suspect, community impact, etc).

Specialist support

The SIO will often call upon specialists to assist the investigation. These could come from a multitude of sources. Some of the more common ones are as follows:

- forensic service providers;
- crime scene investigators;
- imaging or photography expertise;
- specialist search teams;
- criminal intelligence units;
- forensic pathologist;
- house-to-house enquiry teams;
- trained interview specialists;
- tactical firearms unit;
- covert tactical specialists and resources;
- National Policing Improvement Agency (Crime Operational Support Team).

6.4 Effective Resource Management—Logistics Co-ordination Units (LCU)

Some enquiries may pose substantial logistical challenges such as those involving serial offending and cross-force boundary enquiries (ie NIM level II type). These will potentially require the skilful management and control of large numbers and different types of assets, eg mutual aid and/or specialists such as surveillance units and search teams. A separate logistics cell (or Logistics Co-ordination Unit) may prove useful to manage all the various required resources by administering and organizing accommodation, catering vehicles, equipment, finance, IT support, duty rosters, travel arrangements, welfare and personnel matters, expenses, cross-charging with other forces, procuring specialist services etc. Teams of trained briefing officers could also be incorporated into the unit to provide continuous briefings and updates to large numbers of staff in line with the SIO's objectives and requirements. Personnel to fill key roles can be selected and sourced from existing administrative departments that are used to dealing with these sorts of human resources administrative matters on a regular basis. Staff could be temporarily seconded to the LCU for the duration of the enquiry and/or for as long as is necessary. The LCU could be managed by someone sufficiently experienced with the requisite skills to run the unit on the SIO's behalf and who may also have to be answerable to a gold commander for the efficient management of resources and finance throughout the duration of the enquiry/operation.

Any logistics support through an LCU should always be closely linked to the enquiry MIR to avoid duplication of effort to record all details of their activities through the HOLMES2 system. This is also to ensure the SIO and the management team can always maintain control and that there is an effective audit trail of all activity and functions performed by the LCU.

6.5 Investigation Team Structure

Dependent on the type and size of enquiry under investigation the SIO may wish to consider who and what is required and how the investigation team should be structured. There is no 'one size fits all'

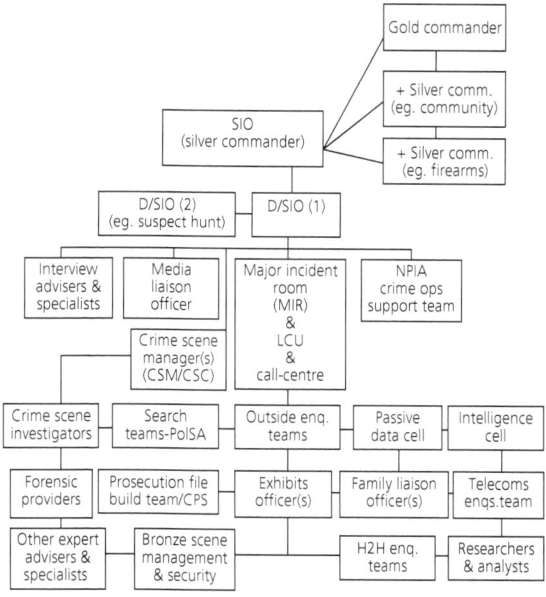

Figure 6.1 Team structure flowchart

solution to how SIOs should structure their investigative resources. However, it is worthwhile giving early thought to this and producing a flow-chart is often the simplest way to present an enquiry-team structure, which may look something like Figure 6.1.

Note: An SIO can, if required, assign ownership of any or all of the various areas of responsibility to nominated and selected individuals and supervisors who will be required to 'project manage'. This is a useful management method that allows important areas of responsibility to be delegated to carefully chosen individuals. The SIO can discuss and agree policies and procedures and obtain updates on progress at regular intervals. The SIO must always have confidence in their team members to deal with their allocated task in an effective and responsible manner.

6.6 Main Lines of Enquiry (MLOE)

These are a means of setting and focusing clear investigative priorities that aim to establish the facts, find the evidence, and arrest and convict the person(s) responsible for the offence. The SIO formulates a list called the 'Main lines of enquiry' in the policy file and ensures that all staff engaged on the enquiry are fully aware of what these are and in which direction the investigation is heading. The enquiry must always remain focused on these and not become too bogged down with other actions and enquiries that are the result of an administration and management system that may sometimes produce workloads that do not reflect the SIO's main priorities.

Some of these enquiries will be obvious and stand out from the information available and the circumstances of the offence under investigation. For instance, known key witnesses who need to be interviewed quickly, or potential exhibits that can be forensically fast-tracked for the offender's fingerprints or DNA, or the securing and viewing of some CCTV footage that may provide images of the persons responsible. These will provide the SIO with immediate and clear lines of enquiry. However, in some cases these priorities will not be so obvious and more thought and consideration may be needed as to how the necessary information and evidence is going to be acquired.

In formulating MLOE an SIO has to ask the question: where is the necessary evidence to solve this crime likely to come from?

The answer normally lies in a relatively small list of sources from which such material can be obtained:

- victims/witnesses;
- suspects (eg admissions or implicating others);
- forensic/fingerprint and expert evidence (including specialist subjects such as ballistics, palynology, entomology, pathology, etc);
- passive data sources (eg CCTV, communications data, credit card records, etc);
- circumstantial evidence (ie evidence of circumstances surrounding the offence which provides inferences, eg failing to furnish credible alibi).

A point to note is that for the purposes of formulating main lines of enquiry the SIO is free to use all available information and material (eg intelligence) and not just material that is admissible as evidence.

Any lines of enquiry that appear to have the best potential to reveal useful material and fill one or more of the aforementioned requirements should therefore be prioritized in the MLOE list. Any information relied upon must, of course, be properly evaluated and analysed to determine reliability and suitability. This rule applies to all sources of information, whether from witnesses, electronic/scientific sources, or whatever. In so doing the A B C principle must be applied:

A	Assume nothing
B	Believe nothing
C	Challenge/check everything

It is always useful to consider the use of an *analyst* as a professional adviser to help the SIO in evaluating the material available and making an assessment as to accuracy and significance of the investigative information. The analyst can also be tasked with highlighting information or knowledge gaps. These can be identified by applying the 5 × WH + H formula (Who, What, Where, When, Why, and How), explained more fully in Chapter 2.

It must be remembered that setting too many main lines of enquiry may lead to low productivity due to overload. A key skill is to determine and judge the relevance and value of all available information in order to make sound judgements and distinguish between good and bad potential leads. In the initial stages this may need to be done under time constraints. If so, the SIO should try to create some 'slow time' to consider these carefully and not act too hastily (investigative decision making is discussed in more detail in Chapter 2). The SIO needs to complete this task at the earliest opportunity so that the investigation is heading in the right direction, correct priorities are applied, and best use made of resources.

It is essential that the MLOE remain under constant review throughout the life of the investigation. There will always be changes—some will drop off the list once they have been dealt with or found to be not leading anywhere, or the investigation may change direction altogether. It is advisable to make regular reference to, and entries about, the MLOE in the SIO's policy file, together with satisfactory rationale as to why some feature and others do not. The SIO must show responsibility and good control of the investigation and be confident about dropping or abandoning initial lines of enquiry.

KEY POINT

Ensure that the main lines of enquiry listed have rationale recorded against each one in order to explain why they have been included. This should be recorded in the SIO's policy file.

What the list should contain is entirely dependent on the individual circumstances of each case and investigation; this will differ from case to case. However, there is a good chance similar 'main lines' will appear regularly in most investigations. Here are some typical examples:

The list is a guide only and each case will require a unique list of MLOE, which may vary from week to week. Probably included

Checklist—MLOE examples

- Tracing and interviewing (TI) significant witnesses.
- Obtaining a full profile of the victim N1 ('victimology').
- Establishing cause and manner of death.
- Scene (1)—forensic scene examination and PolSA search.
- Conducting H-2-H enquiries (in set parameters).
- Intelligence strategy (eg identifying intelligence gaps; biographical profile of gangs, their activities, habits, methods, etc; open source intelligence; community intelligence; tactical initiatives, etc).
- Determining the 'relevant time', ie likely time of death of victim.

- Determining movements of all persons at scene (1) (between — and —).
- Determining movements of victim N1 (between — and —).
- Determining movements of any declared suspect (between — and —).
- Pursuing TIE actions.
- DNA or fingerprint/palmprint elimination methods (eg through TIE procedures).
- Establishing motive—eg sexual, robbery, hate crime, etc.
- Researching and analysing any potential linked crimes or precursor incidents.
- Formulation of a media strategy.
- Telecommunications data strategy.
- Passive Data recovery and viewing strategy.
- Family liaison strategy.
- Making use of covert pro-active tactics (eg use/conduct authorities for tasking of covert human intelligence source (CHIS)).
- Use of community advisory/support groups (eg independent advisory groups (IAGs)).
- Publication of a reward.
- Use of an anniversary reconstruction and/or road checks in locality.
- Identifying and prioritizing modus operandi (MO) suspects.
- Making use of National Policing Improvement Agency (NPIA) Crime Ops Support.

will be some quite specific main lines that the SIO feels strongly about, eg trace/interview Peter Sutcliffe potential significant witness who may have seen incident occur.

All the team must be kept fully aware of what is on the MLOE list and kept up to date with amendments or additions. The list should be displayed or kept in a prominent position for everyone on the enquiry to see and/or circulated to each and every team member. (Note: sensitive covert tactics may need to be left off the list for confidential reasons—if so, this can be explained with reasons and justification in a 'sensitive policy file' entry—see 6.14.1. below.)

KEY POINT

When determining main lines of enquiry the SIO should have in mind para 3.4 of the Criminal Procedure and Investigations Act (CPIA) 1996,

Code of Practice, which states that an investigator must pursue all reasonable lines of enquiry whether they point towards or away from the suspect.

6.7 Investigative Strategies

The SIO should develop and define what are known as 'investigative strategies', which should link in with the SIO's main lines of enquiry list and explain how the MLOE are to be conducted. Investigative strategies comprise of carefully determined activities and tactics that produce a cohesive plan for delivering important elements of the investigation. Each strategy 'title' is a means of linking or grouping activities and setting a specific objective of importance under a particular theme or heading. Some examples include:

- Forensic evidence recovery strategy (this may be further subdivided into particular areas such as Scene (1), victim's body, suspect's house, etc).
- Search strategy.
- Victim/witnesses interview strategies.
- Suspect identification and arrest strategy.
- H-2-H/CCTV/telecommunications data (passive data) strategies.
- Intelligence strategy.
- Media strategy.
- TIE strategy.
- Family/community liaison strategies.
- Overt pro-active strategy (eg high-profile policing in area of scene).
- Covert pro-active strategy (eg surveillance).

Investigative strategies should combine and contribute towards identifying the offender(s) and producing the necessary evidence. They should be fully discussed and agreed (eg at briefings) by the SIO and their management team and all enquiry staff (ie the team approach). It may be that expert advice has to be requested for some areas, such as interview advisers, media liaison officers, PolSA search co-ordinators, CSMs, etc. Clear objectives should be laid down, recorded, and agreed for each strategy and relayed to the teams. For example, the objective for an intelligence strategy may be 'to obtain all possible intelligence regarding rival criminal associates of the victim and establish who was responsible for the offence'.

Earlier it was stated that it is optional for the SIO to assign ownership for each strategy to an individual and/or team. Those with supervisory responsibility are usually best placed to take on any large or substantial tasks, including the deputy SIO. They can be allocated a key task and those given them should be fully briefed on the overall objectives of the strategy and how the SIO expects them to be completed. For example, CCTV (passive data) collection and viewing if on a large scale can be allocated as a project to be managed by a nominated supervisor (eg Detective Inspector/Sergeant with a dedicated team to undertake the task and provide regular updates to the SIO on progress). This decision should always be recorded in the policy file, together with terms of reference, agreed methods, parameters, staffing, and resource levels.

Each individual strategy will require a themed strategy meeting, if not several. These are usually chaired by the SIO (or deputy in their absence), with an agenda pre-determined and the contents minuted/recorded. The purpose of themed meetings is to assemble key stakeholders for the particular strategy to discuss, determine, and review the tactics, progress, and policy. For example, for the 'communications data strategy' the SIO and/or deputy may be present, plus the nominated Communications Liaison Officer(s) from the enquiry team and an authorized SPoC (single point of contact) plus an analyst.

Investigative strategies must remain under constant review to ensure they remain relevant, appropriate, and are making good progress. Investigations are extremely dynamic in nature and frequently require subtle changes in direction and priorities; therefore investigative strategies need to reflect and remain supportive of any such amendments or shifts.

KEY POINT

'It is not an admission of personal failure to change investigative direction in the light of new material'.

Murder Investigation Manual (ACPO Centrex, 2006), 57

6.7.1 Implementation of investigative strategies

Each strategy will contain investigative key actions and activities in order to fulfil and deliver the overall objectives. In order to do this, a list of individual 'actions' is compiled to provide specific detail and instructions about tactical activities and achieve the strategic aims. Some examples follow:

Example 1

Nature of action

'Arrange Level 2 house-to-house enquiries, report on exact areas to be covered as authorized by the SIO, and submit a plan of the details' (H-2-H strategy). (The objective is to gather information and identify potential witnesses.)

Example 2

Nature of action

'Arrange fingertip search of Scene (1) and obtain statements from officers involved' (search strategy). (The objective is to maximize all potential forensic opportunities and ensure exhibit recovery.)

Example 3

Nature of action

'Obtain itemized billing for mobile 07718 792651 believed used by suspect's girlfriend N34 Scanlon for period 1.8.09–15.9.09 covering all outgoing calls' (telecommunications data strategy). (The objective is to consider call patterns to identify the contact telephone number of the suspect which can then be used to trace and arrest him.)

In any large and complex investigative strategy, it is best to record all the key details in what is known as a 'stand alone' document, with all the relevant action numbers entered alongside each listed activity. This can be cross-referenced to an entry in the SIO's policy file if necessary and will help enquiry teams understand the strategy and tactical details and enable everyone to keep track of progress.

Note: Some key investigative strategies are further explained in Chapter 8.

6.8 Messages and Information

In a complex enquiry there will be an influx of information to the incident room (and probably commencing even before the room is set up) that needs capturing, recording, and assessing. It should be stressed that *the management of information is of paramount importance to the success of an investigation*. That one 'golden nugget' of information that may solve the case and save hours and hours of police time and effort may come from an early communication to the incident room. Therefore the SIO *must* ensure there are adequate arrangements in place ready to receive, capture, and effectively deal with all calls and information fed into the incident room. Otherwise valuable time will be lost or information may get overlooked, lost forever, enquiry progress will be compromised, or callers may become discouraged from recontacting. *This must not be allowed to happen at any cost!*

When people contact or call into the incident room or via public enquiry offices or communication control rooms, including officers with information, or even where an officer attached to the enquiry wants to submit information that cannot wait for an action write-up, this information needs to be recorded in the prescribed format on a message form. This will ensure that no information gets lost. It can then be assessed, prioritized, and logged onto HOLMES2.

Incident message forms are an instantly recognizable green, self-carbonating document (known as an MIR/6), which include all the details of the information, the originator, time, and date received, and what has been done with it. These are usually handwritten and should be quickly assessed and prioritized.

Once an incident room is up and running, set procedures are laid down as to how these messages are dealt with. They are the life-blood of any enquiry and the SIO should read and check them on a regular basis (daily as a minimum) as the carbonating copies allow each and every one to be forwarded directly to the SIO. An offender's details may be emboldened within a message, so the incident room and SIO must be in a position to spot these quickly—they should not be left on a desk or in an in-tray until someone has had a chance to go through them.

KEY POINT—Hotline facility

Setting up a fixed incident room public enquiry contact telephone number needs to be arranged at the earliest opportunity. This is so that it can be given out externally to the public in media appeals, posters, etc and also internally to officers and staff within forces. This 'hotline' number must be supervised and managed correctly with someone familiar with the enquiry nominated to be available to listen to and/or take calls at all times (ie out-of-office hours). The SIO cannot afford to miss that one vital call from someone who, if not spoken to immediately, may never call back. Arrangements must be made to have the hotline number constantly monitored, even out of hours when the incident room is closed. This can be facilitated by use of a call-forwarding facility to say a mobile phone carried by staff on a rotational basis. An added consideration is to have interpreters available if necessary to cater for any likely callers who may not speak English.

In the early stages the SIO should ensure there are adequate message forms available to record all the information coming in to the enquiry so it does not get mislaid and there is a clear audit trail and record of where it has come from, etc.

KEY POINTS

1. A good tip is to always carry a small stock of the green message forms for when an enquiry gets started.
2. The SIO should nominate someone to assess and prioritize all messages that are received if it is going to be some time before the incident room gets established.
3. There should be some set criteria for prioritizing information and making use of the high, medium, and low ratings to assist. These should be clearly displayed on the front of all messages, and/or with sticky brightly coloured labels or tags to make them stand out.
4. With highly significant information staff should have the confidence to bring it immediately to the attention of supervisors, who should quickly review it and where appropriate escalate it up to the SIO rather than waiting for it to go through the incident room process (emphasizing it should eventually still go through the room as well). The SIO cannot afford to wait any length of time for highly important information.

6.9 Use of 'Call-Centres'

If the investigation is receiving a large volume of messages and telephone calls from the public, eg where the enquiry is of high public and media interest like the Soham killings of Holly Wells and Jessica Chapman, a dedicated 'call-centre' (similar to a Casualty Bureau) may be required to handle the vast influx of information with a senior superviser appointed to manage it on the SIO's behalf. A gold commander would probably be responsible for providing and arranging this facility. Recent developments such as NMAT (National Mutual Aid Telephony), CASWEB, and MIRWEB can provide the ability to deal with the receipt of a mass volume of information remotely through HVM (High Volume Messaging) now embedded within HOLMES2. Facilities such as those provided by MIRWEB allow for the electronic recording of messages across linked forces directly onto HOLMES2 on a mutual aid basis. This new add-on technology was successfully used in the 2006 investigation into murders of five women in Ipswich and positively commented upon in the NPIA (2008) Tactical Debrief: Operation Sumac (see *Tactical Debrief: Operation Sumac* (London, NPIA, 2008).

Note: If using a dedicated call management facility the SIO should nominate dedicated staff to scrutinize all the messages received, prioritize them, identify any potential significant witnesses, and ensure any vital information is recognized and acted upon quickly.

6.10 Action Management

The term 'Action' is defined as: 'Any activity which, if pursued, is likely to establish significant facts, preserve material, or lead to the resolution of the investigation' (*Practice Advice on Core Investigation Doctrine* (ACPO, 2005), 77).

The term 'action' in the literal sense refers to the process of doing something or the performance of an activity. It is widely used in the language and discourse of major incident investigation and referred to extensively in MIRSAP. Actions are numbered on printed documents containing instructions or directions to perform tasks and serve as a method to record, distribute, perform, and manage workloads and tasks that drive an enquiry (denoted as A1, A2, A12, etc).

Actions will detail specific instructions and a course of action, whom it has been allocated to, time and date, its origin, and the enquiry result. This document passes through various supervisory roles in an MIR before finally reaching the SIO, who has to make a decision as to whether to file it as complete, return it for rework, or raise further tasks from it to be completed.

MIRSAP states:

> **4.3 Actions**
> Actions are generated from information gathered during the investigation and may be requested by any member of the major incident room. Actions are raised once authorized by any of the following: SIO, D/SIO, office manager, receiver, document reader. Actions can be raised and registered by any of the indexes. Each action is given a unique reference number which is the next consecutive number prefixed by the letter 'A'.

4.3.1 Action management

Action management should ensure that each action:

- Refers to one specific line of enquiry only.
- Does not contain multiple instructions.
- Contains sufficient detail to inform the enquiry officer of exactly what is required.

Associated documentation must be made accessible to complete the task. Action result text completed by the enquiry officer should contain:

- Enquiries made to trace the subject of the action.
- Information which is not recorded in any of the accompanying documentation MIRSAP (ACPO Centrex, 2005), 84–5.

The raising, allocating, resulting, and reviewing of actions is the process by which all enquiry team workloads and activities are organized and managed. Actions are generated from information received or gathered during the investigation and should be raised and authorized only by specific persons within the enquiry, usually the SIO/DSIO, office manager, receiver, document reader, or nominated action writer at SIO instruction (ie during briefings/debriefings).

It is important that, once allocated, actions must be properly supervised, a function normally undertaken by a person appointed to act as an action manager. If this function is not done correctly, the efficiency of the enquiry will suffer. All allocated actions must remain under constant supervision as to:

- who they have been allocated to;
- what workloads/numbers of actions each staff member has;
- length of time allocated (usually 14 days is sufficient time to complete medium/low-priority actions);
- whether the actions are achievable;
- the skills/training or experience required to carry out the tasks required.

It is worth considering the acronym SMARTER—all actions/tasks should be:

S Specific
M Meaningful
A Achievable
R Realistic
T Time-specific
E Ethical
R Recorded

The person who performs the action manager role must, on behalf of the SIO, maintain an awareness of staff workloads and match skills and experience to the right tasks. This role needs to draw upon good planning and organizing skills to prevent potential problems, such as staff going on leave, courses, court commitments, etc and to ensure tasks are completed in a timely and efficient fashion.

KEY POINT

Pre-planned enquiries should not be undertaken without an action first being raised and allocated under the SIO's direction. However, this may not always be the case and the SIO/MIR has to remain vigilant to ensure all work undertaken is done through the correct channels and under the full control and supervision of the enquiry management system (HOLMES2).

6.10.1 Action abbreviations

The following abbreviations are used when creating actions and are recognized by the HOLMES2 database:

- TIE—trace/interview/eliminate
- TI—trace and interview
- TST—take statement
- TFST—take further statement
- RI—re-interview
- OBT—obtain
- ENQS—make enquiries
- NOMINAL—number used to identify a person (eg N12)
- UF—unidentified female
- UM—unidentified male
- UU—unidentified unknown
- UV—unidentified vehicle
- PDF—personal descriptive form
- AQVF—alibi questionnaire verification form
- M—message form (eg M14).

6.10.2 Prioritizing actions

Priority levels should be assigned to all actions raised on major incidents. Each action should be assigned a high, medium, or low priority. The parameters for these priorities are set by the SIO and recorded in the SIO policy file. Suggested parameters are:

- **High priority (HP)**—a fast-track action requiring immediate allocation and completion within a defined timeframe.

- **Medium priority** (MP)—an action that directly relates to a main line of enquiry.
- **Low priority** (LP)—an action that may not currently support a main line of enquiry and should not ordinarily be allocated as a matter of routine.

One practical point is that if all actions are raised as the same priority, eg low priority, this is not a very helpful way of enabling staff to understand what priority levels should be attached to their workloads. Conversely, there is no point in making all the actions high priority as this will add little value and confuse the whole prioritization process.

Any decisions and markers should, of course, be regularly and dynamically reviewed throughout the course and progress of the investigation.

6.10.3 Early action allocation and recording

As a general rule most major investigations will require similar actions being raised and allocated in order to conduct early important enquiries. In order to speed up this process various templates have been devised that contain lists of generic actions used or considered in order to kick-start the enquiry. These are often referred to as the 'first 50 [or similar amount] actions'. They are pre-prepared in order to facilitate and ensure swift allocation and registering.

The sooner actions can be raised and allocated to teams, the easier and quicker it becomes to keep track of and manage the initial and subsequent investigation. Therefore any pre-determined list or system for having these readily to hand is a good aid for the SIO. In the initial stages HOLMES2 will usually take a while to become established and fully functional. It takes time to set up and arrange indexing and supervisory staff with requisite administrative procedures (and sometimes the necessary hardware) in place. Therefore an initial 'paper action management system' may have to suffice, and it is advisable to get this up and running as soon as possible. It also enables any subsequent back-record conversion on HOLMES2 to be speedily arranged once it has been implemented.

In order to commence a quick and simple paper system, a pre-prepared matrix/table can be put into use almost as soon as the SIO takes charge of an investigation. Some initial actions can be automatically considered from a pre-determined list as initial tasks and aide memoires to save time. However, any other necessary actions can also be entered onto the matrix in numerical order to keep a record of what activities have been or need to be allocated. As the details of the actions are recorded together with whoever they have been allocated to, the list can be used to keep an ongoing log of all the investigative work that is being/has been allocated.

KEY POINT

The SIO would be wise to appoint an action writer at the earliest opportunity to record and populate a matrix chronologically of all actions raised and allocated, when, and to whom. This will avoid duplication of tasks and hasten any back-record conversion process onto HOLMES2. The matrix will make any handover to another SIO much simpler and show what the initial SIO has done so far. An example of the matrix is shown in Appendix B.

Note: Unlike the matrix, 'actions' are produced onto standardized forms (MIR/5), examples of which are contained within the MIRSAP manual appendices.

KEY POINT

The SIO must retain an awareness of actions that are being raised on their behalf by an action writer or incident room personnel. Increasing the number of actions increases workloads and, once raised, a decision has to be taken to do something with them. Therefore, only relevant and focused actions should be raised. Care must be taken to ensure the investigation is not becoming overloaded with tasks that are not going to take the enquiry any further forward. Once raised, however, the actions do not necessarily have to be allocated. They are there for if and when the need arises and so information does not have to be revisited continuously to see whether actions should be raised.

What this guards against is the duplication of tasks during the initial stages. Keeping track of what has been done, who by, when, where, and what still needs doing, can be an enormous task unless a system similar to this is implemented quickly. It can even be utilized while a (de)briefing session is in progress. A list of tasks can be populated as information is being received, which will save precious time at the end with actions ready to be allocated immediately. An example follows.

Example—Briefing—Action generation and prioritization

Mrs Davies from Number 12, Gould Street heard what she thought were raised voices coming from outside Number 8 (Gould Street). Her husband, Paul Davies, came home shortly afterwards and told her he had seen a young female with blonde hair standing crying at the end of the street. An ambulance attended and treated a male with head injuries who was lying on the footpath. An unknown hysterical female was trying to administer first aid to the victim before he was taken to hospital. The victim, we now know to be called Mark George, later died of his injuries.

Actions from this initial briefing can start being entered onto a matrix almost immediately.

1. TI TST from Mrs Davies, occupant of 12, Gould Street, who may have heard raised voices coming from outside Number 8. (MP)
2. TI TST from N3, Paul Davies, occupant of 12, Gould Street, re sighting of UF young female with blonde hair standing crying at end of the street. (MP)
3. TIE and consider suitability for significant witness status N4 U/F with blonde hair standing crying at the end of the street. (HP)
4. TI TST from ambulance crew who attended victim and consider recovery of any relevant forensic samples and notes made. (MP)
5. TIE and consider suitability for significant witness status hysterical U/F believed attempting to administer first aid to the victim. (HP)
6. Conduct background checks on victim N1 Mark George. (MP)
7. Arrange treating of victim's body at hospital as a crime scene. (HP)
8. Arrange forensic recovery of all clothing and possessions taken from victim at hospital and obtain pre-transfusion blood sample, if applicable. (HP)
9. Obtain hospital medical notes for treatment of victim upon arrival. (LP)
10. Arrange inner and outer cordons for scene (1) believed to be on Gould Street where victim treated by an ambulance crew. (HP)

11. Conduct initial H-2-H enquiries in the immediate vicinity of scene (1) on Gould Street. (MP)
12. Appoint family liaison officer and fully brief on circumstances and arrange provision of immediate family support and notification of next of kin. (HP)
13. Debrief initial response staff and collection of all notes made. (HP)
14. Notify local policing commander and discuss command and control requirements for enquiry and community impact assessment. (MP)
15. Check for any precursor or linked incidents. (MP)
16. Trawl area for CCTV footage overlooking the scene (MP).
17. Obtain copy of the initial 999 call.

6.10.4 Fast-track and High-Priority actions

These are a useful and effective way of prioritizing and allocating urgent and time-critical enquiries. The *Murder Investigation Manual* (ACPO Centrex, 2006), 41) defines fast-track actions as:

> Any investigative actions which, if pursued immediately, are likely to establish important facts, preserve evidence or lead to the early resolution of the investigation . . . Fast track actions are often used during the first twenty-four hours of an investigation, but they may be required at other stages, for example, where another scene is discovered, a significant witness is identified, or a suspect is identified.

They are an invaluable tool for complying with the 'golden hour(s)' principles (the initial period where vital actions are necessary). It is also a responsibility of the SIO to *review* any fast-track actions that are already allocated or in the process of being allocated. This is one of the three strands of the important A B C principles of investigation, where the C stands for 'challenge/check everything'. The SIO must be satisfied that fast-track action allocations are based upon sound and valid reasoning and good judgement to avoid taking the enquiry off in the wrong direction. As the enquiry progresses, even in the initial stages, any critical actions must be regularly reviewed against changing circumstances as and when any new facts and information become available.

KEY POINT

On HOLMES2 accounts all High Priority actions should have 'HP' prefixed to the action text. This is because the action manager when viewing actions using the Action Queue manager function on HOLMES2 is only able to view the first 72 characters of the action text.

An important point is to set a controlling policy over how and when there must be updates provided on fast-tracked enquiries and/or completion timescales. There is little point in allocating prioritized actions if they do not get completed and resulted quickly. Therefore, there should be clear instruction and guidance on when and how to return them. For example, an SIO may stipulate they require an update or completion provided verbally within 24 hours (or less), and a written or printed version within 48 hours, for all fast-track actions. Some examples of 'fast track' actions are:

Checklist—Typical fast-track actions

- Locating and arresting suspect(s) (consider making requests for sightings, etc).
- Conducting significant TIE enquiries.
- Tracing/interviewing important witness(es).
- Arranging formal identification of the victim.
- Notifying next of kin and arranging FLO support.
- Obtaining background and lifestyle details of victim.
- Identifying, securing, and protecting any crime scenes.
- Determining intial scene search strategies and forensic examinations.
- Implementing urgent PACE road checks.
- Locating Passive Data (eg CCTV) sites and preserving/securing recordings (eg tapes and hard drives).
- Setting initial media strategy (eg immediate holding statement).
- Establishing cause and manner of death (eg post-mortem examination).
- Setting up a 'fast time' intelligence cell.
- Initiating covert/overt pro-active tactics (eg surveillance).
- Arranging/conducting debrief of all staff involved in initial response.
- Arranging preservation and collection of victim's pre-transfusion blood sample and personal property including clothing from hospital.

6.10.5 Action 'write-ups'

Actions are the principal source used to evaluate the outcome of an enquiry made and also the effectiveness and efficiency of the completing officer(s). A well-presented response to a task, accompanied by an accurate and readable report, reflects professionalism and underlies success.

Attached to each front sheet outlining the nature of an action and who it is allocated to should be an official report on the result from those who have carried out the instruction or enquiry. Good reports indicate a well-managed approach to the investigation and are important because they constitute disclosable material for the purposes of the prosecutor, defence teams, and any subsequent reviews or public enquiries.

Different SIOs may have their own preferences and styles for the way they prefer action write-ups to be completed. There are, however, some important rules to follow and the SIO must ensure that all their staff are aware of what is/what is not required and acceptable. This is particularly important if staff and teams have been assembled and brought in from different units or other force areas. Below is a useful list of rules for completing Actions.

Checklist—Action 'write-ups'

- A good report requires a solid piece of investigative work. No amount of rhetoric or waffle will disguise a poor and shoddy approach and outcome.
- Opinions should not be included, eg 'I don't think this person is telling the truth', only observations based on fact should be, as should evidence, eg 'there are inconsistencies in the account of this person because she says she was at home during the alibi times when three of her associates say she was with them'.
- The facts should be presented in a clear and logical order.
- They should always include the time, date, and place of any interview conducted, plus full details of persons interviewed.
- Any information cited should be accompanied by an explanation as to the provenance (source) and a clear distinction made between hearsay, opinions, and facts.
- Any rough notes made should accompany the action write-up, for the purposes of disclosure (it is well worth reviewing these in detail as they can often contain more accurate details than the write-up itself).

- There must be a true and complete account of all the facts and information, whether they are favourable to the SIO's particular theory/hypothesis or not.
- They should include details of all investigative steps taken/not taken, with their results.
- They should include any information relevant to the enquiry that should be brought to the attention of the SIO.
- They should include details of any exhibits and property seized and give details of all documents attached to the action, eg witness statements.
- There should be use of clear and concise language, good use of double spacing, and if hand-written they should be easily decipherable.
- There is no point in replicating witness accounts when they are contained elsewhere, eg in statement form.

KEY POINT

In a large-scale major investigation, investigators are generally too busy in the early stages to complete action write-ups. In which case the SIO should ensure that they are still kept updated with useful and interesting developments and the progress of actions through oral briefings and at team briefings.

Case study—Terminology Issue

A male was ambushed by seven masked offenders in a house where he had attended in order to settle a drugs debt. Each offender was armed with a weapon, amongst which were four firearms. The victim received numerous fatal gunshot wounds and died later. After the attack all offenders fled from the rear of the house along a canal bank, witnessed by a neighbour who became a main prosecution witness. However, all the offenders were white males and the witness described one as being dark skinned after noticing the colour of his hands.

The witness made a statement and during her evidence in court retracted the aforementioned detail, stating she was now unsure about the colour of one of the offender's hands. The defence team argued that she had changed her evidence to suit the prosecution case. To support their contention they produced an Action write-up which contained the words 'the witness is sticking to her story about the colour of the offender's hands'. This unfortunate choice of words was used by the defence to accuse the police of trying to get the witness to change her account, and although it was vehemently denied, some damage had been done to the integrity of the witness-handling procedure.

6.11 The TIE Process (Trace/Interview/Eliminate)

The objective of a TIE process is to identify and process individuals who realistically could have committed the offence under investigation. It is also a method by which individuals can be eliminated against a criterion set by the SIO and can be instrumental in leading to the identification of the offender(s) or witnesses. Those who cannot be eliminated are subject to further enquiries aimed at establishing if there is material that would enable them to be implicated in the offence. TIE enquiries are particularly useful in cases where there is no obvious suspect and a large number of people have characteristics that mean they could be potentially involved. The process should then produce an ever-reducing pool of individuals on which the inquiry can focus in order to identify the offender(s).

A key feature of the TIE process is to populate TIE categories with relevant individuals identified by the MIR from information processed from enquiries, house-to-house (H-2-H), calls from the public, intelligence research, search activities, etc.

One of the important main lines of enquiry should be to pursue TIE subjects who have been identified and categorized by the SIO in order to try to eliminate them against set criteria, which should be carefully determined and recorded in the policy file. The *Murder Investigation Manual* (ACPO Centrex, 2006), 250 states:

> Being in a TIE category does not mean that individuals are suspected of the crime, merely that the group is one which, in theory at least, could contain the offender . . . Following enquiries, TIE subjects should be regarded as being either eliminated or un-eliminated from the TIE category, not as being eliminated or un-eliminated as the offender.

Other than enquiries aimed at tracing and arresting declared 'suspects', TIE actions tend to be the next most significant in terms of status and importance to an enquiry. They should only ever be raised either directly or in the name of and under the authority of the SIO. This is because:

- They demand a higher level of time and effort from the personnel who have been allocated the task of conducting a TIE enquiry and are therefore resource-intensive. Often they require two officers to complete each one because of the amount of work involved.
- There is often a requirement to conduct a high level of research and produce a risk assessment before embarking on the TIE of a subject. Some may have criminal backgrounds and reside in places where risks are greater to staff and the public. A supervisor should be nominated to oversee the conduct of these actions and the level of research required.
- It is absolutely vital that they are conducted and completed to a very high standard, otherwise mistakes can happen, with offenders being mistakenly eliminated.
- They are very intrusive for those who are made subject(s) of the TIE process.
- They tend to attract the attention of the legal process through both the Crown Prosecution Service and defence teams and can become a problem in undermining cases if not managed effectively.

In order to facilitate the effective allocation and management of TIEs, they are placed into categories or groups on HOLMES2. Those people who are contained in any TIE category are then known as 'TIE subjects', not TIE 'suspects'—it is very important to differentiate between the two. This is because the term 'suspect' for obvious reasons holds a very different and special status.

Some typical examples of TIE categories are as follows:

- TIE persons named as being responsible (normally through intelligence reports, information messages or ongoing work via the enquiry teams, MIR, or other sources).
- TIE all persons aged 10 yrs+ within the scene or vicinity of the scene (as defined for HOLMES2 indexing purposes) between . . . and . . . (define time parameters).
- TIE any persons aged 10 yrs+ at/or who had access to scene (1) between __ and __ (define time parameters).
- TIE modus operandi subjects (ie those who have exhibited similar criminal behaviour to the offence under investigation).
- TIE registered sex offenders.
- TIE recent prison and bail hostel releases (including tagged offenders).

- TIE known associates of or persons linked to the victim.
- TIE relatives of the victim.
- TIE anyone who fits the description of the offender(s).
- TIE lone males residing within half mile of victim last sighting.
- TIE anyone who has committed or attempted suicide or self-referred to a mental institute (stipulate time and area parameters).
- TIE anyone at the SIO's discretion (to ensure sufficient latitude for those who do not fit into any of the other categories but it is decided for stipulated reasons they should be included).

Note: The SIO should formulate categories specific to their inquiry (ie bespoke), and the more TIE categories a subject is linked to, the more likely they are to be of interest and therefore worthy of closer examination.

6.11.1 TIE elimination methods

The effectiveness of TIE enquiries rests on the thoroughness of the enquiries made in relation to each individual. In order to effectively eliminate any TIE subject it is necessary to set some criteria to eliminate against. Various methods will help satisfy the HOLMES2 and MIRSAP elimination criteria discussed later and will be determined by individual circumstances and the amount of information available, eg the description of a suspect or forensic evidence found at the crime scene, such as tyre or footwear marks. Some examples of TIE elimination processes are as follows:.

- Forensic elimination, eg DNA mouth (buccal) swabs/elimination fingerprints/footwear impressions/vehicle tyre marks or impressions/pedal cycle description and tyres, etc.
- Personal description forms (PDF) of subjects, eg physical appearance, distinguishing features, accent, gender, ethnicity (usually by completion of personal descriptive form—PDF).
- Account and verification of movements between alibi times (stipulated times) and completion of an Alibi Questionnaire Verification Form (AQVF) if alibi confirmed.
- Vehicle details and type/model checks.
- Verification of identity (photo on driving licence/passport, question re antecedents/criminal history, and compare with criminal records held).

- Search on a voluntary basis (or with magistrates search warrant) of their home address, vehicles, land/gardens, adjacent buildings, work premises, linked addresses, etc.
- Seizing all mobile phones and relevant telephone numbers.
- Any other requirements at the SIOs discretion (eg forensic searches or clothing to be seized such as footwear).
- Obtaining photographs of all TIE subjects.

Additional notes

1. An SIO should formulate justifiable, proportionate, and necessary requirements specific to their inquiry.
2. TIE policies for recovering items or samples should be a standing agenda item at forensic and exhibit and review meetings to check for appropriateness and relevance.
3. It is possible to use a checklist for each TIE, with all elimination criteria listed so that they can be 'ticked off' as completed.

Note: PDFs are used to record the personal details and description of any subject, including vehicle details, mobile phone numbers, unusual characteristics, etc. The SIO should decide who they wish their staff to obtain PDFs from, and normally include TIE and/or TI subjects.

6.11.2 Setting alibi times

TIE subjects should be questioned about their movements during any alibi times set by the SIO. These are to coincide with significant events applicable to the incident under investigation and determined by, for example, witness information, CCTV, or time of death indicating when the offence occurred. The time parameters may need to be set wide enough to include other factors such as events before or after the incident that may be significant also. However, the wider the times are, the more work is involved in trying to alibi a subject over a longer period.

Enquiry teams should include in the AQVF where the TIE subject was and details of any person(s) who can verify their movements, ie alibi witnesses, who should be seen and interviewed. Their details should be fully recorded on an AQVF, which should normally be completed if an alibi is to be confirmed, and signed by the alibi witnesses as proof of verification. Alternatively, if the witnesses do not confirm the subject's alibi, then this information should be confirmed in witness statement form.

6.11.3 Mode of TIE interview

The method of TIE interview is important and must be stipulated by the SIO. Depending on the nature of the enquiry, the SIO may wish to stipulate that all TIEs are visually recorded, audio-tape recorded, or contemporaneously recorded on notes signed later by the subject, in order to safeguard the accuracy and integrity of the process. This is important as TIE subjects can turn into either suspects or witnesses.

The SIO should also set a 'refusal policy' to provide guidance in the event of a refusal by TIE subjects to provide information, samples, and details. For example:

1. Ask and note reason for refusal.
2. Ascertain whether DNA/fingerprints/photograph already held by the police.
3. If previously obtained, ascertain level of verification of identity.
4. Create intelligence database entry—request to obtain photo/fingerprints/DNA and cross-reference with action number.
5. Consider possible grounds for search warrant/further action.

6.11.4 MIRSAP elimination criteria

Based upon the information obtained from the TIE methods mentioned earlier, on conclusion of each individual TIE action MIRSAP standard elimination codes 1–6 will be recorded against each subject's nominal record on HOLMES2 in order that an assessment of the level of elimination is available for reference purposes. Care must be taken to ensure these are completed correctly. These categories are:

1. forensic elimination;
2. description;
3. independent alibi witness;
4. associate or relative alibi;
5. spouse/partner or common-law relationship alibi;
6. not eliminated.

Investigators, incident room staff, and managers must determine from the action report what level of elimination from the list applies. The important point about this criterion is that these markers can be changed depending on new information if it becomes available, for example an associate changes their initial alibi account or it is disproved.

6.11.5 Prioritizing TIEs

When there are a large number of TIE subjects there will be a necessity to prioritize them. In order to do this and ensure the most significant and relevant TIEs are conducted before the less important ones, they may need to be put into order by prioritization. This can be based upon such criteria as age range, gender, or proximity to the scene. For example, it may be that males of a certain age are more significant if the profile of the offender is believed to be that of a male. This will make them easier to manage.

6.11.6 TIE Scoring matrix

In order to assist in prioritizing TIE subjects, a scoring matrix may be developed and introduced. This will allow for certain criteria that are specific and directly applicable to the circumstances under investigation to provide a numerical score against which the list of TIEs can be sorted into a more manageable priority list. The SIO may wish to enlist the services of key members of their team to assist with this process as it can be complex and each category and allocated score will need some reason recorded against it. If possible a Behavioural Investigative Profiler (BIA) should be used to provide added support for drawing up the matrix scores and categories. A brief example follows:

> A 70-year-old male is found battered to death at his home address between 1.00 pm and 3.00 pm. He had recently retired and was rumoured to keep large amounts of cash at his home address, some of which was subsequently found to be missing. He lived alone and had very few associates or close family.

The TIE scoring matrix for this case may look as follows:

Subject Criteria	Score (1–10)
Has previous intelligence or conviction for burglary in a dwelling, in particular distraction type MO.	(6)
Has previous intelligence or conviction for aggravated burglary, violence or similar offence (eg street robbery, theft from the person)	(9)
Is linked to the victim or relative or associate of the victim	(8)

Subject Criteria	Score
Is linked (offending, intelligence, family member, known associate, stop-checks, or otherwise) to geographical location within a radius of one mile from the vicinity of the scene as determined by the SIO	(8)
Has previous conviction for daytime offending	(4)
Is known to target or select elderly or vulnerable victims	(6)
Is linked to the offence through intelligence	(10)
TOTAL	

The skilful part comes in determining what score each of the criteria should attract. Clearly those TIE subjects who attract the highest scores should get priority to be dealt with.

There are some dos and don'ts with the scoring matrix process, which are as follows:

DOs

- Provide specific direction to those doing the coding—if necessary giving specific 'operational definitions' of what is meant by each of the terms, eg what is meant by 'daytime offending'.
- Test cases at the end to see if the right people are coming out with the highest scores who are wanted there, if not they may need re-weighting.
- Seek help if possible, particularly from an NPIA BIA.
- Leave some flexibility for the coder and/or SIO to have their own 'captain's picks' as long as there are not too many otherwise the whole point of prioritization via a matrix becomes redundant.

DON'Ts

- Consider this an easy or quick task, ie do not just give it to an analyst to get on with alone. The weighting is vital and if incorrect could waste a vast amount of resources and the offender may never get looked at.
- EVER eliminate anyone/anything with this process, it is a means of PRIORITIZATION only.
- Score everyone with the same points—the idea is to distinguish and prioritize TIEs rather than have a big 'chunk' of persons to look at.
- Ever re-use a prioritization matrix—they should be done on a case by case basis. Even if the offence seems similar the background of the offender may not be the same.

6.11.7 'Significant TIEs' and/or 'persons of interest'

The terms 'significant TIE' and 'person of interest' have worked their way into police investigation language in recent times and are sometimes used by SIOs when it is necessary to create a higher status or category of TIE subject. The added importance is aimed at helping prioritize certain types of TIE subjects who have a higher potential to be the offender and allows the SIO to maintain a heightened focus on this class of persons. It may be that a more stringent set of elimination criteria are attached to these types of TIE subjects, such as enhanced background research and a high level of search criteria of their homes (eg using forensic scientists to check clothing or footwear and more detailed work on alibi evidence provided). The SIO should constantly review the status of any significant TIE subject and ensure that the strict TIE elimination criteria is applied.

It is, however, important to draw the distinction between a 'significant TIE' and a 'suspect'. Once a person is declared a suspect any subsequent questioning should of course fall under the provisions of arrest under PACE, whereas the investigation of a 'significant TIE' subject does not fall under the provisions of PACE unless they are later declared a suspect. A 'person of interest' could also perceivably be a witness, and therefore the integrity of any conversation or interview should be carefully recorded. Interview advisers may also be used to develop interview strategies for all significant TIEs which would include method of interview etc.

At any subsequent court hearing an SIO may have to explain precisely what these terms mean and why, for instance, such an individual was not afforded the protection of a caution, legal representation, and custody safeguards laid out in PACE. Nevertheless, the terms are, by and large, useful provided they are not overly abused and care is exercised so that boundaries between one or the other do not become too blurred or procedurally confusing.

6.11.8 Reviewing TIEs

All outstanding TIEs need to be regularly reviewed in order to manage them effectively. Any list of TIE actions should be reviewed periodically and methodically assessed to determine which of the TIEs are currently of most importance. These decisions should be formally recorded in the SIO's policy file, or by using a printed list of each and every TIE action and putting alongside each one, with reasons, the order of priority.

Also, whether they should remain allocated or become allocated (if they remain in the 'for allocation' queue).

The TIE criteria and categories should also be reviewed at regular intervals and redefined if appropriate to ensure they are relevant and appropriate.

6.11.9 Use of TI actions (Trace and Interview)

Any action that is outside the scope of the TIE criteria is just given the status of a trace and interview T/I. These can be used for a variety of purposes, for example:

- TI N257 Brown who rang incident room and who may have information to assist the enquiry.
- TI N123 Langridge who heard shots while standing outside front door of home address.
- TI N186 Lopez re alibi of N54 Sutcliffe.

TI actions can also be placed into categories for ease of reference and management. These can be tailored to fit the needs of the specific investigation. Examples of these are:

- Persons near to scene (1) outside TIE parameters.
- Any action related to CCTV enquiries.
- Any action related to H-2-H enquiries.
- Actions relating to forensic examinations of exhibits.

6.12 Statement Policies

The SIO must decide when written statements will be required to be taken from persons interviewed. These may be subject to further considerations depending on the type of witness or the age and/or nature of the individual concerned. A clear policy needs to be established and recorded within the policy file to give some guidance to teams who are interviewing people. This might not just be directly as eye-witnesses to the offence under investigation, and can also apply, for example, to TIE subjects or alibi witnesses.

All those engaged on the enquiry need to be informed as to what the SIO's statement policy is, for example statements must be taken from:

1. Any person at or near scene (1).
2. Any relatives/associates of the victim and other persons who may have any useful background information.

3. Any person who has relevant information for the purposes of the investigation.
4. Any alibi witnesses.
5. Any others at the SIO's discretion.

6.13 Defining the 'Scene'

In addition to the usefulness of defining a 'scene' with particular emphasis on parameters and cordons, etc for the purposes of forensic examination and searching (see Chapter 5), there is also a requirement to define each crime scene for the benefit of the incident room in order to index onto the HOLMES2 database. The SIO will have to determine not only what forms the parameters of the scene but also the 'vicinity' of the scene. This enables TIE policies to be specific as to elimination criteria, for example a category may be to 'TIE all persons within scene (1)', or 'TIE all persons within the vicinity of scene (1)'. The latter category enables the SIO to widen the geographical area for the purposes of TIE identification and criteria.

6.14 Record-Keeping (Policy Files/Books/ Decision Logs)

Policy decisions made by the SIO will always be of the utmost importance in determining the outcome of an investigation. Some would say the professionalism of a major crime investigation can be measured against the quality of the policy file. It must be recognized, however, that a good policy file does not always guarantee a good investigation unless the contents of the file and direction of the investigation are properly communicated to the enquiry teams and staff on a regular basis. For this reason the SIO's policy file should be regularly and openly used as part of the SIOs briefing content and method.

A policy file or 'decision log' is normally a bound book, A4 in size (and/or typed directly onto HOLMES2) that is numbered on the front, internally paginated, and labelled with the full details of the investigation or operation it refers to. It also includes details of the SIO and deputy and the date the enquiry commenced. Each and every entry is sequentially numbered for ease of reference. Quite often these books are designed and printed specifically for this purpose with self-carbonating pages, instructions, and prompts contained within the first few pages.

Each and every one of the SIO's policies and decisions must be comprehensively recorded in the file in a legible and durable format for audit purposes. This should be done contemporaneously wherever practicable, ideally at the SIO's dictation by a logist working alongside the SIO. All policy entries must be timed and dated (ie both when the decision was made and when the entry was made, if different), and signed by the person making the entry and the person making the decision (if not the SIO—the SIO should countersign to say they agree to the decision and have noted the policy file entry).

In practical terms the SIO will normally commence rough note taking and record early decisions in a 'day book' during the frantic first few hours of an incident which can then be transferred into the policy file at a more convenient time. However, it should be stressed that the SIO must start a policy file at the earliest opportunity to avoid any unhelpful backlog of material which will require updating and to ease enquiry handover purposes when there is an exchange of SIO (eg when handing over from on-call duties). Once a policy file has been started and brought up to date then the process of regular entries made directly into the policy file can be maintained.

KEY POINT

A large number of important policy decisions will be made in the early stages of an investigation, which is why it is useful to nominate someone to record them on the SIO's behalf so they can be recorded accurately and contemporaneously.

The content of a policy file/decision log is a matter which will ultimately be at the discretion of the SIO but should always accurately reflect each and every important strategic and tactical decision made during the course of an investigation. These include the main lines of enquiry (MLOE) and investigative strategies, for example:

- forensic examination, including fast track tests
- search strategy
- suspect arrest strategy
- witness strategy
- communication and media strategy
- family liaison strategy
- house-to-house enquiries.

The systematic recording of the SIO's policies is one of the most important aspects of management for any major investigation. This is a vitally important skill all good SIOs have to acquire. Policy files should be skilfully constructed and maintained to serve as a vital record and audit trail of the rationale associated with each and every decision and outline the overall management strategy and tactics for a major crime investigation. The SIO does not have to work in isolation in deciding and recording policy. Consultation can be had with the enquiry management team or other experts, with details of that consultation recorded in the policy file. At the conclusion of an enquiry the policy file must be retained and stored with the case papers, even if it has been typed and formally registered as a 'document' onto HOLMES2.

KEY POINTS

1. Policy files tend to play a particularly important role in helping any review team understand and reconstruct the important components of an investigation. Any omissions or lack of clarity and detail are likely to be spotted quickly. They also serve as a permanent point of reference for the SIO to rely upon in any subsequent court proceedings, public hearings, enquiries, or inquests. The recording of reasons for various lines of enquiry being pursued or not pursued is critical to enable SIOs to convincingly explain and support their decision making at any later stage.
2. All decisions in the policy file should identify the decision maker to support their integrity and act as a permanent audit trail afterwards. If someone other than the SIO makes a policy decision, the entry should be countersigned at an early stage by the SIO, to confirm that they agree with and have ratified the decision made on their behalf and that they have always been fully involved in and in control of the enquiry and decision-making process.
3. A policy file should be maintained on a regular basis throughout the life of the investigation, including up to the trial and beyond if an appeal is likely, or to a case review process if necessary.

Policy file entries may need to be cross-referenced to other stand-alone documents that are in existence, for example if there is a separate arrest strategy, or CCTV recovery and viewing strategy, or forensic strategy, which may be lengthy documents in their own right. It may be preferable to make reference to their existence rather than repeat the details in the file. The documents themselves can be completed in a format similar to a policy entry, with the decision and accompanying reasons included, signed and dated by the SIO, then registered as a formal document onto the HOLMES2 database and cross-referenced against the appropriate entries in the SIO's policy file. The recording of such a cross-referencing process will provide reassurance to the SIO that the stand-alone strategy document has been registered onto HOLMES2 and also provide an easier means of locating any relevant strategy documents which they may wish to refer to or review during the investigation or any time thereafter,

KEY POINT

There are three important elements to policy file decisions and entries. The first two relate to the decision itself and the reasoning behind that decision. The third is equally important and should be linked to the first two, ie a record of what information was known, available, and relied upon by the SIO at the precise time the decision was made.

Case study—The Stephen Lawrence Enquiry

'The policy file contains nothing to show when or why the decision not to arrest was made. Nor does the policy file contain any reference to the establishment of surveillance, which the SIO indicated was to be part of the alternative way ahead. This in itself is a glaring omission' (Sir William Macpherson of Cluny, *The Stephen Lawrence Enquiry* (HMSO, 1999), ch 18).

6.14.1 Sensitive policy files

As a general rule all members of the enquiry team should be made aware of any policy decisions and allowed access to the policy file. The contents of the SIO's policy file should be shared with all members of the investigation so everyone understands the direction of the enquiry. This is much simpler if the policy decisions are quickly transferred onto HOLMES2, normally under the document reference of 'D1', making access to everyone that much easier.

However, there are occasions when more than one policy file may need to be kept. An additional 'sensitive' policy file may be required if there are confidential matters and/or material that needs to remain protected due to its sensitive nature (eg sourced from an informant/CHIS). Examples include references to sensitive investigation techniques, covert tactics or intelligence (for which access has to be restricted to protect the integrity and likely success of the tactic and welfare of the source), and/or witness protection issues. If this kind of policy file entry is required, the level of access must be determined by the SIO in order to safeguard the material effectively. For example, the first line in the sensitive file may state that only the SIO, deputy SIO, and office manager are permitted access to the contents of the sensitive file. If using HOLMES2, restrictive access levels can be agreed and arranged through the HOLMES2 account manager.

This is often an area that causes differences of opinion as to what should be restricted and whether it should be entered onto HOLMES2. It can become even more complicated if an independent review team examines the case. A point worth considering is that sensitive material may have to be preserved for a long period of time, including after the investigation has ended. Sensitive documents, important as they are, often end up stored in 'murder libraries' (ie storage of archived case material) for which long-term access can be difficult to control. Once preserved with restrictive markings on a computerized database such as HOLMES2, it becomes less susceptible to being lost and there is a clear audit trail of those who have accessed it.

6.14.2 Content and structure of policy files

The content of the policy file is a matter entirely at the SIO's discretion, set against national guidelines. It is vital that the SIO, or an officer nominated by the SIO (eg a logist), systematically and wherever possible contemporaneously records all relevant policy decisions. This means recording why various lines of enquiry were pursued or not pursued. The detailed recording of those decisions and the reasons for making them is critical, as is a reference to the information that was available and known at the time each decision was made (see earlier keypoint). It is difficult to be too prescriptive when providing guidelines on the construction of a good policy file, which is a core skill of an SIO, other than to comment on the requirement for the SIO to ensure that all decisions are recorded contemporaneously, accurately, and with sufficient explanatory reasons and rationale.

The MIRSAP manual (ACPO Centrex, 2005, 66–7 and 245) states that policy file entries should be written in a decision/reason divided format with only one entry per page. There is also a stipulation that a separate file be maintained that contains a sequential log of events as the enquiry progresses.

The authors' preference is to combine both requirements (decisions and log of events) in one book in a more open, free-text narrative format. This makes progress of the enquiry easier to follow and decisions remain in chronological order alongside events as they occur in sequence. On a practical note, it is much simpler to complete one rather than two separate files/logs. More importantly, decisions can be made alongside developments as they occur which helps show the information that was available at the time the decision was made. When this method of record keeping is adopted, a typical page may look something like the example below.

Consec. no and time/ date entry	Log entry	Cross-ref
47. 13.20 hrs 23.4.2010	At 10.00 a.m. on 23.4.2010 the SIO held a forensic strategy meeting in the SIO's office in the Major Incident Room to discuss the current progress of examinations that have been submitted and results that are still awaited. The agenda and minutes of the meeting, including all details of those present, have been fully recorded and submitted into the incident room for registering as a 'document'.	D.72 refers
48. 14.35 hrs 23.4.2010	Decision: A search warrant shall be obtained for the address of 53, Kings Road, Crompton, and executed today. A full operational order has been prepared (see D.75). Date and time of decision: 14.30 hrs 23.4.2010. Reason: The SIO has reviewed a recent intelligence log (D.74) rated B24 relating to items of blood stained clothing from the suspect N.7 Johnson believed hidden under a bed at 53, Kings Road, Crompton. Research has shown that this is the address of Johnson's half-brother Stephen Smith born 21/05/75. Officer making entry: (signature) DC James (Logist) Officer making decision (if different), (signature) D/Supt Bell (SIO)	Intelligence Log D.74 refers Operational order for search D.75

6.14.3 Suggested content of policy Files

Here are some suggested items that may be included in the SIO's policy file.

Investigation set-up

- Appointment of SIO/DSIO.
- Appointment of crime scene manager (CSM) and media liaison officer (MLO).
- Involvement of any gold or silver commanders (including terms of reference).
- Summary of incident.
- Location of MIR and use of HOLMES2 database.
- Management structure of enquiry team.
- Increase/reduction/refusal for increase in staff numbers.
- Identification of key posts in MIR (eg receiver, disclosure officer, etc).
- Appointment of analysts, researchers, intelligence cells, media liaison officers, etc.
- Typing services—documents (eg taped interviews) to be typed and arrangements.

Enquiry management

- Identification, definition, and parameters of any scene(s) and policy for security and eventual release.
- All policy decisions relating to witness statements (ie when required), personal description forms (PDFs), TIE elimination criteria, alibi verification.
- House-to-house (H-2-H) parameters.
- Media conferences, frequency, and information to be released or withheld.
- Deployment of mobile incident vehicles at scene(s).
- Criteria for research on any suspect and TIEs.
- HOLMES2 indexing policy.
- Liaison arrangements with Crown Prosecution Service (CPS).
- Parameters for all TIE/TI subjects.
- Action management policy (eg how many per team, timescales for submission, etc).

Finance and administration

- Appointment of finance/administration officer.
- Use of a logistics cell.
- Funding considerations—budget allocation/constraints.
- Resources required, obtained, refused (eg mutual aid/liaison from other forces).

- Arrangements for payment and monitoring of overtime.
- Use of police vehicles, mileage allowances, rented vehicles.
- Booking on and off arrangements for staff, tours of duty, leave, and public holiday working arrangements.
- Management of welfare issues.
- Management (eg timing) of briefings/debriefings and management issues.
- Additional equipment required.
- Health and safety issues.

Lines of enquiry

- Outline of all MLOE indicating those with high priority and resource implications.
- Variations on discontinued lines of enquiry (with reasons).
- Details of any declared suspects.
- Details of all investigative strategies (eg witnesses, suspects, intelligence, passive data, telecommunications, H-2-H, FLO, Forensic, etc) and any separate linked policy documents.
- Any important strategic or tactical decisions affecting the enquiry (eg use of national circulation or artists impression of offender).
- Any important events or changes to the direction of the investigation.
- Details of any linked incidents under consideration.
- Use of specialists and/or NPIA Crime Operational Support Team.

6.15 **Conclusion**

This chapter has outlined some vital processes and procedures for setting up and conducting an investigation. These will generally enable the SIO to gain early control of the investigation together with an effective and recognizable management system. Whether the enquiry has a HOLMES2 facility or not is largely irrelevant because the enquiry should, wherever possible, still adhere to these principles and guidelines.

It is hoped that, by implementing the procedures contained within this chapter, the SIO can achieve far more effective management of an investigation. These are *must dos* and should be considered as early as possible: the sooner they are introduced, even in fast time, the easier it will become to record and control every decision the SIO makes and to conduct the enquiry to nationally recognized standards.

Chapter 7
Investigative Briefings and Debriefings

7.1 Introduction

It is the opinion of the authors that this area is so important it merits its own chapter. This is because an SIO must be highly committed to managing briefings and debriefings effectively in order to reap the rewards that will be to the benefit of the investigation. They are a highly valuable investigative and communicative tool and key function and core responsibility of an SIO.

First, it will be helpful to clarify what the terms 'briefing' and 'debriefing' actually mean in the context of this chapter. In a major investigation the term 'briefing' normally refers to occasions when all staff and the management team meet to go through a structured session featuring a discussion of all the important elements of the investigation. There are, of course, other uses of this term in police duties, one of which relates to occasions when teams are 'briefed' before conducting or mounting a pre-planned operation. These types of briefing are slightly different and it is the former rather than the latter which will be the main feature of this chapter.

The term 'debrief' here is primarily concerned with the requirement in the immediate aftermath of an incident and initial response to assemble all those involved and gather as much information as possible. However, this could also include times after a pro-active phase of an investigation has been mounted, for example making arrests or conducting house searches. These, too, would merit a debriefing session to capture all the necessary material of use to the enquiry and should be considered alongside the second section, which focuses on the period immediately following the initial response. Nonetheless the principles are the same.

Secondly, it should be noted that there is a distinction between investigative briefings and counselling/welfare sessions, which are no less important but conducted in order to address any particular welfare needs of individual officers. They may have to take a different format from what will be described in this section and expert advice may have to be sought.

KEY POINT

Investigative briefings and debriefings are an important means of capturing and instantly sharing information, and communicating with the team. They provide an ideal opportunity for the SIO to demonstrate good control and leadership of the enquiry and for all the other staff to make a useful contribution. These are occasions when teams are hearing and seeing the SIO in person and listening to his/her thoughts on the case. Morale, team spirit, motivation, and expectations can therefore be positively influenced by the process. Strong communication is always the language of leadership.

Briefings and debriefings also provide an excellent opportunity to assist the Action management process. Having an Action Writer present and at the ready is an ideal way for the SIO to take early control of the management of the enquiry and begin progressively creating and documenting actions for prioritizing and allocating. This allows the management element of the enquiry to keep pace with dynamic investigations, plus the early production of documents and records that will speed up back-record conversion, ie onto HOLMES2.

Finally, an important matter also touched upon in this section is one of a recurring and important topic throughout this handbook, that of disclosure.

7.2 **Disclosure**

A high proportion of debriefs and briefings will involve cases that are likely to result in court proceedings. In any event it should be treated as though they will do so because the content of operational briefing material falls within the ambit of the Criminal Procedure and Investigations Act (CPIA) 1996.

Throughout debriefing/briefing procedures all staff will need to have due regard for the guidance provided in the CPS Disclosure Manual (2005) which contains details of how the police service have duties to disclose unused material to the defence (see <http://www.cps.gov.uk>).

It is clearly the responsibility of each individual involved in a criminal investigation to ensure that any information which may be relevant to the investigation and which is not recorded elsewhere is *recorded and retained*. This applies to any relevant conversation or discussion and, therefore, applies to all debriefings and briefings. It includes any individual's observations relating to the investigation and any notes or accounts received from witnesses. Therefore all that is said or written can be subject to disclosure.

If relevant information does emerge during a debriefing/briefing, for example where an individual remembers something new or recalls an inaccuracy in a previous note, that information should be immediately recorded and retained in accordance with the Codes of Practice (CPIA s 23(1)). In these circumstances the individual concerned should make a record of the fact, including when this took place and the subject matter.

The SIO and/or any other managers of these sessions should ensure that all participants are aware that the matters discussed will be subject to normal rules of disclosure.

7.3 **Briefings**

Briefings are a key part of any major investigation. It would be extremely difficult for an SIO to manage and control an investigation effectively without them. They are the means by which information is disseminated and shared, ideas, tactics, and hypotheses exchanged, progress discussed, work allocated, updates provided on work allocated, and feedback gained. Matters of interest and developments can be discussed, good work praised, issues raised at short notice, and work duties arranged. Overall they serve as a good forum for the vital communications link between the management and enquiry teams.

Briefings are also opportunities to foster good working relationships and engender team spirit, making people feel valued and part of the decision-making process. All the team members can be introduced to each other and any new members welcomed and made to feel part of the team.

The contents of briefings are a key component of the investigative process. Apart from discussing the information and material currently available, they provide a good forum for collective discussions to fill the 5 × WH + H matrix. The SIO should want to try to use the team briefing to fill in the missing 'intelligence gaps', share the result of intelligence and evaluation of information, and share the 'what do we know, what do we need to know?' principle.

At the same time briefings serve as a subtle means of providing a means of accountability, with updates and progress results openly fed back to the SIO in the presence of team managers, supervisors, peers, and colleagues. Questions, opinions, suggestions, and requests for clarification of concerns and issues that arise can and should be encouraged in this forum. Monitoring and evaluating requirements are facilitated through the briefing process provided there are good communication skills in use.

The SIO must hold regular briefings during an enquiry—in the early stages probably on a twice-daily basis, then maybe once a day thereafter. The nature of workloads and circumstances of each case will dictate as and when they should be held. All those involved in the investigation should be required to attend and the lead always taken by the SIO, or the deputy SIO in their absence. They should be seen as an excellent opportunity to demonstrate good leadership and gain the respect, trust, willing co-operation, and shared enthusiasm from the team.

KEY POINTS

- It is advantageous to have nominated key roles and responsibilities, and have pre-determined important staffing issues before the first briefing is held. Other preliminary meetings such as those affecting media, FLO, or crime scene strategies can also have been dealt with beforehand, as they are time-critical and key decisions and policies that may arise can be presented at the briefing.
- It is also important before the briefing commences to have met with the management team and major incident room staff (if applicable) in order to have agreed policies and parameters, such as TIE elimination criteria (alibi times, etc), together with the initial main lines of enquiry and objectives for the investigation. These can then be made available and presented at the briefing, creating a good impression of managerial efficiency. (Note: heavy debating or signs of disunity among management team during briefing should be avoided.)
- If there is to be a handover from one SIO and/or investigative team to another, they should all be invited to attend the initial briefing so that important issues are not missed.

- There should always be a focus on the positive aspects of the case. The SIO's delivery strategy will have an important impact on the morale of the team. Use of strong points rather than negative ones can be emphasized and an explanation on how these will help move the investigation forward.

7.3.1 Planning and conducting briefings

Usually, anyone involved in the investigation or who may be able to contribute should be invited to briefings, depending on the subject matter (eg if sensitive issues are to be discussed, attendance may need to be restricted). However, briefings can also be subject or activity-specific, such as forensic searches or arrest operation, when not everyone may need to be present. If it is a full-team briefing then as well as the SIO/DSIO everyone should usually be there, for instance crime scene managers, outside enquiry teams, search co-ordinators, incident room staff (indexers, etc), analysts, media liaison officers, local police managers/commanders (gold/silver/bronze commanders), field intelligence officers, community liaison officers, forensic scientists, etc.

Those due to attend should be warned well in advance and know what is expected of them, particularly if they have a major input to provide. They should also know the time and location of the briefing with a message that, with very few exceptions, attendance is obligatory.

The SIO should thoroughly plan and prepare for the briefing with an agenda that is focused and structured. If possible this should be circulated beforehand. It should be made inclusive by ensuring all team members can submit important items for discussion. The agenda for an initial team briefing may look like the specimen below.

Briefing agenda

No	Subject
1.	Introduction of SIO/DSIO and management team
2.	Outline of case circumstances
3.	Background information, community details, and issues
4.	Current and emerging lines of enquiry
5.	Explanation of witness/suspect strategies

Briefing agenda

No	Subject
6.	Outline of family liaison and media strategies
7.	Forensic update, searches, H-2-H, CCTV (ie all investigative strategies)
8.	Allocation of key enquiries and actions to staff
9.	HOLMES2 policies (TIE criteria, etc)
10.	Risk-assessment policies (eg police and community concerns)
11.	Administration issues (duties, briefing times, etc)
12.	Any other business

Briefing rooms should be adequately equipped, with sufficient space for everyone to be comfortable and able to see and hear what is happening. It is appreciated some incident rooms and police premises are not fortunate enough to have purpose-built briefing facilities. The SIO should organize finding a suitable location and venue that is fit for purpose. If large numbers of staff are involved in a major enquiry, this may pose a problem. Sometimes training establishments which have lecture theatres or large conference facilities can be utilized, bearing in mind extra parking facilities may be required.

The SIO may need to use maps, plans, marker boards, flip charts, analytical charts, or overhead projectors that will display visual images such as CCTV, crime-scene shots, or aerial photographs. Other diagrams or scenes can be hand-drawn to explain and illustrate the position of witnesses, etc, which can then be added to and built up over time. Good facilities and equipment make a briefing appear more professional and are more effective and simpler to follow, particularly if staff from outside the area lack local knowledge.

Note: Disclosure rules are relevant once more—any marker boards, flip charts, etc need to be kept or photographed to comply with the retention of material guidelines.

The SIO should take good notes during the briefing and/or arrange a contemporaneous record of the proceedings. In some cases it may be good practice, wherever practicable, to audio- or visually-record key briefings in order to capture precise detail and the nature of the content which can also be useful for briefing those who cannot be present. This is something regularly undertaken in major operations such as those involving the tactical firearms or public order units, particularly when detailed information, instructions, or risk assessments are involved.

Sufficient time should be allowed for the briefing. Some may last as long as 2–3 hours (may be even longer) depending on the nature of the enquiry. If so, allowances should be made for comfort breaks. Attention spans dwindle after a short time and it is necessary to maintain everyone's 100 per cent focus and attention throughout the whole period.

The appropriate use of humour is sometimes not a bad thing as it lifts team spirit and encourages good listening. However, there should be no room for sarcasm, pessimism, or derogatory remarks which do not produce an ideal environment for a briefing or which may dissuade people from making contributions.

KEY POINTS

- Interruptions should be prevented and distractions eliminated by choosing a quiet room with disconnected telephones. There should be a notice placed on the door stating that an important briefing is taking place. The SIO should avoid being called out to see people or answer urgent calls. This can be avoided by nominating someone to screen calls and visitors on their behalf with an instruction not to be disturbed unless absolutely necessary. The staff present should be informed to do the same thing and to *switch mobiles/pagers etc to silent mode.*
- When asking for updates or information, people should be selected at random to ensure everyone is paying attention.
- The SIO should take the lead and effectively manage the briefing, remaining at all times in full control and adhering to the agenda. Effective leadership and communication skills are essential, making good use of the 5 × WH + H formula. Everyone should be encouraged to contribute with nobody dominating or taking too much time to explain a piece of information, thus rendering the session monotonous—contributions must be *relevant and precise.*

The SIO should at all times remember one other important rule, constantly referred to in this handbook and known as the ABC principle: **A**ssume nothing, **B**elieve nothing, **C**hallenge/check everything.

In practice this means it should never be assumed that a task has been completed thoroughly. For example, if an enquiry team states during a briefing that they have tried everything possible to trace a TIE subject and failed, it should not be assumed that obvious possibilities have been considered—for example, early morning visits or checking neighbours either side of last known address for sightings or information. It remains the role of the SIO to ask challenging questions and to probe everything.

KEY POINTS

1. Staff present at briefings should make notes for reference purposes and seek clarification when a point is not clearly understood, so that records are maintained accurately. All notes are eventually handed to the disclosure officer and are open to subsequent scrutiny, hence the requirement, in addition to operational professionalism, for accuracy.
2. Some staff may become overly-eager to please the SIO and impress supervisors and colleagues. They may be tempted to embellish facts or information to look or sound good. The SIO has to remain vigilant and not assume anything. Checking and challenging is more likely to guarantee factual accuracy and clarify provenance and reliability of information.

Checklist—Briefings

- Find and reserve a suitable venue for holding briefings, with adequate equipment.
- Prepare and circulate an agenda.
- Allow sufficient time for the briefing.
- Have no distractions—all phones/pagers to silent mode or switched off.
- The SIO should positively lead, control, and manage the briefing.
- The SIO should set the right standard and tone by speaking confidently, always looking interested, and projecting enthusiasm and energy.
- The content should be kept relevant by tactfully avoiding dominating, monotonous, or extraneous contributions.
- Reports/updates/feedback from staff should be taken randomly to keep everyone's attention.
- Use the A B C principle—role of SIO is to probe and question everything.
- Do not let people dominate on key issues, give everyone a chance to contribute.

- Appropriate humour can be useful and encourages active listening.
- Briefings are a good forum for giving praise and recognition.
- Briefings are a good opportunity to gauge the effectiveness of the team and focus on task, team, and individual needs (see also Chapter 3).
- Check levels of understanding of important information and policies.
- Make good use of props such as marker boards, flip charts, maps, and plans.
- Show images such as CCTV, etc wherever possible to make the content more realistic and interesting (consider electronic presentation, eg Microsoft PowerPoint for key briefings).
- Appoint an Action Manager to allocate/raise new actions during briefing.
- Beware of embellishments and domination from staff eager to impress. Refer to original words used by the witness from a statement or notes of interview.
- Demand and check *detail, detail, detail*.
- Make an accurate record of the content of briefings and all attendees.
- Check staff understand all information and their responsibilities.
- Identify and communicate risks and appropriate action required to minimize the risks.
- Delegate tasks to individuals commensurate with their abilities, training, and experience, and any personal development requirements.
- Fully record any decisions, actions, options, and rationale.
- Identify any welfare needs.
- Invite others to briefings to make them feel part of the team, for example nominated representatives of the Crown Prosecution Service, forensic scientists, pathologists, etc (who can also play an active part by explaining points of law or scientific evidence).

7.4 **Debriefings**

A debriefing is a meeting aimed at obtaining as much detailed information as possible from those who have been involved with an incident, particularly the initial response. This involves clarifying the chronological breakdown of events as they occurred, the people who did them, and the outcomes. They are an early opportunity for the capture of important and significant information or evidence from the aftermath of the incident concerned. Debriefings should therefore significantly contribute to the formulation of urgent actions and potential lines of enquiry, and also the development of useful intelligence.

So-called 'hot debriefs' as they are sometimes known form a major source of vital information to the SIO in the early stages when staff need to impart their information in order for the 'golden hour(s)' principles to be achieved.

Arranging a debriefing session should be among one of the first tasks for an SIO, because sometimes staff finish duty and become unavailable. The wealth of information to be gained from those who were involved in dealing with an incident needs to be obtained as quickly as possible to benefit an effective and dynamic investigation.

The SIO will have to cater for difficulties in getting all the staff together and recognize that debriefs cannot always be achieved under near-perfect conditions. People who have worked long hours cannot be kept waiting around for ever so that everyone can be spoken to simultaneously. Some may also be witnesses or engaged in handing over clothing, vehicles, or exhibits for forensic examination. Therefore, in some circumstances there may have to be more than one debriefing session, which is far from ideal.

Wherever possible conducting debriefings should not be delegated. Unless totally impracticable they should be undertaken by the SIO. The timing of a debrief will depend on individual circumstances and the SIO will have to accommodate fulfilling the task despite other urgent responsibilities that may need to be attended to.

The primary objective of a debriefing session is to identify what action has been taken and by whom, and to capture all possible information that will assist the investigation, for example details of potential witnesses, useful observations or comments from bystanders, information and opinions regarding possible suspects, suspicious circumstances that may be linked, any persons or vehicles of interest, possible intelligence, etc. A debriefing also provides an opportunity for:

- focusing the deployment of resources to best effect and prioritizing;
- checking on welfare of staff;
- identifying community tensions;
- considering risk assessments for further activities;
- recognizing good work.

Checklist—Debriefings

- Debriefs are one of the most important early functions of the SIO.
- The task *should not be delegated* unless in exceptional circumstances.
- All those who have been involved in the initial response should be required to attend—people should be notified *before going off duty*.
- Those in attendance should have completed any notes, pocket books, etc *before* attending the debrief to avoid collusion of evidence (ie 'pooled memory') and compromising integrity.
- A designated person should be nominated to record the proceedings to capture all information.
- Select a suitable and early time for the debriefing.
- Select a suitable venue which needs to be large enough to hold all those concerned and have available necessary basic equipment available, eg marker boards, plans, and maps.
- All relevant documents and exhibits should be handed in by staff (copies of notebooks, etc) at the end of the session.
- Records must be kept of all those present.
- Obtain details of actions taken and a résumé of individual roles at the scene.
- Everything should be recorded for the purposes of disclosure rules (Criminal Procedure and Investigations Act 1996).

7.4.1 Extra notes for the SIO

The SIO should:

- Make good notes during the debrief contemporaneously for immediate reference purposes.
- Nominate an action writer to record any relevant actions the SIO wants raised *during the debriefing process*.
- Recognize those members of staff who have been on duty for a long time and take account of the need to debrief them as

soon as possible. (Note: the debrief process itself may involve overtime payments to retain staff on duty—this will be money well spent!)

KEY POINTS

1. The debrief process can produce a package of documents and raised actions suitable to begin a major incident room (HOLMES2) administrative system and manage the investigation.
2. All notes that have been completed and handed in should be carefully scrutinized. They may contain things that are not said during the debriefing session and provide very useful information.

Debriefings can be supplemented by the use of a *pro forma* disseminated in order to record the involvement of individual staff in a consistent and methodical fashion. This does not need to be overly complicated and returns can be handwritten on a single sheet of paper if necessary. It must, however, be completed before attending the debrief session.

An example of a de-brief form may be as simple as the following:

DE-BRIEF FORM

Name and rank/position..

Incident details...

Time and date...

Copy of all notes made attached (Yes/No)

Any exhibits recovered (Yes/No)

If 'Yes' to above, details of exhibit and where it is located ....

....

Details of action taken:

(Include details of potential witnesses, sources of information, vehicles/persons seen, anything of interest, etc)

a few leaders (continue on separate sheet if necessary)

Time and date completed ....

Signature of person completing ....

Chapter 8
Investigative Strategies

8.1 Introduction

To complement the SIO's main lines of enquiry and in order to progress the investigation, useful investigative strategies can be utilized. This chapter outlines some which are considered to be relevant and useful. Those included are:

- H-2-H enquiries;
- passive data sources (for which the two most common are explained in more detail, ie CCTV and communications data);
- intelligence;
- use of analysts.

Each investigative strategy should be underpinned by a clear statement of the linked objectives that the SIO is trying to achieve. These objectives must be explained and recorded in the policy file.

The SIO should provide a broad outline of the methods by which objectives are to be achieved and the resources they anticipate will be required to carry them out. Once investigative strategies are allocated they should be regularly reviewed in light of any new material that comes into the investigation. The SIO should also ensure that strategies become increasingly more focused as the investigation progresses.

The SIO needs to ensure that the investigative strategies are constantly discussed with all members of the investigation team. This will help the team to understand the direction of the enquiry and the rationale behind the SIO's policy and decision making. All investigative strategies and associated decision making must be entered into the SIO's policy file; and if they are recorded onto 'stand alone' documents then a cross reference should be made within a policy file entry.

8.2 House-to-House (H-2-H) Enquiries

Conducting H-2-H enquiries can be used effectively as an investigative strategy in order to identify witnesses, gather local information and intelligence, or as part of a community reassurance or crime prevention policy. A combination of these (H-2-H to find witnesses and public reassurance) can also be used.

The SIO should try to become familiar with the geographical locations involved as it is vital to set realistic and appropriate parameters for H-2-H enquiry teams. It is good practice for the SIO and/or deputy SIO to visit the surroundings of the scene(s) to assist in this decision-making process. A H-2-H manager (bronze commander) should be appointed and should accompany the SIO during the process. Each road, street, house, flat, business premises, or other building that needs to be included in the parameters should be duly noted. In addition to local knowledge the SIO needs to be aware of any local neighbourhood intelligence about any locations within the H-2-H zone.

In most forces there are standard forms for completing H-2-H enquiries and these are kept in folders for ease of reference. For example, there is the street form with space for a number of addresses to be recorded. Having gained access to an address, the enquiry team officer should endorse the street form with the total number of questionnaires required for the number of persons at the address. Then there is the house occupants form and also the questionnaire itself.

A good map of the selected area can be used for marking the boundaries of the H-2-H requirements and then entered as a document into the major incident room (and registered on HOLMES2). This is preferable to verbally describing the chosen areas and can be linked to a policy file entry explaining the reasons why such boundaries and locations have been chosen.

If a large area is involved, it can be divided into phases in order of priority (phase 1, 2, 3, etc). This will help teams conducting the enquiries understand what the most important areas are to target that suit the SIO's preferences, and to allocate resources to the most important areas first. Natural boundaries can be utilized to set parameters, such as roads, rivers, walls, railway lines, etc, although a more scientific approach is preferable.

To help determine parameters, use should be made of all available intelligence and information. Police officers, PCSOs, special constables, etc and people from the community who may have specific local knowledge can be useful assets. This will add qualitative detail to the task. Looking at a map or location does not always provide sufficient information to work with, for example local shortcuts, meeting places, locations where vehicles or stolen cars are dumped. Other resources such as geographical profilers can also be considered to help formulate appropriate parameters.

In major enquiries where the H-2-H requirements may be resource-intensive it is worthwhile considering the timing of the tactic. If there is insufficient information regarding a certain line of enquiry, it may be prudent to wait and avoid having to revisit the location(s) to ask additional questions. However, this may be unavoidable as knowledge about the incident increases.

Good use of prompts is helpful, such as significant events or lists of TV programmes to jog memories for the date and time in question. It is also a good idea to leave leaflets or small posters at the locations with details of how to contact the incident room.

8.2.1 H-2-H co-ordinator

In a large major investigation a H-2-H co-ordinator can be appointed to assume overall management responsibilities for this area of the enquiry. This individual can be co-located at any temporary-sited incident vehicle being used at or near the scene (eg a mobile incident caravan) so they are near to the teams and enquiries under their supervision. Any information received should be recorded and fed into the incident room by this supervisor, but no further action should be taken without prior approval of the SIO (significant information should, of course, be relayed without delay). This is to avoid the duplication of tasks and to ensure that any potential leads are properly supervised in accordance with the SIO's priorities.

The co-ordinator should ensure the officers engaged in H-2-H activity are regularly briefed, and the co-ordinator should attend the SIO's team briefings to cascade information down to their own teams. It is important they are kept highly motivated to perform the task enthusiastically. The SIO should try to visit and speak to the teams whenever down at the incident caravan or in the area to praise them for their efforts and remind them how important their task is.

The H-2-H teams must appreciate what they can and cannot say to the public they will be coming into contact with, and others who may ask questions of them (eg members of the victim's family or the media). It can be a tiresome responsibility to perform, but those concerned in the task should be made aware that this is often a highly successful method of obtaining information and engaging with the local community.

A practical point is that the H-2-H co-ordinator should be supplied with a reliable communications link (eg mobile phone or office number) that can be left at any premises where there is no response. This allows people to contact the co-ordinator directly rather than the incident room in order to arrange a re-visit at a suitable time and provides a vital link for the incident room.

8.2.2 Fast-track H-2-H enquiries

It is a valuable tactic in most major investigations to conduct early and/or initial H-2-H enquiries in the aftermath of an incident (during the 'golden hour(s)'). Even if no particular parameters have been determined, it is still a means of quickly requesting general information and capturing any immediate line of enquiry. It is important that accurate records are kept of all premises visited and persons spoken to, including any negative responses (inaccurate details undermine any prosecution).

Officers should initially be directed to addresses **within the line of sight** of the main crime scene, or within any other known locations of interest, such as escape routes, or at any linked scenes, eg abandoned vehicles. Any opportunity to capture witnesses and information should not be wasted and H-2-H enquiries should commence as early as possible.

At some stage a specific list of questions will be required for a questionnaire that enquiry officers carry with them as they conduct the H-2-H enquiries. However, in the initial stages they can simply make a general request for information at each address visited and to each occupant—have they seen anything? Do they know what happened? Do they have any information whatsoever? And so forth.

There are standard forms for conducting H-2-H enquiries (MIR/2 etc). These include occupants' details—such as appearance, distinguishing features, clothing worn at material time, whether they visited the scene, if they know the victim, vehicles owned/used—and details of all occupants and visitors to the address. These should be used whenever possible.

The SIO should determine and/or agree specific H-2-H questions. For example:

1. Were you in between 10.30 pm Friday 13.4.10 and 02.30 am Saturday 14.4.10?

2. Did you hear a disturbance at (address/location)?
3. Do you know anything about an incident that took place at that location?
4. Do you know the occupants at that address?
5. Did you see anyone or anything suspicious at or near this address between these times?
6. Have you any further information that might assist?

8.2.3 Identifying witnesses

H-2-H can be used by the SIO to try to identify the following.

- People who may have witnessed the incident under investigation.
- People who may have witnessed related events, eg the area where a getaway vehicle has been stolen from or abandoned.
- Sightings of the victim or offender before or after the event, eg along the likely entry and exit routes of the offender(s).
- Sightings or information regarding relevant property, eg clothing or items of significance that may have been disposed of.
- Sightings of potential witnesses or unidentified persons seen by others or elsewhere. For example, where witnesses are captured on CCTV, enquiries can be made by use of H-2-H tactics to try to identify them.

KEY POINT

H-2-H enquiries can produce information on offenders who tend to be less careful when they believe they are away from the crime scene, and make mistakes such as changing or discarding clothing, dropping or concealing weapons, hiding stolen property, etc. If a stolen vehicle has been used then later abandoned, H-2-H should be used in both locations to try to identify potential witnesses who may have seen the offenders prior to or after commission of the offence.

8.2.4 Community reassurance

In an enquiry that generates a lot of public and media attention it is possible to use this tactic to deliver important messages. This is particularly the case if enthusiastic media reporters are knocking on doors and spreading their own messages. In such circumstances this may link into any of the SIO's media or communication strategies by forewarning residents this may be the case and offering advice.

H-2-H enquiries could include the mass distribution of relevant crime prevention or personal safety advice. The SIO should ensure that any reassurance messages are consistent with those contained in any media strategy, otherwise there may be a conflict of interest from any reassurance perspective.

8.2.5 H-2-H resources

The size of area to be covered, plus the number of scenes and the objectives for the strategy, determine what level of resources is required. When conducting fast-track enquiries, any available staff can be utilized, particularly local detectives with assistance from their uniform colleagues. Sometimes people prefer plain-clothes officers to attend at their address rather than uniformed personnel. Large-scale enquiries, however, will require dedicated resources and in most forces there are officers (including co-ordinators) trained and able to do this.

The SIO should be mindful that, if H-2-H enquiries are likely to occupy a lot of time and resources, there could be inconsistencies in the personnel allocated to the task. This is not helpful and the co-ordinator must minimize adverse effects by close supervision and regular briefings with new staff deployments.

The level of H-2-H enquiry will be set by the SIO; the higher the level, the more time consuming the task (ie level 1 highest). Therefore careful consideration should be given to determining the appropriate level. Usually level 1 should be considered only in exceptional circumstances because of the amount of time and resources required.

H-2-H enquiry levels

Requirement	Purpose
1. Full documentation as per ACPO guidelines together with optional additional questionnaire for all persons in given area.	1. Identify witnesses. 2. Identify possible suspects. 3. Collate information for future analysis as new facts come to light.
2. Full documentation to ensure all persons are seen but with amended questionnaire or substituted questionnaire for individuals in a given area.	1. Identify witnesses. 2. Identify possible suspects. 3. Tailor questionnaire to the enquiry when certain information is established, eg detailed description of offender or identity of offender.

Requirement	Purpose
3. No documentation to ensure all persons identified but a questionnaire to suit purpose of particular enquiry in a given area.	1. Identify witnesses. 2. To identify suspect from description or other information pertinent to the enquiry. 3. To identify property.
4. Complete specific requirements of a raised action for specific premises within a given area.	1. To obtain the result of a specific enquiry by questionnaire aimed at specific premises.
5. Undertake delivery of mail-shot campaign in given area.	1. To bring to the attention of persons within a given area certain facts pertinent to the enquiry.
6. Following briefing and instructions visit addresses in given area. No documentation completed but message submitted through MIR if any relevant information received.	1. To complete a trawl of an area. 2. To quickly establish any useful information pertinent to the enquiry, eg area adjacent to scene following discovery of body.

Checklist—H-2-H enquiries

- The SIO should instigate immediate fast-track enquiries in the golden hour(s) period, eg anywhere within *line of sight* of the scene. Ensure accurate details are recorded.
- Clearly identified parameters must be set and recorded (eg around crime scenes, escape routes, etc).
- The timing of enquiries may be important—weekdays in the early evening is probably the best time to get people at home and available.
- Consider a management policy of two evening visits then leaving a letter for occupants where no reply (pre-paid envelopes can be used).

- Consider extended area for mass leaflet distribution using PCSOs and area officers to assist, with a free-phone number and/or MIR telephone number.
- Coincide H-2-H visits to coincide with anniversary of incident (eg exactly one week or month after) for maximum impact and publicity. Vehicle stop checks and/or roadside questionnaires can also be utilized.
- Use of a mobile police station is good as a focal point for public and can be used as temporary office for H-2-H staff.
- All documentation must be carefully recorded and submitted to the MIR in a timely fashion, then thoroughly scrutinized and any appropriate actions raised.
- Any HP information should be fast-tracked into the MIR for the SIO's attention.
- When drawing up a H-2-H strategy, the SIO should prepare a 'no reply' policy.
- If questionnaires are to be used the SIO should create a bespoke document using open questions.
- Consider background intelligence checks for each H-2-H zone and complete risk assessments.

8.3 **Use of Passive Data Sources**

The term 'passive data' is one referred to in both the MIM (ACPO Centrex, 2006, 179–85) and the Core Investigative Doctrine (ACPO Centrex, 2005, 94–5) and means information that is obtained from automated/mechanical systems, hence the term 'passive'.

The MIM lists some examples of passive data generators:

- CCTV and other images (eg captured on mobile phones);
- financial information;
- personal computer information;
- communications data (eg telecommunications);
- voice-recording systems;
- customer information (eg subscriber details);
- access systems;
- tachographs;
- automatic number plate recognition (ANPR) and GATSO (speed camera) systems.

Note: Others might include satellite navigation systems (which store data and addresses, language used etc), electronic tagging devices, fuel cards, or satellite tracking systems fitted in some commercial vehicles, similar to a 'black box' recorder that reports a vehicle's location via mobile phone networks to tracking centres where records are stored.

These can be rich sources of information and/or evidence for progressing an enquiry. When added to evidence gathered from more traditional sources, they can be a great source of independent corroboration. The two passive sources most commonly used in major investigations are CCTV and communications data.

8.3.1 Closed circuit television (CCTV)

There has been a widespread increase in the public and private use of CCTV surveillance systems. Consequently it is a very cost-effective evidence-gathering tool and can speed up enquiries. This has led to the regular production of a fast-track or early line of enquiry (often listed as one of the initial actions to consider) to ascertain whether there is any CCTV located near to crime scenes that may contain images (and in some cases audible recordings also), and to secure this.

Use of CCTV images can greatly improve media appeals and often there is more chance of attracting public attention if there are good images to release. This tactic can be used to encourage potential witnesses to come forward and help the enquiry by identifying people, and/or to prompt more general assistance.

There are numerous examples of murder, rape, covert operations, child protection cases, missing persons, and terrorism investigations where CCTV has been invaluable, even if the incidents themselves were not captured on camera. As well as recording some element of the offence, people may pass in front of cameras on the way to/from committing crimes, or when making phone calls reporting incidents. Some footage may also show that alleged serious incidents did not take place at all, or may disprove alibis.

Not all CCTV is of good quality or totally reliable because of poor images or equipment. The dates and times and integrity of capturing and recording systems need to be fully analysed and checked thoroughly. Before relying completely upon the material an SIO must be ready to question and challenge the accuracy as it could be damagingly misleading. This brings the fundamental ABC principle into play once more:

A	Assume nothing
B	Believe nothing
C	Challenge/check everything

Often the images, data, or equipment have to be seized quite quickly in order to prevent destruction, loss, or overwriting. It may be that officers in the initial stages are in the habit of seizing as much CCTV material as they can get their hands on. However, while there are some potential benefits in seizing CCTV, there are also practical issues to be mindful of:

- There are a lot of different types of recording system in existence (eg for CCTV there are VHS cassette tapes and/or digital, multiplex), therefore some may be difficult to size or view.
- There may be a storage issue if large amounts of data and exhibits are recovered.
- Under the CPIA rules, usually all data recovered will have to be examined to establish whether there is any material which is *relevant to the investigation*. The same Act places duties of *disclosure* on the prosecutor which means CCTV recordings may have to be copied and made available to the defence (could be significant amount if more than one defendant).
- CCTV must be able to be presented at court if necessary, which may require specialist equipment and/or expert witness testimony.
- CCTV quality—the range and type of images vary greatly and the usefulness often depends on the standard of the equipment and recordings (eg some systems overwrite and are rotated on a regular basis to make them cost effective).
- CCTV date and time stamps are often inaccurate (BST should always be checked).
- Audit trails have to be strictly maintained, particularly when copies are made and original seals are broken (eg for examination purposes).
- Some agencies have CCTV control rooms with strict protocols in place governing how and when the CCTV may be handed over to the police, and a good relationship with the local police is necessary in gaining co-operation.
- Some digital systems may require a degree of expertise to recover.

CCTV strategies

When making a policy decision relating to any CCTV recovery there has to be clear delineation of what the recovery parameters and strategy are. The strategy must be explained in unequivocal terms. For example:

- What premises are to be checked for systems, that is, private residences, public and business premises (eg shops, petrol stations, public houses, etc).
- How the checks are to be made, ie whether a visual check will suffice or if some form of H-2-H type enquiries should be made to ask if there are any hidden systems.
- How the CCTV is to be recovered, ie clarification of checks with the times and dates on the recording system before removing the data (eg comparing with the speaking clock for accuracy and making a written note and/or checking whether there is a maintenance policy for checking when the time was last reset).
- Making a note of the camera angle, position, type of recording equipment (eg if time-lapse or continuous), location captured in the image, and the terrain immediately around it to identify blind spots.
- Completion of a CCTV recovery form for each and every item.
- Completion of a CCTV recovery schedule, outlining precise location and details of where all systems and data have been found and recovered.

KEY POINTS

- Public appeals can be made for the details of any CCTV systems within a certain vicinity. This should form part of the SIO's media strategy.
- It is vital to set parameters for the early retrieval of CCTV material. Tapes are often used continuously and record over old material, sometimes in a 24-hour period. Consider fast-track actions for rapid recovery of useful material.

There are different forms of CCTV and most recent systems seem to utilize digital technology. These record images not onto tape but onto a hard drive. This causes additional considerations as to if and how the drive that contains the original recording should be seized. There may be cost implications as the system may not be able to continue to function without one, and the police may have to provide a replacement. If the system concerned is part of a large security network then recovering the hard drive may not be a simple and straightforward matter, so the SIO should be mindful of this when tasking out the full recovery of all data. The CCTV policy also needs to recognize and safeguard the integrity of any subsequent exhibit, as to continuity and preservation of the material if engineers or experts are required to retrieve data and copy it onto a secondary device.

The policy to recover CCTV material may produce an added problem of how it is going to be viewed to see whether anything of relevance has been captured. There may be a great deal of footage to examine, which can take up valuable time and resources.

The SIO will have to nominate staff and acquire the correct and appropriate equipment and suitable accommodation. Different CCTV systems produce different requirements for ease of viewing, and suitable arrangements will have to be made. How much data has been recovered will determine what staff are required to do the viewing.

The staff selected should be conversant with the circumstances of the case (if they are brought in specially for the viewing duties) and what they are expected to search for. The accurate completion of viewing logs (often on a dedicated form) is an important element of the policy and procedure while the viewing takes place.

KEY POINTS

Dedicated staff, experienced in this field, can be used to log each viewed CCTV exhibit. A viewing officer can become an expert in recognition after viewing many hours of footage and could be called upon in court to show the continuity of images of an individual suspect (*R v Clare and Peach* (1995) 2 Cr App R 333).

Notes: Any identification of a suspect captured on CCTV should be made under strict guidance outlined in Code D of PACE.

The SIO must set some clear objectives and parameters for seizing and viewing, and prioritize the material into phases. For example, consider the following.

Objectives of CCTV viewing

- Identify the persons responsible.
- Identify anyone entering or leaving the crime scene.
- Identify victim's movements prior to the offence.
- Assist in the implication or elimination of any persons in the TIE category or anyone else at the SIO's discretion.
- Identify possible witnesses.
- Identify sightings of any vehicles.

Note: This should be accompanied by an instruction that any potentially useful images should be brought to the attention of the SIO for consideration of enhancement to assist in subsequent identification.

Examples—Setting and recording CCTV parameters in policy file

Phase I—Between (time/date) and (time/date) within the area highlighted on the map depicting the zone for phase I (Document Reference).

Phase II—Between (time/date) and (time/date) within the extended area highlighted on the map depicting the zone for phase II (Document Reference.).

Note: The parameters may change as the enquiry progresses; if so, a clear record should be made in the policy file to this effect.

Case study—CCTV

A Murder enquiry involved premises being set on fire in a city centre. At the time of the incident CCTV captured numerous people at or around the locus.

One of the challenges was to identify all persons who appeared on the CCTV at the locus around the time of the incident. A policy decision was made to digitally photograph every witness who could have been at or around the locus at the material time. The photograph was then attached to the witness statement and passed to the CCTV viewing team who used the photographs and contents to identify all the individuals.

8.3.2 Communications data

These days the majority of major crime investigations have some element of communications data information strategy particularly around the usage of mobile phones. Traditionally communications data strategies have focused on the use of fixed line and mobile devices. The use of emerging technology poses many challenges for the investigator and the SIO should be aware of the varied methods of communication that are being used in the twenty-first century. The following points will be of use to the SIO.

- The SIO should consider at the earliest opportunity the appointment of a trained Communications Liaison Officer (CLO) within the enquiry team, who should make contact with the nominated Communications Data Investigator (CDI) SPOC. Each law enforcement agency (LEA) provides a unit of individuals who are trained and accredited to access communications data from Communication Service Providers (CSP). This will ensure that the most effective use of communications data can be considered.
- Any communications strategy meetings should include the same CDI SPOC wherever practicable. A helpful matrix can be prepared to assist with strategy meetings and should be completed by the CLO and circulated to persons present (see Appendix D). This will be useful to keep track of all the data being acquired, that which is still pending results, comments, etc.
- Consideration should be given to the objectives for obtaining communications data and what is sought to be achieved, rather than obtaining the data in order to secure it. The CSPs retain data in the main for a period of 12 months.

Role of the communication liaison officer (CLO)

The appointment of a communications liaison officer (or whatever title is used within the particular LEA) by the SIO is a designated role within an enquiry team and considered best practice. It ensures a degree of consistency and the same person or persons (if it is a very large-scale enquiry with lots of communications data issues) should perform this role throughout the duration of the enquiry wherever possible. Some officers have built up a lot of knowledge and expertise from performing this role on a number of enquiries. The role involves the following.

Checklist—CLO duties and responsibilities

- The CLO is responsible for all applications for the acquisition of communications data and must be fully conversant with legislation that allows this, ie RIPA 2000.
- The CLO should maintain an index of requests made and received and be in a position to make assessments and judgments of the data obtained.
- The CLO should be able to proactively advise the SIO from an investigator's perspective on present or emerging tactical opportunities for using communications data and examining recovered devices to assist the enquiry.
- All CLOs should be fully briefed on all aspects of the investigation to ensure that all applications they submit are factually correct and the application details fully cover all the reasons for applying for specific data.
- The CLO should work closely with the analyst (if appointed) to analyse the data and seek out information and evidence of use to the enquiry.

Role of the CDI

The CDI SPOCs are trained and accredited and promote efficiency and good practice in ensuring only practical and lawful requirements for communications data are undertaken. Their function is to provide objective judgment and advice to SIOs, applicants, and designated persons. They not only provide a 'guardian and gatekeeper' function, ensuring that law enforcement agencies act in an informed and lawful manner, but also advise on the latest techniques and services available.

The CDI is responsible for the management of all issues regarding the acquisition and retention of communications data. This includes information relating to the use of a public communications service but does not include the content of the communication. For a full definition of communications data, see the Regulation of Investigatory Powers Act 2000 (RIPA), s 21(4).

Duties of a CDI involved in an investigation include:

- Continuous liaison with the CSPs and regular workshops to ensure that the CDIs are aware of latest techniques, trends, and developments and as such are in a position to provide the most up-to-date advice to SIOs and CLOs.
- Involvement in all aspects of communications data applications, strategies, and, where the data is required evidentially, in that process also.

- Dealing with all communications data requests, even where RIPA 2000 is not the legal mechanism for obtaining data. This refers to where data is requested by means of court order, witness summons, MLAT (Mutual Legal Assistance Treaty) etc.

The full responsibilities of the CDI are defined in 'The Acquisition and Disclosure of Communications Data', Draft Code of Practice, which is available via the LEA CDI unit.

What type of data can be recovered?

- Communications data includes all types of data gathered during the course of a communication. It must be stressed that communications are increasingly becoming more sophisticated with the rapid development of both devices and software applications. Device capability is a challenge that investigators should have awareness of. An increasing percentage of communication is carried in other than what is regarded as the 'traditional' manner. Communications data increasingly is becoming IP based (internet protocol), including web usage, email, and voice over internet protocol (VOIP) communications. CDIs will be in a position to advise on the different communications devices there are and the implications this has for an investigation.
- There is a wealth of communications data available, depending on what is being sought and what the objectives are. The CDI should advise the CLO and SIO on a strategy that will address the requirements of the investigation.
- Communications data can provide information in relation to an individual to whom the communication facility is provided and can provide information in relation to lifestyle, movements etc. SIOs should be mindful of all methods of communication when considering a communications data strategy, such as email address, social network presence, as well as the individual's phone numbers.
- In accordance with the provisions of the COP to RIPA the majority of CSPs charge for the data they provide to LEAs. The CDI will be in a position to advise on the cost of data required.

Using data evidentially

- As a general rule the majority of communications data can be used evidentially.

- Attribution of a communication device is always an important consideration, ie proving that a person was using the device at the time of a significant communication. This can be done through supportive CCTV images, witnesses, or supportive analytical products etc.
- Certain confidential techniques can provide useful, and at times crucial, information which can assist in the investigation of serious crime. If this data is later required evidentially there are criteria which must be adhered to (the CDI can advise on the criteria and the process for this, and will be involved in the gathering and presentation of the evidence).
- CSPs provide some data which should not be used evidentially. The CDI will be able to advise in relation to this.

Case study—Murder at a public house

One Sunday afternoon a group of people had gathered in a public house to watch a televised football match. Two males wearing balaclavas and carrying firearms entered a public area and opened fire, seriously wounding customers. After a struggle the two were chased out of the premises, having at some point also been shot in retaliation. They ran onto a grassed area where they collapsed and died. A third male approached and checked the bodies, then fled the scene in a getaway vehicle.

An important part of the investigation surrounded analysis of mobile phone use. Communications data indicated that, on the day of the incident, the phone attributed to the male in the car was in constant use. One of the numbers that featured on the recovered call data was a number attributed to a female who had been in the pub when the attack took place. This came from careful analysis of calls made from this phone and cell-site data.

Analysis of the phone used by the male in the car showed a pattern of travel from his home address to other significant locations, culminating in the phone located in the vicinity of the pub at the relevant time. The phone data also showed contact between him, the two deceased, and the female before, during, and immediately after the shootings occurred. No contact could be identified at any other time.

Communications data, in the form of likely location, top-up information, and call data records, proved crucial to the prosecution case. It helped show how the male in the car had arranged the attack, sending two armed men into the pub, who had subsequently been shot dead while escaping. It also showed how the female had acted as a 'spotter' inside the pub, helping direct them to a target. Both the male and the female were convicted of conspiracy to murder and received life sentences.

Communications data device examinations

- There are many different types of mobile devices including conventional landline and mobile phones. In addition to these there are many devices that provide a communications capability including smart phones, voice over internet phones, USB, and wireless dongles etc. They provide access to voice and messaging services as well as internet access including social networks.
- The examination of a mobile device can provide information in respect of its use.
- The examination can provide details of associates (from contacts) and content of any text messages still on the device (ie not deleted by the user).
- The examination also provides details of call data (calls received and made) but cannot be considered as accurate and call data must in all cases be obtained from the CSP by means of application under RIPA 2000.
- In relation to the seizure of mobile devices, advice should be sought from the mobile device examiners as to the most appropriate methods and the information that may be available.

Note: Devices may also provide additional forensic examination opportunities for tracing blood, DNA, fingerprints, gunshot residue, etc.

8.4 Intelligence

This section explains and outlines how intelligence can be gathered and utilized to assist the investigation to solve the crime under investigation. This will form an investigative strategy in its own right for the SIO and enquiry team.

8.4.1 Initial 'fast-time' intelligence

The SIO should aim to establish an intelligence cell as quickly as possible. Any early research and intelligence opportunities must be maximized. This is a core function required to respond to initial actions that the SIO may raise, some of which may be high priority (HP).

While it is desirable to establish an 'intelligence cell' with dedicated officers performing the role in the first instance, it may not always be practicable to do so. Therefore the SIO may have to rely upon nominated persons from whoever is initially available with the requisite skills and knowledge to conduct urgent intelligence checks in 'fast time' and feed the required information back to the SIO.

For example, the SIO may want some quick research enquiries to find the answers to some important 5 × WH + H questions, such as:

- Who is the victim and what is their background?
- What other incidents can be linked to the one under investigation (ie precursor incidents)?
- When was any previous linked incident?
- What is known about any named suspects?
- What is the background of any witnesses?
- What are the nature and background of the area in which the incident has occurred?
- Where did the offence occur and what is known about it (eg history of previous police or other agencies' involvement with premises or locations)?
- What intelligence searches can be conducted on certain vehicles, nominals, or descriptions?

8.4.2 Role of an intelligence officer/cell

An intelligence officer (or intelligence cell) is established to obtain and develop information and intelligence as part of the intelligence strategy. Depending on the scale and type of enquiry, the size and nature of the intelligence potential will vary. In some instances one person performing the role will suffice, in others there may be two intelligence officers, a dedicated researcher, an analyst, and internal assistance from specialist officers from the force intelligence unit on temporary or full-time attachment to the enquiry.

To get the best use out of the cell, the SIO needs to appoint a supervisor to take overall charge within the management team (eg the deputy SIO). The intelligence strategy needs to be formulated, agreed, and recorded either in the policy file or within a separate document registered on HOLMES2. As with all the investigative strategies this should be regularly reviewed and updated.

The SIO should ensure that a major requirement of the intelligence cell is to be *pro-active* in order to be of maximum benefit to the enquiry. They should be instructed to be mobile as well as static in seeking information of interest and in establishing useful contacts from which information can be gleaned. The function involves much more than just sitting behind a computer terminal analysing whatever may be electronically available. Intelligence officers have to get around to find information and establish/maintain useful contacts. For example, they must ensure that whoever is the nominated point of contact at any centralized intelligence unit is kept updated on developments in the enquiry, with an ongoing summary of information or intelligence gaps regularly communicated to them; otherwise vital information may not be passed on to the enquiry team. This may include maintaining close liaison with other agencies and their intelligence units (eg SOCA).

The intelligence officer/cell could also take responsibility for the following.

Checklist—Intelligence officer/cell responsibilities

- Research of victim's history (victimology).
- Any suspect's background, criminal history, etc.
- Preparing bulletin circulations.
- Preparing CHIS tasking requests.
- Assisting the SIO to prepare briefings.
- Liaising with the force intelligence unit and other agencies (eg SOCA).
- Researching relevant databases as and when required by the SIO, eg for all TIE subjects.
- Researching all H-2-H information.
- Researching all messages in the incident room that name persons, addresses/locations, or vehicles.
- Researching and making good use of any prison intelligence and releases.

The SIO should ensure that the intelligence officer/cell brings to their attention all new intelligence received within the major incident room each and every morning, prior to briefings or as soon as possible. This intelligence could be disseminated to all the enquiry teams during the daily briefing. All new intelligence should be entered into the incident room either as an intelligence log or on a message form, so that appropriate actions may be raised and an audit trail is maintained for disclosure purposes.

It is a consideration for the SIO's intelligence strategy that the intelligence officer should receive all the carbonated copies of all message forms received into the MIR. It is an optional function of the intelligence cell to research the information contained within the message, for example any named persons, addresses/ locations, or vehicles.

An intelligence strategy must stipulate when and how intelligence meetings are to be held, for instance on a weekly basis or more frequently, depending on the requirements of the SIO's policy.

KEY POINT

Where there are lots of items of intelligence, a good practical tip is for the intelligence officer to prepare an ongoing log in a simplified table format with a résumé of all available intelligence, together with its evaluation code. This can be distributed to the enquiry teams and updated on a daily/weekly/bi-weekly basis.

8.4.3 Setting the intelligence requirement

The SIO and enquiry team should be in an early position to identify intelligence gaps in the enquiry which need to be filled and this forms the basis of the intelligence requirement. An analyst may be tasked with assisting to do this (see 8.5 Role of Analysts below).

The intelligence requirement remains dynamic and focuses not only on priorities but also on other key information and research requirements to service the needs of the investigation (eg risk assessments for TIE subjects). The intelligence requirement should remain under continual review and any amendments should be recorded by the SIO.

The SIO should be mindful of avoiding information overload. When requesting information, specific terms and parameters should be recorded in the strategy and/or policy file. For example, if the victim has a notorious criminal background: 'the SIO requests all intelligence logs held by the force intelligence unit that mention the victim between (date) and (date)'.

8.4.4 Potential sources of intelligence

The following is a (non-exhaustive) list of potential sources of intelligence.

Checklist—Intelligence sources

- Regular (eg daily) searches on locally held intelligence databases and crime reporting systems for items of significance (eg similar offences or MOs).
- Specific research, eg 'research incident logs in specific areas and intelligence logs going back to (date) in order to seek intelligence which may provide a link to the incident'.
- Establishment of a separate database (or intelligence folder if intranet-based) relating solely to the incident under investigation where any relevant information can be internally posted (the existence and details must be widely communicated).
- Maintaining close liaison with local and force intelligence co-ordinators and field intelligence officers.
- Checking for other operations by units, departments, or agencies that may be gathering intelligence of use to the enquiry.
- Specific tasking of CHIS through requests to the Authorizing Officer (and other service/agency taskings).
- Force and regional liaison through the Force Intelligence Branch/Unit (usually known as FIB) for onward transmission of any pertinent level 1 and 2 intelligence (may need their assistance with level 3 intelligence from sources such as SOCA, Interpol, and Europol).
- Arranging intelligence interviews with persons in custody. Parameters need to state what sort of persons are to be targeted, eg:
  —Offenders with a similar MO to the offence under investigation.
  —Possible associates of the suspect or offender(s).
  —Gang members or members of associations linked to the type of offence.
  —Persons from same geographical area or community where offence was committed.
  —Any other person considered suitable for intelligence visit from whom useful intelligence might be gained.
- Linking in with pro-active campaigns by source-handling units to recruit CHIS (eg posters with a free phone number requesting information posted in custody offices).
- Community intelligence (see end of checklist below*), ie local information such as that obtained from local area beat officers, neighbourhood policing teams, traffic and tactical units, PCSOs, community wardens, and outside agencies,

eg local authority workers. This is a very important source of information and should be high up on the SIO's list of requirements.

- Scanning of open sources of intelligence such as the internet and social networking sites (sometimes there is a specific website opened relating to the incident under investigation), also other potential sites (eg <http://www.youtube.com>).
- Use of passive data systems, eg ANPR at strategically selected or placed sites.
- Searching of previous police pro-active operations and street intervention records (eg stop and account/search).
- Checking archived HOLMES (1 and 2) databases for similar enquiries.
- Crimestoppers and Neighbourhood Watch information.
- Checking crime and incident reporting systems.
- Child abuse case files and domestic violence reports.
- Hate crime case research.
- Fixed penalty notices and other traffic enforcement.
- Firearms licensing.
- Community and partnership information.
- Custody records.
- Case files, criminal justices/case building units.
- External agencies data.
- Prison intelligence.

*Community Intelligence is 'Local information, direct or indirect, that when assessed provides intelligence on the quality of life experienced by individuals and groups, that informs both the strategic and operational perspectives of local communities' (HMIC, *Policing with Intelligence* (Home Office, 1999), para 7.13.2).

KEY POINT

Local officers and contacts are an invaluable source of information. The SIO should create an intelligence gathering strategy that caters for the dissemination of important information for which further detail or development is required, eg during electronic bulletins or shift briefings. Local officers or those with particular knowledge of the area or community should be invited to attend the incident room briefings and encouraged to contribute as part of the team, including those who work in or who have particular responsibilities for specific areas, such as those related to lesbians/gays/bisexuals/transgender (LGBT), minority ethnic groups, sex workers, etc.

Research levels of subjects

As part of the intelligence strategy the intelligence cell will be required to conduct research for background details of nominals of interest (eg TIEs or suspects). The intelligence searches can be conducted according to a grading system (or levels) set or agreed by the SIO. As there are numerous amounts of research and databases potentially available from which searches can be made, a degree of consistency is required. When the research is requested on a nominal (named/recorded subject), the level required should also be stipulated. For example:

Level A	Basic search criteria
Level B	Intermediate search criteria
Level C	Specific search criteria
Level D	Advanced search criteria

Each level becomes more detailed as it goes up the scale. The search criteria should be fixed according to the requirements of the investigation and range from local checks such as crime-recording systems, the police national computer (PNC), local intelligence systems and HOLMES2, stop/search records, summons/warrants, Department for Work and Pensions, etc (ie basic criteria), to finance companies, Passport Office, Serious Organized Crime Agency (SOCA), UK Border Agency (UKBA), address links archived in HOLMES2, and so forth.

Covert sources of intelligence

There are a number of confidential and sensitive sources of covert intelligence that cannot be highlighted further in any great detail. The SIO needs to seek specialist advice in this regard. Most are governed by provisions contained within RIPA 2000, for example:

- covert surveillance and other covert operational options
- CHIS (source) information
- communications data (ie certain covert types)
- technical support units.

The SIO should also consider as wide a menu of covert pro-active intelligence-gathering options and methods as possible.

Information and intelligence evaluation

Once information is received it should be analysed and allocated an evaluation rating. This includes source evaluation and handling code/risk assessment, commonly known under the National Intelligence Model (NIM) as the 5 × 5 × 5 rating system (eg B/2/5) See Appendix E. The SIO should decide on a policy for dealing with intelligence ratings which are scored highly. For example, if there is any intelligence which has a particularly high rating, the SIO may be tempted to use it as the basis for directing significant activity, such as searches or arrests.

It therefore may make practical sense to have highly rated intelligence re-examined (eg by a CHIS controller) before total reliance upon it. Experience shows that mistakes can happen when intelligence is incorrectly given a high rating. Also it is always preferable to have receipt of the printed intelligence in tangible form rather than accepting the information through less reliable means (ie verbally). This ensures there is no misunderstanding as to the precise wording and content of the intelligence.

Validating intelligence

Wherever possible an SIO should want to satisfy themselves as to the reliability of information from which intelligence is derived. This can be achieved once again by the effective use of the 5 × WH + H pronouns. For example in a piece of CHIS information check:

- What is the provenance of the information?
- Where does it originate from?
- What is the intelligence rating?
- When has the source proved reliable in the past?
- Why does the source not know outstanding pieces of relevant information?
- How can the information be corroborated?
- Why has the source provided the information?
- How has the source come into possession of the information?
- When has the source come into possession of the information?
- Why has there been a delay in providing the information?
- What is the motive for providing the information?

Local force policies will determine how best this is going to be achieved. If the source is CHIS information then contact should be made with the Force Authorising Officer (who has the ultimate responsibility for CHIS management) or at least at a very senior level.

8.4.5 Sensitive or 'need-to-know' information

'Need to know' is a security principle which states that the dissemination of classified information should be no wider than is required for the efficient conduct of the enquiry, and should be restricted to those whom the SIO deems appropriate. A balance must be struck between making information as widely available as necessary to maximize potential benefits, and restricting availability to protect the security of sources, techniques, and information.

Information held on a HOLMES database is mainly non-sensitive, but some information may be confidential. Confidentiality usually relates to the origin of the material. For example, information obtained from covert human intelligence sources (CHIS) or from other types of deployment would usually attract a general protection in law from disclosure. This is known as public interest immunity (PII). Such information is protected because disclosure would destroy or endanger the source, or would be against the public interest in future law enforcement activity and therefore becomes sensitive.

The SIO should liaise with the DSIO and Office Manager to agree levels of access to confidential or sensitive material registered on HOLMES2. The decision should be recorded in the SIO's policy file. Some information may be deemed so sensitive that it needs to be kept in a secure cabinet throughout the duration of the enquiry and cross-referenced in the sensitive policy file. This is entirely at the SIO's discretion, remembering that access levels can be arranged on the HOLMES2 database (with only designated persons able to view policy), and the danger of misplacing 'lost' sensitive information that creates a significant challenge to the integrity of the enquiry.

8.4.6 Recording sensitive intelligence

Intelligence logs which have a restricted handling code should also be accompanied by a risk assessment or conditions as to the reasons why it may be dangerous to disseminate any further or to act on the information. This can change and intelligence that is highly rated one day may not be at a later time (when the risk to the source decreases or the information becomes more widely known). Thus intelligence logs can be regraded in consultation with the SIO and the originator. If this occurs, the HOLMES2 database should reflect this, showing both ratings and the relevant date changes.

Recording onto HOLMES2

It should be noted that sensitive documents typed onto HOLMES2 can be given the protection of 'Restricted Level One'. The SIO should agree at the start of each enquiry, whilst setting the intelligence strategy, which members of the team should be afforded Level One access.

KEY POINT

Sterile corridors must be implemented to protect the source of covertly obtained material and to establish confidentiality when sharing and disseminating intelligence, both internally and externally. This means that there are adequate safeguards to protect the material and restrict who has access to it.

For further guidance see *Manual of Guidance on the National Intelligence Model* (2005) and *Practice Advice* 'Introduction to Intelligence Led policing' (ACPO Centrex and ACPO, 2007).

8.4.7 Intelligence dissemination and sharing

During the course of an enquiry it is highly likely that the HOLMES2 database will accrue intelligence that may be of some benefit to other policing operations and/or units. The SIO should include in their intelligence strategy a means of feeding back and sharing useful information into the force intelligence unit and/or local units, so that it may be of assistance elsewhere. The SIO can instruct the nomintaed intelligence officer to conduct intelligence briefings with all other interested departments and provide a verbal and documented exchange of information whenever and wherever necessary.

Note: A risk assessment must be conducted before intelligence is disseminated anywhere to ensure that it is handled and managed appropriately.

Intelligence disclosure policy

For any investigation that has intelligence within the incident room and on the HOLMES2 database (in some circumstances there can be substantial amounts), a policy is required for disclosure. The nominated disclosure officer (DO) must refer to the policy to determine the procedure for any relevant intelligence material. This of course relates only to circumstances where disclosure is required, ie in the event of a 'not guilty' trial, which is the norm for serious cases.

KEY POINTS

- The *CPS Disclosure Manual* (2005) provides a practical guide to disclosure principles and procedures, building on the framework of the Criminal Procedure and Investigations Act 1996, the Code of Practice and the Attorney General's Guidelines. It assists investigators and prosecutors to perform their disclosure duties effectively, fairly, and justly. The manual is to be regarded as the authoritative guidance on practice and procedure for all police investigators and CPS prosecutors (see <http://www.cps.gov.uk>).
- The Code requires that material of any kind, including information and objects, which is obtained in the course of a criminal investigation as defined by the CPIA 1996 and which may be *relevant* to the investigation must be retained.
- Non-sensitive unused material should be described on the MG6C form which is disclosed to the defence.
- The disclosure officer must describe on the MG6D any material, the disclosure of which they believe would give rise to a *real risk of serious prejudice to an important public interest* and the grounds for that belief. This form is not disclosed to the defence.

Policy is required not only to comply with the CPIA rules but also for ensuring that all material is correctly gathered and sanitized where necessary before being listed on the schedule. The SIO must ensure that suitable arrangements exist to guarantee that all relevant material is collected either from sensitive, confidential, or other sources. This process must be able to stand close scrutiny at a later stage. Reasons for sensitivity may be identified as:

- material revealing police techniques
- material given in confidence
- confidential internal police communications
- confidential internal police information/intelligence.

In most forces the 'clearing house' for intelligence is the force intelligence unit. Therefore a representative from that unit should be nominated to assist the disclosure officer in checking force databases and gathering all relevant material. Experience has shown that, in the case of sensitive sources, eg CHIS material, a heavy reliance is placed upon persons not directly connected to the enquiry to search for and furnish all the relevant material (eg CHIS controllers and/or the force Authorizing Officer). The SIO should be pro-active in gaining the full co-operation of these post holders for compiling accurate lists and gathering together all the relevant documentation for PII hearings.

Some intelligence logs may have to be reproduced in a sanitized format to enable them to be served on defence teams and legal representatives. If so then the unsanitized version is likely to be the type of material contained within the MG6D schedule because of its sensitivity and it is always advisable to liaise with the originator of the material in all cases of doubt.

KEY POINT

The SIO must check that all the available relevant force intelligence is made available and presented in a suitable format to the disclosure officer and the Crown Prosecutor. Any PII hearing that is required must be closely supervised as mistakes do prove very costly, with the potential to inflict irreparable damage on a prosecution case.

8.4.8 Financial intelligence

There can be significant benefits from using financial information as an intelligence source. It can reveal details about a suspect's or victim's lifestyle, financial status, and the identification of a suspect's associates. Financial information can be developed and analysed to establish patterns and trends, fill intelligence gaps, and contribute to intelligence profiles. The use of financial information can sometimes negate the need for expensive alternative methods of information gathering, such as surveillance.

The SIO should not ignore any opportunities to use any asset recovery powers and legislation as part of the investigation, and to apply for forfeiture of any proceeds of crime.

For more information on financial investigations see *Practice Advice on Financial Investigation* (ACPO, 2006).

8.4.9 Sex offenders and other 'dangerous' suspects

Depending on the nature of the offence under investigation, the SIO may want the intelligence cell to tap into significant intelligence that may already be available. If so it is important that the cell maintains strong liaison with units such as the Police Public Protection Referral Unit (PPU) or force equivalent. PPU officers working with multi-agency public protection arrangements (MAPPA) obtain large amounts of information relating to sexual or violent offenders, as well as on other types of case.

The information generated from the management of sexual or violent offenders can be used to identify details about a person's lifestyle, associates, and links to other areas of interest to the investigation. The Violent and Sex Offender Register (ViSOR) and the Impact Nominal Index (INI) hold nationally shared information on sexual and dangerous offenders. These systems can be a key source of information that may be researched, developed, and analysed further in order to fill intelligence gaps and identify potential lines of enquiry.

The SCAS facility

The Serious Crime Analysis Section is available through the National Police Improvement Agency. It is made up of crime analysts and specialist police staff who analyse crime under specific criteria—essentially rape and serious sexual assaults, and motiveless or sexually motivated murder cases.

The SIO may wish to consult with them (depending on the nature of the crime under investigation) as part of the intelligence-gathering process and for other operational reasons (see <http://www.npia.police.uk>).

8.5 Role of Analysts

The usefulness of an analyst in complex major crime investigations cannot be overstated. Analysts have become key players in the decision-making process when investigating major crime and can assist in prioritizing and setting main lines of enquiry and making the best use of available resources. (It is analysts who help military leaders decide when and where to fire missiles!)

Analysts are important members of the SIO's team and they should be included and integrated as such. This means ensuring they attend and participate in all briefings and appropriate management meetings, and are shown crime scenes in order to help them get a feel for the incident and fully understand the location(s) of the offence. They should be co-located within the major incident room, not kept hidden away or isolated in a distant office.

They need to be made to feel part of the team on a daily and permanent basis. This should not preclude them from having access to specialist equipment such as large printers located elsewhere.

Much of this chapter has focused upon using or seeking further useful information from which to set priorities, organize strategic and tactical plans, and lead the investigation to the offenders. Whenever practical and as soon as all this material is available (eg witness statements), it should be provided to the analyst so they can begin their work without undue delay. They are expected to seek out further information by researching intelligence systems and databases wherever appropriate. Their work can be expertly plotted and charted using specialist software and technology that makes the interpretation of information so much easier to present and understand.

KEY POINTS

- The appointment of an analyst and their terms of reference should be recorded in the SIO's policy file. As the case develops these may be subject to review and amendment. If so, the new terms of reference also need to be recorded.
- Only the SIO or deputy SIO should be involved in tasking the analyst. Other staff must not commission them to do tasks without the permission of the SIO.
- The trick is knowing what to ask analysts to do. In order to do this the SIO should get an understanding and appreciation of what they can produce and what software products they work with.

8.5.1 Role of the analysts and terms of reference

The SIO must meet, discuss, and agree with the appointed analyst what their terms of reference are. These must synchronize with the main lines of enquiry and investigative strategies. The analyst should be able to advise the SIO on what analytical products they can use and likely time scales for completion.

All analytical work requested should be recorded on actions and allocated to the analyst for completion. This will help to keep an accurate record of all tasks allocated and completed and the actions should reflect what is contained within the analyst's policy document.

An analyst can also be utilized for preparing suspect interview schedules and the SIO should consider whether it would be worthwhile involving them in any 'downstream monitoring' suspect interview process. They can also be invited to case conferences when the enquiry is approaching trial stage and be tasked with preparing evidential charts for court and/or jury packages, and when required give evidence to support their findings and charts at court.

8.5.2 Types of analytical product

There are a variety of 'products' that analysts can generate which may be of use to an enquiry. Once material has been researched and analysed, the analyst can use these methods to display results and findings, which are useful in formulating hypotheses, identifying interesting inferences and conclusions, and identifying any intelligence gaps that may complete the investigation picture. They can be used in most complex cases, and particularly in cross-border offences and linked series criminality. Some examples of these products are as follows:

Checklist—Analytical products

- *Network charts.* These depict association links between victim, offenders, gangs, companies, drug networks, etc.
- *Timelines/sequence of events charts.* Which portray a chronology of events for matters of interest such as victim or offender movements over a stipulated period of time or even the known events leading up to the incident itself.
- *Statement comparison charts.* These can allow a précis of the salient points from witnesses or suspects to be analysed and compared for evaluation of facts and evidence, and to show discrepancies and similarities.
- *Spreadsheets.* A simple and effective way of collating and presenting material so it can be clearly understood (eg itemized telephone billing data).
- *Comparative case charts.* Used where similarities and differences are compared between other cases or incidents of interest, such as the modus operandi or description of offender(s).
- *Maps.* An ideal way to display and examine geographical points of interest, proximity of significant locations and routes taken, phone cell-site locations, etc.

8.5.3 Identifying and filling intelligence gaps

The usefulness of employing the 5 × WH + H formula has been highlighted repeatedly in this handbook. It is an effective investigative tool, especially when contained within a matrix. This can be used to chart and display information using the interrogative pronouns in order to highlight and analyse intelligence (or information) gaps. This is done by applying the principles 'what do we know?' and 'what do we need to know?' (see also Chapter 2.3). This process is not just the preserve of the SIO or analyst, but shared amongst the team, who must be included in attempting to fill the gaps, particularly during briefing sessions.

Any requirements for filling gaps should be relayed to the SIO and the teams so that enquiries can be prioritized to find the required information. For example, in the time line for the victim, a period may be highlighted when it is unclear where the victim was between certain times. The SIO can then direct actions and resources at activities to find the missing detail, such as re-visiting relatives and associates, or viewing CCTV during the relevant times, or checking itemized telephone billing data, making media appeals, and so forth.

8.5.4 Developing inferences

The analytical interpretation and analysis of information and material can lead to an analyst being able to draw inferences and conclusions. These should be presented to the SIO with an explanation of the reasoning and logic that supports them. For example, after producing a network analysis chart, the inferences may be that some interesting associations can be highlighted, or there may be some conclusions about business or financial links.

An SIO can request the provision of inferences from the analyst if they are not volunteered. Neat charts and diagrams are of little use when there is no conclusion or interpretation. As part of their training analysts are expected to examine all the available material, plus whatever else they can get from research, and present their findings to the SIO. This is the service the SIO should expect from an analyst and is valuable to the investigation.

8.5.5 Using the problem analysis triangle

Analysts can use the problem analysis triangle[1] for focusing their skills and developing products and information to assist an

[1] L Cohen, and M Felson, 'Social Change and Crime Rate Trends: A routine activity approach', (1979) *American Sociological Review*, as cited in *Major Incident Analysis Manual* (ACPO Centrex, 2005), 119.

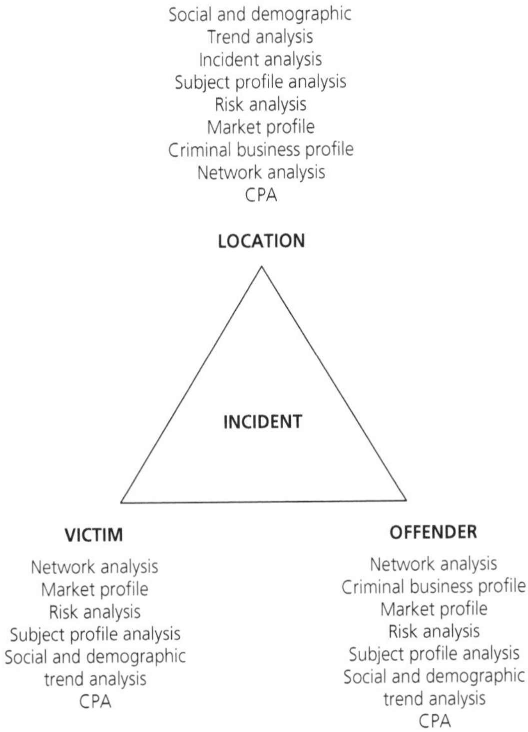

Small text shows examples of research that analysts can do to obtain additional information

Figure 8.1 Problem Analysis Triangle

investigation. It is also a useful principle for the SIO to consider. It relies upon the theory that most incidents contain a combination of three pivotal features in an enquiry and that focusing analytical work on them should produce information that will help progress the investigation.

An analyst can then concentrate on using the products mentioned earlier to produce information about the three linking features, for example analysing previous incidents and mapping the geographical location with other significant events in the case and the location, and producing a network analysis chart for the victim and offender.

8.5.6 Use of analysts for examining communications data

One of the most important tasks for any enquiry using communications data as an investigative strategy will be to analyse the (often vast) amounts of data available. The analyst can be tasked with analysing the material as one of their core functions. They must then be involved in all communications strategy meetings together with the SIO, CLO, and SPoC. They should also work closely alongside the CLO during the investigation. A checklist of their responsibilities for a communications strategy is as follows.

- To research and analyse the data in conjunction with other information emanating from the investigation.
- To liaise closely with the CLO and the SIO and be directly involved in communications data strategy meetings.
- To assist in the examination and analysis of all communications data and help the CLO to identify any further requests for data.

8.6 Conclusion

Some highly relevant and useful investigative strategies have been outlined in this chapter—those relating to house-to-house enquiries, the use of passive data sources such as CCTV and communications data, intelligence strategies, and the use of analysts. These have been selected for inclusion because they are typically used for most major enquiries and usually feature on the SIO's main lines of enquiry.

Chapter 9
Family and Community Liaison, Independent Advisory Groups, and Community Impact Assessments

'Lose the family, risk losing the community, lose the community, risk losing the investigation.'

9.1 Introduction

The issues covered in this chapter have taken on much greater importance in recent times. Certain high profile events, changes in policing methods, and the shifting internal/external attitudes towards greater local accountability have led to significant changes in the police approach.

Policing in England and Wales is now underpinned by the principle of public consent. Without the support of the public reporting crimes and incidents, sharing what they know about perpetrators, or identifying where tensions may be raised, the police cannot operate effectively. Gaining and maintaining this consent is reliant upon the levels of confidence that the public have in the police, both locally and nationally. Securing and maintaining public confidence is therefore a key challenge facing the service and SIOs when investigating serious crime

Not surprisingly there is now a far greater emphasis on the need for the police to ensure that effective relationships are maintained, not with only families of victims but also with the wider community. Terms such as teamwork, partnerships, communication, support, and increasing trust and confidence are often used to describe the aims of the citizen focus and neighbourhood policing (CFNP) programme.[1]

The SIO has a pivotal role not only in leading the investigation but also in taking a more strategic perspective. They are expected to help local policing teams meet their objectives in maintaining good relationships, particularly when major incidents occur amongst vulnerable or hard-to-hear/reach groups. These may be issues for which a gold commander takes the lead who will want to ensure the work of the investigation complements ongoing community engagement activities, policies, and objectives.

Therefore the SIO should never isolate themselves from the importance of contributing to local policing objectives. The enquiry team will effectively become the public perception on policing and local policing teams will still have to work in the locality after an enquiry has concluded. So the attitude, behaviour, and activities of all those engaged in an investigation and their relationship with the victim's family and public must not leave behind a bad legacy. It should be remembered throughout the course of an investigation and beyond that there are much wider issues to consider.

This chapter will now deal with some significant and important responsibilities which more often than not will be incorporated into investigative strategies. They can significantly help strengthen (or weaken) the relationship with victim's families and support of the local community and assist (or hinder) the SIO and the local NPTs to maintain or gain co-operation and support from the public.

There are some serious pitfalls to avoid for an SIO in areas which will be touched upon in this chapter. The success of not just future police/community relations but also the investigation and the reputation/career of the SIO will depend upon the successful handling of these important responsibilities. Providing a professional, supportive, and appropriate service to the families of victims and the community as part of the investigation is most certainly a core responsibility of an SIO.

[1] Neighbourhood policing is a key component of the CFNP programme (see <http://www. http://cfnp.npia.police.uk/neighbourhood_policing.aspx>).

KEY POINTS

1. Solving major crime such as homicide frequently depends on family and community support because it has an impact on the victim's family and potential witness co-operation. Having in place a trusting relationship encourages people to come forward to assist an enquiry.
2. Demonstrating to local officers, elected public officials, and other interested parties such as the media that the work of an enquiry team is positively impacting on public trust and confidence will reap rewards. For example, local people seeing and hearing about lots of extra police presence and activity, eg pro-active operations, arrests, search warrants, H-2-H enquiries etc in their area (via the media etc) will improve the public's perception of the police and assist the SIO in securing and keeping the necessary support and resources for their investigation.

9.2 **Family Liaison**

Family liaison is one of the most important and demanding areas of responsibility performed by an SIO, particularly in homicide and other fatality cases. One of the most significant relationships the police will develop is the one with families of victims at what is a difficult and distressing time of their lives. Much higher expectations are expected and demanded and the accountability of the SIO and FLO roles have never been so great. Therefore these responsibilities must be managed and performed professionally throughout an investigation and in some cases have an ongoing commitment and unique relationship that may last several years.

The Home Office Code of Practice for Victims of Crime (2005) states (<http://homeoffice.gov.uk/documents/guide-for-victims>:

> Where a victim has died as a result of criminal conduct or suspected criminal conduct, the police must assign a family liaison officer to any relatives which the police consider appropriate and make a record of the assignment.

The Stephen Lawrence Inquiry (Macpherson Report 1999) was a defining moment in the role of the police for providing an effective response to families. The recommendations now form the basis of the National Guidelines contained in the *ACPO*

Family Liaison Strategy Manual 2003, as revised by ACPO NPIA Family Liaison Officer Guidance 2008. Included in the recommendations were that:

- The police service should ensure that at local level there are readily available, designated, and trained FLOs.
- Training of FLOs must include training in racism awareness and cultural diversity, so that families are treated appropriately, professionally, with respect, and according to their needs.
- FLOs, where appointed, shall be dedicated primarily if not exclusively to that task.
- SIOs and FLOs be made aware that good practice and their positive duty shall be the satisfactory management of family liaison, together with the provision to a victim's family of all possible information about the crime and its investigation.
- Good practice shall provide that any request made by the family of a victim which is not acceded to, and any complaint by a member of the family, shall be formally recorded by the SIO and shall be reported to the immediately superior officer.
- The police service and victim support units should ensure that their systems provide for the pro-active use of local contacts within minority ethnic communities to assist with family liaison where appropriate.

The manual confirms that the family liaison strategy in providing support to the family of the deceased is one of the most important considerations for the SIO to address throughout the investigation. The initial priority must be to establish communication with the family as soon as practicable in order to furnish them with any information that they require, in accordance with the needs of the investigation.

KEY POINT

'Family liaison has developed from an intuitive craft skill into a professional practice ... It is important to remember that family liaison is primarily an investigative role that must be conducted sensitively in a manner that respects the dignity and needs of a bereaved family. Properly selected and well managed FLOs are essential to the effective investigation of homicide, road-death and mass fatalities ...' (Simon Foy, Commander MPS SCD1 and ACPO Lead for Family Liaison (ACPO NPIA FLO Guidance, 2008), 3.

9.2.1 Family liaison strategy

A family liaison strategy should always appear near the top of an SIO's main lines of enquiry list. An effective and comprehensive strategy must be devised and recorded in the SIO's policy file and must include all aspects of the FLO relationship and tactical planning for maintaining close contact with the family and keeping them apprised of progress and developments in the investigation. An overarching objective should be to maximize benefits for the investigation by servicing the needs of the family for information and support, and to treat them as an integral part of the investigation team.

A main component of the strategy should be to keep the family constantly updated whenever and wherever possible. Victim's families need regular information on what is happening in the investigation, plus answers to a whole lot of questions constantly on their minds. These will probably be the same 5 × WH + H which the SIO and the enquiry team are also working on (eg what happened? why did it happen? who did it? how did they do it? etc).

The family are dependent on the SIO (through the FLOs) for providing them with accurate information; otherwise they have to listen to rumour, gossip, and the media. Public conjecture and supposition may not be accurate or to their liking, and they should be encouraged to feed it back into the incident room via the FLOs. It must be remembered that this is where the FLOs depend heavily on the SIO and where the mutually dependent lines of communication must not break down.

The main aims of a family liaison strategy are to:

- analyse the needs, concerns, and expectations of the victim's family in order to identify all relevant and realistic action that should be taken into the context of their human rights;
- work with the family in order to comply with their right to receive all relevant and up-to-date information about the incident and its investigation (subject to the needs of the investigation);
- gather material from the family in a manner which contributes to the investigation and preserves its integrity (eg victimology, lifestyle, and behavioural information);
- provide information to and facilitate care and support for the family who are themselves secondary victims, in a sensitive

and compassionate manner in accordance with the needs of the investigation;

- secure and maintain the confidence and trust of the family thereby enhancing their contribution to the investigation.

(Also cited in *Family Liaison Officer Guidance* ACPO NPIA, 2008), 5–6.)

KEY POINT

The SIO should beware of giving information to the FLO to pass to the family at too early a stage, before being certain the information is correct. It is better to say, 'we can't answer that question at the moment but as soon as we can we will give you the answer', rather than having to apologize later because the information was incorrect. Misinformation would make the enquiry team appear unprofessional and untrustworthy.

9.2.2 Identification of the family

Identification of a victim's family should be considered in the broadest sense and generally includes partners, parents, guardians, children, siblings, members of the extended family, and any others who may have had a direct and close relationship with the victim. This can, however, become complicated with split marriages, ex-partners, and children dispersed across geographic locations, or involve the victim's possible association with a particular cultural or lifestyle diversity, eg gay, lesbian, bisexual or transgender community, or a religious group. As much information will be needed as possible including many cultural or lifestyle considerations, religious beliefs, language barriers, or disabilities.

The SIO should be mindful of the sometimes complex and sensitive make-up and relationship of some families that can complicate the police relationship. For example, if the parents are separated or divorced, communication with each would need to be managed tactfully so as not to cause undue friction by showing favour to one rather than the other.

9.2.3 Role of the FLO

It must be appreciated at all times how difficult and demanding performing the role of FLO is. The SIO must ensure that the rest of the team do not see or refer to them in derogatory or demeaning terms (which can sometimes happen). This will only serve to undermine their position and make them feel less valued while doing a difficult task. The authors speak from experience in stating that FLOs are extremely valuable assets, people who take an awful lot of pressure off the SIO where managing the demands of the victim's family are concerned.

The role of the FLO should be formally recorded by the SIO and form part of the family liaison strategy. It should be stressed, however, that the role of the FLO is not to comfort relatives, but to assist and support them wherever possible, and (not to be forgotten) to assist the investigation. The family's main requirement is usually for the police to quickly solve the case and arrest those responsible, the success of which tends to give the most comfort of all.

The following points should be considered:

Checklist—Role of the FLO

- Provide the family with full background and updates about the incident and the investigation as directed by the SIO. The FLOs should not disclose any information to the family that has not been agreed by the SIO.
- Provide reassurance the investigation is being conducted diligently and expeditiously.
- Give or facilitate practical support for members of the family.
- Inform the SIO/DSIO of any threats or concerns for their personal safety and welfare.
- Assist in arranging and escorting the family for identification of the body.
- Convey any requests for organ donation to the SIO (see also Chapter 12).
- Gather antecedent information and evidence of identification of the victim. (FLOs should not usually interview a family member as a significant witness or as a TIE subject, unless there are exceptional circumstances.)
- Record any information provided by the family and submit it to the incident room without delay.
- Offer victim/family information and advice re supporting agencies (eg Home Office pack 'Information for Families of Homicide Victims' and victim support at

<http://www.victimsupport.org.uk>) and facilitate access to medical services for severe trauma cases.
- Closely monitor and apprise SIO on relationship between family and the police.
- Deal with any requests or complaints made by the family, eg visiting the crime scene (these should be brought to the attention of the SIO).
- Establish liaison with the Coroner's Office and assist in the arrangements for release of the body following the final post mortem.
- Consider funeral arrangements and refer to SIO for organizing police attendance, eg SIO/DSIO, plus delivery of flowers with suitable message of condolence from enquiry team (but not to get over involved to the detriment of investigative impetus at what may be a crucial time).
- Liaise with family and SIO in relation to media issues and try to protect them from unwarranted media intrusion. (Note: It is important the family are aware of any new information prior to its release to the media. They should also be offered the services and support of a police media liaison officer (see also Chapter 13)).
- Consider an exit strategy at an early stage (this does not necessarily mean implement at an early stage but the family must be prepared early on for the FLOs to eventually leave them).

The FLO should keep a comprehensive log of all their dealings and involvement with the family and their meetings and instructions from the SIO. Some forces have special log books designed for this purpose with carbonated tear-out sheets so the incident room can have quick sight of their contents. FLO log books should ideally include comprehensive guidance notes.

Mentioned in the list is a requirement for the FLO to include details of a family/police *relationship assessment*. The FLO should continuously update the SIO on this so that a critical assessment of the relationship can be monitored throughout the investigation to check it is stable with no ongoing or anticipated problems. The FLO should also comprehensively record any complaints or concerns they may have and bring them to the attention of the SIO at the earliest opportunity. This links in with the requirement for the *SIO in person* to have regular periodic meetings with the FLO (face to face) to maintain direct communication and to discuss any concerns from either them or the family. This is in addition to their contact with the Family Liaison Co-ordinator (where applicable).

KEY POINTS

1. It is important that FLO logs are kept relevant and tight and must be checked and properly scrutinized. There is usually a space for a superviser's signature on the log and the SIO should nominate someone to maintain close supervision of the content, which may later pay dividends. FLO logs may at sometime be handed over to agencies such as the IPCC and/or subsequently the family and possibly the media who will put their own interpretation on the meaning of entries contained within (therefore the logs are not the place to record opinions).
2. Material such as intelligence is not for the FLO log and should be submitted in accordance with the SIO's intelligence policy and graded accordingly. This is another reason why the FLOs should be competent investigators as they need to know what to do with sensitive material.

9.2.4 Appointment of the FLO

In selecting and appointing an FLO, the SIO needs to consider a number of factors:

- The main role of the FLO is as an investigator and for this reason they should be PIP level 2 accredited.
- The needs of the family—eg the deployment of officers who reflect the culture, lifestyle, religion, or gender of the victim (as far as is practicable) or, for example, when dealing with a child murder, a non-English-speaking family, a gay/lesbian victim, etc (though the SIO should beware of any temptation to match culture and lifestyle at the expense of training and skills). Competence is first and foremost as the FLO response can be supplemented with assistance from cultural specialists etc if necessary).
- FLOs must always be deployed in pairs, with one taking the lead role. It is not always essential that both should be present on each and every visit unless corroboration is required or a risk assessment determines it should be so.
- The scale and nature of the incident—there may be a need for multiple FLOs because of multiple victims and the level of media/political attention (and a resilience requirement to cover annual leave commitments etc).

- The training and previous experience of the FLOs (and frequency of recent deployment)
- Their current workload, commitments, and availability (eg if there will be pressure for them to soon return to their normal duties if they are not full-time FLOs).
- Whether they have suffered themselves any recent bereavement or other major trauma.
- Necessary equipment required (eg vehicle and mobile phone).
- If a 'suspect' is in the family, what additional risks this will pose.
- The prevention of any unnecessary friction by avoiding the selection of officers who may have previously arrested family members, or have had previous contact and relationship with the vicitm's family, or resides or works near to the family's residence (for professional objectivity and to assist their exit strategy).

9.2.5 Deployment during initial stages of an investigation

FLOs should be deployed at the earliest opportunity after a risk assessment has been completed. However, in the very early stages of an investigation a fully trained FLO may not always be immediately available. If this is the case then experienced officers should be temporarily allocated the responsibility to liaise with the family, providing a vital line of communication between them and the SIO until trained FLOs can be deployed. The nominated officers should treat this as their primary responsibility and not get involved in witness interviews, other enquiries, or evidence recovery, etc.

This initial period is a time when the family of the victim are at their most vulnerable and distraught. It is also a time when they will form early opinions of the police response and professionalism of the people they are putting all their hopes and faith in. So they must be treated with the utmost sensitivity and given support from the outset. This is also a time when a relative (husband, wife, son, daughter, etc) may still be lying dead at the scene within a protected area the family cannot enter. The reasons why they cannot go into the crime scene must be tactfully explained to them.

If the SIO is not in a position to make the initial contact themselves because of other pressing commitments, they should personally brief those temporarily allocated FLO duties to ensure they know exactly what is required of them. This briefing must be recorded by the SIO and the officers concerned. A handover process can follow later, with the new FLOs being debriefed on the action taken and information supplied to the family thus far.

KEY POINTS

1. The SIO must identify and address the family's immediate needs and provide information about the deployment of trained FLOs. If they are not immediately available, arrangements should be made for other officers to remain with the family to provide support and act as liaison between them and the police investigation prior to trained FLOs being deployed. The SIO must keep in regular contact with those who are performing this role to ensure it is being done effectively.
2. An introductory meeting with the family and the SIO must be a main priority. It is essential, wherever practicable, for the SIO to make early contact with them in person (in accordance with the family's wishes), thereby establishing personal links with the family and ensuring their needs are being met. If this meeting has to be delayed for whatever reason this must be recorded, with reasons in a policy file.
3. A personalized letter of condolence from the SIO to the family outlining roles, contact details and what the family can expect from the police is a good suggestion (giving consideration to any language or cultural issues).

9.2.6 Briefing the FLO

It is recognized good practice for the SIO to meet and brief the trained FLOs prior to their deployment, discussing in full the family liaison strategy and incorporating details of previous contact, their likely expectations, and how they will be managed.

The briefing should include objectives, role, and responsibilities and cover the following:

Checklist—SIO's FLO briefing

- What is known about the circumstances of the incident and what is already in the public domain.
- What the family already know.
- Known background details of family and victim (including cultural, lifestyle, and religious details),
- Any known tensions or breakdowns in the family.
- Whether the identification of the victim has been done and if so by whom, where, how, and current location of the body and the viewing procedures and facilities.
- Whether a post mortem has been completed or when it is scheduled for.
- Precise details of what the FLOs can tell the family about the injuries, cause, and manner of death, or course of the investigation. This will require constant updates and continuous dynamic review.
- Whether the family can visit the body, what restrictions there are (if any), and what are likely time scales for release of the body for burial purposes.
- Whether anyone is under arrest and, if so, what the family can be told.
- Whether there is anything known about the victim's lifestyle, drugs, convictions, etc and how any sensitive details are going to be handled (eg circumstances and nature of the victim's death and revealing a lifestyle the family may be unaware of).
- Location and telephone number of incident room and details of the SIO/DSIO (if not already known).
- Role and responsibility of the Coroner.
- If a deceased person was not alone when the incident occurred and if they were with other members of the same family, the FLO *must* be made aware of their location and condition.
- Risk assessment details.
- Any fast-track taskings/actions.
- Resources and equipment available (vehicles, mobile telephone etc).
- Reporting chain, supervision, and support mechanisms (eg SIO, DSIO, FLO Coordinator).
- Expectations as to briefings attendance, regular contacts, submission of paperwork, etc.

9.2.7 Risk assessment and welfare

There is a statutory duty of care on the SIO to ensure the safety of all officers and staff, including of course FLOs. The SIO must complete and record a risk assessment for the FLO, which should include control measures to cover risk or potential risk caused by people, action/activity, location, and environment. This must remain under dynamic review during the course of the investigation, the results of which should be recorded in the policy file.

Note: A nationally approved document is now in use for this process which should be agreed and signed by the SIO/DSIO, which once completed is marked as 'restricted'. These forms should be available via local force arrangements.

Being an FLO is an arduous and emotionally challenging task. The SIO has an ongoing responsibility to look after the welfare of the FLOs. Regular meetings should always include checks on their well-being and they should be encouraged to report any emerging problems immediately to the SIO.

Suspect/ TIE in family

If there is the potential for a suspect to be amongst members of the victim's family, an increased level of risk assessment is required. Regardless of individual force policy or preference that may stipulate the required numbers of FLOs to be deployed on an investigation, if there is a suspect in the family it must *never* be a single FLO in these circumstances—always two for safety reasons.

In these circumstances care must be taken to ensure an FLO does not stray into the area which is similar to the role of being a Covert Human Intelligence Source (CHIS) when dealing with families. FLOs are always overt investigators and subject to the requirements of PACE, CPIA (disclosure rules), RIPA and human rights considerations. The SIO may therefore wish to plan for how any intelligence and evidence gathering is going to be managed resulting from the FLO's interaction with a family which contains potential suspects.

The SIO should record the decisions in the policy file in relation to the deployment of the FLOs in these circumstances. The level and amount of disclosure of information given to both the FLOs and the family must be controlled and reviewed to prevent undermining the prosecution case. The FLOs should not be utilized for the purposes of arrest or searching.

If it becomes necessary to TIE members of the victim's family, the method of approach will need to be reflected in the FLO strategy (although the FLO should not conduct the TIE). This can cause unnecessary distress and requires managing. One option is to delay the process until an appropriate time and explain why the process is necessary. Outlining the reasons (eg that it is necessary for elimination purposes) usually helps in accepting the process. However, recent high-profile cases where family members have been suspects may make this potentially more difficult. The SIO must try to anticipate problems, ensuring that a planned approach is made, and an unsuspecting and ill-prepared enquiry team officer is not given the task of turning up at the family home unexpectedly to, for example, take their fingerprints.

Case Study—Operation Paris

'In this case the two FLOs were very experienced investigators who had a clear view that their role in this operation was to apply their skills and experience to the task of gathering material from the family that would assist the aims of the operation. This was not compatible with providing support to the family but did enable them to focus, from an early stage, on the inconsistencies in Karen Mathew's accounts and take appropriate action to ensure the material she provided was accurately recorded ... The decision to video-record the account of Karen Mathews was not the most obvious one given that at that stage in the enquiry no one could have suspected what her real involvement was. However, given the inconsistencies in the accounts she gave and the central role that she could potentially play in providing the investigation with information about Shannon, ensuring that her accounts were recorded in this way was good practice' (*Strategic Debrief Operation Paris: The Investigation into the Disappearance of Shannon Mathews* (NPIA, 2009).

9.2.8 Victim background enquiries

'Find out how the victim lived and you'll find out how they died.'

An important task for the FLO is to obtain as much detail of the victim as possible (sometimes referred to as 'victimology'). This may include asking personal and intrusive questions that will require careful and tactful management. It may also necessitate a search of the victim's belongings and/or room, house, etc to look for useful information that may help the investigation. The reasons for doing this must be carefully explained to the family, informing them how it can be valuable to the success of the enquiry.

The victim's background and lifestyle should feature in the SIO's main lines of enquiry list, and obtaining these details more often than not is an initial 'fast track' action. It is an unfortunate by-product of being a victim that investigations have to delve through their personal life to sift out useful clues. However, these enquiries can and often do help generate good leads, and it may be helpful to enlist the services of an analyst to chart any complex information—eg timelines of last movements, association charts, and/or family trees.

A checklist of victimology-type information is as follows:

Checklist—Victimology information

- Victim's full description (and recent videos or photographs), plus social background, home address details, and previous addresses.
- Victim's lifestyle, previous convictions, current criminality, previous incidents of note, employment, habits, current and previous relationships, associates, personality, hobbies, vehicle details, likes and dislikes, drug abuse or other vices, secrets, sexual preferences, risk-taking likelihood, financial details, any vulnerabilities.
- Victim's routines, daily activities, places visited, who they came into contact with and when, last known movements, when last seen and what they said and their mood, any recent incidents of note.
- Personal possession details, where they kept money and expensive items, who had access to their belongings, any missing items.
- Medical details and history, details of doctor (GP), any illnesses, level of fitness and health, any operations, prescribed medicines, deformities, unusual marks or scars, dental history, and details of dentist.
- Any specific queries, such as if victim female have they ever been pregnant or had a termination.

Note:

- When searching premises connected to a victim it may be necessary to compile a full inventory of each and every item. This will enable the list to be checked against any items later believed to be missing. The SIO may want a PolSA to be used for the search—see also Chapter 5.
- In the case of children and teenagers, victimology type enquiries should not be restricted to the family (eg with teenagers how much of what they get up to do they let their parents know?). It is not usually the task of the FLOs to interview friends of the victim but merely to get the information from the family and identify who are the best people for the enquiry team to speak to.
- If it is suspected the victim may have been having an extra-marital affair then the family/spouse may be the worst-placed people to ask questions of. In this case the FLO should be identifying best/close friends of the victim from the family to get the right sort of accurate information.

9.2.9 Maintaining SIO contact with the family

If the SIO has not met the family in the initial stages, it is essential to make contact and arrange to visit the family alongside the FLOs as soon as practicable. This personal touch cannot be overemphasized and is always good practice to develop and nurture the relationship between the SIO and the family. Also emphasized once more is the need to ensure their needs, hopes, and expectations are considered. The police–family relationship must be dynamically reviewed throughout all stages of the investigation, covering significant events such as:

- initial police response and media coverage
- media headlines on the case or investigation
- any significant police activities, such as mass searches
- arrest of suspects
- release or charging of suspects
- release of the body
- the funeral
- court appearances and pre-trial issues
- criminal trial phase (conviction or acquittal and sentence tariff reviews)

- Coroner's court hearings
- post-trial issues and (renewed) media coverage
- any appeals
- if undetected, long-term contact
- any referral to the Criminal Cases Review Commission (CCRC) or Independent Police Complaints Commission (IPCC)
- any cold case investigation
- in the event that any other similar offences occur, particularly in the same area/city/town.

The SIO should stress to the family that the FLOs are very important members of the enquiry team. If the SIO does not acknowledge this, it may be that for the rest of the enquiry the family will want to engage only with 'the boss', thus taking up the SIO's valuable time. The FLO is the vital link between the SIO and the family—this is what they are trained for and how it should remain. This does not prevent the SIO/DSIO from visiting the family regularly as and when appropriate, but the family should not directly contact the SIO. If this happens, the FLO has been 'cut out of the loop' which is not how it should be.

No opportunity should be wasted in keeping a good relationship going, creating a good impression, and keeping the family involved (such as helping to distribute publicity posters) and regularly updated. A good suggestion is for the FLOs to offer a guided tour of the incident room and to meet members of the enquiry team, remembering to remove things the SIO may not wish the family to see (eg details of sensitive lines of enquiry or post-mortem photographs). Ensure staff are available to meet them and fully briefed beforehand (so they know what they can/cannot say).

Case Study—Operation Fincham (murder of Holly Wells and Jessica Chapman)

'On the Wednesday I escorted the families to the deposition site to show them where their girls' last resting place had been. It was very emotional all round. When showing the families the scene from the investigation we considered very carefully the presentation of both ourselves and the scene itself. It is clear from Kevin Wells' book that this simple gesture made an impression that had a lasting impact on the family' (quote: "Det Supt Russell Wate meets our group. Like all the scenes of crime officers he is dressed immaculately in suit and polished shoes, as a mark of respect. Given the quagmire around us it is a gesture that we appreciate deeply").

R Wate DCS, Cambridgeshire Constabulary, 'Deposition sites: case studies Operation Fincham and Operation Sumac', 2008 4(2) *The Journal of Homicide and Major Incident Investigation*; and K Wells *Goodbye Dearest Holly* (Hodder, 2005).

9.2.10 Managing expectations

Worth highlighting is the importance of managing the vicitm's family's expectations. There are usually high hopes to quickly find and charge the offenders and the SIO must be careful not to raise expectations unduly. This is particularly important if the case is complex or difficult.

An SIO can get drawn into a moral obligation to solve a case, often through a mixture of professional pride and emotional pleas from the victim's family. This will naturally produce disappointment—and sometimes resentment—when the results are not so forthcoming. While the SIO should never appear overly pessimistic or negative about the likelihood of a successful outcome, they must remain totally honest and realistic regarding the difficulties and complexities of the investigation. The fact is that some cases are hard to solve, and for one reason or another sometimes the police cannot always secure the vital piece of evidence (fortunately in the majority of serious cases, particularly homicide, they do).

The family will also be eager to arrange an early funeral or retrieve personal items from the victim. However, there may be a period of several weeks before the coroner is willing to release the body, and then only after a second (or third) post mortem has been completed. The SIO must work closely with the coroner and defence solicitors where appropriate to expedite early release. Together with the FLO this must be discussed and incorporated into the family liaison strategy, with the provision of ongoing updates of realistic and likely time scales, but no firm guarantees.

The return of property such as personal possessions (eg necklaces and rings) is something that may help a grieving family recover. The SIO and CSM/forensic experts should try to expedite and prioritize any victim's possessions that need to be examined so they can be swiftly returned (provided they are not required for court). The SIO through the FLO needs to explain to the family the reasons for any prolonged retention of personal items belonging to the victim. It should also be considered how the family want property to be returned, eg cleaned and properly presented. Health and safety issues must be taken into account also.

KEY POINT

In order to prevent any embarrassment or compromise of the role and position of the FLO, the SIO should always ensure the FLO is involved and consulted on any planned contact with the family and the SIO or enquiry teams.

9.2.11 Needs of family v needs of investigation

There will be times during an enquiry when an SIO cannot pass information on to the victim's family for fear of compromising the investigation. For example, when planning to deal with suspects or staging arrests, such details need to be treated confidentially to maximize the element of surprise and evidence recovery opportunities. On such occasions it is understandable and justifiable not to inform the family beforehand, in order to safeguard the integrity of the activity.

The SIO should aim to strike a balance between the competing needs of the investigation and those of the family. In consultation with the FLO, they should plan for a briefing of the family that will not provide any potential compromise and explain at a later stage why the information was withheld. If it is explained that it was for the good of the investigation they will normally understand. This decision and procedure should be recorded in the policy file with accompanying reasons.

9.2.12 Media handling/intermediaries and the victim's family

If the media are interested in reporting an incident they will undoubtedly try their level best to interview and photograph family and friends of the victim. In some instances (eg high-profile cases) the media can become a major problem, with high levels of intrusion and interference, and even harassment and distress. At other times the family may enjoy and encourage media attention, something that also warrants close monitoring and controlling wherever possible (this issue is also covered in Chapter 13).

KEY POINT

The SIO, FLOs, and MLO (Media Liaison Officer) must anticipate in advance and *act quickly* to control any likely media intrusion to the family and relatives of the victim. The family must be given support and protection from the media, and any statements or media appeals from the family should be tightly controlled in order to prevent any compromise of the SIO's communication and media strategy.

The family may also approach or be approached by people who wish to act on their behalf, such as solicitors or community interest representatives. The SIO should be aware that sometimes these well-meaning people can disrupt or affect the important communications link between the enquiry team and the victim's family. They may also have a different agenda to the family and/or police. While the family's wishes are always of uppermost importance, the SIO may wish to outline their concerns and seek advice from local policing commanders and/or the gold commander or IAG wherever possible.

9.2.13 Exit strategies

An exit strategy is always part of an entrance strategy, ie the entry level contains a list of objectives and when those are achieved an exit must be considered. Victim's families often become very attached to and over reliant on their nominated FLOs and it will not be in their long-term interest for recovery and moving on with their lives to maintain permanent FLO contact. Resources in any event would not allow it. The exit tactics need careful management and timing to avoid damaging relationships. It should be a gradual process, planned for well in advance and conducted tactfully rather than abruptly. Good use can be made of other organizations, such as the Victim Support Scheme, after withdrawal of the FLOs.

It is worth mentioning to discuss quite early on that the FLO will at some point have to return to normal duties, although in some instances it may be a long time before this actually happens. It is important that the matter is not first mentioned at a time that coincides with the FLO leaving the family.

Where there is a prosecution case pending, the case officer who has eventual responsibility for the court trial process (normally a Detective Sergeant) can be introduced to keep the family fully updated with progress and developments in the case (including any post-trial contact), although the FLO will be required to assist the family during the trial process and be available to support them at court if they wish to sit through the trial.

9.2.14 Family liaison advisers and co-ordinators

In some forces there are appointed and dedicated family liaison advisers and/or co-ordinators whose role is to select, deploy, and support family liaison officers. They can also assist the SIO in developing tactical options and provide specialist advice (such as advising on how many and which FLOs to deploy). They will also assist in compiling a risk assessment for the deployment of FLOs, act as a channel for welfare, occupational health, support and monitor workloads, and promote and facilitate mutual FLO peer group support.

9.2.15 National family liaison adviser

As part of the National Policing Improvement Agency (NPIA) Crime Operational Support Directorate there is a full-time national adviser who can provide advice on complex investigations, particularly where there are suspects within the family or other sensitivities. The national adviser has an excellent knowledge of national guidelines and good practice and advises and assists UK police forces (and Interpol) in the development and delivery of family liaison strategies at both strategic and tactical level, and training in relation to family liaison. The National Family Liaison Adviser may be contacted through the Specialist Operations Centre on 0845 000 5463 or email <soc@npia.pnn.police.uk>.

9.3 Independent Advisory Groups (IAGs)

Most forces have recognized the benefit of community advice and guidance in major crime investigation. Service delivery is normally arranged through processes that make use of Independent Advisory Groups (and also Neighbourhood Policing Team Meetings and local networks). IAGs on the whole have been provided with relevant and regular training and practical inputs to ensure they have a clear understanding of a police response to major crime. They are now universally acknowledged as an effective means of working with members of the community to solve problems, in particular dealing effectively with critical incidents.

They were largely introduced following criticism outlined in the Macpherson Report of 1999 into the death of Stephen Lawrence. The report highlighted the need for the police to engage with black and minority ethnic communities in order to provide feedback on how policing policy affects those communities. IAGs are now in place across the country and form a vital part of the efforts to maintain trust and confidence in the police service.

IAGs are made up entirely from members of the public. They represent the views from a wide range of local communities and provide lay advice and feedback on all issues of policing, ranging from strategic advice on local operational policy to tactical advice in dealing with critical incidents and major crime investigations. In the event of a critical incident or during the course of a major crime investigation the SIO may access the relevant IAG via the locally agreed protocols.

The role of an IAG in a homicide investigation is contained in section 18.4 of the *Murder Investigation Manual* (ACPO, 2006):

> To review the investigative strategy and advise the SIO on relevant diversity issues which may impact upon, or be affected by, the crime itself and any subsequent police action. In addition to providing investigators with an understanding of community issues they may, in some instances, act as a conduit to the community to prevent rumour or misinformation from damaging the investigation and the police relationship with the community. SIOs should, however, exercise caution if attempting to use the IAG as a means of communicating with the community. IAGs act as a voice for the community and the role of community members is to represent particular social groups to the police. Attempts to reverse this role and turn IAG members into police representatives within their own community may cause significant difficulties for the individuals concerned, and impact on their willingness to participate.

9.3.1 Objectives of IAGs

Each force will have drawn up its own objectives for IAGs. Here is a summary of some of the usual ones:

- To assist the police in improving the quality of the policing service provided to all members of the community by offering independent advice on all aspects of their business.

- To assist in the identification of institutional discrimination with recommendations on how to tackle such issues and promote race equality.
- To inform the police on issues that affect local communities.
- To work towards improving and building upon constructive relationships between communities and the police.
- To help towards increasing the public's trust and confidence in the police.
- To advise on critical/major incidents.

An IAG member can be a useful asset in the progression of the investigation but the SIO must establish key objectives from the outset. They must clearly understand what their role is and not be allowed to become directly involved in the investigation or become compromised as to confidentiality, particularly if they are obtaining information (in which case they may stray closely towards CHIS status).

An adviser can give guidance on cultural issues of the community involved, advise on communication with family members and witnesses within the community, and provide strategic advice on policy, including the impact it may have on that particular group. However, they are not investigators, mediators, advocates, or intermediaries. An adviser should not be asked to speak to witnesses or allowed to attend a crime scene during the early stages of an investigation without the approval of the SIO. In all cases a risk assessment should be considered and recorded in order to ensure the safety and welfare of the adviser. These further guidelines can also be useful:

An adviser can:

- Give strategic advice about the policing of the incident.
- Advise on the impact of the incident in the relevant community.
- Advise how particular police activities are likely to be perceived.
- Provide details of people who may be able to assist the police in community issues.
- Comment on how policies may affect communities and cultures, in particular when dealing with members of the victim's family and witnesses from within that community.

An advisor should not:

- Visit the crime scene during the initial response stage of the investigation without the authority of the SIO. (If this is considered then a fully documented risk assessment must be completed first.)
- Speak directly to witnesses or attempt to persuade them to give evidence.
- Speak to the media on behalf of the police or be used to validate tactical decisions made by the SIO.
- Make enquiries or investigations on behalf of the SIO.

9.4 Community Impact and Public Reassurance

Part of the SIO's investigation strategy is to maintain the support of the community. Any major or critical incident will be subject to a great deal of scrutiny from the media, the public, and diverse communities. The effectiveness of the response from not just the police but all agencies is likely to have a significant impact on the confidence of victims, families, and/or the community. In some extreme cases that impact may be profound and problematical.

Where an incident has been deemed 'critical' (see definition in Chapter 1) a community impact assessment (CIA) should be completed. Individual force policies will dictate the precise criteria for how and when these should be prepared. For the purposes of the SIO this section outlines some helpful guidelines.

Mostly all murder enquiries and some major investigations will be deemed critical incidents, so it is important for an SIO to understand what the CIA entails. They are applicable to any pre-planned as well as spontaneous or unexpected activities and events that may also be identified as critical incidents, eg search warrants being executed in high-tension or sensitive areas, or consideration of 'not guilty' verdicts.

9.4.1 Purpose of a community impact assessment

A community impact assessment (CIA) records the actual or likely impact that a significant incident/investigation will have or has had on communities. The purpose of the CIA is to cater for and manage the impact particularly on those of a minority or vulnerable make-up. It draws upon analysis of available intelligence and in doing so creates new knowledge and perspective, which in turn becomes a source of information. The impact of an incident is dependent upon a range of factors including the inter-relationships that may exist between areas that make up a community, thus creating a range of potential hubs in which impacts and tensions may develop and emerge. It must be remembered that particular incidents can and do lead to high levels of fear and anxiety, and in some cases a backlash and victimization for those perceived to be connected. The main purposes are:

- enhancement of investigative effectiveness;
- protection of vulnerable individuals and groups;
- promotion of community confidence;
- development of community intelligence.

The assessment is informed through effective community engagement and consultation with IAGs and community representatives, partner agencies, and NPTs. The completion of a CIA is a strategic means of considering the extent of any adverse effects on communities and recording what actions are taken (if any) to reduce and manage or control the impact from a policing and partnership perspective, thereby maintaining public confidence.

KEY POINT

Having good relationships with the public is not only good for winning support and co-operation, it also raises and maintains morale amongst the enquiry team.

A CIA is a contingency plan that will effectively facilitate and record the dynamic assessment and control measures for any community tensions. These are affected by not just local but also regional, national, or global events. The planes that flew into the World Trade Center on 11 September 2001, for example, serve to show how international terrorism has a major impact on community tensions across the world. Local policing and community cohesion was and still is affected by such an atrocity.

KEY POINT

It is useful to understand the concept and meaning of the term 'community'—it can be vague or misunderstood because not all communities are homogeneous. At the basic level the term refers to a collection of people within a geographical area within certain boundaries, locations, or territories, eg neighbourhoods. However, it can also indicate a sense of identity or belonging that may or may not be tied in with a geographical area, and includes networks or inter-relationships such as the Hell's Angels community.

The SIO with a responsibility for leading a major investigation is understandably focused on their own area of responsibility: bringing offenders to justice. However, they must also recognize and appreciate the considerable impact that such crimes have on community reassurance and security. For those who normally have very little contact with the police and then experience a major crime in their community, the result will bring extra pressures and tension. So the objective for the police is two-fold: solving the crime and returning the community to normality.

This is why it is important for the SIO to work alongside the local policing commander who has a wider responsibility for engaging with and policing the community. The local policing commander will not want to damage working relationships or partnerships that will have been carefully nurtured. Unfortunately critical incidents have the potential for upsetting the equilibrium and disrupting everyday business. In many scenarios the response phase to a major or critical incident can be relatively short in comparison with the recovery phase, which in some cases can take weeks, months, or even years.

The SIO must therefore liaise with the policing team regularly in order to work together and record/update the CIA. If an incident occurs in the early hours, whoever is the senior duty officer takes that responsibility on behalf of the commander. This may be an on-call uniform superintendent or even duty inspector/sergeant who should effectively take a role of silver and/or bronze commander for local community issues. This responsibility is continuous for the local police unit and should not be totally handed over to the SIO, who has other equally important and competing responsibilities.

Checklist—Risks in a CIA

- Conduct a profile of the community (can be residential or transient groups that frequent area, includes religious, cultural, historical, political, lifestyle, and ethnicity considerations).
- If pre-planned, check whether there are any other agencies or forces involved in the operation and liaise with them.
- Establish what the risk factors are for community tensions (eg high media attention, revenge attacks, public disorder, or likelihood of further offences).
- Determine what internal consultation is required (eg local commander, media liaison, gold commander).
- Determine what external consultation, advice, and assistance are required (eg family/victim, independent advisory group, any other outside agencies such as the local authority, or any minority support groups).
- Grade the potential impact on community tensions (high = possible outbreaks of crime and disorder; low/normal = limited or no issues or raising of tension).
- Check whether there are any additional risk factors.
- Check what other communities will be affected, eg local, regional, national, or international.
- Gather community intelligence that will help monitor the attitude and response of the community.
- Monitor the media and any relevant internet information and discussion groups.

9.4.2 **Control measures**

Adequate control measures may need to be introduced to control the risks and maintain community cohesion. They should be recorded in the CIA document held by the local commander in consultation with the SIO. The record needs to remain a 'living document' throughout the life of the investigation and sometimes beyond, depending on the circumstances. Further CIAs may be required as the event/incident/operation progresses.

There are generic-type intervention or control strategies but an important point is that different types of community will require different strategies to provide adequate reassurance.

Some examples are as follows.

Checklist—Community control measures

- Undertake an assessment of recovery needs, priorities for action, and formulation of recovery plan.
- Monitor tension indicators and intelligence (eg community intelligence).
- Reinforce a strict investigation policy for all linked offences (eg race/hate crime) and encourage/introduce effective reporting processes.
- Identify the right key messages.
- Implement strategic communications policy, eg distribute information via media messages, meet with local groups and representatives to promote reassurance messages, and explain the nature of police action and the reasons why it is/was necessary (rumour control).
- Use high visibility and/or increased reassurance patrols and community policing (take advice from community involved to check appropriateness).
- Place a mobile police station in the area where incident occurred.
- Establish community consultation, eg through IAGs.
- Form a consequence-management cell (constantly monitors the ongoing situation).
- Establish multi-agency strategic co-ordination through the appointment of a gold group.

The SIO has to be involved in this process so that any specific requirements of the investigation can be met without the need to create or heighten any tension in the community or compromise the investigation. If covert tactics are deployed, the SIO should monitor and assess the balance of community safety (ie detecting the crime) against community reassurance (ie not being able to declare what is being done).

9.4.3 **Public meetings**

As part of a CIA control measure and for the purposes of an investigation a public meeting may be necessary in order to:

- address public concerns about a case;
- appeal for witnesses;
- develop community intelligence;
- provide information regarding police actions and intentions.

Meetings should be prepared in line with the SIO's investigative and media strategies and of the CIA and may involve consultation with:

- victim's family members;
- IAG members and/or mediators/intermediaries;
- community representatives;
- gold group members.

Note: Beware that members of the media may try to gain access to the meeting. Plan to keep admittance strictly controlled if the community do not want them present. Liaise with the media via the media liaison officer.

9.4.4 National Community Tension Team (NCTT)

ACPO has established a National Community Tension Team that undertakes tension monitoring and community impact assessments, publishing weekly intelligence bulletins on community tension for police forces and partner agencies including government departments. The NCCT, for example, has the operational lead for the 'Prevent' strand of the national Counter-terrorism strategy. The NCTT at ACPO can provide advice and assistance on the management of community impact. The NCTT has given advice to all forces on impact and tension assessments. The team website can be accessed through <http://www.acpo.police.uk> or by email at <nctt@acpo.police.uk/nctt>. (See also <http://communityengagement.police.uk>).

9.5 Conclusion

The purpose of this chapter has been to encourage SIOs to think carefully about the incidents with which they deal. It has covered some obvious and not-so-obvious areas of responsibility for the SIO. They are nonetheless vital and must not be forgotten or placed lower down the priority list when leading a major investigation. The quote at the beginning of the chapter should remain with the SIO throughout the course of the investigation. Basically, success largely depends on winning and maintaining the cooperation of the victim's family and the community affected by the incident and enquiry. All related post-event management must be right from the start and remain so throughout the course of the investigation, and sometimes beyond.

Further reading

Family Liaison Strategy Manual (ACPO, 2003) as amended by *Family Liaison Officer Guidance* (2008)
Code of Practice for Victims of Crime (Home Office, 2005)
Murder Investigation Manual (ACPO Centrex, 2006), 211–21 <http://www.npia.police.uk>

Chapter 10
Managing Witnesses

'Witnesses play a vital role in helping the police to solve crimes and deliver justice. The criminal justice system cannot work without them'.

cited in CJS on-line <http://www.cjsonline.gov.uk/witness>

10.1 Introduction

Witnesses are often the most important line of enquiry in any investigation. If and when witnesses are traced and interviewed, their evidence plans a major contribution to the outcome of a case, either positively or negatively. Therefore witnesses should be treated with respect and dignity, and the way they are treated will have a significant impact on whether and how they will co-operate with the investigation and any subsequent prosecution.

Although crime scenes yield an abundance of potential information and evidential material, the identity of an offender(s) is usually uncovered through the competent identification and interviewing of witnesses. Obviously the person who witnessed the criminal act is the most valuable (and in some circumstances can also be an offender!). However, other witnesses may hold important information which contains circumstantial evidence, such as supplying the motive for the crime, or disproving the alibi or personal account of a suspect.

> Witnesses are defined in s 63 of the Youth Justice and Criminal Evidence (YJCE) Act 1999 as '. . . any person called, or proposed to be called, to give evidence in the proceedings'.

Victims themselves (if not murdered) are also essential witnesses and can usually provide valuable information about the crime under investigation. So too are those who report crime being committed on others, and a key point to remember is that the person reporting a crime should always be treated as a potential witness. This includes police officers who are first on the scene and may see some vital evidence first-hand.

For practical policing purposes a witness means anybody, except a suspected offender, who is likely to give evidence in a trial. The definition is clearly not restricted to direct eye or ear witnesses to the incident itself. The effect of this is that people in a position to provide circumstantial evidence that implicates a suspected offender would also be witnesses (eg people who witness the disposal of a weapon or other property associated with the offence).

The *Code of Practice for Victims of Crime* (Home Office, 2005) that came into effect in April 2006 adds further clarity to this definition when it draws a distinction between vulnerable victims and vulnerable witnesses. The Code does this by providing for an enhanced 'service' for vulnerable victims (paras 4.2 and 4.6) and enhanced 'support' for those victims who are likely to give evidence in court, ie witnesses (paras 1.6 and 5.8). From this point of view, the Code effectively defines victims as people who have suffered the effects of crime and witnesses as people who give evidence in court; not all victims are witnesses, not all witnesses are victims.

In 2002, the Home Office published 'Achieving Best Evidence in Criminal Proceedings: Guidance for Vulnerable and Intimidated Witnesses' (commonly referred to as 'ABE'), a document that replaced and extended the 'Memorandum of Good Practice' to take account of the new legislation and the developments in research and practice that had taken place during the course of the previous 10 years. A number of related Action for Justice programme publications, including *Vulnerable Witnesses: A Police Service Guide* (Home Office, 2002), were published at the same time. *Vulnerable Witnesses: A Police Service Guide* is of particular significance because it sets out a number of prompts intended to assist the police in identifying vulnerable and intimidated witnesses.

Therefore, when devising witness strategy guidelines, an SIO has to consider some important legislation, policies, procedures, codes of practice, doctrines, and guidelines for conducting interviews with victims and witnesses as part of an investigation. This is an area that has seen great changes over recent times. Fortunately help is usually to hand in the form of trained interviewers and local and national advisers.

KEY POINT

Encouraging members of the public to volunteer to come forward as witnesses has not got any easier. It is often the single most difficult barrier to overcome during a major investigation, particularly when there is little or no chance of finding evidence from other sources such as forensics. Any assistance the SIO can get must be accepted respectfully and enthusiastically, provided the motives are genuine.

10.2 Witness Identification Strategies

One of the SIO's main lines of enquiry should be to introduce strategies aimed at identifying potential witnesses. Good witnesses are the mainstay of an SIO's primary prosecution evidence and they should be afforded every available resource and remain an absolute priority at all times.

Taking account of the circumstances and timing of the incident under investigation, the nature and geography of the area, together with the type of community, will be the initial considerations. This information will provide some pointers as to what witnesses are likely to be available and where they may come from. For example, offences that occur in the early hours of the morning may exclude some but include significant others such as delivery people, night workers, party-goers, taxi drivers, trades people, etc who are unlikely to be around at other times of the day. An early assessment as to the types of people to target initially will help prioritize resources.

A degree of initiative and skill is required for identifying potential witnesses. Each case will differ and the SIO should be proactive in looking to exploit all available opportunities. Association charts may indicate people and places linked to suspects and so suggest where witnesses may be found. People who become victims themselves may have a change of heart about assisting the police, if not managed carefully. Those who have called in with information should be examined closely—listening to any 999 calls for background noises that provide clues as to who they are or that put them at a scene; or where people ring in to say they have heard or seen something, for example 'heard gunshots', which may be a cover story for actually being present and witnessing the incident.

KEY POINTS

1. It is vital to try to identify and interview witnesses *as early as possible*. People are usually more willing to co-operate when an incident is still fresh in their mind. They may feel strongly about what they know or have seen, but this may wear off over the passage of time, or if they talk to others who have a negative influence on their willingness to assist and/or contaminate their recollection.
2. Witnesses can include:
   - eye witnesses
   - victims
   - persons who found victim
   - person who made report to the police
   - last person to see victim alive
   - background witnesses
   - first officers at scene, etc.

Thus the SIO *must act quickly* to seize upon any opportunity to secure witness co-operation. In some areas it is very difficult to find willing witnesses, so when an opportunity presents itself, prompt action must be taken. This means acting quickly to gain their trust and secure their evidence with an approach that demonstrates a determination on behalf of the SIO to safeguard their welfare and not compromising them within their own communities. This can be achieved by using simple but effective measures and tradecraft similar to the tactics and techniques adopted in CHIS (informant) handling. Such measures must, of course, be recorded within a separate 'sensitive' SIO policy file to ensure confidentiality and security, and retained on a *need-to-know basis* within the team.

There are various methods that can be utilized to identify witnesses:

Checklist—Witness identification methods

- Collecting as much information as possible during the initial response stage. If people refuse to give their details, note their descriptions (including vehicle details) so they can be traced or eliminated. (Taking a digital photograph of them is one option, and/or the use of *pro formas* to simplify recording details of large numbers of people.)
- Considering early deployment of visual evidence-gathering/ mobile visual units at the scene to record all those present, particularly when crowds are involved.

- If the media are present, checking whether they have any witness details or useful recordings or film footage (particularly interviews) of witnesses (or even suspects).
- Making media appeals—emphasize that witnesses may not realize they have seen something of importance and to let the police decide whether information is significant (also make request for any mobile phone shots or personal digital visual-recordings from bystanders at the scene).
- Setting up an early public 'hotline' number (which needs to be constantly monitored).
- Making other public appeals (at public meetings, leaflet drops, high-visibility patrolling, handing out small posters, use of large posters in public places, etc) in appropriate languages.
- Conducting H-2-H enquiries.
- Conducting TIE enquiries (may reveal witnesses as well as suspects see Chapter 6).
- Passive data examination (eg checking CCTV, ANPR, social networking sites, club membership lists etc).
- Enquiring in local public places (eg shops, bars, transport routes to/from scene).
- Locating a mobile police station at or near the scene.
- Using a reconstruction to jog people's memories.
- Using cognitive prompts (eg offence occurred when important sporting event played, or at time of popular TV programme broadcast).
- Family liaison strategy may be able to assist with information and witness seeking.
- Community liaison strategy (eg use of leaders and intermediaries) may be able to assist with information and witness seeking.
- Intelligence gathering (eg use of CHIS tasking).
- Placing an 'intelligence database alert marker' on the records of potential witnesses in case they are dealt with for some other matter.
- When searching significant addresses, considering conducting H-2-H enquiries or using leaflet/poster drops at addresses adjacent to or in the vicinity of the location to seek potential witnesses.
- Making enquiries at significant geographical locations significant to the circumstances of the case (eg on potential routes taken by offenders or the victim).

- Trawling incident logs to see if any potential witness details have been recorded and listen to recordings of any callers as call-handlers sometimes summarize what they believe a caller has said missing out important detail.
- Challenging allegiances or explore opportunities which may change them (eg partners or close associates of suspects suspected of 'culturally unacceptable' offences).

10.2.1 Initial contact with witnesses

Initial contact with witnesses is not confined to the early stages of an incident or investigation and might occur at any point during the course of an investigation, including those that are re-opened after a number of years (eg 'cold cases'). The SIO should set objectives to ensure that the members of the investigation team and any other police staff who could have initial contact with witnesses, understand the important significance of their actions if and when they encounter a witness. First impressions of how they might be treated or dealt with may impact on a witness's willing co-operation or otherwise to provide evidence.

10.2.2 Initial brief accounts

Much is said in this chapter about the procedures for interviewing witnesses and victims by visual/audio means. These interviews, however, cannot happen instantly, planning and preparation is required beforehand. Trained staff, equipment, available interview rooms, etc will be required, although in some instances portable equipment can be arranged.

However, these procedures must not prevent witnesses/victims from being spoken to in order to gain an initial and brief account. This is the only way their evidence can be assessed and a decision made about their category and status (eg significant witness, intimidated or vulnerable). This information will be required immediately in order to identify high-priority lines of enquiry, such as the arrest of an offender or identification of an additional crime scene. If the information is not secured at this time, some difficulty may be encountered in obtaining it later if they change their minds about co-operating with the police. A more detailed account can be left until a more formal and pre-planned interview takes place but at least the intial account will help with prioritizing the order of such interviews where there are a number to be conducted.

KEY POINT

Obtaining an initial account is in compliance with the 'best evidence' rule—the longer you wait, the more chance there is for the witness to become influenced, eg by media reporting or discussions with others.

It is completely acceptable for a witness to provide an initial account, accurately recorded by the officer concerned. This should ideally be done through the use of open questions, ie without prompting or probing. A witness should be invited to sign any notes made immediately afterwards as a true and accurate record. If there is the potential to use a small recording device (eg portable digital recorder), this could be a useful viable option provided the SIO and interviewee agree. It would have to be decided whether the device should be used together with or instead of written notes. It must be remembered that all recordings must be fully transcribed, although initially a summary may suffice.

The subsequent interview under the guidelines and procedures can incorporate the initial account and notes taken. This will be in order to confirm what was said and probe more thoroughly any details that have been included.

KEY POINT

Depending on the nature of the incident under investigation it may be of value to arrange a diagram, digital recording, or reconstruction showing exactly where and how a witness was positioned when they made their important observation. This will help preserve this detail and put things into context at a later stage, particularly if the environment concerned changes in the meantime.

10.2.3 Allaying any fears of witnesses

The above list gives some indication of how to trace potential witnesses. Equally important, is persuading them to offer up their evidence and eventually become court witnesses. The SIO must try to be proactive in making appeals for witnesses and explaining the special measures that can be used to help persuade those who may be frightened or even apprehensive about coming forward. There is sometimes an unhelpful perception amongst individuals and communities that being a police witness involves an extreme change of life, such as adpoting a new identity or moving address location.

This can be dispelled by the right message being put across by the SIO and supported by other influential people in the community. Smaller-scale measures can be explained to prevent unhelpful misconceptions, such as the possibilities of using anonymity and pseudonyms where appropriate. People may need reassuring that providing the police with information will not lead to them being harmed and there are a number of ways that SIOs can approach this problem.

10.2.4 Anonymity in investigations

Part 3 of the Coroners and Justice Act (CJA) 2009, Ch. 25, which came into force on 12 November 2009, allows the police to apply to a court for an 'investigation anonymity order'. This is an order made by a Justice of the Peace in relation to a specified person prohibiting the disclosure of information:

(a) that identifies the specified person as a person who is or was able or willing to assist a specified qualifying criminal investigation; or
(b) that might enable the specified person to be identified as such a person.

10.2.5 Qualifying offences

An offence is a qualifying offence for the purposes of this chapter if it relates to either (a) murder, or (b) manslaughter, and the death was caused by one or both of the following:

(a) being shot with a firearm;
(b) being injured with a knife.

Under the Act it is an offence for a person to disclose information in contravention of an investigation anonymity order and a person guilty of this offence is liable on conviction on indictment, to imprisonment for a term not exceeding five years or a fine, or both. A person who discloses information to which an investigation anonymity order relates does not contravene the order if:

(a) the disclosure is made to a person who is involved in the specified qualifying criminal investigation or in the prosecution of an offence to which the investigation relates:
(b) the disclosure is made for the purposes of the investigation or the prosecution of an offence to which the investigation relates;

(c) the disclosure is in pursuance of a requirement imposed by any enactment or rule of law;
(d) the disclosure is made in pursuance of an order of a court.

10.2.6 Conditions for making an order

A Justice of the Peace may make such an order if satisfied that a qualifying offence has been committed and there are reasonable grounds for believing that the following conditions are satisfied:

(a) The person likely to have committed the qualifying offence is a person who was aged at least 11 but under 30 at the time the offence was committed.
(b) The person is likely to have been a member of a group engaged in criminal activities in which it appears that the majority of the persons in the group are aged at least 11 but under 30 at the time the offence was committed.
(c) The person specified in the order has reasonable grounds for fearing intimidation or harm if identified as a person who is or was able or willing to assist the criminal investigation.
(d) The person specified in the order is:
    (i) able to provide information that would assist the criminal investigation as it relates to the qualifying offence, and
    (ii) is more likely than not, as a consequence of the making of the order, to provide such information.

10.2.7 Witness anonymity orders

The Act also allows the police to obtain a 'witness anonymity order'. This is an order made by a court that requires such specified measures to be taken in relation to a witness in criminal proceedings, as the court considers appropriate to ensure that the identity of the witness is not disclosed in or in connection with the proceedings. The kinds of measures that may be required to be taken in relation to a witness include measures for securing one or more of the following:

(a) that the witness's name and other identifying details may be:
    (i) withheld;
    (ii) removed from materials disclosed to any party to the proceedings;

(b) that the witness may use a pseudonym;
(c) that the witness is not asked questions of any specified description that might lead to the identification of the witness;
(d) that the witness is screened to any specified extent;
(e) that the witness's voice is subjected to modulation to any specified extent.
(f) the order will not allow the witness to be screened to such an extent that the witness cannot be seen by:
 (i) the judge or other members of the court (if any), or
 (ii) the jury (if there is one).

Note: This new legislation means previous witness anonymity powers under ss 1 to 9 and 14 of the Criminal Evidence (Witness Anonymity) Act 2008 now cease to have effect.

10.3 Witness Protection and Victim Support

The SIO may wish to consider supporting an essential witness who is critical to the success of a prosecution, and to whose safety substantial risk exists. An enormous duty of care is placed upon enquiry teams that rely upon witnesses who are or maybe under threat. Most forces and some local authorities have existing arrangements for offering support to witnesses, which operate on a sliding scale depending on the perceived seriousness of the threat.

KEY POINT

It must be clearly understood that witnesses should never be offered an incentive, inducement, or any guarantees to provide a statement of evidence or promise of special treatment. Any support must not be seen to significantly increase their current standard of living.

The tactics of witness support measures are highly confidential and cannot be expanded upon. However, when considering potential candidates for any support scheme, an SIO may wish to consider:

- If the witness is an aggrieved person or victim, have they contributed to their own predicament?

- Background and make-up of the witness's family.
- Is any threat 'real' or 'perceived'?
- Has the witness or their immediate family any criminal record?
- Could others give the same evidence as that of the witness who is believed to be at risk?

As a general rule the SIO should seek expert advice before embarking upon these issues. Usually there are experts available who can advise on such sensitive issues and who should be consulted at the earliest opportunity so they can plan for any involvement they may eventually have.

Victims who are also witnesses may need support from an appropriate victim support scheme, a matter which should not be overlooked. Such a consideration should also be given to witnesses who may also be 'secondary victims' because of the traumatic effects of what they may have seen.

KEY POINT—Victim Support Homicide Service

Victims of crime in England and Wales can now get improved help and support. The Victim Support Homicide Service was established in 2010 and can now provide emotional support, information, and practical help to both victims and witnesses. They can be contacted at <http://www.victimsupport.org> and on the supportline 0845 30 30 900.

10.3.1 Media response to witness protection issues

As a general rule an SIO should never comment on particular cases where assistance has been given to witnesses, or in regard to any operational element of witness support. To do so would risk compromising people who have benefited from these arrangements themselves. It is usually inappropriate to comment on the specific details of any cases which remain a matter for the police, prosecuting authorities, and the individual(s) concerned.

However, the SIO may wish to make a public statement that reinforces the commitment to protecting witnesses. This would be in an effort to encourage people to have confidence in the support they will receive to come forward. It is always advisable to seek assistance from a Media Liaison Officer (and witness protection advisers wherever applicable) who may wish to advise on a suitable comment. This may be to reinforce the message that the police, Crown Prosecution Service, counsel, and people responsible for the conduct of criminal trials have successfully brought prosecutions in a number of (perhaps quoted) serious cases where witnesses have had the benefit of such arrangements.

10.4 Reluctant Witnesses

One of the hardest things in any investigation, particularly in communities where there is a mistrust of the police or there are some hard-to-reach minority groups, is to persuade people to become witnesses when they are reluctant to do so. Coming up with initiatives and methods to break down barriers and win the confidence of potential key witnesses is a major challenge for the SIO and their enquiry team. The myth and perception in some communities around 'grassing' to the police can be a major hindrance.

There is no wonderful cure or magical doctrine that will automatically overcome such barriers. Obviously it is important to try to establish what the fears and concerns are, then try to overcome them. Experience has shown that it is the careful selection of the personnel with good interpersonal skills to deal with key reluctant witnesses that invariably makes the difference. (People often buy things just because they like the sales assistant!) Careful thought and planning with good research and a profile of the individual concerned, their background, previous dealings with the police, finding someone who they have trusted before, makes the vital difference. Winning the trust of isolated and intimidated people is never easy; sometimes the time taken to choose the right individuals with the appropriate communication skills can make all the difference.

Intermediaries can be used whom the people trust, such as community leaders, members of independent advisory groups, family, friends, and relatives, or religious people, to help break down barriers of mistrust or anxiety.

Whatever strategy is developed, the SIO must log everything to ensure there is an audit trail of all policies, tactics, and approaches to reluctant witnesses so there can be a firm rebuttal of any accusations later. It is best practice to have a separate policy log for each witness including a sequential log of events of all dealings and communications between them and the enquiry team.

Case Study—DVD witness appeal

During a murder investigation an SIO was seeking to make progress with a significant witness who was reluctant to make a written statement. The SIO decided on an innovative strategy to approach the witness with an appeal for his assistance. This appeal was made in the form of a DVD in which the parent and sister of the victim appealed to this witness to assist the investigation. The parent also wrote a letter to this witness seeking their assistance. The CPS were also consulted for early advice before implementing the strategy.

10.4.1 Reluctant witness court procedure

An SIO needs to be aware of the following legislation whereby a reluctant witness can be required to attend magistrates' court, either by summons or warrant, and be required to make a deposition before court. This power should be considered only in exceptional cases, having regard to the following.

1. There must be a person already charged with the offence in question.
2. The witness has provided information to the police which is of value to the prosecution case but has refused to provide a witness statement.
3. The procedure does not place them at unacceptable risk if the evidence is produced which cannot be catered for by special measures (eg anonymity, screens, etc).

Paragraph 4 of Sch 3 to the Crime and Disorder Act 1998 defines the power of justices to take depositions.

(1) Sub-paragraph (2) applies where a justice of the peace is satisfied that:
  (a) any person in England and Wales (the witness) is likely to be able to make on behalf of the prosecutor a written statement containing material evidence, or produce on behalf of the prosecutor a document or other exhibit likely to be material evidence, for the purposes of proceedings for an offence *for which another person has been sent for trial* under section 51 by a magistrates court and
  (b) it is in the interests of justice to issue a summons under this paragraph to secure the attendance of the witness to have his evidence taken as a deposition or to produce the document or other exhibit.

(2) In such a case the justice must issue a summons addressed to the witness requiring him/her to attend before a justice at the time and

place appointed in the summons, and to have their evidence taken as a deposition or to produce the document or other exhibit.

(3) If a justice of the peace is satisfied by evidence on oath of the matters mentioned in sub-paragraph (1), and also that it is probable that a summons under sub-paragraph (2) would not procure the result required by it, the justice may instead of issuing a summons issue a warrant to arrest the witness and to bring them before a justice at the time and place specified in the warrant.

(4) A summons may also be issued under sub-paragraph (2) if the justice is satisfied that the witness is outside the British Islands, but no warrant may be issued under sub-paragraph (3) unless the justice is satisfied by evidence on oath that the witness is in England and Wales.

(5) If:

(a) the witness fails to attend before a justice when summoned under this paragraph;

(b) the justice is satisfied by evidence on oath that the witness is likely to be able to make a statement or produce a document or other exhibit as mentioned in sub-paragraph (1)(a);

(c) it is proved on oath, or in such other manner as may be prescribed, that he has been duly served with the summons and that a reasonable sum has been paid or tendered to him for costs and expenses; and

(d) it appears to the justice that there is no just excuse for the failure, the justice may issue a warrant to arrest the witness and to bring them before a justice at the time and place specified in the warrant.

(6) Where:

(a) a summons is issued under sub-paragraph (2) or a warrant is issued under sub-paragraph (3) or (5); and

(b) the summons or warrant is issued with a view to securing that the witness has his evidence taken as a deposition,

the time appointed in the summons or specified in the warrant shall be such as to enable the evidence to be taken as a deposition before the relevant date.

(7) If any person attending or brought before a justice in pursuance of this paragraph refuses without just excuse to have his evidence taken as a deposition, or to produce the document or other exhibit, the justice may do one or both of the following:

(a) commit them to *custody* until the expiration of such period not exceeding one month as may be specified in the summons or warrant or until he sooner has his evidence taken as a deposition or produces the document or other exhibit,

(b) impose a *fine not exceeding £2,500*.

10.5 **Offenders Assisting Investigations and Prosecutions**

Defendants too, in some circumstances, can also become witnesses and a plan may have to be considered for exploiting any opportunity to utilise their evidence. Sections 71–75 of the Serious Organised Crime and Police Act 2005 (SOCAP) provide some useful legal options that an SIO might wish to consider for using persons who are offenders or defendants to support a prosecution case or investigation. These are summarized as follows:

- s 71—Granting of a conditional immunity from prosecution for assistance.
- s 72—Provides 'restricted use undertaking' option for any information an individual provides for a prosecution or investigation.
- s 73—Grants powers to a court when sentencing persons who plead guilty to take account of their undertaking to assist an investigation or prosecution.
- s 74—Grants powers for the person sentenced to be referred back to court for discounted sentence when they assist an investigation or prosecution.
- s 75—When dealing with sentencing under s 74, courts can exclude people from court or impose reporting restrictions.

These can be really useful options and should not be considered merely in terms of primary offenders or obvious accomplices, but also for those who may be further down the chain such as facilitators or aiders-and-abettors (ie minor roles). These can also be useful witnesses who could be tempted into taking advantage of these provisions in order to reduce their sentences. Early consultation with the CPS is important before any action is taken.

10.6 **Treating Victims/Witnesses as Crime Scenes**

Sometimes victims or witnesses should be considered and treated as crime scenes. This is in circumstances when they come into close contact with offenders or evidential items linked to offenders (such as vehicles or weapons) and there is a potential to recover trace evidence from any cross-transfer that may have occurred. An obvious example is when a victim is assaulted or attacked (sexually in particular, or when the victim has been involved in a 'crime in action') and must always be treated as a crime scene. Less obvious occasions are when a witness attempts to detain an offender, or comes into close contact with them before or after the offence is committed (eg in cases where there is a likelihood of cross-transfer of fibres, DNA, fingerprints, body fluids from offender to witness).

If a witness is to be considered as a crime scene, the SIO needs to ensure any examination or seizure of clothing and possessions is done tactfully in order to safeguard their welfare and maintain co-operation.

10.7 Witnesses Who Admit Criminality

Sometimes witnesses may admit criminality during the course of an interview. This can range from minor drug abuse to the extreme, such as helping to move or store weapons such as firearms. The SIO should be provided with an idea of the type and nature of witnesses, their background, and the nature of their evidence. This information should give an indication of the likelihood for this to occur.

Ideally, interviewers need to be prepared for such an eventuality so that they know how to deal with it professionally and in accordance with the SIO's directions. A policy entry should be made after consultation and agreement with the Crown Prosecution Service that outlines what the procedure should be. Depending on the extent of criminality admitted, the CPS will advise on setting boundaries for what is in the public interest not to pursue and what is so serious it warrants further investigation.

Case study

During an investigation into a series of serious sexual assaults and rapes in a red light district it became necessary to interview as potential witnesses a large number of sex workers. In anticipation of admissions of minor drug offences the SIO sought agreement with a senior member of the Crown Prosecution Service who agreed on a policy of taking 'no further action' provided the offences admitted were of a very minor type and classification. Each case would be judged on its own merits but it meant that, when faced with any minor drug abuse admissions during the course of the witness interview, the interviewers could continue as they knew how to respond as there was a pre-prepared policy in existence.

10.8 Role of Investigative Interviewing

Given that the interviewing of victims and witnesses (and suspects) is central to the success of an investigation, the highest standards need to be upheld. Interviews that are professionally undertaken and quality assured can realize several benefits. In particular they can:

- direct an investigation, which in turn can lead to a prosecution (or early release of an innocent person);
- support the prosecution case, thereby saving time, money, and resources;
- increase public confidence in the police service, particularly with witnesses and victims of crimes who come into direct contact with the police;
- prevent the loss of critical material, unsolved crimes, lack of credibility and loss of confidence.

Therefore an SIO needs to take account of the advantages of recording (visual or audio) interviews with certain categories of witnesses. This is because it safeguards the integrity of the interviewer and the interview process, and perhaps more importantly provides the SIO with a 'best evidence' quality product. It may also provide strong and compelling evidence in cases where the witness later becomes a suspect, though it must be remembered that people who are 'suspects' at the time of the interviews should be subject to an entirely different approach under the Codes of Practice (PACE 1984).

As stated above, effective investigative interviews professionally conducted will help direct an investigation, support the prosecution case, increase public confidence, and maintain a professional standard. They are always to be treated as an integral part of the SIO's investigative toolkit and a core feature in any witness strategy.

It is, of course important that appropriate consent is obtained from a witness before an interview is recorded. The witness should be informed about the process, the advantages of recording, and the purposes for which it shall be used, and who might have access to it.

A National Investigative Interviewing Strategy (2009) has been produced by the NPIA on behalf of and endorsed by the Association of Chief Police Officers (ACPO). This document revises and replaces ACPO (2004) National Investigative Interviewing Strategy (NIIS) to take account of changes in operational practice and developments in implementation.

10.9 Competency Framework

The National Investigative Interviewing Strategy (NIIS) has now been incorporated into the Professionalising Investigation Programme (PIP) and effectively replaces the former NIIS tiered structure of skill levels such as Tier 3, Tier 5 etc. The implementation of the NIIS is now an intrinsic aspect of PIP. The new framework can be summarized as follows:

PIP Level	National Occupational Standards (NOS)	Notes	Former NIIS Tier
1.	CJ101 Interview victims and witnesses re priority & volume investigations.	Expected standard for volume investigators (eg patrol officers).	1
	CJ201 Interview suspects re priority & volume investigations.	Does not preclude level 1 investigators achieving higher level of interviewing skill where their role requires it.	
2. (core functions)	CJ102 Interview victims and witnesses re serious and complex investigations.	Must have demonstrated competence in CJ101 and CJ201 as a prerequisite.	2
	CJ202 Interview suspects re serious and complex investigations.	Expected standard for those conducting serious investigations (eg CID officers and others in specific investigation roles).	

PIP Level	National Occupational Standards (NOS)	Notes	Former NIIS Tier
2. (specialist roles)	CJ103 Carry out specialist interviews with victims and witnesses.	Must have demonstrated competence in CJ102 as a prerequisite. Expected standard for those conducting specialist interviews with victims and witnesses (eg interviewers of witnesses with severe learning disabilities).	3
2. (specialist roles continued)	CJ301 carry out specialist interviews with suspects.	Must have demonstrated competence in CJ202 as a prerequisite. Expected standard for those conducting specialist interviews with suspects (eg interviewers of suspected Cat. A murderers).	3
2. (specialist roles continued)	CJ301 Manage & coordinate interviews for serious, complex or major investigations.	As a minimum prerequisite must either be: 1. Competent in CJ103 and knowledgeable about CJ203; or 2. Knowledgeable about CJ103 and competent in CJ203. Expected standard for interview advisers.	5

Note: A full copy of the NOS is available on the Skills for Justice website: <http://www.skillsforjustice.com>.

10.10 Role of Interview Advisers

The SIO should try and make good use of interview advisers by getting them involved in the case at the earliest opportunity. The adviser can help the SIO to determine appropriate strategies and formulate policy on determining correct categories of witness and the interviews themselves. They will help take some responsibility off the SIO by 'managing the process' in a similar manner to a crime scene manager. The adviser should also be able to help select appropriate officers for conducting interviews and can manage and support them throughout the process. All agreed policies must be committed to an entry in the SIO's policy file.

KEY POINT

Even when an interview adviser is involved, the SIO must satisfy themselves that any interview is being conducted to their requirements by remaining in control of the process and being continually updated on progress and developments. It must be remembered that advisers are there to do just that, with the final decision always resting with the SIO.

Those selected to conduct interviews with witnesses should be trained to PIP level 2 and the corresponding NOS competency framework. Consideration should also be given to the appropriate competence, background, and experience of those selected to conduct interviews in comparison with the nature of the offence under investigation, and any individual welfare issues that may arise (ie child death investigations for example).

10.11 General Witness Interview Strategies

An interview strategy is a high-level overview of the witness interview process in the context of the overall investigation. It should not be confused with an interview plan, which is more tactical in its composition. This is usually discussed and agreed through extensive discussion between the SIO, the interview adviser, and trained interviewers. A general witness interview strategy is mainly applicable when it is required to manage a number of potential witnesses and should be considered early in a enquiry, although one can be developed later during an investigation if appropriate.

The components of a general witness interview strategy are:

1. Witness categorization:
   - vulnerable
   - intimidated

- significant
- other (ie none of above).

2. Management of intial contact
   - purpose (eg to obtain initial brief account or to aid categorization)
   - process of intial contact (eg under ABE guidelines)
   - any relevant briefing material (eg source of witness info, eg message form).
3. Method for prioritizing interviews
   - witnesses referred to interview adviser to asses importance (particularly if multiple witnesses).
4. Method for co-ordinating interviews
   - methods for preventing repeat interviews (eg within small communities).
5. Resources
   - skills of interviewers accessible to enquiry team
   - location and means of gaining access to interview suites and portable recording equipment.

10.12 Specific Witness Interview Strategy

A general witness interview strategy should be adequate to cover most of the witness interviews in any given enquiry. Circumstances may, however, arise in which a strategy needs to be developed for an individual witness. Such a specific witness interview strategy tends to cover the interview of an individual witness as a result of either (a) the likely nature of their evidence (eg importance to the investigation, inconsistencies with other material, or hostility), or (b) an issue that has an impact on the ability of police interviewers to communicate with them (eg young, traumatized, incapacitated, or disabled).

The componenets of a specific witness interview strategy are:

1. Witness Assessment.
   - the category or categories the witness falls into (vulnerable etc)
   - any issues likely to have an impact on capacity of witness to give informed consent to interview
   - probable significance of witnesses account (based on initial account and assessment)
   - extent to which witness is likely to be co-operative, reluctant, or hostile

- any practical considerations (eg medical/psychological condition).

2. Sources of advice
   - subject matter experts
   - people who know the witness well
   - CPS in context of 'early special measures discussion'.
3. Information important to the investigation
   - matters of general investigative practice, including:
     - — comprehensive account from the witness
     - — points to prove
     - — case law (eg *R v Turnbull and Camello* (1976) 63 Cr App R 132)
     - — any other people present at time of incident
     - — anything said by witness to third party after incident.
   - Case specific material, including:
     - — probable location of any items used in commission of offence
     - — significant evidential inconsistencies
     - — nature and background of any relationship—witness and suspect
     - — anything that might enhance or detract from credibility of witnesses account (eg alcohol or drugs consumed)
     - — information regarding likely witness intimidation.
4. Other investigative strategies
   - Potential impact of other strategies, for example:
     - — forensic strategy
     - — identification strategy
     - — media strategy
     - — family liaison strategy
     - — arrest strategy.
5. Interview structure and style.
6. Method of recording
   - visually recorded (essential if evidence is to be used as evidence-in-chief)
   - audio (secondary choice for accuracy and integrity where witness is classified as significant)
   - notes (last resort if visual/audio not practical or not consented to).
7. Resources
   - personnel:
     - — interviewer
     - — interview monitor
     - — reserve interviewer
     - — equipment operator

— witness intermediary (if appropriate)
— interpreter (if appropriate)
— interview supporter (if appropriate).
- Equipment and facilities
— interview suite
— visual recording equipment
— aids to communication (if required).

8. Timing and location for the interview
   - taking account of witness's normal routine
   - impact of fatigue
   - effects of any medication taken
   - effect of any medical or psychological condition.
9. Objectives.
10. Interview management
    - briefing
    - planning and preparation
    - preparation of witness
    - monitoring and co-ordination
    - debriefing and evaluation.

10.13 Important Investigatory Information

This is something to consider when interviewing witnesses and generally falls into two categories: general investigative practice and case-specific material. The first includes any points to prove for the alleged offence or matters relating to identification evidence, eg *R v Turnbull and Camelo* [1976] 63 Cr App R 132 This is embodied in the mnemonic ADVOKATE *(Practical Guide to Investigative Interviewing* (Centrex, 2004)):

A Amount of time under observation
D Distance from the eyewitness to the person/incident
V Visibility—including time of day, street lighting, etc
O Obstructions; anything getting in the way of the witness's view
K Known or seen before; did the witness know, or had he or she seen the alleged perpetrator before?
A Any reason to remember; was there something specific that made the person/incident memorable?
T Time lapse; how long since the witness last saw the alleged perpetrator?
E Errors or material discrepancies.

The second (case-specific material) deals with the following:

- Where any items used in the commission of the alleged offence were disposed of (if the witness might have knowledge of this).
- Significant evidential inconsistencies between anything said by the witness and other material gathered during the investigation.
- Significant evidential omissions from any account given by the witness in respect of other material gathered during the investigation.
- Where the witness has knowledge of an alleged victim or a suspected perpetrator, an exploration of their relationship, background history, places frequented, and any events related or similar to the alleged offence.
- Any background information that might enhance or detract from the credibility of the witness's account (eg the amount of any alcohol consumed, the nature of any drugs taken).
- Any information that the witness might have about the likelihood of witness intimidation (this should be dealt with after the witness's account has been covered, to avoid confusion).

10.14 PEACE Interview Model

The PEACE model of interviewing is recognized as best practice when interviewing victims, witnesses, and persons suspected of offences. It is implemented nationally amongst all police services in the UK. It has been utilized for a number of years and has a proven track record. All parties involved in establishing the facts during an investigation promote the use of the PEACE model of interviewing. It provides a chronology of events for the interview process and for ease of reference the acronym is outlined here:

P	Planning and preparation
E	Engage and explain
A	Account, clarify, and challenge
C	Closure
E	Evaluation

10.15 **Categories of Witness**

There are three categories of witness for whom there is a requirement to visually record witness testimonies, provided they consent. The first two also present other opportunities for 'special measures' when giving evidence.

1. vulnerable
2. intimidated
3. significant.

10.15.1 **Special Measures**

The Court of Appeal judgment in the case of *R v R* (2008) EWCA Crim 678 overturned the phased implementation timetable for special measures for vulnerable (Youth Justice and Criminal Evidence Act 1999 (YJCEA), s 16) and intimidated (YJCEA, s 17) witnesses as set out in Part 2 of YJCEA, notably visual-recorded evidence-in-chief and live TV link.

The effect of the judgment is that *vulnerable* and *intimidated* witnesses are both now eligible for the following special measures in magistrates (including youth) courts and Crown Courts:

- use of screens (s 23)
- live TV link (s 24)
- giving evidence in private (s 25)
- removal of wigs and gowns (s 26)
- use of visual-recorded interview as evidence-in-chief (s 27).

Vulnerable witnesses are also eligible for the following special measures:

- communication through intermediaries (s 29); and
- use of special communication aids (s 30).

The legislation suggests that access to special measures depends on a three-stage test:

1. Does the witness fit the definition of one who is vulnerable or intimidated? If so,
2. Are special measures necessary to enable the witness to give his/her best evidence? If so,
3. Which particular special measures are most likely to help the witness give his/her best evidence?

Even though some witnesses may now be eligible for these measures, it is important to remember that different witnesses have different needs. It is a matter of judgement based on a consideration of these needs, as well as the circumstances of the alleged offence, as to which special measures may be appropriate in any given case.

KEY POINT

If the witness is eligible, the court must determine whether any of the special measures would be likely to *improve the quality of the witness's evidence*. If so, the court must then decide which of those measures, or combination of measures, would be likely to *maximize the quality of the evidence*. In arriving at its decision, the court must take account of the witness's own views and the possibility that the measure might inhibit the evidence being tested effectively.

10.15.2 Use of visual-recorded interviews as evidence-in-chief

The use of visual-recorded interviews as evidence-in-chief (YJCEA, s 27) should not become routine practice; it should rather be viewed as an exception to the rule in which evidence is given live in court. The overarching aim is to maximize the quality of the witnesse's evidence and in some cases this might mean that other special measures such as live evidence-in-chief from behind a screen via television link will be of more assistance to them.

Where an interview is visual recorded with a view to it being played as evidence-in-chief consideration should also be given to the guidance set out in *Advice on the Structure of Visually Recorded Witness Interviews* (National Strategic Steering Group for Investigative Interviewing, 2010).

KEY POINT

The whole point of allowing visually recorded interviews to be used as evidence-in-chief (and the range of other special measures) is to encourage witnesses to provide their vital evidence. This is something worth remembering when trying to coax witnesses into assisting the case.

10.15.3 Vulnerable witnesses

Vulnerable witnesses are essentially those defined as such by virtue of their personal characteristics, as recommended in *Speaking up for Justice* (Home Office, 1998), plus those defined as vulnerable as a result of their youth. This definition is set out in s 16 of the YJCEA, as follows:

- all child witnesses (ie under 18 at time of the hearing); and
- any witness whose quality of evidence is likely to be diminished because they:
  - — are suffering from a mental disorder (as defined by the Mental Health Act 1983); or
  - — have a significant impairment of intelligence and social functioning; or
  - — have a physical disability or are suffering from a physical disorder.

The courts must take account of the views of the witness in determining whether a witness falls into this category. In addition to this, when determining whether the quality of the witnesses evidence is likely to be diminished in these circumstances, the court has to consider the likely completeness, coherence and accuracy of that evidence (s 16(5)).

10.15.4 Child witnesses

Child witnesses are automatically 'vulnerable', although the extent to which they qualify for special measures as a result of this categorization varies according to the nature of the offence. Section 21 of the YJCEA goes on to effectively create the sub-category of child witnesses 'in need of special protection', with reference to those who are witnesses in cases of 'sexual' or 'violent' offences. The upper age limit has now been raised from 17 to 18 by virtue of s 98 of the Coroners and Justice Act 2009.

In the case of offences committed on after 1 May 2004, 'sexual offence' means any offence contrary to:

- Part 1 of the Sexual Offences Act 2003, or
- the Protection of Children Act 1978 (as amended by s 45 of the Sexual Offences Act 2003).

In the case of offences committed before 1 May 2004, 'sexual offence' means any offence contrary to:

- Sexual Offences Act 1956
- Indecency with Children Act 1960
- Sexual Offences Act 1967
- s 54 of the Criminal Law Act 1977
- Protection of Children Act 1978.

'Violent offence' means:

- any offence of kidnapping, false imprisonment, or an offence under ss 1 or 2 of the Child Abduction Act 1984
- any offence under s 1 of the Children and Young Persons Act 1933
- any other offence involving:
  — assault on;
  — injury to; or
  — a threat of injury to a person.

The sub-category of child witnesses 'in need of special protection' is important because s 100 of the Coroners and Justice Act (CJA) 2009 amended ss 21 and 22 of the YJCEA by making it a rebuttable presumption that they will give their evidence-in-chief by means of a pre-recorded visual and that they will be cross-examined via live television link. The effect of this is that investigative interviews with child witnesses 'in need of special protection' should always be visually recorded unless they do not consent or there are other insurmountable difficulties (*ABE in Criminal Proceedings: Interviewing Victims and Witnesses, and Using Special Measures, Office for Criminal Justice Reform 2007*, para 2.77).

10.15.5 Intimidated witnesses

'Intimidated' witnesses are those that are classified in *Speaking Up for Justice* (Home Office, 1998) as being vulnerable as a result of the circumstances. This classification has been developed by s 17 of the YJCEA where intimidated witnesses are defined as those whose quality of testimony is likely to be diminished by reason of fear or distress.

Witness intimidation is defined as: 'Threats to harm someone, acts to harm them, physical and financial harm; and acts and threats against a third party (such as a relation of the witness), with the purpose of deterring the witness from reporting the crime in the first instance, or deterring them from giving evidence in court' (*Speaking Up for Justice* (Home Office, 1998)).

KEY POINT

Witness intimidation is an offence under s 51 of the Criminal Justice and Public Order Act 1994 and can occur before the crime is reported, during the course of the investigation, or even after the case is heard at court.

In determining whether a witness falls into this category, the court is obliged to take account of:

- the nature and alleged circumstances of the offence
- the age of the witness
- where relevant:
  - the social and cultural background and ethnic origins of the witness
  - the domestic and employment circumstances of the witness
  - any religious beliefs or political opinions of the witness
- any behaviour towards the witness by:
  - the accused
  - members of the accused person's family or associates
  - any other person who is likely to be either an accused person or a witness in the proceedings.

Complainants in cases of sexual assault are defined as falling into this category *per se* by s 17(4) of the Act. Section 101 of the CJA 2009 now gives complainants to sexual offences greater access to visually recorded evidence-in-chief in Crown Courts (ie not magistrates' courts).

Vulnerable Witnesses: A Police Service Guide (ACPO and Home Office, 2002) also lists a number of prompts aimed at helping the police to identify witnesses who are, potentially, intimidated. Given that intimidated witnesses are, by virtue of the definition originally set out in *Speaking Up for Justice*, those vulnerable by circumstance, these prompts focus on:

- the nature of the offence (sexual offences, domestic violence, racially motivated crime, and repeat victimization);
- the relationship between the witness and the alleged offender (eg a carer);
- the living conditions of the witness (living in a place where there is a history of hostility towards the police or living in close proximity to the alleged offender or his/her associates);
- the background of the alleged offender (notably, where s/he has a history of violence or intimidation).

The Guide suggests that elderly and frail witnesses should also be regarded as intimidated when the court takes account of their age, as required by s 17 of the Act. It also suggests that witnesses to racially motivated crime, domestic violence, and repeat victimization may also fall within this category.

Since the publication of the Guide, the *Code of Practice for Victims of Crime* (Office for Criminal Justice Reform, 2005) has extended these prompts a little further by including the families of homicide victims in the intimidated category.

KEY POINT

Experience and research suggest there seems to be a poor track record for the police in identifying vulnerable and intimidated witnesses. This could be for reasons of complex (and changing) definitions, lack of ability to recognize or admit disabilities (eg mental illness or learning disability), or lack of training aimed at improving the ability of officers to identify vulnerable and intimidated witnesses. The SIO must ensure this does not happen for reasons of ethics, greater effectiveness, correct adherence to policy and legislation, and above all the key issue of quality of evidence under ABE principles.

Levels of intimidation

There is a useful 'intimidation framework' to consider outlining three levels of intimidation, as shown in Figure 10.1.

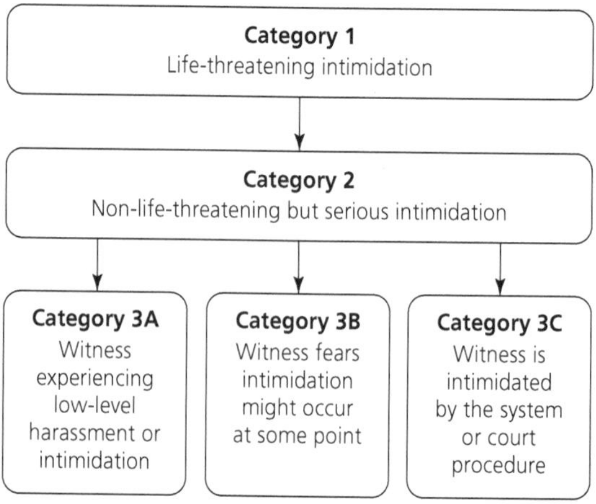

Figure 10.1 Levels of intimidation

These are further outlined in the *Working with Intimidated Witnesses* manual, published by the Criminal Justice System (see <http://www.cjsonline.gov.uk>), November 2006, where there is a lot more information on this subject.

There are a number of witness support services provided by key organizations other than the police, for example the Crown Prosecution Service, Victim Support and witness service (<http://www.victimsupport.org.uk>), National Witness Mobility Service (<http://www.cjsonline.gov.uk/witnesses>), housing organizations, local witness care units (WCU), local support organizations, and national helplines (eg Victim Support line), or a combination through joint agency working. There may be other support services required, such as breaking down language barriers (use of Language Line service or an interpreter).

10.15.6 **Significant witnesses (SW)**

Significant witnesses (SW) are the category the SIO is most likely to use for the purposes of an investigation. It is a key function and responsibility of the SIO to identify and designate those witnesses who should be afforded SW status. Such a decision should be recorded in the policy file and contained within a witness strategy. In some cases it may also be necessary to explain why a witness has *not* been granted SW status in order to pre-empt questions, should they be asked later (eg in court proceedings).

> Significant witnesses are defined in para 4.7 of *Achieving Best Evidence* (ABE) *in Criminal Proceedings: Guidance on Interviewing Victims and Witnesses, and using Special Measures* (Office for Criminal Justice Reform, 2007) as those who:
>
> - 'have or claim to have witnessed, visually or otherwise, an *indictable offence*, part of such an offence or events closely connected with it (including any incriminating comments made by the suspected offender either before or after the offence); or
> - stand in a particular relationship to the victim or have a central position in relation to an indictable offence.'

There is no statutory provision for visually recorded interviews with significant witnesses to be played as evidence-in-chief until s 137 of the Criminal Justice Act 2003 is implemented. Therefore these interviews are visually recorded for the purposes of accuracy and integrity only and are not intended to be played as evidence-in-chief.

There is a fundamental difference between the ACPO definition and s 137. ACPO does not specify a time scale for when the alleged offence/events occurred whereas s 137 requires that the visual interview should be conducted soon after the commission of the offence/event, when it is still fresh in the witness's memory, thereby providing an early and reliable account.

There is a temptation to concentrate on the obvious witnesses who fall into this category, such as a person who sees a crime in the act of being committed. However, the SIO may wish to consider other suitable recipients for this status that are less obvious, such as the first officer to attend the crime scene who may observe some important events and circumstances, or even paramedics.

Nonetheless, this category of witness needs to be applied sensibly. Interviewing a large number of witnesses as 'significant' by either visual or audio means can be resource-intensive and should therefore be used sparingly and sensibly. Also, having numerous accounts recorded can have a detrimental effect on the enquiry as they will need to be transcribed/typed before entering the major incident room. This may hinder the management system from keeping pace with a fast-moving enquiry. On a practical note the SIO may need to take appropriate steps to speed up the process, for instance arrange a faster turn-around in transcribing and typing time scales.

Significant witnesses should always be visual recording interviewed unless they do not consent. Alternatively, they may be interviewed on audio-recording equipment, also by means of consent. If both are refused, written notes can be attempted, including an explanation that the interviewee has refused with reasons, and a record made ideally signed by them to that effect.

As the recording cannot be used as evidence-in-chief (although this may be introduced at some stage) the evidential material captured needs to be transferred into a format acceptable to the courts, usually into a full s 9 Criminal Justice Act witness statement (Form MG11). This is usually done by using the recording as an accurate guide, and a subsequent statement can then be read and signed by the witness which should also be recorded to accurately capture any amendments or alterations. This should be completed very soon after the initial interview to avoid the witness being unduly influenced prior to reading and signing (eg maximum delay period 72 hours).

Note: The options for converting material gleaned from interviews with significant witnesses are described in para 4.8

of *Achieving Best Evidence in Criminal Proceedings: Guidance on Interviewing Victims and Witnesses and using Special Measures* (Office for Criminal Justice Reform 2007). These options are referred to as 'exhibited transcript' and full 'MG11']

The purpose of introducing and adopting this interviewing process is to preserve and ensure the *integrity* and *accuracy* of the witness interview process, eliminating any later suggestions that a witness has been unduly influenced or coerced. In summary, the only occasions when pre-recorded visual evidence can be used as evidence-in-chief in a criminal case is when the witness meets the definition of 'vulnerable' or 'intimidated'. However, on some occasions a significant witness may feasibly change status, moving into either of these categories at a later stage and then becoming eligible for the special measures considerations.

10.15.7 **Early Special Measures Discussions**

The SIO should inform the Crown Prosecution Service of the potential need to make an application for special measures through an 'early special measures discussion'. This used to be called a 'meeting' but it has since been recognized that it does not have to happen face-to-face, and can be, for instance, over a telephone or other communications link. Practical guidance in relation to early special measures discussions is set out in *Early Special Measures Discussions between the Police and the Crown Prosecution Service* (Ministry of Justice, Home Office and CPS, 2009).

Early special measures discussions are aimed at considering how evidence will be presented to the court. It is important for these discussions to take place either before or as soon after the interview as possible so that a Criminal Justice Act statement can be prepared while the witness's memory remains fresh if it is decided not to proceed with an application to play the visual recording as evidence in chief. To prepare a statement at a later stage risks exposing the witness to unnecessary trauma and could be counter-productive since some of the details of the witness's memory are likely to change as time goes on.

Following an early special measures discussion, the police should ask a witness who is required to give evidence if they wish to meet the CPS prosecutor. The purpose of this is to discuss matters relating to special measures decisions (see also *Special Measures Meetings between the Crown Prosecution Service and Witnesses—Practice Guidance* (Ministry of Justice, Home Office, CPS, 2009)).

10.16 **Witness Intermediaries**

An intermediary is someone who the court approves to communicate to the witness the questions that the court, the defence, and the prosecution teams may intend to ask, and to communicate the answers that the witness gives in response. Intermediaries can assist at all stages of the criminal justice process from police investigations and interviews, through pre-tiral preparations to court. They provide communication assistance in the investigation stage and can:

- assist in victim and witness interviews and trials in which the interviewee has limited expressive and/or receptive communication abilities as a result of age or disability;
- carry out an assessment to evaluate the abilities and need of the witness, deciding whether they have the correct skills and experience to act as the intermediary in the case, and establish rapport with the witness;
- following initial assessment, provide advice on how to get the best evidence from the witness (eg types of questions to avoid, types of questions most likely to get accurate response, whether they will require breaks in questioning etc);
- directly assist in the questioning process by asking interviewers to rephrase questions the witness does not understand, or rephrasing questions themselves if necessary;
- help to communicate the witness's answers;
- assist in pre-trial preparation for the witness.

There is a witness intermediary team based within the NPIA Specialist Operations Centre who can provide support to SIOs in the use of Registered Intermediaries and offer advice on interview strategies. They can be contacted by email at <soc@npia.pnn.police.uk> or on 0845 000 5463.

10.16.1 **Service standards**

The use of witness intermediaries complies with the minimum standards of service for witness's under the Witness Charter, which is a commitment to witnesses on how they should be treated by the criminal justice system to meet the needs of witnesses.

10.17 The Witness Charter

This was rolled out in April 2009 by the Home Office Criminal Justice System and is a document that outlines the 34 standards which set out the level of service that witnesses should expect to receive at every stage of the criminal justice process, right through to giving evidence at trial and post-trial support. It is aimed at ensuring every witness receives a level of service that is tailored to their individual needs so that witnesses are more likely to stay involved with helping the case and attending trial to give evidence. This is a document that is essential reading in developing and maintaining adequate knowledge levels for performing the role of an SIO (see <http://www.frontline.cjsonline.gov.uk>).

10.18 Use of Interpreters

In some circumstances it may be necessary to use the services of an interpreter to interview witnesses. The SIO needs to be aware that there are some important guidelines for working with interpreters. Some useful ones are listed below:

- The identification of the interpreter should always be verified (eg on arrival at a police station).
- The interpreter should be isolated from other members of the public and anyone connected with the case.
- Interpreters should be supervised at all times when conversing with witnesses.
- They should only work in the language they are fully qualified so to do.
- Whenever possible, witness statements written in another language should be translated into English at the police station.

10.19 Conclusion

This chapter has looked at the practical and legislative considerations when seeking out and dealing with witnesses. It will always be a challenge for any enquiry team to coax witnesses and persuade reluctant communities to part with their information. However, new legislation and procedures that have recently become available have provided new alternatives that can and should be used for the maximum benefit of the investigation.

Witnesses can now be afforded greater protection by the courts. Methods of obtaining their evidence are now also far more professional, with trained interviewers and advisers available as resources for the SIO. The entire process has undergone significant changes that must become integral to the success of the investigation. This also means that the process of managing witnesses and their evidence will now come under greater scrutiny.

Because the subject of investigative interviewing and interpretation of the guidelines is a highly specialist area, there is a greater need for the SIO to have access to trained advisers who can be relied upon to provide effective tactical and strategic guidance. Although the final decision always sits with the SIO, the aim should be to strive for obtaining the best possible evidence, and the higher the quality of investigative witness interview, the greater chance of success for the prosecution case.

Further reading

K Smith and S Tilney, *Vulnerable Adult and Child Witnesses* (Blackstone's, OUP, 2007).

Chapter 11
Managing Suspects

11.1 Introduction

An essential focus for any investigation is the identification of the person(s) responsible, making arrests, conducting interviews, and bringing charges. These processes require careful strategic and operational planning, with consideration of:

- methods of identifying suspects;
- determining how and when the arrest(s) will be made and legal powers;
- maximizing forensic capture opportunities;
- managing detention arrangements and custody time limits;
- preparing and conducting investigative interviews;
- charging and processing procedures.

In some instances an SIO is presented with circumstances where arrests have already been or are about to be made, without the luxury of time to formulate a carefully thought through and pre-planned strategy. The principles nonetheless are the same; plainly faster decisions and actions will be necessary and communicated by the SIO in a more rapid and spontaneous fashion to avoid missed opportunities.

The focus of this chapter is to cover the main phases of suspect strategies and tactics for the SIO to consider. These begin with the identification of suspects and legal considerations to meet the requirements of the Police and Criminal Evidence Act 1984 (PACE). In addition we look at issues surrounding the decision to declare 'suspect' status, the making and timing of arrests, detention and interview strategies, recovering forensic evidence from the suspect in custody, moving on to some practical points on ways to conduct effective pro-active hunts for suspects.

11.2 Suspect Identification

Details of suspects can emerge from the result of witness interviews, forensic evidence, passive data such as CCTV, admissions, qualitative information/intelligence, or prompt actions taken at or near a crime scene. Any one or more of the SIO's main lines of enquiry or investigative strategies could reveal the identity of a suspect(s) in an investigation and that is precisely what they are supposed to. Sometimes it becomes clear from an early stage who the suspect(s) is/are, and depending on the quality of the evidence or information this may present the enquiry team with an early opportunity to make an arrest.

KEY POINT

Prompt action taken at the scene can lead to the identity and/or location of an offender. The initial police response should incorporate a search for suspects, such as the use of a human scent dog in the immediate aftermath. The checking of local hospitals in case the offender(s) is/are injured is also worth considering. Care should be taken, of course, not to destroy any forensic opportunities in whatever initial actions are taken.

Where witnesses are concerned, the term 'identification' takes on its more literal meaning and formal identification procedures must remain of paramount importance. Accurate descriptions should be obtained not just of the individuals but also of their clothing, vehicles, direction of travel, where/when last seen, etc. These are critical and must be carefully obtained and recorded. Any errors at this vital stage will prove costly and undermine the investigation. Witnesses cannot always be relied upon to get things right, but mistakes in failing to record details properly or elicit accurate information due to lack of care or professionalism are inexcusable.

KEY POINT

Mentioned in Chapter 10 and repeated for ease of reference here is *R v Turnbull and Camelo* [1976] 63 Cr App R 132 embodied in the mnemonic ADVOKATE (*Practical Guide to Investigative Interviewing* (Centrex, 2004)):

A Amount of time under observation
D Distance from the eyewitness to the person/ incident
V Visibility—including time of day, street lighting etc
O Obstructions; anything getting in the way of the witness's view
K Known or seen before; did the witness know, or had he or she seen the alleged perpetrator before?
A Any reason to remember; was there something specific that made the person/incident memorable?
T Time lapse; how long since the witness last saw the alleged perpetrator?
E Errors or material discrepancies.

11.2.1 Identification by witnesses

Code D (para 3) of PACE deals with the important provisions concerning the practice and procedure of the identification of a suspect by a witness. These fall into two categories.

1. If the *identity of the suspect is known* or suspected to justify an arrest, for example after being named by a witness, there are opportunities to consider later that will assist in the formal identification of the suspect by the witness, eg video identification, identification parade, or group identification.

KEY POINT

A witness must not be shown photographs, computerized or artist's composite likenesses, or pictures (including 'E-Fit images') if the identity of the suspect is known and the suspect is available to take part in video identification.

2. The procedures are a little more complicated if the suspect's details are not known and identification evidence is sought. This commonly occurs where an offence has been recently committed and there is an opportunity to take a witness to the area where the offender may be located in order to identify them, eg after a large-scale disturbance in a town centre.

In the latter circumstances there may be a useful opportunity to identify and arrest the offender(s) while still fresh in a witness's mind, and PACE Code D3.2 allows for it. The swift capture of suspects is always preferable, enabling forensic samples and clothing to be quickly secured. The conditions are that, insofar as possible, measures should be adopted to guard against mistaken identity and preserve the integrity of the process, and where practicable:

1. An accurate and legible record should be made of the first description of a suspect given before a witness is asked to make any identification.
2. The witness's attention should not be directed towards any particular person.
3. If more than one witness they should be kept separate to maintain their independence.
4. Once there is sufficient information to justify the arrest of a particular individual for suspected involvement in the offence, eg after the witness makes a positive identification, the provisions for when the identity of a suspect is known then apply for any other witnesses in relation to that individual.
5. A detailed record should be kept of the proceedings by the police staff accompanying the witness, including as much detail as possible (date, time, place, how the identification was made, and conditions at the time as to weather, distance away, and lighting, whether the witness's attention was drawn to the suspect and the reason for this, plus any comments made by the witness).

11.3 Declaring 'Suspect' Status

Declaring 'suspect' status is a very significant step in an investigation. It amounts to a formal declaration from the SIO that the enquiry is focusing on a particular individual (or plural) and should be considered very carefully. Such a decision must be based upon solid justification and rationale, supported by reliable information and/or evidence and clearly recorded in the policy file (and registered on HOLMES2). If a suspect is wrongly identified this can have a detrimental effect on the enquiry by deflecting resources and attention from the true suspect, and will also affect team morale.

Generally speaking, suspect status should only be given where:

- tangible evidence exists to directly link a person(s) with involvement in the offence, eg physical/forensic evidence, eyewitness testimony, CCTV; or

- circumstantial evidence exists of sufficient strength to warrant the arrest of that person, ie reasonable objective grounds for suspicion based on known facts or information relevant to the person to be arrested/under arrest (see s 24 PACE below); or
- there is a strong intelligence case supported by supporting material containing a highly graded and dependable evaluation/rating marker (ie using the 5 × 5 × 5 intelligence rating system).

If too many suspects are declared and arrested this may give an impression the SIO has little or no idea who is actually responsible—particularly if there is believed to be a small number of offenders involved. It can also produce contradictory or undermining evidence when the offender(s) is/are eventually arrested and charged and face prosecution. The declaration of a suspect is invariably picked up on and reported by the media and/or community because it is viewed as a highly significant development in the investigation. Hopes and expectations then rise towards a positive outcome and if a number of people are being arrested as suspects only to be later released without charge this wil inevitably produce negative connotations.

Nonetheless, when the time is right and the SIO is satisfied there are sufficient grounds for declaring a person a suspect, then the SIO should be bold and decisive enough to do so. This will be a defining moment in the investigation and one that invariably lifts the morale of the victimís family, the local community, and the enquiry team.

KEY POINT

Sometimes there can be confusion over the terms *suspect* and *subject*. This can occur when discussing or recording information and making reference to an individual. External agencies, family, media, the Crown Prosecution Service, and the courts can also get confused by a mix up over the two terms. The SIO and incident room staff must remain vigilant to ensure the two words are not mistakenly recorded; there is a great deal of difference between being referred to as a suspect and as a subject!

11.4 Making Arrests

Once a suspect has been identified a decision must be made as to when, how and where they are to be arrested and what for. Legislative considerations for the SIO are contained within s 24 of PACE (as substituted by s 110 of the Serious and Organised Crime and Police Act 2005 (SOCAP)) and Code G PACE Codes of Practice. It is suggested that the SIO knows and understands these because it is not uncommon to be questioned about the use of legal powers such as these under cross-examination by the courts.

11.4.1 Power to arrest without warrant

PACE, s 24 states that a constable may arrest without warrant for any offence where:

1. S/he has reasonable grounds for believing that it is necessary to arrest the person for any of these reasons:
   - To ascertain the person's name or address (including where s/he has reasonable grounds for doubting that s/he has been provided with the real details).
   - To prevent the person causing physical injury to himself or another.
   - To prevent the person causing loss or damage to property.
   - To prevent the person committing an offence against public decency.
   - To protect a child or vulnerable person from the person in question.
   - To allow the prompt and effective investigation of the offence or conduct of the person.
   - To prevent any prosecution for the offence being hindered by the disappearance of the person.
2. The person is, in fact, about to commit an offence, or is in the act of committing an offence, or has committed an offence (whether or not the constable has reasonable grounds to suspect those matters).
3. The constable has reasonable grounds for suspecting that the person is about to commit an offence, or is in the act of committing an offence, or has committed an offence (whether or not the person, in fact, is guilty of such misconduct).

Guidance is contained within Code G as to the meaning of the phrase 'reasonable grounds for suspecting' in (3) above. Note for Guidance 2 states: 'there must be some reasonable, objective grounds for the suspicion, based on known facts or information which are relevant to the likelihood the offence has been committed and the person to be questioned committed it'.

11.4.2 The meaning of 'reasonable grounds to suspect' (the three-part test)

This was explained by Woolf LJ in *Castorina v the Chief Constable of Surrey*, (1988) *The Times*, 15 June; local government reports, 30 March 1996, 241 (where it is fully reported) at 248 (in a passage quoted in part in *Chapman v Director of Public Prosecutions* (1989) 89 Cr App R at 190):

> I suggest that, in a case where it is alleged that there has been an unlawful arrest, there are three questions to be answered:
>
> 1. Did the arresting officer suspect that the person who was arrested was guilty of the offence? The answer to this question depends entirely on the findings of fact as to the officer's state of mind.
> 2. Assuming the officer had the necessary suspicion, was there reasonable cause for that suspicion? This is a purely objective requirement to be determined by the judge if necessary on facts found by a jury.
> 3. If the answer to the two previous questions is in the affirmative then the officer has a discretion which entitled him to make an arrest and in relation to that discretion the question arises as to whether the discretion has been exercised in accordance with the principles laid down by Lord Greene MR in *Associated Provincial Picture Houses Ltd v Wednesbury Corporation* [1948] 1 KB 223.

11.4.3 The meaning of suspicion

The classic statement of the meaning of the word suspicion in the context of the phrase 'reasonable suspicion' is that of Lord Devlin in *Hussein v Chong Fook Kam* [1970] AC 942, (PC) at 948:

> Suspicion in its ordinary meaning is a state of conjecture or surmise where proof is lacking: 'I suspect but I cannot prove'. Suspicion arises at or near the starting-point of an investigation of which the obtaining of prima facie proof is the end. When such proof has been obtained, the police case is complete; it is ready for trial and passes on to its next stage. It is indeed desirable as a general rule that an arrest should not be made until the case is complete. But if arrest before that were forbidden it could seriously hamper the police. To give power to arrest on reasonable suspicion does not mean that it is always or even ordinarily to be exercised. It means that there is an executive discretion. In the exercise of it many factors have to be considered besides the strength of the case.

11.4.4 Timing of an arrest

Usually, the sooner suspects are arrested, the less chance or opportunity they have for destroying or contaminating evidence or witnesses, plus there may be financial and resource benefits in reducing costs from lengthy investigations. A duty of care for safeguarding the welfare and safety of the general public needs to be taken into account also.

If there is an opportunity to make an *early arrest* based on available information then usually it should be made. This is simply because the closer to the time the offence was committed that the arrest is made, the more opportunity there is to recover forensic evidence or any other useful items or material. It also prevents the offender from concocting an alibi, threatening potential witnesses, destroying evidence, or committing further offences. It is also a good tactic for providing victim and/or community reassurance, increasing trust and confidence in the police service and preventing any temptation for people 'taking the law into their own hands'.

The SIO should determine the most advantageous time and place to make an arrest which will depend entirely on the circumstances. There are a number of matters that could influence that decision, for example, the SIO may wish to coincide an arrest operation with a tactic to try and approach potential witnesses, who hitherto the arrest of a suspect(s) may have been withholding their information for a variety of reasons, eg fear of intimidation.

A further point, however, is that the 'golden hour(s)' principle supports a view that offenders are at their most vulnerable nearest to the time of the offence, and more likely to make mistakes or admissions when interviewed. This is when they are less able to claim they 'cannot remember' what they were doing or where they were at the material time, especially if the time lapse between offence and arrest is minimal.

Case study

In a murder investigation following a violent attack on a victim who was severely beaten about the head and body, the identity of the suspect was made public via the news media. This was a bold decision taken by the SIO and incorporated into a personal police appeal for a particular named individual to hand himself in at the earliest opportunity. The tactic paid off as the following day he presented himself with his solicitor at a police station, whereupon he

> was arrested and charged with the murder. The SIO's policy decision to use this tactic was justified on the basis that the suspect had a violent history and was considered a danger to the public. There were also concerns about revenge attacks by the victim's family and friends who were actively seeking to do him serious harm.

The Core Investigative Doctrine contains practical advice on determining the timing of an arrest. It states:

> . . .The decision about timing depends on a number of factors. These factors should be kept under continuous review. If the circumstances should alter, the decision to make an immediate arrest or to delay it may have to be amended and the reasons for this recorded.
>
> These factors are:
>
> - Does the suspect pose a serious risk to the safety of the victim, witnesses or the general public?
> - Is there a likelihood that the suspect will commit further or more serious offences?
> - Is the suspect likely to destroy, conceal or falsify evidence that will obstruct the investigation?
> - Is further surveillance or other covert means of surveillance required?
>
> The timing of an arrest provides the investigator with an opportunity to plan searches of the suspect's home address (or other premises) and their vehicles. It may also provide opportunities to recover incriminating or corroborating material before it is altered, disposed of or destroyed. A search of a suspect's premises may also identify property from other offences or intelligence which can be used to identify other offenders or associates (*Practice Advice on Core Investigative Doctrine* (Centrex, 2005), 105.

There are, of course, other ways in which to conduct searches of premises without the need to make formal arrests, such as by a search warrant. Section 8 of PACE as amended by ss 113 and 114 of SOCAP provides the grounds and procedure to be followed when applying for a search warrant for an indictable offence. It also provides a power to seize certain incriminating items.

11.4.5 Delaying arrests

There are sometimes good reasons for delaying an arrest. It may, for instance, be advantageous not to arrest immediately if such a course of action would frustrate other enquiries. Delaying an arrest may reduce the need to pre-charge bail a suspect, will produce a better position to conduct a meaningful interview, and reduce any delay in bringing the case to court.

There are other reasons for delaying, for example when trying to maximize evidence-recovery opportunities. If, for example, there are multiple suspects, then it is usually preferable to arrest all simultaneously to limit the chances of their disposing of evidence after collaboration and being alerted to the police interest in them. A delay may therefore be required in order to synchronize the arrests. In other circumstances the SIO may need the suspect to remain at large to allow them unknowingly to 'assist' in gathering evidence against them, for example when conducting surveillance to locate premises or property, or to lead enquiry teams to a location where a victim or body may be held or stored.

KEY POINT

The SIO should always record their decision and reasons for making or delaying arrests in the policy file. Once an arrest is delayed it should always remain under dynamic and continuous review.

One of the dangers in delaying an arrest is that a suspect is potentially placed in a position whereby they may not be afforded their statutory rights (eg being cautioned and allowed access to independent legal advice) should they be interviewed and consequently placed at risk of implicating themselves. This must be catered for in the SIO's policy file and adequate control measures taken to prevent it happening, eg instructions that there should be no direct approach or interview by enquiry team officers. There is a further danger that the offender may commit other offences; if so, it may be difficult to justify any delay.

11.4.6 Planning and preparation for arrest, reception, and detention

Wherever practicable, before any arrest is made thorough preparation should be made beforehand, with an appropriate operational plan agreed by the SIO. The SIO should nominate a member of staff with the requisite skills, training, and experience to produce a research package containing all known details of the suspect(s), to include in addition to the usual name, date of birth, description, photograph, etc a detailed analysis of known associates and criminal background, modus operandi, and any warning indicators. This task is sometimes given to an intelligence officer/cell within the enquiry team.

The SIO should request a 'target profile' containing all this information. Depending on the circumstances of the investigation, special details may also be required. Background information on a suspect may show a link to other premises, such as where they work or frequent (eg a social club or gymnasium). These may also need to be considered for searches or location checks (eg lockers). The profile should also contain information about their previous bad character, eg outstanding case files, previous offending, current intelligence, lifestyle, associates, similar fact evidence. Interviewers may later wish to introduce this information during the interview process.

An operational order that is produced should contain identification and assessment of all risks, with accompanying control measures aimed at reducing them. The order can be structured using the nationally recognized IIMARCH formula (see below) as the basis for planning and recording the arrest tactics.

The arrest operation should include a detailed plan for making the arrest, the precise day and date (as above—timing may be very important), method of transport of the prisoner(s) to a nominated custody office, reception arrangements upon arrival, and detention and interview thereafter. The precise wording for the arrest needs to be agreed by the SIO with an officer being nominated and briefed to make the arrest. The following is a checklist of considerations.

Note: If a PIP level II interview adviser is appointed, they will require early involvement in the planning/execution process.

Checklist—Arrest, reception, and detention

- Nominate appropriate officer to make the arrest and consider who is best person to do so (eg whether this should be independent of the interviewing officer or one and the same—there can be advantages/disadvantages for both).
- Determine exact wording and powers for the arrest.

- Decide which custody suite will be used (eg convenient location and good interview and monitoring facilities).
- Consider whether separate custody offices required for different prisoners.
- Decide on mode of transport to custody office (independent officers are usually best to avoid accusations of interference en route; use a vehicle that will be searched before journey and afterwards).
- Ensure correct procedures followed for any unsolicited comments/significant statements and that they are not encouraged.
- Brief custody officer well in advance so they know suspect is expected, the reason and correct wording for the arrest, and grounds for the custody record.
- Brief any custody clerks, supervisors, or handover shifts in a similar way (may require production of custody staff handover summary document).
- Appoint officer from investigation team to act as liaison with custody office to co-ordinate all activity (particularly if multiple arrests).
- Plan for recovery of forensic exhibits and samples from the suspect and nominate people not connected with the enquiry to obtain them (*avoid any cross-contamination—sterile areas/cells may be required*).
- Ensure swabbing and sampling kits are available for use with the suspect (eg firearms residue kits).
- Plan for recovery of prisoner's clothing and ensure there are replacements available.
- Consider suspect's religious beliefs/faith considerations and plan for appropriate replacement clothing, dietary and religious requirements, or texts.
- Plan for medical examination of suspect and brief/debrief the surgeon involved (request body mapping on a diagram).
- Plan for early photographing of suspect for injuries or unusual features.
- Plan for fingerprinting of suspect.
- Plan for collection of any special samples (eg firearms residue, DNA swabs, pollen).
- Ensure adequate communications link between arresting officers, custody suite, and incident room; so SIO can monitor progress.

- Ensure all details of information provided by detainee (eg addresses, intimation details) and possessions are relayed back to SIO for appropriate decisions (eg mobile phone examination, house/vehicle key checks, diaries etc).
- Arrange home address search strategy and consideration of treatment as crime scene (if not done already), and any other linked addresses of interest.
- Obtain early background/cultural details on prisoner (intelligence cell task) and stipulate requirements (eg any link to victim, crime location, other known places frequented that may need to be searched).
- Consider family liaison strategy, media, and community impact re details and news of the arrest.

Case study—Prisoner transportation

A suspect who returned to the crime scene as an onlooker was arrested and conveyed to the police station in an unmarked CID vehicle. Clothing taken from him later forensically linked him to the crime scene. The defence team requested production and examination of the police vehicle logbook used to transport the suspect, which was found not to have been completed correctly for the time/date in question. They contested the police could not prove the sterility and integrity of the vehicle and transportation process; therefore someone else who had been to the scene could have left the forensic traces in the car. The mistake of not completing the vehicle logbook proved to be a costly issue and undermined the forensic evidence in the case.

11.4.7 IIMARCH briefing method

The strategic planning for the arrest operation is a key element and start of the whole process. The acronym IIMARCH (pronounced 'aye aye march') provides a useful template and framework for producing an 'operational order' containing all the essential information, policy, and procedures from which to brief the staff. It should contain all the essential instructions and details in a logical sequence and ensure every team member is aware of the tasks and role they will perform. This serves as a permanent record and should be used and referred to during a briefing by the officer in charge of the operation (eg SIO). It should be retained in the major incident room and registered on HOLMES2 as a document.

Here is an outline of the IIMARCH format with brief examples to illustrate the meaning of terms:

IIMARCH operational order

I Information	Use of 5 × WH + H in order to brief fully on all pertinent circumstances. To include details of suspect research work (description, warnings, vehicles, associates, etc) and addresses being targeted.
I Intention	The intention should list the aims and objectives of the operation, which should be in accordance with the SIO's strategy (eg locate and arrest named suspect and search address for trace evidence, etc).
M Method	The method should outline the roles and responsibilities of all personnel involved in the operation and how it is to be conducted (eg premises to be secured front and back, then entry gained by force if necessary). Entry and search by warrant. Nominated team to effect arrest, conduct initial prisoner search, and convey to custody office by uniform prisoner van, etc).
A Administration	Should contain all the logistical arrangements for the operation (eg warrant to be obtained under PACE and suspect to be arrested on suspicion of (offence details and powers)). Silver control room to be run from major incident room, OIC (eg SIO/DSIO) (include start times, (de) briefing times and location, vehicles, equipment, overtime). (RIPA authorities).
R Risk Assessment	Details of all associated risks plus control strategies eg *risk* = violent criminal background of suspect, *control strategy* = all officers to be safety trained and wear protective body armour, carry batons and CS spray.

IIMARCH operational order (continued)

C	**Communications**	For example, airwaves radios to be used on dedicated Channel 5. Individual mobile phone numbers listed in Appendix 1.
H	**Health and Safety**	This should include any additional issues such as instructions not to climb onto a roof or use ladders to go in lofts without appropriate training.

KEY POINT

All staff involved in the arrest operation must be properly briefed and fully understand their role—there should be no ambiguities. If during the course of the operation it becomes necessary to interfere or breach any aspects of the Articles contained within the European Convention for Human Rights, this needs to be recognized in the order stating the Article affected, the legal power, and the rationale for the decision.

11.5 Legal Powers and Considerations upon Arrest

Code C of PACE provides legal guidelines for the detention, treatment, and questioning of persons in police custody by police officers. A quick checklist of the important ones for the SIO to consider and be aware of is as follows:

Checklist—PACE detention considerations

- Rules regarding 'significant statements' (see also Chapter 4).
- Right not to be held incommunicado.
- Right to legal advice.
- Citizens of independent Commonwealth countries or foreign nationals.
- Conditions of detention/care and treatment.
- When a caution should be given.
- Interviews/interview records and urgent interviews with vulnerable suspects.

- Use of interpreters.
- Reviews and extensions of detention.
- Charging detained persons.
- Testing for presence of specified Class A drugs.
- Intimate and strip searches (Annex A).
- Delay in notifying arrest or allowing access to legal advice (Annex B).
- Restriction on drawing adverse inferences from silence (Annex C).
- Written statements under caution (Annex D).
- Provisions relating to mentally disordered and otherwise mentally vulnerable people (Annex E).
- Countries with which bilateral consular conventions or agreements requiring notification of the arrest and detention of their nationals are in force (Annex F).

KEY POINT

The arrest and detention of suspects may provide investigative opportunities that are catered for under Part III of the Police Act 1997 and Part II and s 26(3) of the Regulation of Investigatory Powers Act 2000. These should, wherever possible, be planned well in advance and the relevant resources and authorities arranged.

11.6 Treating the Suspect as a Crime Scene

Each and every suspect must be treated as a potential crime scene and is a source of vital evidence to prove or disprove their involvement in the offence. The time scales between incident and arrest will of course vary in each case; however, the sooner the arrest and detention, the better in terms of evidence recovery. Crucial forensic material can come from the suspect and therefore it is vital to arrange for the recovery of their clothing, footwear, and other samples as quickly as possible.

Apart from obvious fingerprints, DNA, and recovery of clothing and footwear, the suspect can provide a wealth of forensic evidence, from transfer of hair, blood, semen, paint, soil, gunshot residue, glass fragments, fibres, pollen, etc. The SIO needs to make the most of evidence recovery opportunities that may link a suspect to a crime scene.

Sometimes it may be necessary to obtain these samples or seize clothing at the point of arrest, rather than wait until arrival at the police station. Firearms discharge residue in particular needs to be recovered as soon as possible after a firearms-related incident, and in some cases the covering of exposed areas such as the suspect's hands is necessary to increase the likelihood of success. The SIO should take advice on all forensic recovery issues and contamination avoidance from a CSM/CSI before planning the arrests.

As a minimum standard, all the suspect's clothing and footwear should be screened for blood. Other considerations may be swabbing for gunshot residue from hands. It is best practice for a suspect to be medically examined by a police doctor upon arrival at a police station. Checks should be made for any cuts, scratches, or other injuries (eg marks on the hand from the recoil firing mechanism of a semi-automatic handgun) which may link them to the crime. A full body map profile should be completed and any marks found should be photographed.

Note: The planning process should include checks to ensure all the necessary swabbing and sampling kits are plentiful and readily available in the custody suite where the suspect is to be detained. An Exhibits Officer should be tasked with preparing all the necessary kits, forms and equipment required in advance.

KEY POINTS

1. It is worthwhile ensuring any suicide deaths found post-incident have their full details (eg DNA, fingerprints, and description of deceased) sent to the enquiry team for comparison against any outstanding and known suspect details. A strategy to capture this information needs to provide for adequate notification of offenders who, after committing the offence may decide to take their own life, particularly if they do so in locations far enough away from the area in which the incident is under investigation.
2. If suspects have clothing brought into a custody office for them, it must be checked to see if it is what any of the searches (eg home address) are looking for.

11.6.1 Legal powers—taking samples from suspects in custody

Intimate samples

Section 62 of PACE creates a power to take intimate samples from a person in police detention. Examples include anal swab, pubic hair, nose swab, wound swab, penile swab, urine.

(1) Subject to section 63B an intimate sample may be taken from a person in police detention only:
(a) if a police officer of at least the rank of inspector authorizes it to be taken
(b) if the appropriate consent is given.

(1A) An intimate sample may be taken from a person who is not in police detention but from whom, in the course of the investigation of an offence, two or more non-intimate samples suitable for the same means of analysis have been taken which have proved insufficient:
(a) if a police officer of at least the rank of inspector authorizes it to be taken; and
(b) if the appropriate consent is given.

...

(6) The duty imposed by subsection (5)(ii) above includes a duty to state the nature of the offence in which it is suspected that the person from whom the sample is to be taken has been involved.

(9) In the case of an intimate sample which is a dental impression, the sample may be taken from a person only by a registered dentist.

...

(9A) In the case of any other form of intimate sample, except in the case of a sample of urine, the sample may be taken from a person only by:
(a) a registered medical practitioner; or
(b) a registered health care professional.

If consent is refused without due cause, then in any subsequent proceedings adverse inferences may be drawn by a court, judge, or jury (s 62(10)).

The suspect must be made aware of the possible consequences and be reminded of his entitlement to free legal advice.

Non-intimate samples

Section 63 of PACE as amended by s 10 and Sch 37 of the Criminal Justice Act 2003 provides powers relating to the taking of non-intimate samples. Examples include saliva, head hair, mouth swab, nail cuttings.

(1) Except as provided by this section, a non-intimate sample may not be taken from a person without the appropriate consent.
(2) Consent to the taking of a non-intimate sample must be given in writing.
(2A) A non-intimate sample may be taken from a person without the appropriate consent if two conditions are satisfied.
(2B) The first is that the person is in police (or SOCA) detention in consequence of his arrest for a recordable offence.
(2C) The second is that—
  (a) he has not had a non-intimate sample of the same type and from the same part of the body taken in the course of the investigation of the offence by the police or SOCA, or
  (b) he has had such a sample taken but it proved insufficient.
(3) A non-intimate sample may be taken from a person without the appropriate consent if—
  (a) he is being held in custody by the police [or SOCA] on the authority of a court; and
  (b) an officer of at least the rank of inspector authorizes it to be taken without the appropriate consent.
(3A) A non-intimate sample may be taken from a person (whether or not he is in police detention or held in custody by the police (or SOCA) on the authority of a court) without the appropriate consent if—
  (a) he has been charged with a recordable offence or informed that he will be reported for such an offence; and
  (b) either he has not had a non-intimate sample taken from him in the course of the investigation of the offence by the police (or SOCA) or he has had a non-intimate sample taken from him but either it was not suitable for the same means of analysis or, though so suitable, the sample proved insufficient.
(3B) A non-intimate sample may be taken from a person without the appropriate consent if he has been convicted of a recordable offence.
(4) An officer may give an authorisation under subsection (3) only if he has reasonable grounds—
  (a) for suspecting the involvement of the person from whom the sample is to be taken; and
  (b) for believing that the sample will tend to confirm or disprove his involvement.

...

(7) The duty imposed by subsection (6)(ii) includes a duty to state the nature of the offence in which it is suspected that the person from whom the sample is to be taken has been involved.

Note: The Criminal Justice Act 2003 expanded police powers to re-take DNA samples without consent from detainees provided the two conditions in 63(2B) and (2C) are complied with.

11.7 Custody Time Limits, and Warrants of Further Detention

In the planning and preparation phase the SIO needs to anticipate how long the detention proceedings are likely to take in order to plan for exceeding custody time limits. It should be established in advance which (PACE) duty senior officers are likely to be tasked with the responsibility of considering extending any custody time limits and/or authorizing the taking of intimate samples, so they can be fully briefed and prepared with the facts of the case and likely requirements.

Experience suggests that custody time limits need very close monitoring throughout the entire period of detention. It is helpful to produce a live-running 'time line' of events and activities for each and every detainee and to nominate a person to assume responsibility for monitoring and updating it. Ideally this will be the same person who is nominated to supervise and manage the detention and interview process on behalf of the SIO to ensure everything is managed and co-ordinated efficiently. This information can be used as the basis for any warrant of further detention hearings to show how enquiries are being progressed diligently and expeditiously.

When dealing with warrants of further detention, wherever practicable the SIO should appear in person to make the application. If this task is delegated to someone else the person who attends court to apply for the warrants must be properly briefed by the SIO, and made aware of all the circumstances of the investigation and any likely areas of contention. It is very important, particularly if they are someone who is not directly involved with the investigation, that they are involved in team briefings post arrest and kept updated on any evidential finds or intelligence updates. It may also be useful to have the interview adviser present when the warrants of further detention hearing takes place. It should be remembered, however, that during these hearings the defence team may wish to extract information from the investigation team that has not yet been declared in an interview. This may be because it has been withheld as part of an interview strategy. A tactical response may have to be anticipated in advance.

Note: In order to avoid multiple suspects all hearing the evidence against each other, the SIO may wish to consider requesting separate hearings for each detainee.

11.8 **Interviews with Suspects**

This is a vital part of the arrest and detention strategy after having made the arrests and completed all other necessary considerations. The SIO must *play an active role* in not only the devising of a suitable interview plan but also its implementation, and consideration should be given to using the services of a trained PIP level II Interview Adviser and PIP accredited interviewers (see table in Chapter 10).

The SIO needs to be satisfied about the appropriate selection of officers who will be conducting the interview(s). It should not just be a case of choosing someone who is trained and 'next in line' for doing a complex interview, but rather choosing people based upon their suitability. Reserve officers should also be chosen in the event of unforeseen circumstances.

This interview process is an area where very detailed and careful planning is required. A briefing should be provided to the interview teams (particularly if they are not completely conversant with the investigation), and if necessary they should visit the crime scene to familiarize themselves with it. This may be of assistance if admissions are made or detail provided by the suspect that requires an appreciation of significant locations.The PEACE acronym is used as the basis for structuring interviews and is worthy of mention once more:

P	Planning and preparation
E	Engage and explain
A	Account, clarify, and challenge
C	Closure
E	Evaluation

The aims and objectives for the interview should be determined. These can be separated into 'phases' if there are different areas to cover. Separate objectives should be set for each phase. For example, if there is DNA evidence that puts the suspect with the victim, the aim of the first phase of the interview may be to see whether the offender denies ever being in company with the victim. When the DNA evidence is revealed during later phases of the interview it makes it much more difficult for the offender to allege innocent contact with the victim.

All disclosure items need to be agreed and decided and the structure and timing of the disclosure process may be crucial to getting the most out of the interviews. Whenever vital evidence is put to the suspect (eg witness evidence, DNA, or fingerprint evidence at a scene), the timing, method, and wording of any disclosure will be extremely important. The SIO should consider appointing a separate disclosure officer to deal specifically with all the disclosure for the interview and thus take away this onerous responsibility from the interviewing officers.

The process should be fine-tuned to ensure everyone involved knows what the interview plan is. If necessary it could be rehearsed by the interview teams to the SIO's satisfaction, with suitable individuals playing out the roles of suspect and solicitor.

It is good practice to 'downstream' monitor the interviews on a visual or audio link, depending on what is available. Suitable custody facilities should have been chosen that provide the best possible resources. The SIO and Interview Adviser (if applicable) should be within easy reach of the interview location so that any matters arising or developments can be easily and speedily discussed.

The interview plan must remain flexible throughout the process and this is why the SIO needs to be involved in monitoring the process. It may be important to review, restructure, and amend the interview plan as things progress because of things said by the suspect or admissions made, or changing attitudes and opportunities. Recent interview-training methods tend to focus on delaying all 'challenges' (as per the PEACE model) towards the end of the interview. This may not always be the best tactic if there is an opportunity to put a good point across at the right time in order to make the most impact at the right time of any available evidence or material.

Case study—Timing of challenges

A 20-year-old female being interviewed for a fatal assault was being strongly defended by her solicitor who was advising her to say 'no comment' throughout the interviews. There was some witness evidence from one of her associates stating she had not been where she said she was at the time of the incident. This was being saved until the 'challenges' phase. The SIO changed the initial strategy after sensing the female wanted to tell the truth and the evidence was put to her earlier than originally planned. The solicitor tried to intervene but when the suspect heard the contents of the evidence she began making tearful admissions about the offence. The SIO was concerned that had they waited any longer the suspect would have been more able to cope with resisting challenges to her original false account and that her solicitor was trying to 'run down' the custody time clock.

Note: A Behavioural Investigative Adviser (BIA) and/or clinical psychologist from the NPIA can be requested to help formulate the interview strategy and help in the monitoring process, advising the SIO on how to get the best out of the interview. See <http://www.npia.police.uk/cos>.

KEY POINTS

1. If a suspect is arrested at such a time when it is impossible to have pre-planned or prepared for a structured interview, or due to the time and nature of the arrest it would be some time before such an interview could take place, it may be necessary to obtain an initial account. This is so that the detainee gets an early opportunity to provide a version of events under caution (with a legal representative if required), and in case they wish to make admissions/denials or impart information for which a delay would cause unnecessary inconvenience. This is a key decision for the SIO and may be vital in certain circumstances, eg if a suspect is arrested late at night and there is no prepared interview team available until the following day.
2. An initial or early interview may be necessary and justifiable as a 'safety interview'. This may apply in circumstances where there are concerns for public safety and information is required urgently from the detainee, such as details of outstanding dangerous offenders, substances or weapons, or the location of any victims who could be rescued.

Note: A planned and structured interview can still be completed at a later stage when it is more convenient to do so.

Whenever possible the SIO should have enquiry teams available (ie on standby) and for the incident room to remain open with access to HOLMES2 during the interview stage. This is so that any information received or comments made can be researched and fast-track actions conducted as the interviews take place. It may be important to speak to witnesses while the suspect is still in custody and prevent any collaboration, for example where alibi details are provided.

11.8.1 Aide memoire for a suspect interview plan

This is not an exhaustive list, but rather an outline of the considerations for interviews with suspects that SIOs, interview advisers, and interview teams should consider.

Checklist—Suspect interview plan

- Full briefing and/or scene visit for interview officers.
- Nature of allegation considered and 'points to prove'.
- Noting any 'significant statements'/pre-interview comments.
- Checking custody records for relevant information on suspect.
- Obtain and consider records of other interviews with suspect(s).
- Consider any medical/psychological issues.
- Have awareness of suspect's domestic/background circumstances.
- Note previous involvement with police and previous criminal convictions.
- Previous/current involvement with other agencies.
- Obtain photos/maps/CCTV, etc of relevance for use during interview.
- Review and assimilate evidence/information/intelligence/disclosure.
- Familiarize with exhibits required for interview and sign labels for continuity.
- Review arrest strategy (impact on interview process).
- Consider any relevant forensic strategies.
- Note any requirements for an 'appropriate adult'.
- Identify witness status (vulnerable/intimidated/significant) and the impact on them of disclosing their evidence.
- Consider whether use of interpreters appropriate.
- Prioritize interviews (multiple suspects).

- Determine method of recording suspect interview (visually/audio).
- Obtain necessary resources (staff/equipment).
- Determine time and location of interview(s).
- Set specific and realistic objectives.
- Consider all PACE issues (custody times/refreshment breaks, etc).
- Identify appropriate interview model (PEACE/Advanced).
- Determine pace of interview, estimate number of sessions.
- Identify areas for clarification (SIO agenda).
- Determine content and format of pre-interview briefing (legal adviser).
- Delivery format of pre-interview briefing (audio/written/oral).
- Consider use and timing of 'special warnings'.
- Determine 'no comment' or 'prepared statement' interview strategy.
- Monitoring of interviews ('downstream').
- Set interview plan and prepare all necessary notes and documentation.
- Determine whether separate interview required for evidence of 'bad character' (under 'previous misconduct' provisions of Criminal Justice Act 2003).
- Note any post-interview comment(s).

11.8.2 Aide-memoire for post-interview considerations

- Debrief interview team(s).
- Analyse and evaluate interview process.
- Analyse and evaluate information from interview(s).
- Assess what impact any information provided has on the enquiry.
- Ensure any necessary fast-track action(s)/further enquiries undertaken.
- Provide constructive feedback to interview team(s).
- Consider further interview strategies.
- Consider further pre-briefing strategies.
- Consider welfare of suspect/interview team(s).
- Consider identification procedures.
- Maintain close liaison with CPS.

11.9 Pro-Active Hunts for Suspects

In some circumstances it may require a large amount of time, effort, and resources to locate and arrest a suspect(s). This is particularly so when there are a large number of offenders involved in the offence under investigation and/or the suspect(s) is/are deemed to be dangerous.

It may be worthwhile for the SIO to consider nominating a suitable deputy to take responsibility for a pro-active arrest operation. This could be the deputy SIO, a senior detective, or another SIO brought in specifically for this task. There is usually a lot of work involved in organizing and managing this proactive part of an enquiry and it may be too much added workload for the SIO to cope with single-handedly at the same time as running the rest of the investigation.

In extreme cases it may be necessary to treat the offender search and arrest as a 'crime in action', similar to the way in which some kidnaps and counter-terrorism operations are managed. If the crime is one that has attracted major public and media attention, and there is a risk to public safety (which is always an overriding consideration), the necessity to swiftly find and arrest the suspect(s), if known, will be of paramount importance.

In proactive arrest operations (particularly those engaged in the hunt for dangerous and/or armed suspects) large amounts of assets and resources may be required, such as surveillance teams, arrest and search teams, firearms tactical intervention teams, intelligence cells, specialist telecommunications advisers, co-ordinators from other forces and regions, and managed media campaigns. Such major operations will require dynamic consequence management of media and community impact. A silver control room with a designated gold commander is likely to be required with the SIO or their nominated deputy playing a key role in all gold group meetings and decisions and maintaining responsibility for any arrest tactics (eg evidence recovery and suspect processing, etc) once an arrest is made. These operations require fast-time control, management, and instant decision making and the necessary command structure, assets, and resources need to be in place. In large-scale operations of this nature more than one deputy SIO may be required to provide added 24/7 resilience.

If a proactive hunt takes on these epic proportions it is easy to understand why the SIO with responsibility for the investigation will require extra resilience themselves. If firearms are a consideration because there is a possibility they may be used or carried by a suspect(s), then a firearms tactical adviser and independent accredited firearms silver commander will most certainly be required to command and manage the tactical firearms operation (and in some instances authorize the use of firearms in spontaneous emergency situations). Planning and preparation for any 'strike arrests' must be fully co-ordinated and the SIO or deputy will need to work closely with and directly alongside a firearms silver commander

KEY POINTS

1. In any proactive operation to trace and arrest suspects, particularly when the suspects are believed to be armed and/or dangerous, public safety is always the most important overriding consideration followed closely by officer safety and lastly the safety of the suspects themselves.
2. Contingency plans need to be made for when arrest(s) are made, such as a nominated hospital for suspects who are in need of treatment and a risk assessment indicates they require an armed round-the-clock police guard to protect them from rivals or vigilante groups. (Note: this may also apply to witnesses who need to be protected once an arrest is made.)

11.10 National Interview Adviser

In complex cases involving multiple suspects or where witness testimony is likely to be the key, the services of the National Interview Adviser and their cadre of deputies is available. They can provide advice and guidance on the interviewing of suspects, victims, and witnesses across a broad range of criminality with particular reference to PACE Codes and national standards. This includes:

- advice and support in establishing interview strategies;
- advice and support regarding planning and preparing interviews;
- analysis of interviews;
- analysis of written statements;
- debriefing of overall interview process.

The adviser works closely with SIOs and interviewing officers to develop bespoke interview strategies. They also contribute to the implementation of the ACPO Investigative Interviewing Strategy, incorporating development of the Professionalising Investigations Programme (PIP), and the delivery of training (see <http://www.npia.police.uk/soc>, or email <soc@npia.pnn.police.uk> or tel. 0845 000 5463).

11.11 Conclusion

Making arrests and charging offenders is a major objective for an enquiry team. This chapter illustrates that there are a lot of important decisions to be made once a suspect is identified and before an arrest is made. Strategic and tactical planning are key elements for the whole process. The chapter has covered a wide range of associated topics, such as suspect identification and status, operational planning for making arrests, legal powers, forensic examination, and investigative interviewing.

Any suspect strategy should always incorporate these tactical phases, which are generally chronological in order, to make the most out of the opportunities presented. The phases can and do sometimes overlap and, as the next phase begins, the previous one does not necessarily end. The golden rule is for the SIO to ensure careful planning and preparation is completed in order to increase the likelihood of success. Conducting a thorough arrest and detention operation will undoubtedly reap rewards for the SIO and their enquiry team when dealing with suspects.

Further reading

P Ozin, H Norton, and P Spivry, *PACE 1984: A Pratical Guide* (Blackstone, OUP, 2006).

Chapter 12
Forensic Pathology and the Role of Coroners

12.1 Introduction

When dealing with unexplained, unnatural, or suspicious deaths and murders, the SIO relies upon a significant contribution from a forensic pathologist. A deceased person is not in any position to offer up any information as to how they met their death; fortunately their physical bodies are still a wealth of information and forensic evidence. They become an important crime scene for the collection of forensic samples and pathological evidence that assist in determining the cause and manner of death.

If there is any doubt or ambiguity surrounding the cause and manner of death, pathology is pivotal in helping reach conclusions. Worrying or aggravating factors at a scene need expertly interpreting and contextualizing, such as unexplained blood around the deceased. A pathologist will help determine what may have been the cause, for example whether linked to natural phenomena, accidental death, suicide, or even homicide.

In some circumstances the deceased's lifestyle or environmental factors can complicate the investigation. Detached limbs, badly burnt bodies, potential 'human'/animal remains, bones, badly decomposed or fragmented bodies can leave very limited material for a pathological examination or finding trace evidence. The deaths of alcoholics, drug abusers, homeless people, persons who have suffered numerous accidental or self-inflicted injuries, or those with mental illnesses often create an impression their death is suspicious based on the general condition of the body or the circumstances in which the body was found. Some persons are generally untidy or unhealthy and create an appearance of some degree of violent attack due to their lifestyles which confounds and confuses the investigation.

Therefore the forensic and pathological examination of a body or body part is a crucial part of the investigative process. The purpose of this chapter is to clarify the roles of the SIO, pathologist, and coroner; also to provide practical guidance on processes and body recovery, the autopsy process and recovery of forensic evidence from the deceased.

12.2 Pathology Explained

The word pathology derives from the Greek words for disease and knowledge. In modern usage, pathology means the scientific study of disease. Pathology is a wide-ranging medical specialism and includes microbiologists, haematologists, chemical pathologists, and immunologists. However, as far as the SIO is concerned there are predominantly two categories of pathologists involved in post-mortem examinations—histopathologists and forensic pathologists.

Histopathology is primarily concerned in making diagnoses from the study of human tissue ('histos' is the Greek word for tissue). This includes the examination of biopsy material from living patients and the examination of the deceased to establish why they died. The latter (forensic pathologists) have additional training and expertise enabling them to examine traumatic or unnatural deaths and present their findings appropriately to the Criminal Justice System (CJS).

12.3 The Role of the Forensic Pathologist

Traditionally in the UK forensic pathologists were called Home Office pathologists, because they were registered with the Home Office. Recently this term has been dropped in favour of consultant Home Office registered forensic pathologists. However, many judges, juries, and lay people will probably still know and understand the older terminology.

Clearly, amongst all other professionals who assist in the investigation into suspicious deaths, the forensic pathologist holds a pivotal role in determining the cause and manner of death.

It follows that there must be close liaison between the pathologist and the SIO, particularly in the early stages of the investigation. There are a significant number of deaths initially investigated as suspicious that eventually turn out to result from suicide, accident, or natural causes. This will not usually become clear until after the post-mortem examination.

An SIO needs to know how to get the information out of the pathologist rather than the SIO having to know about pathology. Nevertheless, pathologists will often use complex medical terminology which may seem confusing for police personnel. Therefore it is best to ask the pathologist to explain his/her findings in clear terms. The SIO should never leave the mortuary or crime scene without fully understanding and being able to explain to others the pathologist's opinions.

The principal role of the forensic pathologist is to determine the cause of death, and as far as possible provide information as to how the death occurred. In England and Wales a post-mortem examination is in fact conducted on behalf of Her Majesty's coroner, or the procurator fiscal in Scotland. The information gained from the examination is obviously extremely useful to assist a police investigation.

The investigation of a suspicious death involves two separate components. The role of the coroner is to identify the deceased and establish cause of death where possible. The role of the police is to investigate any criminal offence that may have occurred. The forensic pathologist is involved in both these investigations. Therefore the forensic pathologist is acting under the authority of, and on behalf of, the coroner but provides evidence and guidance to the police to assist with the criminal investigation.

A forensic pathologist is a medically qualified doctor who is an expert in identifying the patterns of natural disease and unnatural trauma in the human body and uses their skills and knowledge to assist investigations and the legal process. The pathologist is essentially a medical adviser and potential expert witness. Consequently the SIO and pathologist work as a close team, while maintaining the professional integrity and impartiality of the forensic pathologist.

In a living patient the doctor can usually ask the patient about the presentation of the disease and their symptoms: this is known as the history. However, the forensic pathologist cannot rely upon the deceased to provide a history of their symptoms. Therefore they have to rely upon other sources to provide the missing information.

In practice a forensic pathologist should be available on a call-out basis, 24 hours a day, seven days a week, 365 days a year and their role is outlined as follows.

Checklist—The role of a forensic pathologist

- Attend scenes, liaise with police officers and CSIs, forensic scientists, and other such experts (eg fire investigators).
- Make observations at the scene of the body and the context in which it has been found.
- Assist with identification of a body.
- Assist with the estimation of time of death.
- Contribute to the formulation of a forensic strategy to maximize evidence recovery from the body, including prior to removal to the mortuary.
- Advise on what samples should be taken from the body in conjunction with the CSI/CSM.
- Advise on a strategy for removal of a body to the mortuary.
- Advise on what samples should be taken from people dying in hospital.
- Carry out full external and internal examination of bodies and co-ordinate the imaging of any wounds or injuries with a scale by a photographer.
- Advise on what additional tests are required before, during, and after the post mortem, eg X-rays, histology, toxicology, ballistics etc.
- Provide information that will help the SIO initiate early lines of enquiry.
- Advise on health and safety issues.
- Advise on what other experts may be required to assist with examinations, eg paediatrician for child cases, radiologist and/or ballistics expert for firearms and explosives cases, odontologist for dental examinations.
- Provide full briefing for SIO after post mortem and communicate provisional findings to the coroner.
- Provide a detailed witness statement to include not only cause of death but also an interpretation of circumstances surrounding the death.
- Attend briefings as and when required and meet with the prosecution team prior to trial to discuss pathological findings.
- Give oral evidence in court as and when required.

- Provide opinions on non-fatal wounds and/or suspicious circumstances.
- Attend training courses and give useful inputs, etc.

KEY POINTS

- The first priority is always the preservation of life. Saving a victim is the first consideration before requesting confirmation of death by a medical expert. In most cases this is completed well before a pathologist arrives.
- If there is any doubt or ambiguity as to cause or manner of death a pathologist should always be requested because of their expertise in interpreting circumstances, injuries, marks, medical conditions, and crime scenes.
- If unsure after the pathologist attends a scene it remains an option to keep the scene secure and sterile until the result of the post-mortem examination is known. If something is revealed indicating an offence has taken place the crime scene remains available for further examination and consideration (and is recommended as *best practice*).
- The SIO has ultimate authority and control of the scene and the victim's body. It is their decision if and when to call a pathologist, though it should first be discussed with the coroner as only they can authorize a post mortem.

12.3.1 Determining cause and manner of death (COD/MOD)

From an investigative perspective, the medical *cause of death* (COD) is the pathological condition which caused the death; the *manner of death* (MOD) is the instrument, physical agent, or other means used. It is important to distinguish the medical cause of death from the manner of death, which is the determination of the circumstances surrounding the death. For instance, a medical cause of death could be a head injury but the manner may be from a gunshot wound, road traffic collision, hit with a baseball bat, fall off a building etc.

Note: If the case results in an inquest the coroner will also provide a verdict on the death. See 'Role of Coroner' at 12.10 below.

Clearly the medical cause of death and any pathological interpretation as to the manner of death will play a crucial role, either in the verdict determined by the coroner or the outcome of any subsequent criminal proceedings. However, the pathologist may not always be able to determine the manner of death. For example, in a case where a cause of death is determined by the pathologist, eg as a head injury, the manner of death may have to be determined by a coroner's verdict aided by a police investigation. The conclusion could be that there was a fall without third party involvement and verdict of misadventure (eg a person who falls down a flight of stairs); or alternatively unlawful killing from being deliberately pushed (although from a pathological perspective it is usually impossible to determine whether someone has fallen or was pushed, and therefore this evidence may have to come from elsewhere, eg a witness or an admission). This illustrates that sometimes, to establish the manner of death, a combination of a police investigation and pathological findings is needed to complete the evidential picture.

Case study—Cause and manner of death

A male's body was found lying on the car park of some industrial premises next to a disused warehouse. The deceased was found to have extensive injuries and the pathologist was able to give a cause of death as severe trauma to the head and body. The police investigation showed the male had left a suicide note and some possessions at the top of a fire escape adjacent to where the body was found, and a friend was traced whom he had told the day before that he intended to jump off the building and commit suicide. This meant the police enquiry was able to provide the necessary evidence to prove the manner of death, and the pathological examination the cause of death.

12.3.2 Attendance at a crime scene

Attendance and assessment of a crime scene will enable the pathologist to set the post-mortem findings in context. Having a pathologist at the scene also facilitates a good team approach and their advice will be vitally important when formulating body- and evidence-recovery strategies. The early interaction between pathologist, CSI/CSM, other experts, and the SIO will form a solid platform from which to launch the investigation.

Initially the pathologist (and any other experts summoned) will require a briefing about the facts of the case. It is usual for the SIO to contact them personally (ie by telephone) and fully explain the circumstances and reasons for requesting their attendance. This will also allow the pathologist to suggest initial strategies for managing evidential recovery from the body. The pathologist may also suggest bringing in other experts, for instance an entomologist, or anthropologist at an early stage, allowing the SIO to work out a co-ordinated time scale for all the experts to arrive simultaneously.

KEY POINT

Pathologists usually like to speak to the person in charge and experience shows it is not good practice to get someone else to contact the pathologist on behalf of the SIO, particularly if it is in the early hours of the morning!

If other important matters need attention before an approach can be made to the body, such as searches for offenders or initial scene assessment, such a delay can cause the pathologist and/or other experts to be waiting around unnecessarily. It must be remembered that the pathologist will have to conduct a post mortem at some later stage and they will need the necessary resilience and time in order to do so. Provided the fact of death has been medically confirmed and scene preservation arrangements put into place (eg a suitable tent covering the body if out of doors) there is sometimes no need to rush into approaching or removing the body, so the request for a pathologist may not be that urgent. However, persons in custody awaiting interview or dangerous crime scenes may also be issues to consider as well as an early indication as to likely cause of death if it is not obvious.

Points to cover in an initial briefing should include the following.

Checklist—Pathologist initial briefing

Provide details of:

- Who the SIO is.
- Who the CSI and CSM are and details of any other specialists who will be attending.
- Where the incident is believed to have occurred (and where the body is if different) and details of any known health and safety hazards.
- When the incident is believed to have occurred and any other significant times, eg last sighting of victim, time of discovery, time certified dead, and by whom.

- Who the deceased is (identity, medical and social history (if known).
- What the circumstances of the incident are.
- Why the death is being treated as suspicious.
- What has happened since body discovery (eg any disturbance by members of the public, initial officers attending, or medical staff).
- What relevant material or information will be available and whether they can have access to it, eg CCTV footage, witness statements or reliable intelligence.
- What is known about any injuries on the victim or weapon details.
- What the condition of the body was when discovered (rigor mortis, decomposition, insect activity, etc).
- What other assessments from other experts have been made.
- What the scope and priorities of the investigation are.
- What time they are required to attend and where (eg scene, RVP, or police station)
- Where the major incident room is located.
- What the contact details are of all relevant individuals.
- What other details they may require.

(Note: pathologist's notes made during the process are always potentially disclosable.)

KEY POINT

The SIO should be prepared to re-brief the pathologist at such time when further information becomes available, eg CCTV recording of an attack. This includes after the post mortem has been completed, as early information inevitably changes as the investigation progresses and this allows the pathologist to review their intial findings.

12.4 Initial Strategy Meeting

Wherever practicable the SIO should arrange an initial conference for the pathologist, crime scene investigator/manager, scene photographers, and any other experts that have been requested to attend the scene such as ballistics experts, entomologists, palynologists, anthropologists, or forensic scientists. This meeting can be either: (a) at the RVP near the cordon; or (b) at some other suitable location such as a police station or mobile incident trailer or command vehicle. In either case it should always occur *before* an examination is made of the victim's body.

This is a vital meeting to discuss the circumstances and make important decisions and policies on how to enter the scene, approach the body, decide what samples are required from the body while in position and determine how the body will be recovered, packaged, removed and transported, also what imagery recording requirements are necessary (eg still photography, visual digital, or high vantage point shots). The strategy and tactics should be carefully recorded either in the SIO's policy file or in a stand-alone policy document, once agreed, and then countersigned by all those involved in the decision-making process.

12.5 Preservation of Evidence Rule

The strategy meeting must indicate what, where, when, and why samples are to be taken, who by and how. This includes any clothing that may have to be removed and the necessary packaging of the head, hands, and other exposed areas as deemed appropriate. Tapings, combings, swabs, and scrapings of exposed surfaces may be required in order to prevent contamination when the body is being physically lifted and transported to the mortuary. Bodies can and do discharge bodily fluids when disturbed which can obscure or contaminate trace evidence, particularly from open wounds and orifices. So extreme care must be taken when moving them.

KEY POINTS

- Forensic trace work on external or exposed surfaces of a body will almost certainly be carried out prior to any pathological examination. This may slow the body recovery process down and create some delay but will form part of the forensic strategy.
- If ligatures or bindings are involved—the golden rule is not to undo or cut any knot. This is to enable a 'knot expert' to be in the best possible position to examine how the binding has been constructed.

Once ready to be removed from the scene a body should be properly secured in a sealed body bag. **This body bag must not**

be opened until the SIO, CSM, and pathologist are present at the mortuary and it is agreed to do so (this is a vitally important rule, see below).

> **Case study—Body preservation**
>
> The body of a young sex worker was taken from the scene to the mortuary where a mortuary technician began 'preparing and washing the body down' for the commencement of a pathological post mortem. Although DNA swabs had been taken from the body at the scene, only the obvious exposed surfaces had been included. It was not until the body was closely examined at the mortuary that a bite mark was revealed on the victim's right forearm, but it was then too late to swab for DNA. The external surfaces had been contaminated in the preparatory 'cleaning' process. The mark later became very significant to the enquiry and an important evidence-recovery opportunity had been lost.

12.6 Continuity and Identification of a Body

A body needs to be 'identified' to the pathologist and this duty should be performed before a post mortem takes place. There has to be continuity of identification from the crime scene to the mortuary, which is achieved by someone going with the body to the mortuary in order to make an identification. A body is an important exhibit and the integrity of its handling and movement is no less important than any other key item of evidence. The identification can and should happen when the body bag is opened and immediately prior to an autopsy taking place.

Police identification is made by the person who observed the body at the scene, whereas personal identification is performed by a relative or person who knew the deceased. In practice the latter is done at the mortuary in a suitable viewing room once the external examination of the victim has been completed and all necessary external swabs and samples have been obtained. The autopsy can be halted temporarily and the viewing and identification completed. This procedure has the following benefits:

- It allows the formal identification to be completed without having to wait for the full post mortem to finish.
- It allows the relatives of the victim to have an earlier opportunity to see and identify their relative, and most are always

eager to do so at the earliest opportunity, which should be respected wherever possible.

- It allows the viewing to be made before any further medical interference with the body.
- It is an opportunity to establish positive relationships with the family.

This part of the process has to be managed sensitively and tactfully and the SIO should discuss all options and arrangements with their FLO beforehand. Other considerations may be important, such as state of the body, and distress it may cause. If the victim is a young child, and even in other cases, the family may want to touch or hold the victim. If so this will require careful planning and supervision with the pathologist and crime scene manager to ensure there is no compromise of the post mortem and forensic examination process (this topic is covered in Chapter 14).

KEY POINTS

- The post-mortem process may be a distressing experience and everyone must be reminded that a body is that of someone who is a lost relative, friend, and/or loved one. The management of deceased person's bodies requires tactful handling, including concealing the location and exit route from where it is being preserved to prevent journalists and morbid spectators viewing or taking photographs of the removal process. Body transportation should also be managed carefully, employing professional undertakers who have the correct training, skills, equipment, and vehicles to take the body to the mortuary, and displaying at all times proper respect.
- Certain religious death rites may create additional considerations, for example prohibiting males to touch deceased females, or anybody but clerics to handle the body. These are issues the SIO may need to take appropriate advice on.

12.6.1 Methods of body identification

The identification of a body is always a high priority. In most cases it is easily achieved by witnesses or when other information is received by the enquiry. Sometimes, however, the procedure is aggravated by mutilation, advanced decomposition, dismemberment, or where there are very few or no known relatives or friends in existence.

Where the identity of a victim is in doubt, there are a number of alternative methods for assisting with identification. Some of these include:

- facial identification (visual, photographs, facial reconstruction, facial image analysis, or iris recognition).
- personal effects (clothing, jewellery, spectacles, wallets, watches, keys etc);
- external physical characteristics;
- internal organs and soft tissue (eg surgical operations and body art and modification);
- odontology (teeth, gums, contents of oral cavity);
- osteology (study of the human skeleton—a sub-discipline of anthropology);
- biological samples (blood, biochemistry, toxicology, or DNA);
- prints (finger and palm prints);
- radiological imaging (for use in osteology, odontology, and facial reconstruction);
- computed tomography (ie CT scans for 2- and 3-dimensional imaging);
- podiatry (using foot analysis for diseases, walking gait, abnormalities etc);
- environmental information (specialist examinations to identify likely environment within which a person lived, eg stable isotope fingerprinting to identify geographic region, or pollen, soil, and botanical samples to do the same);
- checking missing person reports with the National Missing Persons Database (which will only be successful if the person is already on the database);
- media appeals.

(See Professor G Rutty, *Body Identification: Briefing Guide to Assist in Body Identification* (NPIA National Injuries Database, 2009).

Note: The NPIA Missing Persons Bureau can be contacted at <http://www.MissingPersonsBureau@NPIA.pnn.police.uk> or <soc@npia.pnn.police.uk>.

12.6.2 Estimating time of death (aka time since death)

This can often be a contentious area of pathology and for this reason it is preferable to rely upon factual evidence such as witness testimony of the incident itself, and/or other material such as CCTV. Nonetheless it is still an extremely valuable piece of information (and in some cases supporting evidence) and will also assist in determining TIE elimination/alibi parameters. Any estimation of time of death (whether provided by pathological means or otherwise) is used as the 'relevant time' for a whole host of vital investigative considerations and hypotheses.

There may be complicating factors for the pathologist in trying to estimate a time of death, such as the environment the body has been kept in. Inclement weather, indoor heating, air-conditioning, and the amount of time taken to find the body are all potential further aggravating features when making accurate predictions that rely upon body temperature. Post-mortem changes such as hypostasis, rigor mortis, and decomposition such as putrefaction or skeletalization are other complications for the pathologist to consider.

An entomologist (study of insects) can examine the larvae deposits on bodies to assess the length of time exposed to the open air. Alcohol contents in blood and urine help in providing a 'back-record conversion' in a similar way to drink/driving cases.

Other more traditional clues can be found and utilized, such as dates on unopened mail and newspapers left at the deceased's home address, plus information about when they were last seen alive; and intelligence sightings through informants (CHIS). Also, useful observations made at the scene such as changing weather conditions post mortem, eg rain, where underneath the body is dry.

A useful list of potential methods for calculating time of (or since) death is as follows:

1. Temperature-based methods. Algor mortis (post-mortem cooling) requires a steady core body temperature prior to death, presumed to be approximately 37°C. However, any temperature-based method needs to account for the multiple variables that are experienced in crime scenes such as the effect of different items of clothing and the number of layers worn, the variety of ventilation or artificial heating, and even

the physical position of the body. Submereged bodies and exposure to fires can also alter core body temperatures.

2. Rigor mortis. Muscular rigidity occurs after three to six hours and lasts up to 36 hours, by which time it diminishes. This may also be affected by the temperature of the environment, the degree of muscular activity prior to death, and the age of the deceased.
3. Morphological changes. In the absence of blood circulation red blood cells settle under gravity and therefore livor mortis (hypostasis) develops. The timing of decomposition, however, will depend on factors such as the health of the deceased prior to death, the effects of drugs or medications, the ambient environment (temperature and humidity), extent of animal and insect acrtivity, and degree of perimortem trauma.
4. Muscular excitability. This is determined by external electrical stimulation of muscle groups and requires very specialized equipment that is not widely available.
5. Gastric contents emptying (gastroenterology). This method assumes that gastric contents that have been ingested at clear predictable rates. The theory is that if the time of the last meal eaten is known the extent of gastric (eg stomach) emptying can assist with an estimated time of death. This will depend on the type of food ingested (eg fat content), the physiological and psychological status of the deceased (eg degree of stress or fright) and consumption of alcohol or drugs misuse.
6. Opthalmological changes. This includes such analyses as vitreous humor and the chemical constituents of the fluid within the eye (eg changes in potassium concentration).
7. DNA and ultrastructural changes. Assessment of DNA and denaturation could provide a method of time of death estimation as cells begin to break down with the onset of cellular death. Like other methods the rate seems dependent upon ambient temperature and humidity.
8. Entomological methods. The study of insect life cycles may assist as blowflies such as green and bluebottle flies have a predictable lifecycle. Temperature, humidity, manner of death, and the presence of drugs within the body may affect the results.
9. Botanical methods. The use of plant growth through the study of palynology and botany assume the seasonal specific pollen species adherent to articles of clothing or parts of the body, especially within interred remains. Rootlet infiltration

of remains can similarly aid with perennial plants through their growth stages.

(Taken from Dr B Swift, Consultant Home Office registered forensic pathologist in *Methods of Time Since Death Estimation Within the Early Postmortem Interval,* The Journal of Homicide and Major Investigation, Vol 6, Issue 1, pp 97–107, Spring 2010, ACPO NPIA.

KEY POINT

Methods of accurately estimating time of death can be subject to considerable variation. The SIO should be sure that any expert or specialist who is carrying out any of the above methods can provide good scientific support for their opinions and conclusions.

12.6.3 Examinations of critical victims

With advancements in medical knowledge and treatments, victims who have suffered severe trauma injuries now receive improving levels of treatment. For this reason there tend to be more cases of victims being treated on ventilators and life-support machines even though their injuries initially appear to be extremely severe and life-threatening. This provides an opportunity to consider if any injuries can be assessed while the victim is still alive.

Clearly this is a very delicate tactic and the introduction of a pathologist is probably very unwise when relatives and friends are coping with severe emotional trauma. It also requires informed consent from the next of kin. One option is to explain that a police medical expert could conduct an examination, rather than introducing a pathologist as a suitable alternative. Any such examination would have to be performed very tactfully and not interfere with treatment, yet could prove extremely beneficial to the investigation.

12.7 The Post-Mortem Examination

The powers to authorize a post-mortem examination and remove a body to an appropriate location for examination are held by the coroner (Coroners and Justice Act 2009).

When arranging a post mortem the SIO must be mindful of the following requirements.

Checklist—Arranging post mortems

- The coroner needs to authorize it *beforehand.*
- The coroner needs to know and be kept informed of time/ place of post mortem (in some instances they may wish to attend).
- If there is a suspect in custody, the defence may wish to have a representative present.
- The chosen mortuary needs to be placed on alert that a pathological post mortem is to take place so they have sufficient time to prepare the examination, viewing rooms, and equipment (suitable time and date should be agreed).
- The victim's medical notes and/or hospital records, x-rays etc if taken initially to hospital, must be obtained and made available for the pathologist to read and examine before the post mortem takes place.
- Details of all treatment and drugs prescribed or administered to the victim, and any such items or information recovered from the crime scene or victim's address will be required.
- Details of any infectious diseases, such as HIV or Hepatitis B etc, must be communicated to anyone who may come into contact with the body, eg mortuary staff, coroner's officer, etc.
- The victim's social history and lifestyle (eg if drug abuser, sexual orientation, reputation, etc) will be useful.
- The appointed exhibits officer must arrange for all necessary bags, labels, sample buckets, fingernail-cutting, hair-combing, and plucking kits to be ready and available (evidence-gathering equipment).

12.7.1 Attendance at a post mortem

In most cases the SIO should be present during a post mortem. This is to observe first-hand any significant findings and partake in discussions, as the examination takes place, on all matters that may affect the course of the investigation. In some cases, however, the SIO may wish to delegate the task of attending the post mortem. This may be due to competing demands and other equally important matters that may take precedence or need attending to, being mindful of the length of time taken for a post mortem (usually no less than about four hours).

If this requirement is delegated they should discuss and agree the desired evidence recovery plan with the nominated deputy beforehand. A compromise may also be for the SIO to attend at the beginning and then return before completion in order to discuss the findings personally with the pathologist. The SIO can also be briefed on the telephone as the examination progresses. There is no hard and fast rule; suffice it to say wherever possible the SIO should normally insist on being present throughout this very important examination process. Many times during post mortems questions arise and important decisions are needed as the examination progresses.

Checklist—Persons required to be present for the post mortem

- SIO (or designated deputy)
- pathologist
- mortuary technician/assistant
- crime scene manager/investigator
- crime scene imaging staff/photographic experts (still and video/digital)
- other experts as required (ballistics, paediatricians, forensic biologists, toxicologists, palynologists, odontologists, etc)
- Exhibits Officer.

KEY POINT

Sometimes it may be requested if a medical student can attend and observe the post mortem. This is a judgement call for the SIO, who needs to be mindful of any sensitive issues, or potential leaks of information to unauthorized persons, and a duty of confidentiality to avoid compromising the investigation. Nonetheless these students may be the pathologists of the future and need to begin their training somewhere.

12.7.2 Evidence-recovery strategy meeting

Before commencement of the examination there should be a further strategy meeting (ie in addition to the one at the scene for evidence samples and body recovery) to discuss and agree the forensic evidence recovery plan for the post mortem. The SIO calls and leads this meeting, which usually takes place at a suitable venue within the mortuary with all the persons listed above being present.

The purpose of the meeting is to discuss or re-examine the circumstances of the case and determine and agree what the primary objectives are for the post mortem, what samples are to be taken and in what order, what photography is required and when (eg before, during, and after removal of clothing), and whether any x-rays are required (eg to find bullets, pellets, knife tips, etc). Depending on the type of case, the following are the types of objectives and samples routinely considered.

Checklist—Objectives for post mortem

- Establish or confirm the identity of the deceased.
- Assess the size, physique, and condition of the deceased.
- Determine cause of death (and manner if possible).
- Determine time of death.
- Determine likely survival time after attack.
- Conduct injury analysis (amount of force used, type of weapon used, precise method details, sexual assault indicators, any incapacitation, direction of blows, position of deceased at time of injury, which wound(s) were fatal, whether injuries incurred ante or post mortem, etc).
- Establish whether any indication of self-defence and if offenders are likely to be injured.
- Establish/confirm place of death (eg look for any evidence of movement of body after death due to drag marks evident on feet/ankles).
- Determine lifestyle of victim (eg drug or sexual abuse, health condition).
- Determine if deceased under influence of drink or drugs at time of death.

Checklist—Samples for collection at post mortem

- Further DNA swabs from the body from unexposed areas and/or areas not completed while the body was *in situ* at the crime scene (eg swab all biting wounds for saliva traces and any other likely areas for gripping/holding traces).
- Oral, vaginal or penile, and anal swabs.
- Fingernail scrapings and clippings (tip: if victim has long fingernails, photograph them as offender may have scratch marks).

- Head and pubic hair (or other bodily hair) combings and cuttings.
- Blood, urine, and stomach contents.
- Internal swabs of areas such as the oesophagus (eg for sperm heads).
- Any botanical swabs/samples (advice required from palynologist).

12.8 Health and Safety Risk Assessments

It is in the interests of everyone concerned with the post-mortem process that health and safety issues take precedence; even when there is a conflict with the expediency of the criminal investigation. There is a very real possibility of risk of infection from the deceased and any samples or possessions taken must be suitably controlled. A general rule is all bodies are to be regarded as potentially infective.

KEY POINT

For health and safety reasons, the SIO should allow only those persons who are absolutely necessary into the examination room. Observers can often be accommodated behind glass screens in a viewing gallery.

A risk assessment must be completed at the same time the post-mortem strategy meeting is conducted and before anyone enters the examination room. There is a requirement for the SIO to record this in the policy file in consultation with the pathologist.

The initial duty on the SIO is to provide the pathologist and mortuary staff with relevant information about the deceased and their medical records. This includes lifestyle, social background, drug abuse, known diseases, country of origin, etc.

KEY POINT

The mortuary in which the post mortem is conducted must have sufficient facilities to contain infectious risks, ie adequate ventilation and cleansing equipment. In conjunction with the coroner, the SIO and pathologist can request that a suitable mortuary be utilized.

The following is a list of control measures for the risk assessment at a post mortem.

Checklist—Post-mortem risk assessment

- All those in attendance must have been in receipt of *up-to-date* inoculations for TB, Hepatitis B, polio, and tetanus.
- Full protective clothing must be worn, ie full-length gown and mask, face/eye shield, waterproof non-slip boots/overshoes, nitrile gloves.
- Any staff who at the time has open wounds/cuts/abrasions or skin complaint must be identified and discussed with the pathologist.
- Drinking, eating, or chewing is forbidden.
- Experienced staff should accompany the inexperienced.
- Familiarization instruction on the layout and facilities of mortuary.
- Any accidents during the process to be fully investigated and reported.

Note: It is appreciated there may be bespoke policies and procedures in certain force areas that may need to be adhered to.

12.9 SIO Preparation and Note Taking

The SIO should be well equipped before going into the examination room, with suitable writing and note-taking accessories, including their enquiry notebook. It is always useful to note what the pathologist and other experts say as the examination progresses, and make drawings/sketches that will assist when back at the incident room (for briefings, etc). Useful sketches of injuries or marks can be made and, although photographs will be taken, these may not be printed and available immediately. Paper and anatomical body maps can be used to help indicate the location of significant findings (see Appendix F).

12.9.1 Preliminary procedure

Once a body bag has been opened at the mortuary the body should be examined before any clothing or possessions are removed. The position and condition of the clothing may reveal vital clues, particularly if a sexual attack has occurred. Any cuts, tears, holes, rips, etc in clothing will need to be matched against any injuries. Evidence of missing buttons, fasteners, etc should be checked. A decision should have been made during the post-mortem forensic strategy meeting as to how any garment shall be recovered in order to maximize evidence-recovery potential (eg DNA, blood, fibres, etc) and if/what/how much photography is required during the process.

12.9.2 Completion of examination

A further meeting of all those involved should be held once the examination is complete. This is an opportunity to discuss with the pathologist (and any other experts present such as ballistics or forensic scientists) any findings, interpretations, and conclusions. Any experts' opinions must always be supported by good rationale.

The pathologist should be in a position to summarize findings and provide an initial verbal report on the outcome. It may be, however, that some aspects of the examination are still incomplete. Further tests may be required on samples or parts of the body, eg the brain. Toxicology reports from blood, urine, or stomach contents may be necessary which have to be done separately. Specialist examination of bone fractures may need further analysis. In some instances a further visit to the body may be required to see whether there are any indications of bruising that have been enhanced or changed by the passage of time.

The exhibits officer must ensure that all relevant exhibits are accounted for, packaged properly and labelled with correct evidential signatures from the pathologist and any other expert who has handled them. The list of exhibits recorded should be thoroughly checked with the pathologist so they too have a corresponding accurate record of all items and samples taken.

The pathologist must then be kept up to date with evidential developments that may alter their opinions. In some circumstances they may also wish to revisit the scene before reaching a firm conclusion and ask for any additional information, such as copies of witness statements for instance.

12.9.3 Use of National Injuries Database (NID)

To assist the SIO and pathologist there is a National Injuries Database. This is held at and managed by the NPIA and is a national resource to support serious crime investigations.

The team can conduct research and provide support and advice in determining the cause and type of any injury found on a victim whether dead or alive. They can also assist with providing independent expertise for forensic medical opinions and research, specialist imaging, and court presentations.

It is mainly victim-focused and can search for cases to identify possible similarities between a victim's wound, or specific injury patterns with a possible weapon. This is particularly useful for an investigation in cases where the nature of the injuries is unknown and the weapon has not been identified. The database currently holds over 4,000 cases of suspicious deaths, homicides, and serious assault cases including child abuse, sexual offences, and self-inflictions. It also has more than 20,000 scene, injury, and weapon images.

Note: The SIO should note that, if material is passed onto another agency, it is as a matter of common courtesy to inform the original pathologist (or other expert concerned). Not to do so may alienate the experts involved who may have to eventually meet up. The National Injuries Database can be contacted via email <soc@npia.pnn.police.uk> or by calling 0845 000 5463.

12.9.4 Types of death

Asphyxia and strangulation

'Asphyxia' comes from a Greek word meaning 'lack of pulsation' and in everyday terms means death from an interruption of the process of breathing. Asphyxia may be due to suffocation (blockage of airway), strangulation (external pressure on neck), internal blockage of the airway or interference with the movements of respiration. Asphyxia signs can include:

- petechial haemorrhages in the face, eyes and/or body;
- congestion to the face;
- cyanosis (blue discoloration) of the face.

However, to complicate matters these signs can be mimicked by other events, including heart failure, resuscitation, and hypostasis. Therefore some circumstantial or supporting evidence is always useful.

Strangulation is traditionally divided into ligature and manual strangulation. Pressure may also be exerted on the neck using a 'bar arm' or 'choke hold' with a forearm. Ligature strangulation may be carried out using a variety of methods including ropes, wires, and improvised pieces of clothing (such as a bra). Internally there can be fractures to the larynx or hyoid bone denoting trauma to the neck and internal bruising/haemorrhaging. Manual strangulation can leave fingernail abrasions and localized fingertip bruises to the muscles in the neck (which may also carry marks indicating attempts at defence by the victim).

Firearms cases

There are additional considerations for certain circumstances and offences, such as those involving firearms:

- A ballistics expert should be present at the examination.
- X-rays will be required to locate bullets/projectiles in the body.
- Swabs should be considered for firearm discharge residue from the body (helps determine how far the victim was away from the firearm).
- Discharge residues on the victim's hands can help determine if they handled the firearm (particularly if suicide is suspected).
- There should be an analysis of both entry and exit wounds, which will help a ballistics expert determine direction of travel of the bullets and the angle the victim was shot from.
- Recovery and examination of bullets will assist in determining whether there was more than one weapon involved, and possibly what type of weapon was used (eg shotgun or automatic).

KEY POINT

There are four factors that affect physical appearance of gunshot wounds on a human body: type of weapon, type of ammunition, range from muzzle to body, and any intermediate targets.

Fire deaths

Usually there are local protocols in place for investigating fire deaths which should include arrangements for a tripartite investigation between the police, fire service, and scientific experts. Aspects of fire deaths and pathology to consider are as follows:

- The post mortem is often difficult as fire can cover up injuries or create spurious injuries that mimic an assault.

- One key question is, was the deceased alive when the fire was burning?
- If the deceased was alive during the fire, there can often be carbon monoxide in the blood, soot in the airways, and scorching below the vocal cords. There may be a vital reaction to the burns but this may be difficult to confirm even under microscopic examination.

The presence of flammable liquids and several seats of fire ignition are good indicators of arson. However, meaningful interpretation of these clues must be left to the experts due to the complexity of fire investigation. The SIO will have to rely upon the pathologist to try to interpret what injuries are visible, if any, on badly burned bodies.

Deaths resulting from fire are generally caused by the inhalation of noxious gases and fumes. The victim is usually dead prior to the burning of parts of the body flesh. The pathologist will be tasked with answering the critical question referred to above: whether the victim was alive at the time of the fire.

Case study—Fire investigation

A vehicle fire was quickly deemed to be an electrical fault by the fire service officers in attendance with no suspicious circumstances. This was accepted by the attending police officers which resulted in no further enquiries being made and no SIO or forensic experts being called. However, the fire had been deliberately caused by an explosive device. Therefore cursory examinations by fire and police officers should not be solely relied upon; instead the fire service experts (examination unit) and an SIO should be called.

Bodies in water and drowning

These post mortems are usually more difficult as the body will often be in a poor condition, and the signs of drowning may have disappeared after a few days. Some pointers to consider are:

- The typical signs of drowning are foam in the airways and over-inflated lungs.
- Spurious post mortem injuries may be created by boats, underwater objects, marine life, or the deceased's hands dragging on the bottom of the waterway.

Suicides

Investigatively speaking, all deaths should be treated as murder until the facts prove otherwise. With suicides there are three important things to consider:

1. The presence of a weapon or means of death close to the scene.
2. Injuries or wounds that are obviously self-inflicted.
3. The existence of a motive or intent for the deceased to take their own life.

It must be noted that sometimes weapons may 'go missing' due to either being stolen (eg if in a public place) or removed by family or friends (eg to prevent embarrassment).

Regarding the wounds, certain observations can be made that are obviously not considered as possible indicators of suicide, eg multiple stab wounds in the victim's body. It is sometimes surprising how much a person can injure themselves when intent on suicide. With determined suicidal people wounds are not always superficial and can be severe so increasing their pain threshold if a person is desperate to take their own life. The traditional target areas in a suicide are often called 'sites of election', and include the throat, wrists, chest, and abdomen, or the head if with a firearm. Suicidal gunshot wounds usually are close-range and there should be evidence of firearms discharge residues around the area of the entry wound but not always on the deceased's hand.

The manner of death can be a good indicator of motive and intent: for instance, putting their head on a railway line, or jumping from a building when they have had to pay a special visit to these particular areas. Background information on the deceased should indicate useful clues as to intent especially the existence of a suicide note, provided it is authenticated as the victim's own. Behavioural indicators such as giving away possessions, disregarding their doctor's advice, entries in diaries, text messages, and talking to others about committing suicide in the lead-up to death are also good indicators. Some aggravating features may warrant further investigation such as missing money or personal possessions, or when their lifestyle (eg criminal or sexual) may give cause for concern.

Case study—Murder or suicide?

The badly burned body of a male was found fastened to a tree in a forest by strong thick metal wire, secured after twisting the ends firmly together. A petrol can was found nearby and the body, due to mutilating fire injuries, was very difficult to identify. An initial hypothesis was that a brutal gangland-style torture and execution had taken place. A full-scale enquiry was commenced, with a pathologist and fire service examination team being requested by the SIO to examine the body *in situ*.

The internal examination revealed that the deceased suffered from a malignant tumour in his abdomen. A pair of pliers was eventually found located in the undergrowth near to the body and appeared to be far enough away to prevent release and escape.

It was established that the deceased had purchased the wire and pliers from a local DIY store and was captured on CCTV obtaining a container and fuel from a local petrol station. It was proved to the satisfaction of the coroner that he had voluntarily made his own way to the secluded location, secured himself in such a manner as to prevent escape, poured petrol over himself, and set himself alight. The main seat of the fire was found to be around the area on his body where his tumour was located, as if he was trying to 'burn it out'. The evidence from both the pathologist and police enquiry supported a coroner's verdict of suicide.

Hanging

These are usually suicidal or accidental, as in auto-erotic deaths. Caution should be exercised to ensure they have not been deliberately staged to appear like a suicide, ie homicidal hanging. If the body is obviously dead and there is no need for immediate life-saving methods nothing should be touched, handled, or disturbed until the body and scene have been photographed.

If the ligature around the neck must be removed the knot or tie should not be touched; instead it should be cut in an area which does not disturb the actual knot. The pathologist usually performs this function during the post mortem and the noose does not normally need to be removed at the scene unless there is a possibility the victim is still alive.

12.10 Role of the Coroner

A coroner is an appointed independent judicial official responsible for supervising any violent, sudden, or unexplained death where the cause is unknown. They are independent of both local and central government, and although paid by local councils are not local government officers but hold office under the Crown. They are required to act in accordance with laid-down rules and procedures. Most coroners are lawyers and some may also be doctors. Not all are full-time or have their own coroner's court, although they normally have a team of people supporting them in their work.

As soon as a death is deemed to be suspicious and is under investigation the coroner who covers the area where a body is found must be notified without delay. This is a key requirement of the SIO.

12.10.1 When is a death reported to the coroner?

- When the cause of death is unknown.
- When the deceased has not been treated by a doctor during their last illness.
- When the doctor attending the deceased did not see them within 14 days before they died or after death.
- When the death occurred during an operation or before recovery from the effect of an anaesthetic.
- When the death was sudden and unexplained in suspicious circumstances.
- If there are any unusual or disturbing features to the case.
- If the deceased was detained under the Mental Health Act.
- If the death may be the result of a lack of medical care.
- If the death may be due to an abortion.
- If the death may be due to suicide.
- When the death may be due to an industrial injury or disease, or to accident, violence, neglect, or abortion, or to any kind of poisoning.
- When the death occurred in police custody or prison.

Once a death has been reported to the coroner, the Registrar of Births, Deaths and Marriages cannot register the death until the coroner's enquiries are complete. Initial investigations are normally conducted by Coroner's Officers who are either serving police officers or staff employed by the police/local authority, sometimes from a police background. The coroner may be able to establish that the death was due to natural causes and a doctor may be able to issue a medical certificate as to cause of death. If unable to do so the coroner will arrange for the deceased to be subject to a post mortem at a local hospital to establish the cause of death. If the death cannot be attributed to natural causes an inquest must be held, which is a medical/legal enquiry into the death, not a trial. Therefore the inquest cannot apportion blame for the death to any individual or organization; that must take place in a criminal court.

12.10.2 Duty of coroner to investigate certain deaths

Under s 1 of the Coroners and Justice Act 2009 (ch 25), which came into force on 12 November 2009, the coroner has a duty to investigate all deaths were there are grounds to suspect they are either of the following:

(a) the deceased died a violent or unnatural death;
(b) the cause of death is unknown; or
(c) the deceased died while in custody or otherwise in state detention.

12.10.3 Purpose of the coroner's investigation

Under s 5 of the Act, the purpose of the coroner's investigation into a person's death is to ascertain:

(a) who the deceased was;
(b) how, when, and where the deceased came by his or her death;
(c) the particulars required to be registered concerning the death; and
(d) to avoid a breach of any Convention rights (within the meaning of the Human Rights Act 1998) to establish in what circumstances the deceased came by his or her death.

12.10.4 Coroner's inquest.

The coroner is required to hold an inquest into the death in all cases were an investigation has been conducted, in accordance with s 6 of the Act. The inquest must be held with a jury under the following circumstances:

(a) the deceased died while in custody or otherwise in state detention and that either:
   (i) the death was a violent or unnatural one, or
   (ii) the cause of death is unknown,

(b) that the death resulted from an act or omission of:
   (i) a police officer, or
   (ii) a member of a service police force, in the purported execution of the officer's or member's duty as such, or
(c) that the death was caused by a 'notifiable' accident, poisoning, or disease.

For this purpose, an accident, poisoning, or disease is 'notifiable' if notice of it is required under any Act to be given:

(a) to a government department, for example NHS,
(b) to an inspector or other officer of a government department, or
(c) to an inspector appointed under s 19 of the Health and Safety at Work etc Act 1974,
(d) if the coroner thinks that there is sufficient reason for doing so.

Once an inquest has been held the coroner will send a report to the registrar in the district where the death occurred who will register the circumstances and details of the death. It is the registrar who issues the death certificate. Inquests are held in public and may include a jury. This may involve witnesses being called who are legally obliged to attend and may be penalized if they fail to do so. The coroner may record the cause of death as:

- natural causes
- accident/misadventure
- industrial disease
- unlawful or lawful killing
- suicide
- attempted or self-induced abortion
- dependence on drugs or non-dependent abuse of drugs
- open verdict.

Note: The coroner may also record a 'narrative verdict' which provides far more detail than the terms outlined above.

12.11 Human Tissue Act (HTA) 2004

The law has been changed due to a review following public enquiries that became 'causes célèbre' (eg Royal Liverpool

Children's Hospital, Alder Hey, and the complications leading from hitherto commonplace storage and use of organs and tissue without proper consent). This Act introduced a number of provisions that are of relevance to the SIO. These include the following:

- The storage of the body of a deceased person for the purpose of determining the cause of death must be on premises licensed for that activity by the Human Tissue Authority unless the storage is incidental to transportation.
- The performance of a post-mortem examination may only take place on premises licensed for that activity by the Human Tissue Authority.
- The pathologist undertaking the post-mortem examination must act under the authority of a licence from the Human Tissue Authority authorizing post-mortem examinations on those premises.
- The Coroners and Justice Act 2009 prevents a coroner authorizing a post-mortem examination if doing so would violate s 16 of the HTA 2004.
- Samples may only be taken for the purpose of establishing or confirming the deceased's identity or determining the cause of death if the post mortem has been authorized by the coroner (in non-suspicious cases).

12.11.1 Samples—general

Samples of relevant material may be taken for three reasons. The first two, identification of the deceased and determination of the cause of death, are taken for the purposes and under the authority of the coroner. Thirdly, material required as part of the investigation of crime (ie suspicious death investigations) is taken by the police through powers to seize evidence under s 19 of PACE 1984 and the common law and is not subject to the HTA 2004 restrictions.

12.11.2 Samples—records

All samples taken should be recorded by the exhibits officer and given a unique identifier. This record should make clear those samples taken for the coroner and those taken for the police. Any samples taken at the location where the body was found should be incorporated into this list.

12.11.3 Police samples

Samples held on the authority of the police do not fall within the consent requirements of the HTA 2004 or within the licensing requirements of s 39 of HTA 2004. However, samples held by the pathologist on behalf of the police should, as far as practical, comply with the guidance issued by the Human Tissue Authority. It is also advisable for the police to comply with the guidance and it is reasonable to seek a consistent level of approach.

12.11.4 End of enquiries—samples

The police investigation into a death can end in a number of different ways. It is therefore a matter for the police to determine, in line with relevant guidance, what must happen to samples seized as evidence (under PACE) and how they should be disposed of. This would be different if the samples had been taken and the death not deemed to be suspicious as the HTA 2004 would stipulate they should be returned to the family without delay and/or disposed of as deemed appropriate.

Given the possibly significant period between the post-mortem examination and the end of the enquiry it may be useful to have made an initial assessment of the need to retain samples soon after the examination.

The SIO should also take account of any views expressed to the Family Liaison Officer with regard to this matter.

12.12 Human Rights

Article 2 of the European Convention for the Protection of Human Rights (ECHR), incorporated into domestic law by the Human Rights Act 1998, sets out the 'right to life'. This has been held to require an effective public investigation by an independent official body into any death occurring in certain circumstances.

There has been an increasing awareness of the requirements imposed by Art 2 and, as a consequence, it is accepted that there may be cases where a coroner's inquest must be re-opened after a failed prosecution.

12.13 Organ Donations

The issue arises from time to time when families and relatives may wish to donate organs in murder investigations. This should be resolved through consultation by the SIO with the pathologist and the coroner, who is the only person who can authorize this.

Ultimately it will be a matter for the SIO to take a lead role and collate the necessary information. A record should be made of any subsequent decision and rationale in the policy file. There are some important considerations before reaching any decision; for example:

- A second post mortem may be required.
- The impact on the investigation (which takes precedent).
- The relevance of the organ(s) to the outcome of the pathological and forensic examination.
- The views of the defence if a person is charged.

12.14 Second Post Mortems and Release of a Body

For some time, coroners have authorized the performance of second post-mortem examinations. In many cases this is to facilitate the early release of the body to the family after facilitation of an independent examination. Although the great majority of homicides result in a swift arrest, delays can become acute due to the complexity or difficulty of certain types on investigation, or where there are a number of jointly charged defendants. This may cause undue distress to families and relatives. Therefore the SIO should be keen to seek an early performance of all subsequent post mortems.

The main objectives and features (as agreed by inter-agency agreements between bodies such as ACPO, Coroner's Society, Law Society, and Home Office) for second post mortems are:

- Reducing delays for release of a body for burial or cremation.
- Limiting the possibility of miscarriages of justice.
- Reducing the incidence of multiple post mortems (on the same body).

- Where no one is charged in connection with the death within a month, provision can be made for a second, independent post mortem for use by a defendant in the future.

There is no statutory authority for a person charged in connection with a death to order a post-mortem examination of the deceased. The performance of such an examination, however, has been well recognized by the courts. This examination must only be undertaken on the authority of the coroner.

If a homicide case is still undetected after a period of time, the SIO should liaise with the coroner to discuss and arrange a second autopsy to prevent any further delay in waiting for potential defendant's solicitors to be appointed. Where the coroner is informed by the SIO that it is unlikely that any person will be charged within 28 days from the date of the offence then usually the coroner will agree to arrange for a qualified independent pathologist to perform a second post-mortem examination; and they may wish to discuss and share their findings with the original pathologist. The subsequent report can then be provided to a defendant's solicitors in the event of an arrest being made. The SIO should also have sight of the report and request a copy from the coroner.

It is advantageous for the SIO to nominate a person as liaison officer with the coroner, defence team(s), and pathologist(s). This may be a coroner's officer or someone within the investigation team. The decision should be recorded in the SIO's policy file. The officer should ensure all necessary action is taken to satisfy the coroner that all examinations are completed and the body can be released. A personal call from the SIO to the coroner is advisable and would encourage good working relations.

KEY POINTS

- In all cases the SIO, through the Family Liaison Officer, should always keep the victim's family fully updated on developments and arrangements for subsequent post mortems and when the body is likely to be released by the coroner. A conservative estimate rather than firm commitment is advisable to avoid disappointment and upsetting the police/family relationship.
- The time taken for the pathologist to produce their report is a key factor in the early release of the body. This will influence the decision on whether a second post mortem is necessary. In some jurisdictions reporting is available for the police/Coroner outlining a preliminary cause of death pending further medical/scientific examinations or results.

- In the vast majority of cases an initial post mortem will have been carried out before any person is charged. Therefore defence pathologists will require to be provided with material that will assist them in conducting a second post mortem, such as the initial post-mortem report, x-rays, or other photographic records.

12.15 **Conclusion**

This chapter has looked at the roles for the three main parties involved in a criminal investigation—the police, forensic pathologist, and coroner. Together with any other relevant experts and advisers all three have an important role to play in the investigation into violent and suspicious deaths. Because of the importance of a specific role, there has deliberately been a particular emphasis on the scope of pathology and an explanation of what it can and cannot provide to the investigation. Some common types of death have been summarized and included to help gain a better understanding of the main considerations presented. There has also been an outline of some of the legislative frameworks applicable to this area of the investigation.

It is hoped the content of this chapter will provide useful source material for an SIO called upon to lead an investigation involving a deceased person. This includes deaths in circumstances that are obviously murders and those for which the signs are more ambiguous. Some useful checklists have been included which hopefully will make the appreciation of the roles and procedures much simpler. The final comment is a reminder that the body is a major crime scene, rich in potential evidential material, and every effort should be made to get the most out of the investigative opportunities on offer.

Chapter 13
News Media Management

13.1 Introduction

Many serious crime investigations attract substantial amounts of media interest. Increasing demand for news about serious crime or critical events has had a profound affect on media relations. The police carry an exceptional duty in the public sector for the protection of life and property, and therefore must remain highly accountable. Obtaining and releasing information about police efficiency and effectiveness through media coverage in news outlets is an effective method of police scrutiny and therefore the professional management and handling of the media is extremely important. Publicity helps build and shape images and perceptions of the modern police service, whether they are positive or otherwise, and like it or not the media can and do influence public opinion.

Local, national, and worldwide correspondents amongst a large range of competing outlets cater for what is now a high intensity 24/7 news cycle. The UK alone has experienced a steady increase in local and national radio, cable, digital, satellite and internet channels. Improvements in technology have increased the access, speed, and capability at which news is generated and reported, Breaking news is by nature spontaneous and can become global within minutes appearing on news programmes or in 'ticker tape' fashion at the bottom of television screens.

News gatherers have the ability to rapidly descend on major crime scenes and create a media-feeding frenzy. So called 'citizen journalists' with lightweight portable camcorders and mobilephone recording devices can also capture instant pictures. The murders of Holly Wells and Jessica Chapman in Soham, the missing child Madeline McCann in Portugal or the fraudulent canoeist John Darwin from Hartlepool illustrate the extreme levels of media interest some cases generate. Intense public and press interest can place the SIO in the full glare of the media spotlight, which can be prolonged or resurface at regular intervals (eg the Saddleworth 'moors murders' by Ian Brady and Myra Hindley).

Fortunately the needs of major crime investigations and those of newsrooms can be highly compatible. Journalists like to participate in mutual arrangements to obtain essential information and updates, conduct interviews and photograph opportunities. An SIO too can take full advantage of the free publicity by working with the media not against them; which has become the norm. Without such agreements it would be more difficult and costly to solve crime, gain public trust and confidence, reach out to witnesses and communities, and demonstrate openness, transparency, and accountability.

Effectively managed, the media can make a significant contribution to an investigation by acting as a conduit for information. The media spotlight, however, can place huge time and resource implications on the SIO at critical stages but at the same time play an important role in shaping the public's views on the standard of the investigation, the police service, and the wider criminal justice system.

Handling the media can be one of the most demanding and nerve-wracking tasks for any SIO. Yet in the twenty-first century media engagement is a very important part of the role and the challenge must be faced and handled professionally. The media must always be treated with respect and used effectively they can make a hugely significant contribution to an investigation. Effectively using the media will almost certainly appear in most if not all SIOs' main lines of enquiry. The alternative is to risk journalists and reporters unduly interfering with, meddling in, or maybe even impeding the investigation in relaying right or wrong messages to tens of thousands or even millions of people. Included in those audiences may be the very suspects, witnesses, and sources of information that the SIO will need to reach out to inorder to solve the crime under investigation. This chapter therefore needs to begin with the stark message that news media management is an essential skill of a modern-day SIO, and this chapter is aimed at providing the necessary help and guidance and can be consulted as a good aide memoir even for the most accomplished of those who have to stand in front of the cameras.

13.2 Who the Media Are

There are a variety of different types of media communication, for example:

- television (eg news bulletins by the BBC, ITV, SKY, etc)
- radio stations (local and national)
- newspapers, magazines, journals, leaflets, and posters
- world wide web news sites (BBC, Sky, Reuters etc)
- local community websites
- social networking sites (eg. 'Flickr', 'Facebook', 'My Space', 'Piczo', 'Twitter' etc)
- public meetings, or using local community contact networks.

KEY POINT

The term 'media' (or mass media) refers to the main means of mass communication regarded collectively, especially through newspapers and TV/radio broadcasting.

13.3 Conduct of the Media

The activities of the press and broadcast media can have a profound effect on the success of any investigation and subsequent prosecution. Handled incorrectly the media becomes a major disruption to any investigation because they will inevitably seek contact with victims, witnesses, and investigators. For instance, while the Press Complaints Commission's (PCC) Code of Practice stresses that payment should not be offered to potential witnesses, there have been examples and it is possible to ask the PCC to intervene with editors if there is evidence of this. Do not ignore the media because if the 'beast' is not fed regularly it will feed itself and wreak havoc on an enquiry—for instance by speculating, criticizing, or finding so-called 'experts' to comment, many of whom are not in touch with the latest developments in policing and investigations, and none of whom are sighted on the details of the investigation. Wrong messages can be given out, and evidence (particularly witness testimonies) may be compromised. It is therefore preferable to treat the media as an investigative tool.

It is not uncommon for members of the media to be taken along on police operations. There have also been 'fly on the wall' type documentaries that show policing enquiries and routines. Controlled pre-verdict media briefings are considered good practice and the release of material can be done under embargo to achieve maximum impact and publicity while protecting the integrity of the court proceedings.

If an incident under investigation is of great public interest (eg vulnerable victim, celebrity, part of a series of crimes, or race/hate crime) the media attention will most likely be substantial. Many reporters can quickly get to a scene and may even be interviewing key witnesses. Worse still, they could be with members of the victim's family, causing unnecessary alarm and confusion. Every action and decision made by the police may be publicised by journalists and reported by TV, radio, newspapers, and via the web. The media can quickly mobilize outside broadcasting teams and even helicopters/planes to capture aerial shots. Within a short space of time the local, national, and even international media can spring into action. Some eye witnesses even contact media agencies direct with what they have seen or photographed, or to talk about their perceptions of events and the background to them.

13.4 How the Media can Support Investigations

The media can support investigations by:

- Keeping the public informed.
- Disseminating information very quickly to large audiences.
- Providing accurate and timely information to the public.
- Helping the public understand what the police do and why.
- Making appeals for information and witnesses.
- Identifying victims and/or establishing their last movements.
- Tracing named suspects.
- Putting pressure on offenders to give themselves up and/or admit offences.
- Tracing the whereabouts of missing persons.
- Increasing public confidence in the police.
- Providing reassurance and/or crime prevention advice.

- Developing good relations with the community.
- Providing positive publicity for good work and raising the police profile.

The media can be used to urge suspects to hand themselves in and also to indicate that the police investigation is drawing closer to them. Publicity can be used to appeal to the consciences of those who may be shielding offenders or knowingly withholding information. One useful tactic is to place posters in precise locations directly in the line of sight of suspects or potential witnesses (eg opposite their home addresses). The power and influence of the media should never be underestimated.

Case Study—John Darwin

Huge media coverage in the case of a missing canoeist from Cleveland prompted Darwin to hand himself in at a London police station. The case had become front page news all over the world with one national newspaper publishing a photograph of him and his wife alive and well in Panama. This development, aided by the media, led to Darwin and his wife being arrested, charged, and convicted of offences in connection with fraudulently faking his own death and claiming his own life insurance.

13.5 Avoiding Media Compromise

If the police aren't proactive in providing accurate and regular updates of information the media will conduct their own enquiries. If they do so they may get up to serious mischief by reaching incorrect or inaccurate conclusions that are subsequently broadcast or published in the public domain. This can lead to a misrepresentation of facts or false information being circulated that can seriously undermine an enquiry or destabilizes police/community relations and confidence.

Some examples of this are:

- speculative *links* to other offences/incidents in a region or elsewhere;
- critical comments about the *location* where the incident took place;
- assertions about *motive* or *cause* behind an offence/incident/operation;
- assertions about the details of *offender(s)*;
- assertions about the details and background of *victim(s)*.

This re-emphasizes the importance of managing and working *with* as opposed to *against* the media. If a clear strategy for co-operating, managing, and controlling their activities and information flows is neglected the consequences may wreak havoc. It is not uncommon, for example, for reporters to track down potential witnesses and report their version of events on news bulletins without a thorough evaluation and the necessary evidential safeguards being put into place. Worse still, reporters may approach victims or their family and relatives before the police get chance to do so.

KEY POINT

The media like to make attempts at negative portrayals of or challenges to the integrity or effectiveness of the police or criminal justice system. They may even make links to wider social trends, causes or policy issues, eg increases in gun/knife attacks or sexually motivated crime. The impact of such reporting may be avoided or minimized by working with media agencies and/or feeding them positive information to counterbalance the negativities, anticipating in advance any adverse publicity, and managing it as part of a comprehensive media strategy. (Note: This may require positive rebuttals from other agencies as well as the police.)

13.6 Role of the SIO and the Media

The SIO has the ultimate responsibility for formulating policy and managing the media with regard to the investigation. The local community context also plays a large part in media tactics and strong links need to be developed with local neighbourhood and community officers as early as possible to relay the correct messages. However, the SIO may be required to comply with requests for information and provide interviews that give out not just appeals but also updates on the progress of the investigation.

Media interviews can take up a lot of an SIO's time and often there is not one media agency but lots of them. There may be representatives from different television companies, numerous large or small radio stations, and press journalists, including those who work freelance and sell stories on. Each may demand one-on-one interviews with the SIO and from personal experience this can get repetitive, time consuming and tiring.

The answer is to enlist the help of the Media Liaison Officer to assist in managing this demand on the SIO's behalf.

The SIO should work with the Media Liaison Office (also known as 'press office' in some forces) to link into a wider communications strategy which includes direct communications with certain targeted audiences. The public will want to know exactly what has happened, why it happened, who is responsible, what is being done to catch the person(s) responsible, etc.

13.7 Role of the Media Liaison Officer (MLO)

Sometimes also referred to as 'press officers', MLOs (usually part of a corporate communications unit) have a co-ordination and liaison role. This is not only for media and communications activities, but also marketing and sponsorship to promote and manage the image of the force. MLOs operate at both strategic and tactical levels, communicating with external agencies and providing support to operational staff. This occurs both 'back stage' in facilitating preparation and 'front stage' in acting as an important buffer and conduit between the media and the police. Police media relations are, by and large, far more professional when managed by MLOs who are an extremely valuable asset for any SIO who has to engage with the media.

MLOs can assist in formulating media strategies and are adept at finding the right form of words and choosing the most appropriate methods and timing for communicating with the public. Creative ideas are often better discussed and developed jointly and it is the job of the MLO to spot or create media opportunities or use local contacts to improve media involvement. They also monitor the media and gauge their reaction, level of interest, and accuracy of story lines in order to anticipate media interpretations and reporting of incidents an circumstances. This is an early warning mechanism to give ample opportunity to react and prepare a response. Knowing what has been or is going to be published in the media should influence media strategies.

It is wise to utilize the invaluable assistance of media liaison specialists at the earliest opportunity. Most forces have agreed protocols to do this and the bigger forces should have access to a media officer 24/7. Most of the staff have extensive knowledge and experience of working in the media or as journalists outside the police service. It is best practice to include them as integral members of the enquiry team and to keep them briefed and up to date as the enquiry progresses. They are able to maintain an awareness of local reporting methods and reporters, and will know when there are quiet and busy news days or other events to consider. They should know which reporters can be trusted and which to be wary of.

Recent examples have shown how important this role can be. If the case attracts huge (inter)national attention, such as the Harold Shipman case or the Soham murders, the Media Liaison Officers will be a huge asset to the SIO and their force.

More importantly, they are there to offer protection for the SIO to fend off media interest and attention. This will enable the SIO to concentrate on other tasks. They should collate all the media publications for the use of the enquiry team and for disclosure purposes later at court as it is not uncommon for defence teams to make allegations about what has been said in the media, particularly when misquoting facts provided by the SIO. Such material should also be made available to the victim's family and relatives, etc should the need arise.

Checklist—Role of the MLO

- Preparation and dissemination of information about incidents.
- Analysis of media reporting.
- Liaison with and management of journalists and reporters at scenes.
- Logging information given out to journalists.
- Mediating between the SIO and media over interviews media facilities/opportunities.
- Monitoring all press coverage to check accuracy and interpretation.
- Assisting in development of media strategies.

13.8 Initial Media Management

Not every encounter with the media occurs at major or serious incident scenes but this is where things can go badly wrong if not brought quickly under control. An appreciation of the likely risks and complications is very important, particularly for first responders who will have to take initial command and control.

The media tend to get notified very quickly when serious incidents occur and chances are they will descend on crime or incident scenes very soon after. They may even be present when the incident occurs if already reporting on the event or nearby. Competitive and forceful reporters present an awkward distraction for responding officers especially if TV crews, bulky vehicles, and technical equipment block or commandeer valuable space and obstruct access and egress routes. Reporters invariably try and get as close as possible to get the best shots and hunt around for witnesses and information. They will invariably try and record all police activities at the scene plus casualties, victims, crime scene evidence, or even fatalities and corpses.

In order to manage and control such a situation secure cordons must be quickly put in place around scenes to protect them. This must be done as quickly as possible in order to preserve and protect the integrity of the scene and keep the public and media out. This may include the use of screens to keep certain things out of the line of sight (eg victims).

KEY POINT

The media have a right to be at a crime scene provided they are public places but only in areas outside of a cordon. As long as they are in a public place while they are taking photographs and filming there is no power to ask them to leave or confiscate camera equipment. However, if there is a problem with the proximity of the media and public to the scene the best answer is to extend cordons, not arrest journalists and photographers.

Activities of the media should be managed through an appointed Media Liaison Officer (MLO) (or similar) who should aim to direct the media to an agreed location suitably positioned away from important police activities (ie a media briefing point, see below). This is where and how they are best controlled in order to keep them regularly updated with information to satisfy their needs to inform their viewing and listening public.

It is always the role of an incident commander and/or SIO to assume responsibility for making strategic or tactical decisions involving the media. However, sometimes more junior staff get approached and offered the chance of speaking to a reporter or providing impromptu interviews. This should generally be avoided and/or refused unless undertaken with full permission and approval *beforehand*.

Case Study—Media management

The discovery of the body of a murdered young boy in a park early one morning led to a proliferation of (inter)national and local media reporters and their vehicles and equipment converging on the scene. Large vans with transmitting dishes were soon parked in every available space potentially disrupting scene examination and security. Reporters were keen to interview people from the local community that included potential witnesses and the handling of the incident and investigation was in danger of compromise. The first response officers, incident commander, on-call SIO and Media Liaison Officer acted quickly to put large secure cordons in place and gather all the media together in a location away from the scene to hold an early media briefing to satisfy their need for information and official interviews. There were some 30–40 journalists present at the initial briefing plus supporting technical crews and live pictures were transmitted. Had swift action not been taken to control and manage the media the police would not have kept control of the incident scene or investigation.

Checklist for Media management—initial response phase

1. Put cordons in place as quickly as possible to keep the media and public out of the scene(s).
2. Do not discuss any aspect of the case with representatives of the media. There is limited information at this stage and any disclosure of incorrect information may be magnified by the press and may hinder an investigation.
3. Request attendance of a MLO as quickly as possible and inform reporters that they will be officially dealt with in due course by the MLO.
4. Only the SIO or high ranking/senior officer should engage with the media unless permission is granted and ideally only then when advice and guidance has been taken from an experienced MLO.
5. All staff should at all times remain vigilant for cunning reporters. Any approaches for 'off the record' or 'informal' interviews, apply rule (2) above.

KEY POINT

Media gaffes are often caused by actions of those who say the wrong thing inadvertently at the scene of an incident, or when they are heard talking indiscreetly within earshot of reporters, or photographed in compromising or unprofessional circumstances. This must be avoided at all costs.

13.8.1 Media briefing points

Despite cordons, media crews may still attempt to get into the best vantage points to take shots of the scene and surrounding activities. Media representatives come from a wide variety of agencies and although the majority may be well known and trusted, others from less well-known news agencies have to be treated with caution. If there is more than one scene this will compound matters further and they will be even more difficult to control. The best option is to arrange a suitable media briefing point for all agencies. This is normally sited where journalists can still see some amount of police activity provided it does not impact on the investigation and serves as a place where enquiries can be fielded and formal briefings held. MLOs and/or the incident commander/SIO should consult with the media to negotiate with them if it is felt that any distressing images have been obtained and may be published or broadcast. Broadcasting codes of practice discourage the use of inappropriate images, although the police have no formal powers of censorship.

13.8.2 Holding statements

Usually when an incident occurs the media get to hear about it very quickly and are on the scene and hungry for information. This is usually when there is very little actually known about what has occurred yet the SIO must be prepared to respond with an initial holding statement. Ideally an experienced MLO will also be available to handle all media enquiries. The initial statement allows the SIO to 'buy time' until a more informed response can be made. It usually includes the following detail:

1. Confirmation the police are dealing with an incident.
2. Details of the location.
3. What it is being treated as (eg murder or suspicious death).
4. If and when there is to be a post mortem.
5. Details of incident room location and telephone number.
6. Initial appeal for witnesses/information.

KEY POINTS

1. On first arrival at the scene it is advisable not to discuss any aspect of the case with the media. The SIO may have very limited knowledge at this stage and any disclosure of incorrect information may get magnified by the media and hinder the investigation. The SIO should ensure all officers and staff are also reminded not to discuss the case with the media and that all enquiries should be channelled through the SIO and/or MLO.
2. Details of a deceased person are never released until after formal identification and the next of kin have been made aware.

13.8.3 Devising a media strategy

A media strategy should be incorporated into the SIO's list of investigative strategies and should be discussed and agreed (if possible) with the MLO. The focus of the strategy may change as the incident develops, so it should be regularly reviewed and updated. It may be useful to use a separate policy file for all media decisions if it is a major enquiry. A good MLO will maintain their own log of policy and decisions. Most forces have electronic media logging systems which provide an effective audit trail of activity relating to the investigation.

The policy should include a requirement to monitor all media outlets, which may possibly be linked to the intelligence-gathering function. Swift action may be required to correct inaccuracies in media reporting and a review of the strategy will then be required. A carefully formulated media strategy can be linked to a list of objectives (eg filling information gaps) indicating what media appeals are necessary, how they can be communicated and when, where, why, and by whom. For example, it may a tactic to provide media interviews to appeal for witnesses directly from a location nearby the primary crime scene by the SIO on the second day of the enquiry. The reasons could be recorded in the policy file as:

1. The incident is likely to have been witnessed as it occurred at a time when members of the public were likely to be in the vicinity.
2. This is the most suitable and effective way of getting an early request out for public assistance.
3. Images of the crime scene in the background may jog people's memory.

4. An early opportunity for an appeal is to capture testimonies before recollections are forgotten or contaminated.
5. The SIO will make the appeal as they have the best knowledge and is recognized within the local community as being the person leading the investigation.

The strategy needs to remain dynamic, flexible, and tailored to individual circumstances as things develop and may change as the investigation progresses. It will have to cater for any overt activities or significant events, eg arrests, searches, execution of search warrants, significant dates or anniversaries, potential criticism of policing activity, any subsequent connected incidents, court appearances, etc.

The MIM states the purpose of the media strategy should be:

- Establishing the circumstances of the incident and bringing any offenders to justice.
- Controlling police interaction with the media.
- Maintaining public confidence in the police.
- Minimizing impact on public fear of crime.
- Generating confidence within the investigative team.
- Maximizing publicity opportunities in the search for information (MIM, ACPO Centrex, (2006), 225).

13.9 Media Reporting and the Victim's Family

One of the most important points to consider is the impact the media can have on the victim's family/friends and/or the local community. Therefore it is essential to liaise with, consult, and keep the family informed wherever practicable prior to any statement being passed to the media. ACPO media guidance clearly stipulates that the SIO must adopt a partnership approach with the victim's family and in formulating an agreed media strategy, wherever possible and they should be given help to prevent excessive media intrusion.

It is a continuing responsibility of the SIO (through the FLO) to keep the family informed of any developments and ensure they are fully aware before any formal release of information, pictures, updates etc appear in the media. They should be provided with all copies of any formal media statements *in advance* of publication unless this is absolutely impossible; in which case the information should be given as soon as possible. The SIO should be mindful of balancing the requirement to appease the media demands for information and releases (eg holding an immediate press conference at the scene) against ensuring the victim's family are breifed beforehand.

A balance may have to be struck between the privacy of the victim's family and the needs of the investigation. Sometimes sensitive facts have to be disclosed to the media for the benefit of the investigation. For example, a victim may have had numerous relationships and it may be important to make this clear to the media in order to encourage previous partners to come forward for elimination. This may not be very pleasant for the family and would need careful planning with the FLO.

Previous convictions of the victim, or their lifestyle and background, are other examples. One option is to make a compromise and balance the negative side of the victim's character against the positive, eg how good she was as a mother and carer for two young children as a single parent (despite working in the sex industry). Efforts to maintain the support of the family and sympathy of the public are of paramount importance.

KEY POINT

Anticipating what line of questioning is going to be taken in interviews is vital. Often it can be stipulated beforehand what topics the SIO is willing to answer. If there are local policing issues at stake from a build-up of previous similar incidents, or there are concerns about crime prevention or safety issues, or that any police cordons or activity post-incident are likely to be disruptive, then it may be preferable to have a local uniformed police senior officer to act as a 'talking head' and reassure the public. This leaves the SIO free to concentrate on getting the correct message across about the investigation and appeals for information.

13.10 **Types of Media Interviews**

Whatever the type of media, whether print, radio, TV or internet etc, interviews generally have the following different levels of engagement:

- Formal interviews. These are pre-arranged with the interviewer and likely to have prepared questions and researched areas to discuss. The interviewee gets a chance to fully prepare. Usually recorded in note form, on tape or on camera.

- Pre-recorded interviews. These provide an opportunity to pause and re-record comments that haven't come across well or have been said badly (provided the interviewer agrees). Sometimes for convenience they are recorded down a telephone line. The main disadvantage is they can be edited and important messages, such as public appeals may be blanked out.
- Live interviews. A far more pressurised type of interview as there is only one opportunity to get it right and the interviewer can stray from the agreed areas and ask awkward questions that are difficult to avoid because the broadcast is 'live' (eg about mistakes or criticisms). This is a favoured method in 'breaking news' headlines on news bulletins. Not for the faint hearted or inexperienced, although there are benefits because messages cannot be edited once they have been made by the interviewee.
- Press conferences (or 'media facilities'). The traditional method of allowing a large number of media representatives to hear the same message all at once to save time. Used for significant announcements that are likely to attract a lot of media interest. Prepared statements can be read out and members of the public such as victims' relatives may appear on them. Question and answer sessions can be added if appropriate at the end.

The golden rule is always to clarify what type of interview is being conducted and to establish whether it is live or pre-recorded, and prepare accordingly, remembering that live interviews require more preparation because of what they are!

KEY POINT—Informal interviews

These sometimes occur if a reporter gets a police source to agree (often spontaneously and unprompted) to provide an interview. A superficial, casual, or friendly nature and approach may lull an interviewee into becoming 'off their guard' and saying something they (and the SIO) later regret. Absence of note-taking or recording devices may betray the true intent to use the comments or produce a distorted version. These are also known as 'off the record' interviews and must be avoided at all costs. It is safer to treat everything as being 'on the record' as the reporter may be trustworthy but their news editor may not be! To avoid this occurring an SIO must stress to all their staff that they must not provide any unsolicited interviews to reporters.

13.11 Releasing Details of Victim(s)

Any decision to release details of a person who is a victim should not be made without the authority of the SIO. The general rule is that this should not be until:

- the person(s) has/have been formally identified;
- the immediate family/families has/have been informed;
- the family/families has/have been informed of the intention to release basic details to the media.

13.12 Preparing for Media Interviews

When providing interviews it is helpful to find out what the first question will be, what topics will be covered, how long it will last, and any other likely questions. It must be made clear about what the SIO wants to achieve and *does not* want to talk about. In order to anticipate lines of questioning the SIO should remember that the interviewer, like the investigators, will make use of the interrogative pronouns (5 × WH + H).

KEY POINT

Drafting some key words and messages to say and keeping them on a small piece of paper for easy reference and last-minute rehearsal is a good tip.

The media will have their own agendas and may wish to ambush or embarrass the police with certain lines of questioning. It is good to remember a rule of *turning negatives into positives*. When an interviewer focuses on the negative aspects of an investigation, the SIO should turn it back to the positives. For example, an interviewer may say to the SIO that the enquiry has been running for six weeks and there have been no arrests. This can be turned around by a response along the lines of:

> This is a complex enquiry and we have made such a good start it is taking us time to go through and prioritize all our lines of enquiry. Since we began we have already interviewed and taken statements from a large number of people . . .

Thinking and preparing carefully about the objectives of an interview is important, together with a rehearsal on delivering it beforehand (which is what the professionals do). Then it can be given in a confident, enthusiastic and positive manner.

13.13 Holding Back Information

As a general rule it is advisable to be open with the media wherever possible without compromising an enquiry. Sometimes, however, it can be tactically advantageous to withhold certain unique features or information contained within the knowledge of the investigation. This can be used for investigative or interviewing reasons, or for future appeals for information. Unusual features of the modus operandi are obvious examples and these can include the specific manner in which the attack was carried out, how many bullets were fired, blows struck, what part of the body was hit, how the scene was left, what items were stolen, or what type of weapon was used. In such circumstances it may be worth being open by explaining why certain details are withheld, for example: 'we would not wish to reveal these details as this might prevent us from identifying the offender later on', or 'for operational reasons we cannot reveal that information at this stage of the enquiry'.

> **Note:** Never say 'no comment' as it sounds dishonest or untrustworthy.

Such a tactical decision needs to be made at an early stage and recorded in the policy file. To safeguard the integrity of this tactic, the SIO may also have to withhold the information from most members of the enquiry team to prove it has never been leaked, either wittingly or unwittingly.

The security and integrity of the storage of any withheld information may have to be proved to the full satisfaction of a court at subsequent proceedings, particularly if the offender or a key witness provides information that has been deliberately withheld (therefore increasing its probative value). It may have to be proved beyond any doubt whatsoever there was no possibility withheld information was leaked out, therefore could only have been known by those involved in the incident itself.

This is a useful method of proving veracity of the offender's guilty knowledge, involvement, or subsequent confession. It can also help the SIO eliminate people who wish to wrongly admit their responsibility or mislead the enquiry. Other types of information from intelligence or evidential sources can be eliminated as incorrect if they do not match with factual information that has not been disclosed. Whereas any confession that includes deliberately withheld detail can constitute compelling evidence.

There may also be some instances where releasing information would breach a duty of confidentiality or contravene statutory requirements or national guidance (eg not naming rape victims). These should be carefully considered in line with relevant legislation and guidance. In difficult, sensitive, or exceptional cases the matter should be referred to a more senior officer, eg ACPO rank who will make a strategic decision. A strategic 'Gold Group' may need forming comprising of senior officers and community representatives and other agencies to discuss and agree a media and community impact strategy. Such is the importance in serious cases, particularly critical incidents, of getting the right message across in the right manner at the right time.

In the SIO's policy file the rationale for or against withholding or releasing information should be recorded. Two separate lists of examples of different reasons are as follows.

Reasons for disclosing/witholding information to/from the media

For disclosing to media	For witholding
Gain publicity or make an appeal.	Prevents offender(s) destroying evidence.
Maintain media/public interest in case.	Too many likely respondents.
Assist public in providing information.	Assess misinformation more accurately.
Gives public reassurance.	Confirm offender's guilty knowledge.
May prompt offender reaction.	Reveals sensitive policing methods.
Provide crime prevention advice.	May create 'copycat' offences.
Prevent media speculation.	May create more media intrusion.
Appeal to consciences.	Alerts offender to police activity.
Corrects media misinformation.	May affect fairness of trial process.
	May negatively affect the relationship with the family of the victim to disclose.

Reasons for disclosing/witholding information to/from the media

For disclosing to media	For witholding
	May alarm the public to disclose (note: may need to reconsider if the public needs information to keep them safe). To disclose may indicate or imply identity of an offender or key witness, particularly protected or vulnerable witnesses.

Case study—Damilola Taylor

In the review of the Damilola Taylor murder investigation it was reported that a tabloid newspaper published leaked information about a critical piece of evidence. This was about a finding from the post-mortem examination on Damilola of an object lodged in his windpipe. This leak was found to have a very damaging effect on the case and severely weakened prosecution evidence, because it could no longer be proved that the information could only have been acquired from the person(s) responsible. The confessional evidence that contained this fact was then ruled inadmissible (Rt Revd Sentamu, *et al.*, *Damilola Taylor Investigative Review* (2002).

13.14 Importance of Timing—Media Releases

The timing of media releases is not only of importance to investigative needs but also to avoid causing offence to any victims, family, and close friends and the wider community. It is extremely important that any developments or releases of important information are shared with the victim's family *before* being released to the media to avoid unnecessary or unpleasant surprises.

The release of information via the media must be made at a time that produces maximum benefit for the investigation. It may, for example, be linked into other (eg covert surveillance) investigative tactics. Any release of material such as pictures or CCTV must not compromise witness interviewing strategies by contaminating or influencing recollections. It is worthwhile seeking the advice of the Crown Prosecution Service if in any doubt about the legal implications on identification procedures, for example of photographs or details of possible suspects (note: sometimes parts of images can be pixellated).

To generate maximum publicity it may be advantageous to make appeals that coincide with any significant event, such as the arrest of offenders, execution of search warrants, court appearances, or anniversaries of incidents. These can be useful links to attach appeals to and generate media and public interest.

The wider news agenda must be considered and some form of scanning to see what other newsworthy events or stories are taking place that may compete for media attention. These could be major sporting or political events and anything of a local nature that would occupy the headlines. Print deadlines or publication dates are something else to consider, particularly if it is important to include a popular local media outlet that is not printed daily.

As a general rule:

- The timing of information, messages, and appeals may be crucial to other significant lines of enquiry.
- Chronological events and developments can enhance media attention, eg the arrest of suspects or the finding of crucial CCTV footage.
- The release of information must be *after* the close family, relatives, and friends of any victim(s) involved have been traced and officially informed of the details about the incident (although not possible in every case).
- It is important, as far as possible, to check what other events are taking place that may compete for the same media interest (provided they can be forseen).

Case study—Badly timed appeal

A pre-recorded media appeal regarding the case of a hotel arsonist and double murder investigation was scheduled to go out on news bulletins on a particular day. The appeal was regrettably superseded by an unforeseen major terrorist incident that occurred the same day. Consequently the appeal received very little or no publicity at all. The date was 11 September 2001.

13.15 Levels of Media Interest

It is an unfortunate fact that some cases will always attract more press interest than others. Unusual or aggravating features will always be more popular with the media than 'mundane' or routine cases. Some types of serious crime are just not considered 'newsworthy', eg the media tend not to be as interested in what they refer to as 'bad-on-bad' crime. The way to overcome this is to offer an extra feature that makes it more interesting and eye-catching. For example, providing CCTV or artist's impressions of the offenders may make the case more of an attractive proposition for the media to show some interest. Involving a MLO in the investigation's management team can often facilitate the identification of newsworthy 'angles' to exploit.

13.15.1 Publicity-generating methods

There is generally some criterion by which news producers and gatekeepers (editors and sub-editors) select events to be presented in the news. Matters that are judged 'newsworthy' include things such as the specific characteristics of an offence or incident, the location, the victim's age, status, background, and vulnerability, linked or series crimes, and race/hate motives. Some stories or incidents are major headlines from the very outset, while others are not considered newsworthy at all. Both of these extremes have implications for the investigation either in engaging with the media or getting them interested in sending out any required messages.

Incidents involving major crime such as murder and rape usually attract a substantial amount of press interest, especially in the first few days. Thereafter interest tends to diminish although some particularly newsworthy cases sustain media interest. Not all offences, however, attract the desired level of attention and in these circumstances the challenge is to gain and maximize media interest and publicity.

The media like to incorporate unusual features or anything that adds value or drama to their stories. For example: CCTV footage; pictures of offenders; artists' impressions; details of missing articles (eg clothing); reconstructions; horrifying injuries; personal appeals from a victim's family or close friends; dramatic 999 calls; pictures of police raids; or specialist units such as underwater search teams in full action. All these 'extras' make stories more appealing because they are more dramatic and interesting. They can therefore be used to tempt media agencies into running an appeal.

Sometimes it pays to be creative. There are many methods of proactively putting messages across without the need to provide media interviews. Useful examples of innovative publicity-generating ideas that can be used for witness and information appeals are as follows:

Checklist—Publicity methods

- Full-size billboard posters sponsored by local/national advertising agencies.
- Full-size upright cardboard cut-outs of a victim placed in popular stores and areas in order to attract attention and public assistance.
- Use of celebrities and sports personalities to make appeals.
- Use of modern media outlets on internet sites that attract a certain audience, eg young people (such as <http://www.YouTube.com>, Facebook etc.).
- Use of publications to target specific communities, eg gay/lesbian communities, or medical journals to help identify unusual physical features, characteristics, or operations of patients, victims, or suspects.
- Leaflet drops in specific geographical locations.

KEY POINT

To gain publicity media messages, posters, and leaflets need to be 'hard-hitting'. Here are some examples that have proved useful on major investigations:

- 'We know people saw what happened . . . do you want those responsible to get away with it?'
- 'What if he was your brother, boyfriend, or mate . . .?'
- 'We know people are scared, we can help and work together on this . . . don't let them get away with it.'
- 'Please help the police find my killers' (underneath picture of victim).

13.16 Partner Agencies

The police normally act as the lead agency for crime matters and a co-ordination point for all statements released by other agencies that may also be involved in the incident and/or investigation. It is good practice to ensure all parties are kept appraised of media statements and are given an opportunity for feedback. Partners should, where appropriate, be involved in formatting joint press releases (eg local authority or Crown Prosecution Service). It must first be discussed and agreed with the partner agency as to who has primacy in providing the information. Partners could include the following, although not an exhaustive list:

- local authorities (in particular social services or education departments)
- local schools
- youth clubs
- community organizations
- health authorities, mental health trusts, hospitals, etc
- prison authorities
- UK Border Agency, Home Office, SOCA, etc
- probation service
- Crown Prosecution Service
- other emergency services, such as ambulance or fire and rescue service
- private sector companies, including airports, airlines, retail outlets, football clubs, etc
- other forces, including British Transport Police (BTP).

Good liaison will ensure nothing is issued that could compromise the enquiry. In a major enquiry this may involve very close working arrangements and perhaps even co-location. There may be a requirement for seeking external advice and guidance from bodies such as independent advisory groups regarding specific community issues and formulating the wording of media responses. This may be a vital strategic requirement as badly chosen wording can have a dramatic effect on community relations.

13.17 Reconstructions

A media strategy can include reconstructions in order to remind the public of events and tease out important information. These are always worthy of consideration and serve as a high-impact way of getting a message across. They are also useful for internal communication messages such as electronic briefings and presentations about the case.

From experience, the BBC *Crimewatch* programme and localized crime-appeal programmes have proved to be invaluable means of attracting public support. They attract a large number of viewers/listeners, are very professional in their approach to the appeal, and will do everything they can to get the right message across. This is more of a collaborative type approach to solving the crime rather than just a news story. The team are extremely experienced and will assist in making the appeal very focused in its objectives.

The timing of these tactics is pivotal. Wherever possible they should be planned to coincide with other events of significance. Media publicity should be co-ordinated with other operational activity aimed at identifying or arresting key witnesses or suspects. Subtle messages can be passed through the wording of the appeals, especially if a particular person(s) is/are being targeted. Behavioural Investigative Advisers (available through the NPIA) can be useful in helping develop and phrase messages aimed at the suspect or witnesses.

There is a need to be aware that vast amounts of information from these appeals can result, all of which has to be evaluated and potentially investigated. Any large appeal/reconstruction needs to be as focused as possible—well-intentioned misleading information from the public may take up valuable time and resources. For example, in one case an appeal for the whereabouts of a locally based murder suspect produced sightings all over the United Kingdom, some of which proved difficult to ignore.

13.18 Legal Issues and the Press Complaints Commission (PCC)

Neither the police nor any other agency have any right to censor the media reporting of major crime. For example, if the media decide to obtain photographs of mutilated bodies and publish them, that is their decision. The SIO of course can do a lot to prevent this from happening by adequate control and screening of crime scenes and the careful planning of body removals.

The media approach to witnesses is a contentious subject, especially the offer of financial rewards for stories (aka cheque-book journalism). The matter of publishing photographs is another problem area, particularly where protected witnesses who have been photographed coming out of court are concerned. Usually a tactful approach to the editor by the SIO will suffice. The MLO should also be able to help by positively influencing reporters and editors in such circumstances.

In extreme circumstances inappropriate media behaviour can be reported to the Press Complaints Commission. Once an offender has been charged the media are duty bound by the *sub judice* rule and the provisions of the Contempt of Court Act 1981. This effectively prevents them from prejudicing any future criminal proceedings. Nor can they name juveniles.

The police must be careful with information and anything issued or released must be accurate and should not jeopardize criminal or civil proceedings, compromise investigations, put lives at risk, or impact inappropriately on people's right to privacy (eg ECHR Art 6 *right to a fair trial*, Art 8 *right to a private and family life*, and Art 14 *prohibition on discrimination*).

Any information released to the media must be properly recorded and retained and is potentially disclosable under the CPIA rules (Criminal Procedure Investigations Act 1996). When taking a case to court the Crown Prosecution Service and in most cases defence teams are allowed access to everything, including what has appeared or been stated in the press. For this reason all media interviews and press cuttings need to be retained and stored ready for court, normally a function of the MLO.

When an investigation goes into post-charge phase, the due legal process comes into force. Historically some cases have encountered particular problems over the press gaining access to, and in one case publishing, pictures of a suspect prior to charge or the commencement of the trial. Media agencies invariably have access to their own legal advisers and forces should be willing to draw this kind of behaviour to the attention of the PCC.

Case study—Harold Shipman trial

During the trial of the serial killer Dr Harold Shipman one radio station pre-empted and broadcasted the guilty verdict and was held in contempt by the trial court judge.

13.19 Training and Development

The earlier in a career SIOs get used to talking to the media the easier it becomes and there is generally good support available. The most should be made of any opportunity to get training and practice because it may one day come in useful. Appearing in the media is an ideal way of positively promoting an SIO's image and profile amongst colleagues, supervisors, and the general public, provided all goes well.

13.20 Using Appropriate Language

Using plain 'everyday' language during interviews is always preferable with a strict avoidance of police jargon, buzz phrases, or acronyms. Frequently repeated internal police terms such as 'intelligence-led policing' are not easily understood by members of the public and sound too official when used in media interviews. It is better to use clear and understandable terms that the public can relate to and understand, for example 'females' are women; and 'males' are men. The use of everyday language reaches out to the public a lot better than official terminology or police clichés. The best way to get people's interest and support is to use language that has meaning for them, such as:'What if it was your son, brother or best friend left in agony and bleeding to death on the pavement...?'

When providing interviews or contributing to media releases and publicity material there must be strict adherence to what in some forces is termed 'appropriate language'. This is simply to safeguard against offending certain sections of the community and should recognize issues of diversity, such as faith and culture. The use of discriminatory, prejudicial, or exclusive language indicates a lack of professionalism and encourages the exclusion, devaluing, and stereotyping of groups or individuals. Correct terminology is important together with a strict adherence to force diversity policies (eg knowing what the correct term is for 'gangs' or 'street workers', ie not prostitutes).

Checklist—Media handling and interviewing tips

Here is a guide for easy reference purposes:

The Dos...

- Make full advantage of good advice from a MLO.
- Be clear about the aims and objectives of the interview.
- Retain control of the interview by refocusing on the issues the SIO wants to talk about (and repeat messages as often as possible).
- Ask what type of questions will be asked beforehand so answers can be prepared.
- Prepare and practice thoroughly—identify and remember **3 × key messages**.
- Research any current 'hot topics' in the media. Think what else is current and could have an impact on the line of interviewing.
- Remember the questioner will also use the 5 × WH + H principles—Who? What? When? Where? Why? and How?
- Avoid waffle. Answers will probably be whittled down into 'sound bites' so make sure they're good ones.
- Stay relaxed, confident, and always *positive, positive, positive*.
- Be confident not nervous—treat the interviewer as one individual and ignore how many others may watch or listen.
- Adrenalin is required to produce excitement and stimulation—use it as an advantage.
- Check appearance, hair, tie, etc (if on camera) before the cameras start rolling.
- Check what material is displayed in the background and remove inappropriate or confidential material.
- Ignore noise and/or activity taking place off-camera.
- Look at the person interviewing, not the camera (unless directed otherwise).
- Use straightforward plain language, *not* police-speak or jargon.
- Be clear about the things that cannot be talked about, such as pending or ongoing court cases (or sensitive issues).
- Steer clear of giving personal views on subjects—know your force's media policy and stick to the party line.

- Ensure the victim's family is informed about the contents of any media release or interview *before* it is released.
- Ensure messages are clear and strong, stating exactly what is wanted from the public (ie do not just appeal for 'general information'—be specific).
- Never say 'No comment'—it sounds suspicious. Explain reasons why a question cannot be answered, or information released (useful alternatives are 'It is too early to say . . .', or 'That will be looked into as part of the ongoing investigation ...', or simply 'At this stage we are still unsure . . .').
- Avoid comments that imply guilt or innocence—never discuss the evidence.
- Use cognitive prompts wherever possible (eg such as a major sporting event).
- Emphasize the importance of all information, no matter how trivial.
- Remember to state the telephone number of the incident room (write it down!).
- Ensure there is an appropriate answering-machine recorded message and policy for regularly checking the incident room number, if giving out to the public or media.
- Inform the media as soon as possible when a suspect is charged. This helps to prevent the possibility of them inadvertently breaching the Contempt of Court Act and jeopardizing the case. Confirm the name, date of birth, address, full details of charges, and court date.
- Consider giving positive crime prevention advice along with reports of crime and offer public reassurance and help ease the fear of crime.
- Publicize good work, particularly heroics or important court results.
- Use interesting facets of the case to gain extra publicity and interest from the media (eg some useful CCTV footage).
- If being asked a question on behalf of someone else then tell the reporter he/she must speak to that person.
- Do not be afraid to admit when something has gone wrong but always go on to say what is being done to put the situation right—'ah yes, but . . .' (ie turning the negatives into positives).
- Keep full control of the interview and keep turning the subject back to the topics you want to talk about, follow your agenda not the interviewer's.

The Don'ts . . .

- Allow junior staff to provide information or interviews about the incident to members of the public or media without being authorized by the SIO.
- Wear checked or stripy clothing (they look blurred on camera).
- Fidget or sway on or stare at your feet.
- Stare directly at the camera (unless you are doing a 'down-the-lens' interview where the reporter is at a different venue.
- Drop your guard and make 'off the cuff' remarks as the microphone could be still switched on.
- Respond to the reporter's questions with just 'Yes' or 'No' answers. Try to avoid starting responses with 'Yes that's correct, I think ...'.
- Let the reporter try to put words into your mouth or try to get you to agree to what they are saying. (Instead use phrases such as 'well, that's one point of view but from a force perspective ...').
- Lower your voice or appear disinterested—always look and sound confident, enthusiastic, and in control.
- Ever criticize the criminal justice system or other agencies.

Useful phrases for the more difficult questions

If you disagree with a question then say so strongly and dismiss it, ie:

- 'I disagree.'
- 'No, you are wrong there.'
- 'That is an irrelevant question to what we are here to discuss.'
- 'That is not true.'
- 'That is not the issue.'
- 'That could only be pure speculation at this early stage.'

If being asked a question on behalf of someone else then tell the reporter he/she must speak to that person.

Do not be afraid to admit when something has gone wrong but always go on to say what is being done to put the situation right—'ah yes, but. . .' (ie turning the negatives into positives).

Keep full control of the interview and keep turning the subject back to the topics you want to talk about, follow your agenda not the interviewer's.

KEY POINTS

1. Dealing effectively and confidently with the media is a great way of raising an SIO's profile.
2. Anticipate the line of questioning that will be adopted. For example, local policing issues that may be at stake such as a build-up of previous similar incidents, concerns about crime prevention, safety issues, or where police cordons or activity post-incident are likely to be disruptive.
3. Draft out key words and **3 × KEY MESSAGES**, keeping them readily accessible on a small piece of paper for quick reference or last minute rehearsal.

13.21 **Conclusion**

Media appeals are useful because most major crimes are solved with help from ordinary members of the public. But the massive media response in some cases can either leave the police overwhelmed or force the enquiry in directions the SIO does not really want it to go. Therefore the media is either a burden or an investigative tool, depending on how it is handled.

Unquestionably, the SIO cannot afford to ignore their responsibilities in effectively managing and controlling the media. Modern technology means that news stories are more easily sent rapidly around the globe. So an appropriate strategy will be required soon after an incident occurs, remembering the media themselves are very quick at responding to newsworthy incidents.

The best advice is to request the services of a recognized media expert. In this chapter they have been referred to as MLOs, who are an invaluable asset to the SIO when under pressure from the media. They can substantially help in avoiding mistakes and gaffes in the news. Nonetheless the SIO *must* prepare and be in a state of readiness for any media interviews.

Making good use of the media should be viewed positively. Being able to reach thousands if not millions of viewers, listeners, and readers at no extra cost is a great opportunity to send out the right messages and appeals. An SIO should always take full advantage of opportunities for access to free publicity and support for major investigations in order to reach out and appeal to witnesses and communities. Improving the police image and increasing public support through good use of the media has been incorporated into routine police procedures and has to be at the forefront of the SIO's investigative strategies.

Chapter 14

Investigating Sudden and Unexplained Child Deaths

'Every child who dies deserves the right to have their sudden and unexplained death fully investigated in order that a cause of death can be identified and homicide excluded'.

Baroness Kennedy, SUDI working group, (2004)

14.1 Introduction

Sudden and unexplained[1] child[2] deaths (SUDC) can be extremely distressing and traumatic events that deeply affect parents, carers, families, relatives, and communities. It is hard to imagine anything worse for a family than the sudden death of their child. Unlike older and more mature people healthy infants and children are not expected to die. The stark reality is despite a reduction in infant deaths (eg by education campaigns) statistics show several hundred children in the UK will die before they reach one year of age. The vast majority of these deaths usually occur as a consequence of natural causes such as disease, physical defect or pure accident. Unfortunately a small percentage are also caused by callous and criminal acts of malicious, intentional, and gratuitous violence, maltreatment, neglect, physical abuse, or administered noxious substances or drugs. Children and infants can be subjected to deliberately inflicted head injuries, asphyxiation, stab wounds, hypothermia, dehydration, shaking injuries, methadone poisoning, broken/fractured bones,

[1] The term 'unexplained' means when a doctor cannot issue a death certificate after, say, a long term of illness for which there would be no need for police involvement.

[2] 'Child' means a person under 18 years of age.

drowning, burns, crushing injuries, ruptured/failed organs (liver, kidney etc), or abdominal injuries.

Consequently some children through no fault of their own are extremely vulnerable not only to poor health, disease, and accident but also dangerous parents, carers, or sexual predators. At a very tender age potential victims are extremely unlikely (and unable) to question or notice inherent dangers; nor are they in a position to object to lethal and deliberately administered noxious substances. It is to these unfortunate souls that Baroness Kennedy entrusts her confidence in the investigation process when their sudden death occurs.

Child death investigations, however, can and do pose additional challenges for SIOs due to the hidden nature of tangible evidence and telltale signs. Young infants and children's bodies are tinier than adults therefore indicators of non-accidental injuries are less noticeable. Contact trace evidence in intra-familial child homicides also has limited use unless there are specific blood injuries due to regular contact with the suspect(s). Therefore a requirement to properly diagnose, follow correct procedures, and thoroughly investigate all the circumstances becomes much more important. At the same time a difficult distinction has to be made between parents who are suffering from a tragic loss and those who have committed an extremely serious and grave crime.

It has been widely recognized that added trauma can be caused to innocent parents and families from inappropriate or insensitive handling of child deaths. High profile appeal court cases, for example the Angela Cannings (2002), Sally Clarke (1999), and Trupti Patel (2003) cases produced negative publicity and overturned convictions which severely undermined public trust and confidence. Others such as the Victoria Climbie and 'Baby P' cases produced similar bad publicity for reasons of lack of intervention and action. The media will always seize upon opportunities to present sensational critical headlines and is a backdrop against which complex child deaths are investigated.

Child death investigation procedures are now more sophisticated with a legal requirement to involve a variety of experts and specialists, particularly when interpreting injuries. Consequently it is not uncommon to encounter conflicting expert opinion due to the complex and specialist nature of ascertaining a precise cause of death in infants and children. Unfortunately, traditional methods of investigation can be more limited because unlike adult homicides the chance of using passive data, DNA, and fingerprint (contact trace) evidence are less likely given the home based familial nature and likely frequent contact between the suspect(s) and the child.

Nevertheless every child who dies unexpectedly has every right to have their sudden and unexplained death properly investigated. Any surviving siblings also have a 'right to life' under Art 2 of the European Convention on Human Rights (ECHR). In meeting this requirement an SIO is entrusted with the responsibility of concluding or excluding that a criminal act has taken place and helping to record an accurate cause of death. This chapter is now aimed at preparing SIOs for this challenge and providing (particular for those on-call) a guide for applying the most essential procedures and processes in order to effectively manage and conduct these investigations.

14.2 Classifying Child Deaths

Sudden death enquires are always challenging particularly when there is no medical explanation and the circumstances are uncertain or ambiguous. This is probably more so when a young infant or child dies under the care and supervision of parents in the family home which presents added challenges. A useful starting point, however, is to clarify the different categories or classifications that may apply to the circumstances that will help determine the type of police response required and scale of investigation. Most cases will begin as a category (1) SUDC death and can move up (or back down) the scale as the information changes. In order of seriousness every case will fall into one of the below categories.

Category 1	Not suspicious (ie natural or accidental with no apparent medical explanation or grounds to suspect a criminal act)
Category 2	Suspicious (certain factors raise the likelihood of a criminal act having been committed and warrant a more detailed investigation)
Category 3	Clearly homicide (or other serious criminal offence, see list below)

By definition category (1) cases almost always require a different type of response from those falling within categories (2) and (3). Safeguards, however, need to be incorporated into this level of investigation to safeguard evidence in case the circumstances and classification change. This is vitally important when considering the procedures referred to in sections of this chapter that are inappropriate for categories (2) and (3). For example, in homicide or suspicious deaths the classification for the investigation will change from a 'SUDC' death to a 'murder investigation' and the place where death is believed to have occurred (eg a child's bedroom) will be reclassified as a 'crime scene'. This will trigger standard procedures that are explained in other chapters of this handbook due to a criminal act being suspected (although in the majority of cases unless clearly homicide the body is likely to have been transported to hospital and not remained in position for forensic examination purposes, as explained later). The SIO will also be making early consideration of making arrests, treating witnesses as 'significant', managing the investigation on HOLMES2, conducting H-2-H enquiries, conducting witness trawls etc.

However, if there is nothing clearly obvious to suggest a suspicious death or homicide has occurred—*a very important judgement call*—the term 'SUDC' death will only be used to describe what is likely to be a lesser type of investigative response (though still very thorough, and certainly much more comprehensive than the standard police response to a non-suspicious sudden death of, say, an older person). Category (1) types are covered by guidelines outlined in this chapter while categories (2) and (3) are still investigated in accordance with the additional requirements contained within the *Murder Investigation Manual (MIM)* (ACPO, 2006).

Child homicides and suspicious deaths, however, are not always obvious or easily recognizable and it may be more difficult to initially determine what category to apply. There may be no obvious signs such as wounds or fractures. Head and internal injuries, asphyxiation, ruptured blood vessels in lungs, traces of poisoning, abuse, and neglect can be very difficult to detect in young children, particularly infants. Therefore child death procedures have been consolidated to ensure all category (1) SUDC investigations meet a higher investigative standard. This is to provide not only adequate safeguards for sensitive parent management and support but to ensure every effort is made to establish why a child died unexpectedly and rule in or out criminal involvement. This is, however, required to be done more sensitively; an example being the expectation of a more tactful and less obvious use of golden hour(s) tasks; another is the call for a greater multi-professional approach to the investigation. SUDC procedures ask for a balance to be struck between the requirement for carrying out an effective investigation and the need to acknowledge and cater for the needs of the parents and other children that may be affected. For these reasons an experienced senior detective and/or SIO should always lead a child death investigation, particularly when it is initially unclear as to what category it falls into.

'Infant deaths must be allocated to an accredited SIO, who must retain overall responsibility for the investigation. A detective officer of at least Inspector rank should be tasked to immediately attend the scene and take charge of the investigation, in all cases of sudden unexplained infant deaths, whether or not there are any obvious circumstances. This applies if the child is still at the scene or if the child has been removed to hospital. It is further recommended that this detective has child protection experience' (ACPO Guidelines (2006), Infant Deaths supplementary reading *Murder Investigation Manual*).

Notes:

1. Child death procedures may equally apply to older children. However, due to their age and development sudden deaths in older children are more likely to allow for a simpler assessment and determination of category.
2. A number of different terms are commonly used to refer to child deaths such as 'SUDI' (Sudden Unexplained Death in Infancy—infant meaning up to one year of age); or 'SUDICA' (Sudden Unexpected Death in Infants, Children and Adolescents; 'SUDC' (Sudden Unexpected Death in Children); SIDS (Sudden Infant Death Syndrome) sometimes described as 'cot deaths' which is simply a classification to indicate that after all the investigations have been concluded, the coroner is unable to say why the child died, but there is no indication of maltreatment.

KEY POINTS

1. National child abuse investigation guidance documents (ACPO and Centrex, 2005 and Baroness Kennedy in the Royal College of Pathologists and Paediatrics and Child Health Report, 2004) suggested an

SIO dealing with sudden or unnatural child deaths should be one with experience of child-abuse investigations; or for such an accredited person to be closely involved with the investigation (eg to spot early evidence of child abuse etc). Other staff selected to work on these enquiries should ideally also come from a 'child abuse' type of investigative background.

2. Child deaths are also potential 'critical incidents' meaning a senior detective (if suspicious then a SIO) should assume responsibility and lead the investigation.
3. In addition to establishing whether a crime has or has not been committed there is always a responsibility on the police to assist the coroner in examining the circumstances for the purposes of an inquest.
4. It is vital that correct procedures are followed even when initial suspicions prove to be unfounded. This helps protect everyone concerned, including the parents from unfair and inaccurate speculation.
5. The death of a child is not a police matter in cases where a doctor has issued a medical certificate as to cause of death. This is usually when they have been historically treating the child for a diagnosed serious illness or condition which can be medically attributed to the death, therefore the death is not then 'unexplained' or 'unexpected'.

14.3 Category (3) Type Offences

Below is a list of possible offences for a category (3) type case:

- **Murder**—contrary to common law.
- **Manslaughter** (including corporate manslaughter, eg deaths in healthcare settings)—contrary to common law.
- **Familial homicide** (causing or allowing the death of a child or vulnerable adult)—s 5 of the Domestic Violence, Crime and Victims Act (DVCV) 2004.
- **Infanticide**—s 1 of the Infanticide Act 1938.

Other related or kindred offences might be:

- **Child destruction**—s 1(1) of the Infant Life (Preservation) Act 1929.
- **Administering/procuring drugs/instruments to procure an abortion or miscarriage**—s 58/59 of the Offences Against the Person Act 1861.

- **Exposing a child whereby life is endangered**—s 27 of the Offences Against the Person Act 1861.
- **Concealment of birth**—s 60 of the Offences Against the Person Act 1861.
- **Preventing lawful burial**—concealment of a corpse—dispose or destroy a dead body.
- **Neglect**—death of infant under three years caused by suffocation while infant in bed with person 16 years or over who is under the influence of drink—s 1 of the Children and Young Persons Act 1933.
- **Wilfully assault, ill-treat, neglect, abandon, expose child u-16 yrs**—s 1 of the Children and Young Persons Act 1933.
- **Maliciously administering poison etc or noxious thing so as to endanger life**—s 23 of the Offences Against the Person Act 1861.
- **Attempting to choke etc so as to commit an indictable offence**—s 21 of the Offences Against the Person Act 1861.
- **Drunk in charge of child apparently under seven years**—s 2(1) of the Licensing Act 1902.
- **Child abduction by person connected with the child**—s 1 of the Child Abduction Act 1984 as amended by the Family Law Act 1986 and the Children Act 1989.
- **Grievous bodily harm or wounding with intent**—s 18 of the Offences Against the Person Act 1861.

14.4 Factors Which May Increase Suspicion

Whilst every case needs to be judged on its own merits in SUDC cases there may be surrounding facts or circumstances that may be indictors of suspicion. The following are listed as a guide (some are also cited in 'Guidelines in Infant Deaths' (ACPO, 2006) additional chapter to MIM):

1. History of violence in the family to children.
2. Parents or carers provide an inconsistent account of the events surrounding the child's death.
3. Mental health issues within the family.
4. Previous unusual illness, episodes or recent admissions to hospital.
5. The child is older than 12 months (these unexplained deaths are rare and unusual).

6. Intelligence suggests the child has been 'at risk' or precursor incidents suggest this should be the case, eg child or sibling is on a 'child protection' or 'care plan'.
7. Family of the child are known to the social services.
8. Parent or carer has a criminal record.
9. The child has been dead longer than is stated.
10. Crusted blood on the face of the type associated with smothering and physical abuse rather than the 'pinkish' mucus associated with resuscitation.
11. Unusual bruises or petechiae or retinal haemoraghing eg. in the eyeballs—symptoms of suffocation or shaking (have someone check the eyeballs as soon as possible).
12. Presence of foreign bodies in the upper airway.
13. Child has come from a family in which a previous child has died unexpectedly.
14. The child comes from a family or household with a history of drug, alcohol, or domestic violence abuse.
15. Any inappropriate delay by the parents in seeking medical help.
16. The position of the child, its surroundings, and the condition in which it was found give cause for concern.
17. Evidence of high risk behaviour, eg domestic abuse, drugs/alcohol use.
18. Parent's reaction/demeanour/behaviour.
19. Neglect issues.

KEY POINT

When a child does not die immediately, evidence-gathering and case-building opportunities should not be neglected. This can occur when a criminal act is suspected and a child is in intensive hospital care. As the child has not died there is a risk the investigation may not be treated with the same amount of rigour and must be avoided. A risk assessment and control strategy may also be required if the parents (who may be suspects or even in custody) request to be with their child at the moment of death. If applicable this will have to be managed carefully to avoid compromising the investigation, scene management and security. However, a long term strategic goal is to maintain a good working relationship with other professionals such as doctors, and the impact on that relationship of a perceived insensitive approach by police, must be taken into consideration at this stage.

14.5 Key Multi-Agency Guidance

A leading document when investigating child deaths is: *Working Together to Safeguard Children, A guide to inter-agency working to safeguard and promote the welfare of children* (HM Government); hereinafter referred to as 'Working Together' . This has had a clear impact in the response to and investigation of child deaths. Chapter 7 deals with child death review cases and correct procedures for a 'rapid response' to unexpected deaths of children. These guidelines became compulsory on 1 April 2008 following a number of high profile cases in the UK (where the standard of investigation was hitherto called into question) and now underpin all principles and procedures in SUDC cases. Widespread consultation took place with agencies such as the medical profession, coroner's service, children's social care, government officials, and the ACPO Homicide Working Group to produce these working guidelines. It was highly recommended that all forces contribute to their Local Safeguarding Children Board (LSCB) protocols to ensure that all investigations have a multi-agency approach to them, which is seen as best practice in determining the cause of death and assisting prosecutions.

Chapter 7 also sets out roles for various professionals tasked with enquiring into and evaluating all unexpected child deaths, reaching conclusions about whether and how they could have been prevented and undertaking an overview of the deaths of all children together with clear lines of accountability. It stipulates how, when a child dies unexpectedly, several investigative processes should be instigated, particularly when abuse or neglect are factors. It is intended that the relevant professionals and organizations work together in a co-ordinated fashion in order to minimize duplication and ensure any lessons learnt contribute to safeguarding and promoting the welfare of children for the future.

14.5.1 Definition of an 'unexpected death'

Section 7.6 of the 'Working Together' report states:

> 'An unexpected death is defined as the death of a child that was not anticipated as a significant possibility 24 hours before the death, or where there was a similarly unexpected collapse leading to or precipitating the events that led to the death (Fleming et al., 2000; The Royal College of Pathologists and the Royal College of Paediatrics

and Child Health, 2004). A designated paediatrician responsible for unexpected deaths in childhood should be consulted where professionals are uncertain about whether the death is unexpected. If in doubt, these procedures should be followed until the available evidence enables a different decision to be made.'

Note: The same definition applies if a child is admitted to a hospital ward and subsequently dies unexpectedly while in hospital.

14.6 Guiding Principles—SUDC Investigations (Categories 1, 2, and 3)

It is worthwhile referring to a number of fundamental principles that underpin the work of all relevant professionals, especially responding officers and SIOs when dealing with all categories of sudden and unexplained child deaths. These are:

- The need to maintain a sympathetic and sensitive approach to the child's family, regardless of the cause of death. Police action has to be carefully balanced between considerations for the bereaved family and recognition that a potentially serious crime has been committed.
- Retaining an awareness that innocent parents/carers wrongly accused of harming their child are caused unimaginable suffering as a consequence.
- Retaining an open mind as to how and why the child or young person died. A child with seemingly no obvious signs of external or internal injury could still have been the victim of unlawful killing because the signs may be less detectable.
- A co-ordinated and rapid inter-agency response is required from not just the police but other specialists and service providers who have particular knowledge and experience of child abuse and development (working together/sharing information).
- Communicating clearly and sensitively with parents/carers (who are not suspects) about the need for an investigation, explaining all necessary activities and actions and role of the police, other agencies and the coroner's enquiry.

- Recognizing and understanding that all SUDC deaths require a thorough and meticulous but compassionate standard of investigation.
- Ensure there is a proportionate response to the circumstances.
- Preserve all potential evidence.

14.7 Inter-Agency Collaboration (Rapid Response)

Success for any type of child death investigation relies upon effective cooperation and liaison between the police, essential experts (paediatricians) and certain other agencies all working together (see list below). The death will trigger the coming together of a team of professionals from a number of agencies and is known as the 'Rapid Response'.

This is why in most force regions joint LSCB protocols cater for this and it is advisable for on-call SIOs to be familiar with them. Each agency will also have its own guidelines, which reflect the work done to review child death procedures by the Royal College of Pathologists and Royal College of Paediatrics; detailing a multi-agency approach for the sudden and unexpected death in infants, children and adolescents.

A key point is that all agencies share the responsibility for an investigation to establish the cause of death and a duty of care to the parents and surviving children. An SIO who takes the lead for the criminal investigation will be expected to work alongside highly qualified and experienced professionals, who together must balance the medical, forensic and all other investigative requirements with the welfare of the parents affected and potential risks to other (and future) children.

A multi-agency collaborative approach may involve such agencies as:

- ambulance/paramedic service
- hospital medical and nursing staff
- safeguarding children coordinators
- coroners (and coroner's officers)
- general practitioners (GPs)
- health visitors or school nurses
- mental health professionals

- midwifery staff
- paediatricians
- pathologists
- children's social care service
- education authority
- police child protection teams
- community representatives
- police investigators/SIO.

Between an assembled team of professionals there should be the necessary knowledge, expertise, information, and resources to mount a sophisticated joint investigation into why and how a child or young person died. Any sudden and unexplained death must trigger the coming together of such resources with the SIO ensuring there is trust and confidence amongst the team for a coordinated inter-agency response, particularly in relation to information sharing.

KEY POINT

Recognition of maltreatment related child deaths is not the responsibility of just the police or other groups of professionals working in isolation. Rather it is crucially interdependent on the collaboration among a team of professionals that will include the coroner, police, pathologists, paediatrician, and other health and social care professionals (cited in P Sidebotham and P Fleming, *Unexpected Death in Childhood: A Handbook for Practitioners* (2007), 91).

Each agency and individual will have different areas of responsibility. For example, a paediatrician will most likely focus upon issues that have implications for others such as infectious diseases, in addition to the cause of death. The coroner will focus solely upon the cause and circumstances of the death (ie who, when, where, and how) and the social services on safeguarding the welfare of other children in the family. These various agendas should be inter-twined and viewed as complementary in establishing why a child has died, providing parents and others affected with support, and quickly identifying and investigating any potentially suspicious circumstances.

An overriding consideration for all agencies involved is to safeguard: ECHR Art 2—Right to life of surviving or future siblings.

Checklist—Inter-agency—Investigative responsibilities

- Work together to make rapid enquiries into and evaluate reasons for and circumstances of the death, in agreement with the coroner.
- Undertake the types of enquiries/investigations that relate to the current responsibilities of respective organizations.
- Collect information in a standard, nationally agreed manner.
- Support and follow the death investigation through to conclusion and maintain contact at regular intervals with family members and other professionals who have ongoing responsibilities for other family members, ensuring they are informed and kept up to date with information about the child's death.

14.8 Inter-Agency Case Meetings

In SUDC cases various representatives should meet together for an early strategy meeting to share information, discuss the circumstances of the case, and plan the investigation and support process. Further risks can then be assessed and it should be decided who will assume responsibility for recording, collating, and disseminating all the deliberations and decisions, although each professional concerned should be responsible for recording all their own discussions, decisions, and notes.

The SIO (or where unavailable his/her nominated representative) should fully engage in all multi-agency meetings outlined in chapter 7 of 'Working Together'.

These meetings provide an opportunity not only to review and discuss important aspects of the investigation and findings but also identify key issues for further investigation and discuss information about the child who has died and risks to the remaining family. Together the various agencies can then formulate, agree, and record a cohesive action plan. The plan will stipulate actions, tasks, or responsibilities to be delivered by specific individuals or agencies within a set timeframe.

The SUDC paediatrician should review all medical records relating to the dead child and relevant family members. They should consult the SIO about any information contained in them that could potentially assist the police investigation. This should include medical records held by A&E, hospital paediatrician/consultant, community nurses (includes health visitors, school nurses, and children's community nurses), and the child's general practitioner. If the SIO requires a copy of any medical record for the purposes of their investigation, consent issues for any living person may need to be addressed or other legal authority obtained.

Note: Protocols can be obtained from the CPS website <http://www.cps.gov.uk/publications/agencies/protocolletter.html.>

During the investigation an SIO should liaise closely with any children's services personnel if there is any possibility that care proceedings may be commenced in respect of siblings of the dead child/young person. This will help ensure that any potential criminal investigation is not inadvertently compromised by the disclosure of information during such proceedings. Any family court cases may also produce useful information for the criminal investigation that with leave of the judge can be used in a criminal trial, eg additional medical evidence.

14.9 Hospital Procedures

Child deaths are likely to be reported directly to the emergency services and routed through an ambulance control centre. Sometimes they may even originate directly from A&E units at hospitals. Occasionally a general practitioner will be first on the scene and notify the emergency services. Call handlers are responsible for obtaining as much information from the person reporting the death as possible and organizing the rapid despatch of an ambulance to the scene. In most cases the police will be notified at the same time and could feasibly arrive simultaneously.

Guidelines in 'Working Together' stipulate that after an initial attempt at resuscitation a child should be taken directly to an A&E unit (unless obvious and clear signs a homicide has occurred). Taking a deceased child to a hospital rather than a mortuary is aimed to reduce the impact on the parents and allow them to go with the child and receive themselves any necessary initial support from trained hospital staff. It also facilitates the early examination of the body by a consultant paediatrician in support of the investigation into the cause of death. Once at the hospital a lead clinician will normally contact a paediatrician to arrange contacting other agencies including the police via standard communication protocols.

A member of nursing staff is usually allocated to deal with and support the family. They should also begin obtaining initial details from the family and accurately recording them. Hospital staff will also be fully briefed by the paramedics or ambulance crew who attended and conveyed the child to hospital. The SIO should note that is a highly valuable source of information and probably the first account (other than the call to the emergency services) of what took place. If the circumstances develop into something more serious and suspicious, the paramedics may become significant witnesses for the purposes of determining mode of interview.

Once a child has been certified clinically dead hospital staff will normally facilitate arrangements for the parents to be allowed time with their child. This is usually followed by a more in-depth interview (also known as 'history taking') which is normally done at the hospital with the parents and wherever possible the police should take the lead in this process with a paediatrician involved to interpret all medical and parenting issues. If the parents are suspected of a criminal offence then the SIO shall have to determine whether this should take place at all and instead have them treated as 'suspects'. (Note: If they are 'suspected of a criminal offence' then they must, by definition, be treated as 'suspects'. This doesn't necessarily mean they have to be arrested immediately, but it does mean that once that threshold has been crossed, it will be unlikely that the product of any informal history taking could be used in any criminal proceedings.)

KEY POINTS

1. As with all sudden deaths, suspicious or otherwise, a doctor or qualified paramedic must certify death (also known as 'fact of death'). Most paramedics are qualified to do so and trained to minimize disruption or potential contamination.
2. Only when obvious signs of maltreatment or suspicion and death has been certified will paramedics or ambulance crew leave a child's body in place (or if there is a health risk in movement). It is then for the SIO to determine when and how the body is eventually

transported from the scene. This also applies to all older children who normally would also be taken to an A&E unit unless this is inappropriate because the circumstances of the death require the body to remain at the scene for forensic examination and retrieval.

3. Expert paediatric assessment may reveal the presence of retinal or subdural haemorrhages, bruising or other head injuries that would determine that a criminal investigation should be mounted.
4. A coroner (and/or coroner's officer) should always be informed. Once the death of a child has been referred to the coroner and they have accepted it, the coroner has jurisdiction over the body and all that pertains to it (eg taking of samples).

14.10 Initial Police Response

KEY POINT

How the initial response is dealt with always affects any forensic and evidence gathering opportunities—Fact.

Most of the standard MIM type procedures outlined in Chapter 4 of this handbook will underpin the police response, activities, and actions when dealing with an incident that may involve a category (2) or (3) type death. However, as the majority of unexplained child deaths are not usually the result of criminal acts, ie category (1), the police response needs to be finely balanced between providing the utmost consideration for the needs of an innocent, grieving family and conducting a thorough investigation into the cause of death. Child deaths have added sensitivities, complexities, and challenges, both from a professional and emotional perspective. These can be emotionally demanding events that require a high degree of composure, experience, and tact, therefore using trained child protection/abuse unit investigators is a preferred option, wherever possible. There is also a requirement to look for any factors that may raise suspicion (see earlier) even though everything overtly appears normal. For these reasons only the most experienced staff, supervisors, and senior detectives should be used, whenever possible, in the initial response.

If the initial response requires police attendance at a child's home address it should, wherever possible, be conducted in a 'low key' and unobtrusive fashion. This is to reduce or minimize any undue attention or distress to the parents and attracting the early attention of the community, public, and media. Plain clothes officers, particularly detectives in unmarked vehicles are ideal for using as first response officers if practicable, provided no unreasonable delay is caused as a result (remembering the 'golden hour' principles).

Officers attending should make an initial assessment of not just the scene and circumstances of the child's death but also the safety and welfare of any other children at the same location. Depending upon the circumstances of the death and the conditions in which other children may be found it may be necessary to take prompt action to secure their safety and wellbeing, a decision ideally taken in consultation with supervisory staff and other agencies.

KEY POINT

When attending a scene, including hospitals, police staff should be careful when speaking to colleagues, or using police radios and mobile phones within earshot of grieving parents, carers, or relatives. Overhearing the use of insensitive terms such as 'suspicious death' or 'crime scene' may cause unnecessary distress in being misinterpreted.

If the initial police attendance is to a hospital, the first officer(s) should liaise with any A&E staff that have examined the child/young person or spoken to parents/carers to establish what is known so far. Careful and accurate note-taking of these details is required. They should also ensure that the parents/carers have been informed of the need for police involvement.

It is good practice to give an early explanation for the necessity for police involvement to the parents and the reasons for any action taken. For example, it could be explained that the police are acting on behalf of the coroner who requires an investigation to be carried out for all sudden and unexplained death of any child that occurs with the aim of establishing why the death has occurred. Most parents and carers, however, will welcome the opportunity of finding answers to questions such as 'Why did my child die?' which they themselves need in order to move on with their lives.

When dealing with family/carers there should be an early attempt to recover, label, and secure any nappies, clothing, or possessions taken from the child by hospital staff that may be important to the investigation (being mindful of cross-contamination issues). Items taken should be treated as potential exhibits and packaged separately and properly to avoid any risk of contamination. They may be later required for forensic examination.

KEY POINT

Usually sudden deaths of children and young persons under the age of 18 years are subject to what some forces term 'special procedure investigations'. Local protocols should dictate how the investigation is to be managed and will almost certainly require the early notification and attendance of a senior detective and/or SIO to take command and control, and commence a policy log.

The initial investigation into the circumstances of a child's death includes the obtaining of information and historical details from the parents. This procedure may have already been commenced if the body is at hospital by medical staff (see earlier section under 'hospital procedures'). This process forms an important part of the rapport building with the family, parents, and relatives and for the purposes of an investigation is an ideal opportunity for using essential police tradecraft skills and intuition in order to form an early opinion on whether there maybe any suspicious circumstances.

It must be remembered that the initial response is always within the golden hour(s) period, a time when emotions are running high and people are at their most vulnerable. Offenders in particular are under the greatest levels of psychological and emotional pressure and can make mistakes or give false and inaccurate accounts and details. This is therefore an opportunity to gauge reactions, observe attitudes, behaviour, and demeanour of the parents or carers and look for any suspicious or disturbing signs or comments, flawed explanations that do not add up or give rise for concern. As with any other investigation, skilful handling of people (including significant witnesses), information building, and accurate record-keeping are always essential during the initial stages (golden hours).

Note: If the circumstances for whatever reason have meant that the child's body has been left in place at an address, there is an opportunity for conducting a *visual* (ie without touching) check of the body and its surroundings to look for any obvious signs of maltreatment or information to assist the investigation.

Checklist—Initial responders—first actions at hospital

- Confirm location of child's body and confirm continuity of movement.
- Make early attempt to locate any nappy, clothing, or possessions taken from the child/young person by hospital staff.
- Try to obtain and record details of the person/s who removed the items from the body (or later handled them).
- Treat all items as potential exhibits and package/label them separately to avoid any risk of contamination (they may later require forensic examination).
- Seek the consent of the parent/carer (or owner if different) to retain items—there may be sufficient grounds under s 19 of PACE if a criminal offence has been committed.
- Reassure the parents/carers/owner that the items will be returned to them as quickly as possible and in the best possible condition.
- Ask for the duty SIO to be informed and request them to attend as soon as possible.
- Brief the SIO (or nominated representative) about enquiries made and information obtained.

14.11 Preserving the 'Scene' (or Place Where Death Occurred)

Even when a child death is being treated as non-suspicious, initial response officers should strive to keep the primary 'scene' (or 'place where death has occurred'—remembering to choose words carefully in front of grieving parents when the cause of death is unknown) as sterile and secure as possible for when an SIO and health official arrive to conduct a home visit (inspection). In child deaths the 'scene' is likely to be the room where the child died though this may not always be limited to one room if the child has been moved around or it is not so certain or obvious (it may even be necessary to control the entire household). It might also, however, dependent on the circumstances (eg it may be possible to securely lock the scene), involve an officer controlling the security of a room until a thorough combined examination can take place. The senior detective/SIO is responsible for deciding whether to request the attendance of a CSI and/or photographer (and any other resources as felt necessary), although there is a strong argument for CSIs routinely attending all death scenes with the SIO. The photographing and videoing of the 'scene' is always to be treated as good practice in every case (even if not initially suspicious) as it a way of ensuring there is permanent record in case the circumstances later develop into something more serious (eg in post-mortem results such as toxicology).

Note: Protocols described earlier that cater for taking the child and parents to a hospital emergency unit may render the task of preserving the scene, eg home address, that much easier.

KEY POINTS

1. In order to protect parents from undue public and media attention it is advisable to try and avoid using cordon tape around their home.
2. Arrange video and photographing of the 'scene' as standard procedure in all SUDC cases as a safeguard in case the death subsequently develops into a criminal investigation.
3. Think wider than just the room in which the child died—the whole premises may paint a better picture of the environment in which the child lived prior to death (eg cleanliness, food, clothing, toys, etc).

Vitally important is that in cases where there is no immediate suspicion the preservation process must be handled tactfully and sensitively, particularly if a child's home is involved. This may, for example, require an explanation as to why it is such a necessary process for the investigation (ie it will significantly help determine why the child died and is standard procedure). Some parents may become highly sceptical of police procedures and will require careful management. There is also a need for parents (including carers, relatives, and friends) to be dissuaded (and effectively prevented if needs be) from disposing of anything evidential such as bottles, bedding, nappies, residue food and drink etc that may be useful to the investigation. In extreme cases where parents are obstructive powers under s 19 of PACE (or even ss 18 and 32 if arrests have to be made) may have to be considered.

It can be common practice for officers to seize bedding and sometimes even the cot in which a child died. Yet it is more beneficial for the bedding etc to be left undisturbed so it can be observed by the SIO and paediatrician who jointly attend for a home visit and assessment. In natural deaths bedding can be one of the key items that may hold clues as to how a child died, eg thickness, position, etc). In many ways there is nothing different between these procedures and standard crime scene procedures about preserving and protecting everything as it is found (as explained in Chapter 5). One main difference, however, is the requirement to be more sensitive and tactful for the benefit of grieving parents and distressed relatives, especially when in the majority of cases no crime will have been committed.

KEY POINT

The SIO may deem it inappropriate to remove a child's body from where death occurred, particularly when there are clear signs of suspicion. In most cases, however, it can be anticipated that the body will already have been held, moved, or interfered with by the parent or carer and, therefore, removal to A&E will not normally jeopardize a forensic examination. This is a matter for which advice should be taken from a competent and experienced Crime Scene Investigator/Manager (CSI/CSM).

14.12 'Scene' Assessment and Examination

Regardless of the circumstances an SIO will always need to conduct a thorough and proportionate scene assessment while in a preserved format and arrange for any necessary photographs, visual images, measurements, drawings etc (always seen as a safer measure for preserving an accurate record, whatever the circumstances). Other experts and advisers such as a CSI or plan drawer may also be required to assist the SIO and if believed suspicious then the standard MIM procedures contained within Chapter 5 need to be applied (eg a forensic pathologist required to attend to discuss and formulate a crime scene examination, body recovery strategy, etc). In category (1) SUDC enquiries scene examination tactics may need to be reviewed once the aforementioned 'home visit' has been completed or if more information comes to light (in which case the enquiry may move into a higher category).

The confidentiality requirement must be observed so as not to bring undue suspicion upon or attention to the parents of the deceased child. Visits to the family home (and elsewhere if clearly connected to the parents) should be done as discretely as possible. If a search of the place where death has occurred (non-suspicious) is to be conducted staff involved in the search should be fully briefed beforehand and the process conducted in a highly sensitive manner. Where items are to be removed from the child's house, once again it should be explained to the parents how this is standard procedure that may help establish why their child has died. The SIO should be in a position to justify to the parents/carers the need to remove or seize any item for examination. Assurances should be given that wherever practicable items will be returned to them in the best possible condition (and some forces have special containers for returning keepsakes such as a child's jewellery).

KEY POINT

It is essential to make a diagram/sketch of the 'scene' and the SIO may themselves wish to compose one themselves or enlist expert services. This can be used to show any room measurements, location of doors, windows, heating, any furniture or objects in the room, position of others etc relative position of the child. Consideration can also be given to using computer 3D graphics for mapping and display purposes.

14.12.1 'Scene' investigation—quick checklist

The following represent various scene considerations in a SUDC enquiry:

- Check for delays in getting to or finding the child; signs of alteration or staging by parents/carers.
- Searches should include all potential scenes, multiple rooms and vehicles, and exterior of any dwelling.
- Check for any rubbish receptacles and laundry for discarded items.
- Obtaining photographs, visual imagery, and scaled diagrams of the scene(s) will almost certainly be required.
- Take measurements of furniture and seize any relevant furniture items.
- Look for possible weapons or objects that may have been used to cause harm (eg smothering) especially if there are any patterned injuries found on the child's body.

- Give consideration for recovering trace evidence (fingerprints, DNA, blood, hair, fibres, etc) on possible articles, weapons, drugs, etc.
- Check for evidence of soiling, vomit, illness, colic, messes, or spills, (monitors or devices if a special needs child). (Note: vomit containing 'coffee grain' appearance suggests internal bleeding.)
- Seize any documentary evidence, eg life insurance policy on child, diaries, medical appointments or birth/health records, midwifery papers, etc.
- Check for evidence of neglect, quality of caretaking (food, warmth, clothing, etc).
- Check for baby bottles and baby food containers.
- Evidence of drugs, alcohol usage, domestic problems, debts (things that may induce stress on the parents).
- Child's clothing, bedding, and toys.
- Paraphernalia used and discarded by emergency personnel (eg paramedics) for elimination purposes.
- Any potential toxins and medicines.
- Photographs and videotapes of child showing physical developmental levels.
- Childcare books and magazines.
- Telephone records, computers, phones, emails, social networking sites used.
- Being vigilant for anything that looks out of place.

'PAY ATTENTION TO DETAILS—The smallest seeds hold the biggest truths, physical evidence doesn't lie—people do.'

14.13 **Role of the SIO**

As in all other cases the senior detective/SIO should initially liaise with response officers and/or supervision and methodically go through the briefing/de-briefing process (see Chapter 4) to review what has been done/not done, information known etc. One of the first considerations should relate to confirming the whereabouts of the child's body which may have been removed to hospital. A visual check of the body can then be made and identification confirmed. A paediatrician must also be contacted (if not already done so) to commence an investigation into why the child died (speaking to the parents etc). If the matter is being treated as a homicide or suspicious death then, as stated throughout this chapter, procedures as per any other major investigation should commence and override anything else (eg making early arrests, identifying crime scenes, making significant witness interviews, etc). These procedures are all covered elsewhere in this handbook.

However, where circumstances do not point to immediate suspicion it is recommended a joint investigation is mounted as per the 'Working Together' guidelines with the SIO working alongside an appropriate paediatrician. If the child's body is at hospital a joint interview will usually be conducted with the parents or carers, sometimes referred to in the medical profession as 'history taking'.

It is the role of the senior detective/SIO to explain the purpose and process of the investigation to the parents, and the reason for a post mortem (ie may help determine cause of death and is a requirement of the coroner). However, in most cases the A&E paediatrician will have done this before the police arrive at the hospital.

14.13.1 Personally viewing the body

The SIO should arrange to view the body themselves (preferably with the consultant or SUDC paediatrician at hospital) and record details of any observations. In doing so they will be personally aware of all visible injuries or marks of concern and the state of the body before any post mortem takes place, eg hygiene, nutritional state, whether post-mortem staining and rigor mortis is consistent with early accounts given by parents/carers. This information may be needed to brief the coroner when s/he is considering the type of post mortem to hold.

In gathering and assessing information the ABC rules and the 5 × Wh + H principles are always useful whatever the circumstances (see also Chapter 2). The SIO is wise to use these interrogative pronouns to aid the process of information gathering to identify not only intelligence gaps, but also where the missing information may be obtained from. Questions worth posing may be along the lines of:

Questions to professionals:

- Who pronounced life extinct, where and when?
- Who found the child dead?

- When, how, and by whom the emergency services were called?
- What actions have been taken by the paramedics or medical staff who attended? What is their assessment of the circumstances and what was said to them when they arrived?
- Was resuscitation attempted and if so by whom?
- Were there any responses obtained from the child?
- Where was the body found, who by, and where was it moved to/from?
- What was the exact position of the body? (any evidence of over-wrapping, restriction in ventilation, risk of smothering, potential hazards etc?)
- Were there any suspicious marks or injuries on the child's body?
- What are the parents' explanations as to the circumstances leading up to the death?
- Who was present who may have posed a threat to the child?
- What condition were the parents/carers in (eg drink/drug abuse apparent)?
- What was their behaviour and attitude to the death?
- What evidence is there to suggest neglect such as temperature of the scene, condition of accommodation, general hygiene, people who smoke heavily in the household, and the availability of food/drink?
- What database checks have been conducted and intelligence is available on the child, parents, carers, family, or regular visitors?
- What other agencies or agents are involved (eg Child Protection Register, Legal Order etc)?
- How many times have the police or other agencies been involved with the child or family previously and what for?

Questions to parents/carers during initial accounts and/or 'history taking':

- Who was with the child at each stage leading up to the death?
- How many other people (and who) were present in the premises around the time?
- Who was in the child's room/bed?
- What was the sleeping position of the child?
- Where was the child sleeping in relation to the parents/carers and in what?
- Who saw the child last?

- What condition was the child in then?
- When was the child last fed, how (eg breast fed) what with and who by?
- What was the child's behaviour 48–72 hours prior to death?
- Who put the child to bed, when and in what position?
- How did the child look when found (eg blue, stiff, etc)?
- What was the child's sleeping environment like? Who else was sleeping near the child? What was the location or position of the cot relative other objects in the room?
- What was the health of the child prior to death?
- What previous medical conditions or treatment has the child had? (including disabilities or impairments)?
- Were any health care professionals involved with the child recently?
- What medicine had the child been taking?
- Was there any bedding over/under the child?
- Was an infant intercom/monitor in place?
- How many other children are in the same household or family?
- What are the social circumstances of the child? (Who does the child normally live with—past and present? Do both parents cohabit? Are the parents married? Who is the natural father? Any recent changes in composition of the household? Who has come and gone and for what reasons?)
- What other child deaths have the family/extended family experienced?
- Who is the child's and family's GP?
- What if any sort of special treatment did the child require after birth?

Such questions and subsequent answers may of course trigger other and subsequent thoughts.

(See also *'Guidelines in Infant Deaths'* additional material to MIM (ACPO, 2006).)

KEY POINTS

1. The SIO's objectives are to establish why the child died, what was the cause of death and circumstances, what (if any) offences have been committed or *not* committed and, if so, who was/were responsible.
2. It is important that the family understand the need for an investigation, stressing it is not just to find evidence of guilt, but also of innocence (see also Chapter 2.2—'Objectives of an investigation').

3. In child deaths that are criminally attributable (eg homicide), potential suspects (eg parents) are usually readily identifiable and therefore available for early accounts or significant statements. This is a good time to consider their behaviour, attitude, and response. Strange behaviour or inaccuracies must not, however, be confused with genuine and innocent people who under extreme stress or emotional panic may experience difficulty in recounting details or events.

14.13.2 General actions—SIO checklist

- Assume command and control of the investigation.
- Attend the location of the deceased, usually an emergency department.
- Call out sufficient staff to assist. As a rule of thumb, at least a detective sergeant and three detectives will be a minimum team needed to undertake the fast-track actions.
- Commence a policy decision log.
- Critically assess the circumstances surrounding the death.
- Keep open minded and be alert to suspicious indicators such as 'staging'.
- Confirm death certified (the cause won't be certified if it is unexplained) and by whom.
- Arrange personal viewing of the body.
- Identify and locate next of kin, if not done already arrange for them to be informed of child's death.
- Deploy FLO where appropriate with an agreed strategy (ideally child abuse/death trained) and consider strategy if it is believed there is a 'suspect in the family'.
- Arrange formal identification of body.
- Develop investigative strategies and deploy staff to explore all reasonable lines of enquiry.
- Ensure all staff engaged on the enquiry are, as far as possible, caring and sensitive to those who are grieving (keep them updated with information and explanations of 'what' and 'why').
- Obtain and review contents of any calls to emergency services (eg copy of 999 call or to any medical emergency helplines).
- Arrange early interviewing of all response staff, call takers, paramedics, medical staff etc. (Note: In the case of the paramedics and A&E doctors, this needs to be done by way of careful and detailed statement taking, ensuring all words used by carers and their actions at the home are accurately recalled

and recorded in the statement (eg were they on the mobile phone to anyone during the rescusitation process). It is very important to ensure police investigators speak directly to the individuals involved and not rely solely on their notes. In the case of the A&E doctor this may mean getting them out of bed again!)

- Establish what physical examination has taken place and what if any photographs or written records have been made (eg by hospital staff) and if any suspicious or identifiable marks have been found. (A police photographer should always be deployed if there are any concerning marks on the body—do not rely on hospital photographs.)
- Review rationale for deeming the death suspicious/not suspicious.
- Determine what category and type of investigation is required (ensure there is a proportionate response).
- Establish identification and control of all potential 'scenes' (especially the 'death scene' and child's body if at hospital) and preserve evidence.
- Obtain treatment and medical records of deceased in preparation for post mortem (ie paediatric or joint post mortem).
- Where applicable ensure a pre-transfusion blood sample is obtained.
- Avoid uniform staff attending the home address and using overt cordons.
- Decide whether and when it is necessary to seize any potential exhibits or leave them in place (bedding, clothing, feeding implements, articles used during resuscitation attempts, any evidence of alcohol use in waste bins etc).
- Obtain and record detailed initial separate accounts from parents/carers (may be in conjunction with paediatrician obtain medical history).
- Consider obtaining blood samples for alcohol/drugs from parents/carers (by a force medical examiner—FME). (Note: This should be requested in all cases where overlaying is one of the hypotheses, and or drink drugs are believed to be a factor.)
- Ensure other children and members of household are treated as potential witnesses. Check on welfare, conduct risk assessment, and determine if any immediate protection measures or medical examinations are required for them.
- Establish if there are any potential significant witnesses (if young in age may be vulnerable) and make appropriate interview arrangements.

- Establish what the sequence of events was leading up to the death.
- Determine what personnel requirements and specialist training/experience is required for resources likely to be required.
- Determine what CSI/CSM and photographers/video required for 'scene' examination and recording (good practice in every case).
- Inform coroner of the death and brief on investigative intentions.
- Assess the risks to staff and the investigation (welfare, investigative barriers, etc).
- Make early contact with the paediatrician and agree parameters for the fast joint response phase (as per 'Working Together' report).
- If required consider arrangements for joint visit to 'death scene' (within first 24 hours) but not to be unduly delayed (potential loss of evidence).
- Assess the circumstances of the death, any unusual facts, behaviour, or responses and develop investigative strategies deploying staff to explore all reasonable lines of enquiry.
- Determine whether forensic or standard post mortem required and co-ordinate paediatric post-mortem examination with a paediatric pathologist or pathologist with some paediatric expertise.
- Liaise with local policing commander to complete community impact assessment.
- Work together in a multi-agency investigation and share information wherever possible.

KEY POINTS

1. In non-suspicious deaths the SIO will be expected to follow guidance contained within chapter 7 of 'Working Together'. Any deviation may need to be justified.
2. Specialist evidence may be needed for a prosecution from medical and scientific experts. SIOs must, however, guard against assuming paediatricians and other medical personnel will automatically carry out the appropriate tests, whilst they are expert at healing sick children, they are not necessarily expert in gathering evidence for a criminal investigation. Maintaining a clear dialogue with all professionals involved ensures everyone understands exactly what is required and why.
3. In some circumstances an SIO may wish to consider deeming the person who last saw the child alive the status of significant witness.

The usual guidelines would then apply for making arrangements to ideally record the interview provided the witness agrees.

4. If the SIO considers a parent/carer to be a suspect they should be afforded the usual legal rights and safeguards under PACE. If the suspect is not arrested and interviewed in accordance with Code C, the SIO needs to take into consideration that the product of any conversations (such as their initial account to the police/paediatrician) may not be available in any subsequent criminal proceedings.
5. Witness statements may be required from hospital staff such as nurses or doctors. Care must be taken when these people wish to produce their own statements when it may be preferable for them to be obtained by specially trained police staff.
6. Consideration should be given to any carers being interviewed separately to avoid the possibility of each contaminating the others version of events.

14.14 SIO General Investigative Actions

There are general investigative actions that the SIO might wish to consider when investigating child deaths. These must be decided on a case-by-case basis and as a guide may include actions to seize CCTV or ANPR for any scenes or significant routes to corroborate accounts from parents and showing movements of any suspects, or seizing and examining mobile phones for any calls or text messages of interest. House-to-house enquiries may also prove useful for witness trawls, also relevant are media appeals, significant witness interviews, computer examinations, etc. These are all covered in other chapters of this handbook, and as such shouldn't be ignored simply because an intra-familial child death is involved.

Case study—Use of 'Guthrie test'

An SIO investigated the death of a child in which there was reason to believe a noxious substance had been administered from which death resulted. The SIO used what is known as the Guthrie test—a heel prick blood sample obtained by a midwife soon after the delivery of a baby which is forwarded to the public health laboratory and analysed for conditions such as cystic fibrosis and hypothyroidism. The SIO was able to use this sample to establish if the drug had been in the child's system during birth therefore eliminating a possible defence for the parents of the child.

14.15 Combined SIO and Health Care Professional (Paediatrician) Home Visit—Category (1) SUDC Cases

The place where the SUDC death occurred is always likely to yield important information for the purposes of the investigation and should therefore be kept intact. When a baby or older child dies in a non-hospital setting, and the death is not deemed clearly suspicious (ie not a category (2) or (3) death) the senior detective/SIO and paediatrician should decide whether a joint visit to the place where the child died should be undertaken. This should almost always take place for infants (under 2 years) who die unexpectedly. As well as deciding if the visit should happen, it should also be decided how soon (ie guidelines state it should be within 24 hours) and who should attend. This is in accordance with the guidelines and protocols contained in 'Working Together'. If, for whatever reason this has to be done separately, for example if unnecessary delay might result because of the unavailability of the health-care professional, the SIO may wish to consider going ahead and conferring later. Although 'Working Together' suggests a visit within 24 hours, as a rule of thumb, the SIO and CSI should ideally visit the death scene within the first six hours of commencing the investigation. Whatever is found at the death scene may significantly affect the course of the investigation and early considerations. It is a case of striking the right balance between ensuring evidence is not lost against benefits of a more professional and thorough joint visit and assessment.

If the death, trauma, or collapse occurred in a place other than the home location, consideration should still be given to visiting and examining the family home. Similarly, if the child had been living in different locations in the time leading up to death, consideration should be given to 'joint visits' to them also. As well as deciding if the 'joint visit/s' should take place, it should be decided how soon (within 24 hours) and who should attend. The SIO and SUDC paediatrician can talk with the parents/carers and inspect/assess the scene. The purpose of a 'joint visit' is to identify all possible factors (from both a police and medical perspective) that may help explain why the child died.

The home visit is also designed to enable both the SIO and paediatrician to review the historical information (and any other investigative information that may have been obtained) and put it into context at the scene of death. This allows for maximizing any opportunities for obtaining as much information as possible from the scene, the family, any available witnesses and the environment in which the child has died. The parents are likely to be a little more relaxed in their home surroundings in which to repeat facts and detail and add any further information to assist. Any discussions do not necessarily have to take place in the exact room where the child has died, but will probably necessitate a visit to the room and place at some point so that the parents can describe in detail the circumstances leading up to the death (and the SIO may wish to video record the process).

As with the examination every effort should be made to keep police visits to the family home 'low key' and to a minimum. A comprehensive plan by the SIO (in consultation with the SUDC or 'duty' consultant paediatrician) to capture all potential information or evidence in one visit should, in most cases, avoid any need to disturb the family again. Repeated police visits may unnecessarily increase the apprehensions of the parents/carers that they are under suspicion and potentially cause added concern and embarrassment.

If the SUDC paediatrician has not attended the scene, the SIO can consider using the images captured to brief him/her and, in criminal investigation cases, the forensic pathologist before post mortem.

KEY POINT

It may seem unusual for a paediatrician to be attending, examining, and possibly contaminating a potential crime scene, which if the death is obviously suspicious from the outset may not be appropriate. The majority of SUDC cases, however, are not suspicious and the visit can help the diagnosis of a natural cause of death or otherwise.

14.16 Managing the Child's Family

A recurring theme has been how an official involvement of professionals including police investigators in child deaths may cause a devastating effect on parents, close family, and those connected to them. They will have suffered one of the worst shocks ever imaginable which will change their lives forever with an added complication of the stigma that accompanies it. Grieving parents may consequently exhibit a variety of reactions such as overwhelming grief, anger, confusion, hysterics, disbelief, or guilt. A key rule therefore is that they should be managed *sympathetically* and *sensitively*, remembering that some frustration may be levelled at the police as a manifestation of their distress. There are other guidelines that can be adopted for dealing with the grieving parents of deceased infants and children, such as:

- avoiding undue criticism of the parents/carers either direct or implied;
- not referring to the infant as 'it' but using the infant's proper name;
- avoiding placing children's bodies into body bags;
- allowing parents to see, touch, and hold their loved one provided it does not interfere with clinical care or any forensic examination and only in the presence of a professional;
- dealing sensitively with religious beliefs and cultural differences while remembering the importance of evidence preservation;
- allowing parents/carers an opportunity to ask questions and have explained to them what is happening at every stage;
- allowing the parents/carers to accompany the deceased infant/child to hospital;
- arranging for other children in the household to be looked after;
- giving advice on useful support agencies and resources (eg FSID—Foundation for the Study of Infant Deaths—<http://www.fsid.org.uk>)

The police response and activity can prove very distressing to the family, particularly if there are no criminal offences involved. It should be emphasized, however about the importance and usefulness of a thorough investigation which is beneficial for them in finding answers to important questions and establishing what caused the death of their child.

KEY POINT

Demonstrating sensitivity and tact in handling child death cases does not prevent a shrewd and tenacious SIO from being 'compassionately sceptical' about the circumstances under investigation. How an SIO presents themselves outwardly may have to betray what they are thinking or considering inwardly—which is totally professional. This also complies with the fundamental ABC principle (see also Chapter 2)

14.16.1 Deployment of an FLO

Whatever category of child death is being investigated the SIO may consider it highly appropriate to appoint an FLO (Family Liaison Officer) at the earliest opportunity; although this is not always a routine procedure in category (1) SUDC investigations. Certain circumstances may influence this decision, such as a high level of media interest and/or intrusion. There may also be added complications in dealing fairly and equally with estranged natural parents who may have other partners. The SIO may also decide that in order to ensure the family are fully engaged as partners in the investigation process and/or in order to maintain a sensitive, supportive relationship with them a deployment of an FLO is necessary. If there is, for example, a reliance on tests such as toxicology and specialist examinations of portions of the brain there may be a protracted amount of time for the parents to await the outcome. This can be a very unsettling, uncertain, and stressful time for the parents.

During this period at the same time as providing support an FLO can act as the SIO's conduit within the family and home environment, picking up on any vital evidence that may assist the investigation. This is particularly important if there is a greater reliance on circumstantial supportive evidence, especially if a potential offender(s) comes from within or is connected to the child's family (termed 'intra-familial' see below) with family dynamics that can change or intensify.

Ideally the appointed FLO should be 'child protection' trained (the role of the FLO is described in Chapter 9). There are, for example, useful support agencies for grieving parents and relatives the details of which should be known to trained FLOs and hospital staff (eg <http://www.FSID.org.uk>).

KEY POINTS

1. The requirements to recognize and deal effectively with diversity issues are fundamentally important. Positive and practical support should be given to people who may feel vulnerable and acknowledgement and respect for a broad range of social and cultural customs, beliefs, and values; avoiding prejudice and discrimination.
2. Where a child is living in the UK but their parents live abroad, careful consideration should be given to how best to contact and support the bereaved family members.
3. Parents/carers should be kept up to date with information about their child's death and the involvement of each professional unless the sharing of such information would jeopardize a police criminal investigation.

14.17 Allowing the Holding and Touching of a Child's Body

It is entirely natural for a parent/carer to want to hold or touch the body of their deceased child/young person and is known to help with the grieving process. As a general rule this is normally permitted if the death is not deemed suspicious provided it is supervised by a professional (eg police officer or hospital staff) who should be present during the process.

In most cases it is unlikely important forensic evidence will be lost by the tactful and sensible use of this activity. It is usually trace evidence being sought if someone else (eg a stranger) other than a person who has legitimate access to the child (eg parent/carer) is suspected of involvement or having caused the death. Individual circumstances will dictate whether this is the case. Contact trace evidence in intra-familial homicides, however, has limited use because parents and family members will have had recent and regular access and legitimate contact with the child. Any contamination potential can be carefully managed, eg if clothing is required for body fluids or interpretation then seizing prior to contact with the child would suffice. Any concern about the unlikely possibility of post-mortem injuries being caused during this process can be negated by the ability to easily distinguish between ante- and post-mortem injuries. Thus any external forensic gathering potential should be balanced against the needs of the grieving family; though ultimately the decision rests with the SIO, national guidelines favour allowing parental contact provided appropriate control measures are in place.

A supervised contact session, if and when permitted, is something to be agreed between the SIO, CSM (for advice where possible) and hospital staff. Hospital A&E departments are normally used to dealing with unexpected child deaths and experienced nursing staff should be able to arrange for a child to be protected (eg covered in a blanket) and suitably prepared for the parent/carers to hold. Normally the parents are seated to avoid them dropping the infant and a member of experienced staff present to ensure parents comply with any tactful instructions or in case they become over emotional or unwell during the process.

A comprehensive record of any contact with the body should be made, together with details of those who supervised the session and how. This information should be entered into the SIO's policy file.

KEY POINT

Instructions from an SIO for strict refusal of any request to touch or handle a child's body must be passed to hospital (A&E) staff without delay, especially if the child/young person is already at (or en route to) hospital. This direction must be clearly communicated before it is too late to halt processes that are considered acceptable and agreed procedures.

An SIO must decide on the appropriateness of this course of action, which will depend largely upon the particular circumstances of the case and degree of suspicion falling on the parents. It is beneficial to discuss the process with an experienced CSI beforehand and/or the forensic pathologist/paediatrician. Once permitted the parents should be closely monitored so they do not mishandle or mistreat the body in any way.

Occasionally, the parents may ask to hold the dead child while the initial account is being taken by police and a paediatrician. This should not be allowed as the emotional affect on the professionals involved may be such that they are dissuaded from calmly and carefully asking comprehensive and probing questions.

14.17.1 Requests for mementoes

Requests for mementoes such as prints of hands and feet, photographs, and locks of hair are normally permitted but in cases where there is a police-led investigation and there are concerns and suspicions this should not be agreed until after the pathologist has fully examined the body. The police should only refuse the request (and not every family will want them) if there is good reason to believe it would jeopardize a criminal investigation. The responsibility for arranging the taking and delivery of mementoes from the body (which is always potentially a crime scene) always rests with the SIO. If a decision is made to do so, details of the method adopted and agreed terms must be recorded in the SIO's policy file. However, in non-suspicious cases the parents should normally be allowed to leave the hospital with the requested mementoes, as it can be several days before a post mortem takes place.

Note: 'Training will help SIOs to be confident that in most cases no harm would come from allowing these basic human requests from the family' (J Fox in P Sidebotham and P Fleming (2007) *Unexpected Death in Childhood: A Handbook for Practitioners* (Wiley, 2007), 146).

KEY POINT

Some parents/carers may, for religious, cultural, or personal reasons find the idea of taking mementoes objectionable and/or distressing. For this reason it is important the matter is handled with sensitivity. If they do not wish to discuss the subject then their decision should be respected, but it should be made clear that once their child has been buried or cremated this opportunity will have been lost.

14.18 Post Mortems

An autopsy is one of the most critical elements of a death investigation, particularly those involving the sudden unexpected death of a child. The procedure provides crucial information for the SIO and any other agencies involved in the investigation. The child's parents and family will also want to know why their child died.

After life extinct (or 'fact of death') is pronounced the coroner has jurisdiction over the child's body and as per adult suspicious death investigations the SIO should liaise with the coroner and discuss the arrangements for a post mortem. In child death cases the post mortem should always be undertaken by a paediatric pathologist and if deemed suspicious the SIO should also request a Home Office accredited forensic pathologist (who takes the lead) to carry out the autopsy alongside the paediatric pathologist.

KEY POINT

Post-mortem examinations in young and small infants and children can prove very intrusive with organs often having to be removed for closer examination. These can, in some instances, take several weeks or months to conclude.

As in any other death investigation the SIO should provide a full briefing (and it is advisable to keep a record in case of disputes later) to the pathologist(s) beforehand including the showing of any scene video and photographs (if available) and any information gathered to inform the process. Now that there are prescriptive guidelines for the management of SUDC deaths (history-taking, joint home visit, inter-agency approach, etc) any additional details should also be provided for the pathologist before an examination commences. This will include a summary of the child's medical history including relevant background information concerning the family and any concerns raised by other agencies. This is to ensure the pathologist has as much detail as possible and is intended to be an improvement on previous procedures which often contained far less detailed briefing.

In all cases a full skeletal radiological survey and ideally an MRI bodyscan should be carried out before the autopsy takes place. These scans should be interpreted by a consultant paediatric radiologist.

Child post mortems are different to those conducted on adult bodies, if for no other reason the bodies being examined are much tinier and important areas cannot be examined or viewed with the naked eye so easily. The range of diseases to be considered can also vary from adults as the bodies concerned are still in the stages of natural development. Dependent on the circumstances added histological examinations and samples may be required and a wider range of ancillary tests. For example, if 'shaking' or 'suffocation' is suspected then the brain may need examination by a neuropathologist and eyes by an ophthalmic expert. These added tests may mean the identification of unlawful and malicious acts can be more difficult and/or take longer to detect. For this reason the examination will involve a pathologist who has special expertise such as a paediatric pathologist.

If there is anything to indicate criminality then in addition to a forensic pathologist the SIO will naturally require other resources and experts to be present such as an exhibits officer, CSI, and photographer (procedures outlined in Chapter 12). It must also be stressed that in cases involving a 'non-suspicious' post mortem that subsequently reveals matters of concern, the autopsy process should be immediately halted, the coroner informed and the case referred to an SIO (if not already involved). The coroner will then decide whether to continue or re-convene the post mortem with the additional involvement of a forensic pathologist.

It is mandatory in cases of child deaths, prior to the post mortem examination, for a full skeletal x-ray survey to be performed and interpreted by a paediatric radiologist. Skeletal surveys in older children may also be considered on a case-by-case basis. A paediatric radiologist can interpret any survey conducted. In cases which may inviolve head injury, a CT scan should also be done of the head before autopsy commences.

KEY POINT

'Occasionally the cause of death may be recorded as 'unascertained' where there is a raised level of suspicion. For example, the post-mortem findings may show factors consistent with suffocation that are not conclusive so that this cannot be given as the actual cause of death, although there may be some grounds to suggest this may have been the case, either accidentally or deliberately. With this essential element of a potential offence absent, ie the cause of death, the Crown would be unable to proceed with a criminal prosecution, eg with a charge of child neglect where the child was overlaid by an adult who was intoxicated. (Cited in D Marshall, 'Child Homicides: A Suspect in the Family—Issues for the Family Liaison Strategy' (2008) 4(1) *The Journal of Homicide and Major Incident Investigation* (NPIA).

Under the requirements of the Human Tissue Act 2004 a pathologist is allowed to retain only such tissues as required to ascertain the cause of death. The next of kin (ie parents) must be consulted regarding their wishes about the retention of the tissue for any further research purposes, and the return to them for burial/cremation or sensitive disposal by other means must be a consideration. It may, however, be in the parents' best interests or for that of others for the pathologist to retain tissue samples, especially when a definitive conclusion as to cause of death has not been reached. However, this may be a sensitive area and one that has previously caused some degree of controversy. This does not, of course, apply to samples taken for the purposes of a criminal investigation under s 19 PACE (see also Chapter 12). There can also be retention of samples with permission of the coroner. He/she can authorize retention until an inquest has been concluded.

Case study—Suspicious death of young girl—vagal inhibition

At 7.50 am on a chilly November morning a previously healthy nine-year-old girl was found dead by her mother on top of her bed in their family home. Police officers attended the emergency call, immediately treated the death as suspicious and summoned the assistance of senior detectives. A subsequent post mortem was initially inconclusive because there were no obvious signs to indicate the cause of death other than petechial haemorraghing (small red or purple spots as a result of bleeding) in the eyes. A CSI had also recovered a saliva sample from the victim's chin which was crucially later found to contain presence of spermatozoa. The victim's natural father was later arrested for an unconnected murder of a young prostitute and his DNA was matched to the sperm found on his daughter. It is known that death in a young person can sometimes occur without leaving any physical signs, for example by means of obstruction to respiration and mediated by the mechanism of vagal inhibition, where a victim is placed in a stressful or frightening situation and there is a sudden stopping of the heart mediated by the nervous system. The pathologist was then able to conclude that although the diagnosis on the mechanism of death was initially unascertained, the additional information meant he could conclude the victim most likely died due to the release of adrenalin and fear producing a sudden abnormality of heart rhythm. This was most likely from the father having forced the child to commit an oral sexual act that produced a fatal shock reaction. This conclusion was supported not only by the presence of petechiae and DNA from the sperm, but other supporting circumstantial evidence uncovered during a thorough child death investigation and the father was charged with murdering his daughter.

14.18.1 Hair samples

A useful sample to take from the child victim and/or suspect(s) is head hair. The head hair should be taken from the child's body at post mortem prior to any incisions being made on the child's body to negate any suggestions of contamination. Important trace evidence for drugs can be found in hair such as an indication of a fatal dose of methadone, heroin, or cocaine. If drugs are suspected other samples should also be appropriately obtained such as nail clippings and vitreous humour, including the clear gel that fills the space between the lens and the retina of the eyeball.

14.19 Head Injuries (RADI and TRIAD)

It is important to recognize that head injuries are common in child homicides and the most common type is known in the acronym RADI. This stands for:

R Rotation
A Acceleration
D Deceleration
I Impact

These are common force injuries normally associated with 'shaken baby' type assaults. There is also common reference to a term known as the 'Triad of Injuries' (TRIAD). These are different from those acquired, say, in a short fall and point towards non-accidental causes. The three injuries referred to under this term are:

- Subdural haemorrhages: bleeding beneath the dural membrane.
- Brain encephalopathy (ie swelling): damage to the brain affecting function.
- Retinal haemorraghes: bleeding into the linings of the eyes.

The Cannings judgment ruled that the presence of these three injuries together indicates maltreatment, so it follows that whenever the SIO is informed that the triad is present the case will always be considered suspicious.

KEY POINT

Professionally produced graphics illustrating injuries sustained by child victims can be of great value when presenting expert evidence in court. They allow images that would otherwise be too distressing for jurors to see.

14.20 'Intra-Familial' Child Homicides

This is a term now often used in certain types of investigation where the offender is:

- a family or extended family member;
- a person living in the same household;

- a person visiting the household regularly;
- a person having care responsibility at time of the alleged offence, eg teacher, health or youth worker, baby-sitter, child minder, etc;
- a carer (where the victim is under 18 years);
- a carer when the child is in care, eg foster carer or children's home employee.

14.20.1 Section 5 of the Domestic Violence, Crime and Victims (DVCV) Act 2004

A useful piece of legislation introduced in 2005 created an offence designed to cater for circumstances where there are two or more parents/carers who may be responsible for the death of a child with neither accepting responsibility. Initially evidence will be gathered in order to prosecute for a primary offence of murder or manslaughter but where this is not possible then an offence under s 5 can be considered.

An offence under s 5 provides that members of a household who have frequent contact with a child under 16 years or a vulnerable adult will be guilty of an offence if they:

- caused the death;
- allowed the death, if the following conditions are met:
  - they were aware, or ought to have been, that the victim was at significant risk of serious physical harm (ie grevious bodily harm under the Offences Against the Person Act 1861);
  - they failed to take reasonable steps to prevent that person coming to harm;
  - the person died from the unlawful act of a household member in circumstances that the defendant foresaw or ought to have foreseen.

The offence is limited to where the victim has died of an unlawful act so it does not apply to circumstances where there has been an accident. The offence only applies to members of the household who had frequent contact with the victim, and could therefore be reasonably expected to be aware of any risk to the victim and to have a duty to protect them from harm. The household member must have failed to take 'reasonable steps' to protect the child. The offence only applies to those aged 16 years and over unless they are the mother or father of the child.

Unfortunately the offence is not retrospective and only caters for offences committed after 21 March 2005. The maximum penalty on conviction for an offence under this legislation is 14 years' imprisonment. Suspects can be additionally charged with offences of murder and/or manslaughter if they are suspected of 'causing the death'. The term 'household' is intended to be given its ordinary English meaning and would be unlikely to cover care homes or professional nurseries.

Case examples—Use of s 5 offence

1. A child died as a result of a fat embolism but had numerous non-accidental injuries for which neither parent would admit responsibility. After a trial both parents were convicted of an offence under s 5 of the Domestic Violence Crime and Victims Act 2004 for causing or allowing the death of a child and were sentenced to nine years' imprisonment.
2. A child was murdered by her mother's partner in a domestic violence and child neglect environment. After trial the partner was convicted of murder and sentenced to life imprisonment; the mother was convicted of an offence under the s 5 legislation and was given a two-year community rehabilitation order.

Note: Additional guidance can be found in Home Office circular 9/2005 and a Home Office pamphlet *Protecting Children and Vulnerable Adults—The New Law on Familial Homicide* (HO 2/2005), available at <http://www.homeoffice.gov.uk/about-us/publications/home-office-circulars/circulars-2005/009-2005/>.

14.21 Intelligence Strategies

An SIO should carefully craft an intelligence strategy to compliment the main lines of enquiry (MLOE). Wherever necessary, this should include researching all key persons present around the time of death on police intelligence databases. As with any other investigation all available intelligence on persons connected to the circumstances of the child's death will enhance the quality of the investigation.

Valuable background information may be held about the dead child and any other persons of interest, eg parents/carers, by partner agencies at case meetings. Data protection authorities may be needed by these agencies if the consent of the 'other' persons has not already been obtained. Local data sharing protocols may help in this process.

14.22 'CATCHEM' Database and 'SCAS'

The Centralised Analytical Team Collating Homicide Expertise and Management (CATCHEM) database is held by the NPIA. It holds data on offenders and offences relating to child homicide and long-term missing children, and provides a useful support system for investigating officers. In addition, the Serious Crime Analysis Section (SCAS) based at Bramshill within the NPIA, provides investigative support in cases where there is either an unknown or sexual motive and/or the homicide remains unsolved after a period of 28 days. (For further information see <http:/www.NPIA.police.uk>.)

14.23 National Injuries Database

The National Injuries Database, NPIA, can offer a range of services to investigating officers dealing with child death investigations:

1. The National Injuries Database is held by the NPIA and stores data focused on victims and injuries. This data covers a wide variety of cases including non-accidental injuries in children, suspicious child deaths, and child homicides. The database can be searched to provide intelligence for an investigation team in relation to cause of injuries. Intelligence reports produced from the database can support investigative strategies and the medical experts involved in a case.
2. If an injury is patterned in nature and a particular weapon is suspected to have been used to inflict the injury the National Injuries Database can scope the potential for an overlay which might depict the correlation between the injury and the weapon.

3. The National Injuries Database team have access to the NPIA Expert Advisers Database, which contains, amongst other things details of medical experts covering a wide range of paediatric specialisms. The staff are experienced in assisting investigating officers with sourcing the appropriate medical experts to provide expert medical opinion.
4. A member of the National Injuries Database team holds a portfolio in paediatric cases and keeps up to date with emerging medical research in the field of child deaths. Investigative officers can be provided with updates in relation to prosecution and defence arguments and also given references for informative research and guidance.

14.24 Information Sharing

Some useful pieces of legislation are as follows:

- s 10 of the Children Act (CA) 2004: statutory guidance states that good information sharing is key to successful collaborative working and that arrangements under s 10 CA 2004 should ensure that information is shared for strategic planning purposes and to support effective service delivery.
- s 11 of the CA 2004: places a duty of bodies within the NHS to make arrangements to ensure that their functions are discharged with regard to the need to safeguard and promote the welfare of children
- para 7.4 of *Working Together to Safeguard Children* (HM Government, 2006) sets out the regulations relating to child deaths review functions and this includes collecting and analysing information about each death.
- Art 8(2) of the Human Rights Act 1998: the right to respect for private and family can be legitimately interfered with where it 'is in accordance with the law and is necessary ... in the interests of ... protection of health and morals or the protection of rights and freedoms of others'.
- reg 6 under s 13 of the CA 2004: the sharing of information within the Child Death Overview Processes is a function set out in and therefore is in accordance with the law. It can be seen as a proportionate response in relation to the pressing social need for the protection of health and morals or the protection of rights and freedom of others. (The CDOP process is not the same as rapid response). Common law duty of

confidentiality: the common law provides that where there is a confidential relationship, the person receiving the confidential information is under a duty not to pass on the information to a third party. The duty is not absolute and can be shared without breaching the common law duty if there is an overriding public interest in disclosure.
- Data Protection Act 1998: information sharing within the Child Death Overview Processes is a statutory function and the Data Protection Act therefore permits the sharing of information without express consent of the subjects.

14.25 **Conclusion**

The investigation of child and infant deaths is of such a specialized nature as to warrant the inclusion of supplementary material to the *Murder Investigation Manual* (MIM) (ACPO, 2006). This is not only because in every case where the death is felt to be suspicious, the same thought processes, vigour, expertise, and professionalism, which apply to adult homicides also apply to child deaths, but also because of the added complexities these investigations contain.

It takes a huge amount of callousness to kill a young child and despite feelings of sympathy to the parents being an overriding factor to consider, it is also vitally important that a detailed and professional investigation is launched as quickly as possible. An SIO should take firm control from the earliest opportunity and apply the procedures that the category of the death will require, be they under 'Working Together' and/or the MIM. A sensitive approach is required whilst ensuring a proportional and detailed police investigation is undertaken either to pursue a criminal prosecution or confirm there are no criminal factors associated with the death.

These are invariably difficult investigations that require highly specialized techniques and procedures in respect of all child and infant deaths. It is hoped the material contained within this chapter has proved to be a useful addition to other sections of this handbook.

Further reading

ACPO, Guidelines; *Infant Deaths—Murder Investigation Manual* (Supplement) (ACPO, 2006).

ACPO, *Guidance on Investigating Child Abuse and Safeguarding Children* (2nd edn) (NPIA, 2009).

Department for Children Schools and Families 2006, *Working Together to Safeguard Children* (The Stationery Office, 2007).

Kennedy, Baroness H, *Sudden Unexpected Death in Infancy: A Multi-Agency Protocol for Care and Investigation* (Royal College of Pathologists and Royal College of Paediatrics and Child Health, 2004), Introduction at 1–16 and The Protocol's Executive Summary at 17–27).

Fox, J, Briefing Paper, 'A contribution to the evaluation of recent developments in the investigation of sudden unexpected death in infancy' (Department of Sociology, University of Surrey in association with the NPIA, 2008).

Foundation for the Study of Infant Death, *A Suggested Approach for Police and Coroner's Officers* (FSID, 2005).

Foundation for the Study of Infant Death (leaflet), *When a Baby Dies Suddenly and Unexpectedly* (FSID, 2007).

Foundation for the Study of Infant Death, *Cot Death Facts and Figures* (FSID, 2008).

Fox, J, *The Police Response to Infant Deaths* (2005) 1(1) *The Journal of Homicide and Major Incident Investigation* (NPIA).

HM Government, *Information Sharing: Guidance for Practitioners and Managers* (The Stationery Office, 2008).

HM Government, *Information Sharing: Further Guidance on Legal Issues* (The Stationery Office, 2009).

Marshall, D, Child Homicides: *A Suspect in the family—Issues for the Family Liaison Strategy* (2008) 4(1) *The Journal of Homicide and Major Incident Investigation* (NPIA).

NHS, A *Guide to the Post Mortem Examination Procedure Involving a Baby or Child* (NHS, 2003).

Police Review (18 July 2008), 'New Tricks' (the new s 5 legislation), 18 and 'Defend the Children' (investigating death of a child), 22.

Sidebotham P and Fleming P, *Unexpected Death in Childhood: A Handbook for Practitioners* (Wiley, 2007).

Vaughan, JR and Kautt, PM, *Infant Death Investigations Following High-Profile Unsafe Rulings: Throwing Out the Baby with the Bath Water?* (2009) 3(1) *Policing* (NPIA), 89–99.

Wate R, Marshall D 'Effective Investigation of intra-familial child homicide and suspicious death' (2009) 5(2) *Journal of Homicide and Major Incident Investigation* (OUP).

Appendix A
SIO Aide-Memoire Quick Checklist

Objectives of an investigation

- Establish whether an offence has been committed/not been committed.
- Gather all available information, material, and evidence and adhere to CPIA rules.
- Act in the interests of justice.
- Pursue all reasonable lines of enquiry.
- Conduct a thorough investigation.
- Identify and arrest offenders.
- Present the evidence to the Crown Prosecution Service (CPS).

The 'ABC' of investigation

A Assume nothing
B Believe nothing
C Challenge/check everything

[For example, check detail, detail, and detail again, and also check that things have been done to SIO's satisfaction.]

Initial responders—duties

An SIO must always have an understanding of initial responder actions so they can check what has already been done, or should have been done. A mnemonic often provided to help conduct an initial assessment at incident scenes is SAD-CHALETS:

S Survey (make observations, eg position of a body and any possible injuries)
A Assess (determine what has happened, eg murder or natural death)

D Disseminate (relay information to those who need to know)

C Casualties (determine approximate number and their condition)

H Hazards (eg terrain, public disorder, weather, dangerous buildings etc)

A Access (best routes for emergency vehicles and supporting resources)

L Location (using landmarks, street names, buildings etc)

E Emergency services (present and/or required)

T Type of incident

S Safety (all aspects of health and safety risk assessment)

This handbook also provides the following:

First Response officers—10 x 'Golden Hour(s)' Actions

1. Make any scenes safe and preserve life. Identify and attend to any victims, casualties, or fatalities, and administer first aid and/or check for signs of life. Summon medical assistance where required. If victim(s) obviously deceased, cause as little disturbance as possible and ensure medically certified dead (and note precise time and by whom).
2. Conduct an initial assessment (apply ABC principle) and provide situation report to control room using 5 × WH + H method (eg what happened? how? what additional resources required? where? etc).
3. Identify, protect, and secure all potential crime scenes and any items of evidential value that may be easily lost, destroyed, or contaminated (eg CCTV, weapons, discarded clothing, blood distribution, footprints, or other potential exhibits).
4. Identify entry/exit to scene with only one point of entry, a designated CAP and RVP for other attending resources. Mark out and protect perimeter, eg using barrier tape and cordons. Prevent unauthorized access and cross-contamination and commence incident scene log(s).
5. Note all actions taken and by whom.
6. Establish any victim's identity and next of kin details without disturbing evidence (descriptions, identifying marks/tattoos/features/clothing/vehicles can also be used). If family, relatives, and friends present, deal sensitively, giving preliminary support and advice.

First Response officers—10 x 'Golden Hour(s)' Actions

7. Identify and arrest any suspect(s) and/or their likely escape route/direction and means (eg public transport, vehicle, or on foot). Once arrest made note any replies or significant comments, and treat them as a crime scene.
8. Note details of all persons and vehicles at the scene.
9. Identify and separate witnesses, record details, and get initial accounts.
10. Identify, obtain, and exploit any information-gathering opportunities (apply ABC principle) carefully note the source and 'fast track' any potential or urgent lines of enquiry (eg circulation of vehicles involved or descriptions of suspects etc).

Role of an SIO

- Assume early command and control and begin issuing directions and instructions at earliest opportunity (and record).
- Make an assessment of nature and category of the incident/investigation and review any initial response actions and decisions made
- Focus early thoughts around (1) correct processes and procedures (eg scene preservation); and (2) hypotheses and theories as to what, where, when, why, who, and how.
- Arrange and conduct early debriefing of first responders (ie hot debriefs within first 24 hours of the investigation).
- Provide briefings to all subsequent staff drafted onto the enquiry.
- Arrange collection and evaluation of all relevant available information and material, ensuring it is retained and recorded as per CPIA requirements (perform role of officer in charge of the investigation).
- Assess usefulness, reliability, relevance, provenance, and validity of all information.
- Develop and implement necessary investigative strategies, identifying and prioritizing fast-track actions and determine/review main lines of enquiry (MLOE).
- Transfer/record all decisions into a policy file and provide accompanying reasons.
- Make use of and arrange collection and evaluation of all available intelligence and information sources.
- Conduct and record any necessary health and safety risk assessments.

- Assess any factors likely to impact on the investigation and take appropriate action (eg cultural or language barriers).
- Confirm identities of all victims and potential witnesses and support and manage them in accordance with current legislation and policy.
- Ensure victims, witnesses, and families are kept informed of progress of investigation.
- Pursue identified lines of enquiry fairly and without bias, and take appropriate steps to identify suspects.
- Set up and manage an effective major incident room for the investigation at a suitable location, incorporating information management and decision making systems (as per MIRSAP guidelines).
- Secure and manage necessary specialists and resources (assess work levels to maintain appropriate staffing to process enquiries).
- Remain fully accountable to chief officers (eg gold) for conduct of the investigation and regularly brief them.
- Compile reports and provide updates as necessary for chief officers, the coroner, public enquiries, Crown Prosecution Service, etc.
- Set time scales for review and progress of actions and documents (ie priorities, allocation, and referral).
- Make decisions as to the filing of all documents and processing of exhibits.
- Ensure early engagement of the CPS and counsel where necessary.
- Liaise with other agencies as required (eg fire service or specialist investigators) and arrange necessary exchange of information.
- Make good use of any specialists, experts, advisers or agencies who may be able to assist the investigation
- Deal with all individuals in an ethical and effective manner, recognizing their needs, and comply with legislation and key responsibilities, particularly with respect to race, diversity, and human rights.
- Maximize potential of staff and consider requirements of PIP (identifying strengths, weaknesses, and development needs/opportunities).
- At all times demonstrate high qualities of leadership and always remain calm, composed, confident, and inspirational.
- Stay totally positive and keep staff motivated.

Problem solving (use of 5 × WH + H)

Use interrogative pronouns to obtain and assess information:

- Who was killed? —Victim details (and why this victim?)
- What happened? —Precise details of incident
- When did it happen? —Temporal issues (ie. relevant and significant times)
- Where did it happen? —Geographic considerations (location)
- Why did the crime occur in this way? —Motive for the crime
- How did it happen? —Precise modus operandi details

Command and control

[Note: Obtain full details and record contact numbers for all those mentioned in this list.]

- Establish who is/has been in command and control (eg at the scene), and obtain comprehensive briefing from them and record it in a notebook/daybook.
- Establish who is senior detective in charge (if different) and get a good briefing from them also.
- Assess impact on local community for tensions, threat assessment, and victim care (complete/record Community Impact Assessment ASAP) and implement appropriate control measures.
- Review and update fast-track actions (must continue throughout the investigation).
- Confirm what responsibilities and tasks have been allocated (eg H-2-H enquiries, CCTV capture, witness trawls, arrests etc).
- Appoint core roles and key areas of responsibility (eg inner/outer cordon supervisor, exhibits officer, FLOs, staff officer/deputy SIO, media liaison officer, H-2-H co-ordinator, intelligence cell, CSM/CSI, action writer/manager, enquiries supervisor, traffic manager, resource co-ordinator, RV point manager, etc).
- Ensure there is an adequate communications link between all staff involved at the scene and elsewhere.
- Assess and declare whether major or critical incident.
- Ensure local policing commander informed and briefed.
- Establish if a Gold, Silver, and Bronze (GSB) command structure has been implemented (eg bronze scene commander), if so obtain full details.

- Clarify and/or request strategic directions of gold commander (eg community or media policies).
- Ensure all initial response staff debriefed before going off duty.
- Determine whether specialist silver commanders required (eg firearms silver commander, community silver, public order tactical advisor, etc). If so, discuss/agree tactical options to maximize all benefits for the investigation, eg appeals, evidence recovery, etc.
- Identify and liaise with other emergency responders, eg fire service, ambulance, local authority incident officers, Health and Safety Executive and/or IPCC (if applicable).
- Set up incident room with appropriate resources (eg HOLMES2) in accordance with the MIRSAP manual and determine/release public hotline number.

Personnel and resources

- Account for all staff who have been involved and/or deployed.
- Assess staffing levels and request additional as required (eg uniform patrols and traffic specialists, detectives, trained interviewers, PolSA teams, etc).
- Give clear instructions to staff, eg where to deploy or attend/ personal equipment required.
- Check what other specialists are required (eg interpreters).
- Introduce measures to avoid cross-contamination of scene(s), suspects, and personnel.
- Make early appointment of a resource manager or Logistics Coordination Unit.
- Decide what extra equipment required, eg scene tents, lighting, screens, barriers, catering vans, removal transport, mobile police station, etc.
- Assess what external agencies required (eg local authority, IAG members, fire service investigation team, social care services).
- Ensure provision made for monitoring staff hours worked, welfare requirements, eg hot drinks, rotation of staff for rest and refreshment, etc.
- Confirm personnel have right equipment to perform their role (eg waterproof clothing, footwear, high-visibility jackets, body armour, adequate communications, eg radios).
- Check what risk assessments have been conducted or are required (3 × types—generic, specific, and dynamic).
- Separate risk assessments are required before entry into scenes, approach and removal of bodies, and all searches and arrests.

Categorizing incidents

Determine what sort of incident is being dealt with [examples below]:

- major or critical incident (gold group considerations)
- domestic-related (eg current/former spouse, parent/child, child/parent, sexual rival, extended family members)
- criminal enterprise (eg during course of robbery, burglary, etc)
- gang-related
- child victim
- racially motivated
- sexually motivated
- stranger attack
- serial offence
- argument-motivated
- terrorism-related
- other (eg religious, sectarian, mass homicide, etc).

[Also determine official ACPO category of murder, ie cat 'A+', cat 'A', cat 'B', or cat 'C'.]

Motive

- Gain (financial or otherwise)
- Criminal enterprise
- Personal cause
- Jealousy
- Revenge attack
- Gang-related (eg drugs, territory, or power)
- Racism, homophobia (or other prejudice or hatred)
- Anger or loss of control (rejection, argument etc)
- Crime concealment or witness elimination purposes (eg a court witness)
- Sexual gratification, lust, desire, sadism
- Power, control
- Thrill and excitement
- Mental illness/personality disorders (psychopath, narcissism, paranoid, schizoid)
- Political/religious/ritualistic causes
- Terrorism related
- To cover up or in the process of another crime (eg arson, burglary).

Victim and family liaison

- Primary responsibility for victims is always *preservation of life*.
- If dead at scene, unless obvious, medical staff must pronounce and certify fact of death (ie manage doctors'/paramedics' attendance).
- Victims who survive may be shocked, traumatized, or distressed—if so arrange immediate medical and/or welfare support.
- Obtain full victim details and description (including clothing) of victim(s).
- If victim deceased—check whether dying declaration made.
- Confirm location of deceased's body (treat as a crime scene, even at hospital).
- Next of kin—find out who they are, when notified, who by, when, and where they are now?
- Arrange immediate welfare and support for victim's family, relatives, and close friends.
- If trained/accredited FLOs not immediately available, select other suitable experienced (and briefed) officer(s) to perform role temporarily.
- Brief FLOs before deployment, record specific objectives, and conduct risk assessment.
- Select most suitable staff for FLO duties (always best practice to deploy in pairs).
- SIO should meet family as soon as practicable, introduce themselves and explain role of FLOs.
- Updates must be provided to family whenever possible—ensuring information is always accurate and reliable (provided release will not compromise the investigation).
- Protect families from media intrusion (and manage their media interviews/statements).
- Remember maxim: 'Find out how the victim lived and you'll find out how they died.' Obtain as much detail as possible about the background of the victim (full victimology).
- Try and establish any relationship between victim/scene/offender.

Crime scene examples

- Location where offence took place.
- Body (or body part) recovery site (body itself should be treated as a crime scene and a body recovery strategy carefully developed,

and an evidence recovery strategy should be determined, samples being taken prior to any removal, wherever possible).
[In terrorism cases a body part has been deemed by the coroner to include anything over 5 cm^2.]

- Place where body has been moved to/from.
- Location where a body or object may be suspected of being located.
- Any victim.
- A witness who has come into contact with a victim, an offender, a crime scene etc.
- A suspect.
- An attack site.
- Anywhere there is trace or physical evidence, eg tyre marks, footprints, location of a weapon, blood distribution, clothing, body concealment tools, eg a spade etc.
- Any articles connected to victim(s), witness, or offender(s).
- Vehicles connected to an incident (including those used to transport suspects or victims such as police vehicles and ambulances).
- Premises connected to offender or suspect.
- Access or escape routes to/from primary scene taken by offender(s).
- Casualties or bodies removed to hospitals or mortuaries. (Note: try to prevent hospital staff placing all clothing in one bag to avoid cross-contamination.)
- Location where a crime has been planned or some element of the offence that has taken place.

Note: It is important that the first officer attending any 'scene' is aware of the potential for multiple crime scenes and the need to protect and preserve them also

Scene considerations

- Confirm exact location of scene(s).
- Determine how many crime scenes (and designate/number them).
- Consider complexity of any scenes and sustainability in terms of their potential to deteriorate and likely time available for retention.
- Conduct review of initial bullet actions regarding:
  - Parameters set for the scene
  - Security of the scene
  - Actions taken to preserve material and evidence

  - Adequacy of resources at the scene (and properly supervised and briefed)
  - Identification and security of any additional scenes
  - Record keeping arrangements (scene logs)
  - Health and Safety risk assessments
  - Management of potential contaminators.
- Decide if SIO directly attending scene or initially meeting elsewhere (eg at local police station for full briefing).
- Decide what constitutes the scene(s) and whether there are any others that have not yet been identified or defined.
- Check and amend scene parameters and any search or scene boundaries (if necessary).
- Confirm cordon arrangements for security and protection, ie inner/outer cordons [golden rule—always start big]—record precise locations.
- Ensure adequate resources are in place to protect, supervise, and manage the scene(s).
- Check scene logs are being completed correctly (one for each, ie inner and outer cordon) and that staff completing them have been properly briefed and are being supervised, and that correct forms are being used.
- Check suitability of common approach path (CAP)—must be least likeliest route taken by offender.
- Establish if an RV Point has been nominated for resources to attend at and what logistical arrangements may need to be made (eg parking facilities, briefing/meeting area) plus appointment of an RVP manager.
- Decide what experts and specialists are required and arrange attendance (eg CSC/CSM/CSI, photographers, pathologist, forensic scientists, geoforensics specialists, ballistic experts, etc—the sooner they arrive, the better for maximizing the recovery of forensic evidence).
- Consider and agree the order upon which experts will need to visit the crime scene to avoid any cross contamination or destruction of potential evidence.
- Identify all hazards (complete and record a risk assessment before any personnel enter a scene(s)).
- Determine what emergency services are/have been in attendance and ensure they are fully debriefed and relevant samples obtained (eg vehicle tyres and footwear impressions).
- Identify all other persons who have been in the scene and obtain footwear/vehicle tyre impressions.

- Use tapes, ropes, natural barriers, police vehicles, etc to reinforce cordon boundaries.
- Establish what extra equipment is required (eg scene tent, lighting, screens).
- Reinforce rule—no one to enter scene(s) cordons without permission of SIO, particularly members of the media or senior officers (beware of media aircraft/helicopters photographing)—any unauthorized persons must be immediately removed.
- Check location of police/emergency service and parked vehicles. Instruct to park in places where offender(s) unlikely to have been (eg middle of road, not kerbside).
- Make arrangements to deal with displaced persons, stranded residents/vehicles.
- Ensure anything touched, moved, or altered within scene cordons has been recorded.
- Obtain and record current and short-range weather forecast (if scene outdoors) for evidential purposes and scene examination strategy.
- If scene indoors, note state of doors/windows—open or shut, locked from inside/outside, lights or heating on/off, etc.
- If scene search involves large-scale, complex, or multiple scenes, make early appointment of search co-ordinator who is PolSA trained.
- Regularly check welfare arrangements for all staff at the scene.
- Nominate exhibits officer (may need more than one initially).
- Arrange for entire scene to be photographed and digitally recorded while any deceased remains *in situ*.
- Avoid initial floral tributes—these may contaminate botanical evidence.
- Arrange detailed maps/plans/drawings of scene and area (consider use of 'Google Earth' type maps plus air support unit shots and/or satellite imagery).
- Agree and record evidence recovery plan (in liaison with the CSM/CSI and other experts, eg pathologist).
- Agree and record other (non-forensic) search procedures (eg line searches, PolSA, etc) *after* forensic searches completed.
- Consider arrangements for longer-term protection of the scene.
- **Remember the golden rule not to release any crime scene prematurely.**

Early investigative considerations

- Conduct immediate searches of the scene area and escape routes, eg road blocks, aerial surveillance (heat-seeking equipment), circulations, human scent dogs, etc (stress importance of accurate descriptions for suspects).
- Determine and check likely direction of travel of offender(s). Route will need search strategy. Check for CCTV/ANPR/H-2-H opportunities.
- Check local hospitals for suspects and any other potential victims (if likely to be injured).
- Obtain copy of control room incident log to analyse and raise fast track actions where necessary.
- Obtain and listen to any emergency (999) calls.
- Set up early public message/information hotline number and appoint superviser to manage and monitor arrangements on a 24/7 basis.
- TI/TIE person who first contacted the emergency services (have recording from control room preserved/examined).
- TIE person who found victim (may need to be forensically eliminated, outer clothing seized, may also need welfare support, determine status, eg significant witness or suspect).
- TI/TIE person who last saw the victim alive (same rules as last point apply).
- (Where applicable) inform the coroner.
- Allocate fast-track/HP (time-critical) actions.
- Consider forensic fast-track submissions.
- Consider allocation of 'first 20' actions list on matrix.
- Arrange initial H-2-H enquiries, eg within line of sight of scene, along possible escape routes, around other scenes (parameters and questionnaires required).
- Obtain details/descriptions and accounts of all persons and vehicles at scene (digitally record if necessary) and obtain any personal or media video/mobile phone photography.
- Formulate main lines of enquiry and initial investigative strategies.
- Check for any linked or precursor incidents/crime reports (or useful police operations, eg covert).
- Arrange search and seizure of all passive data generators, eg CCTV (make and record parameters).
- Plan and record arrest strategies and tactics for declared suspects.
- Arrange urgent circulations where required (suspect details).

- Conduct initial intelligence cell checks.
- Consider possible transport links to and from scene by offender(s) (railway/buses/taxis, etc).
- Arrange suspension of local rubbish collection and drains (parameters).
- Use 5 × WH + H questions, eg What do we know? What do we need to know? Where are we going to get it from?

Main lines of enquiry

Examples:

- Tracing and interviewing (TI) significant witnesses.
- Obtaining a full profile of the victim N1 ('victimology').
- Establishing cause and manner of death.
- Scene (1)—forensic scene examination and PolSA search.
- Conducting H-2-H enquiries (in set parameters).
- Intelligence strategy (eg identifying intelligence gaps; biographical profile of gangs, their activities, habits, methods, etc; open source intelligence; community intelligence; tactical initiatives, etc).
- Deterrmining 'relevant time', ie likely time of death of victim.
- Deterrmining movements of all persons at scene (1) (between — and —).
- Determining movements of victim N1 (between — and —).
- Determining movements of declared suspect (between — and —).
- Pursuing TIE actions.
- DNA or fingerprint/palmprint elimination methods.
- Establishing motive—eg sexual, robbery, hate crime, etc.
- Researching and analysing any potential linked crimes or precursor incidents.
- Use of a media strategy.
- Telecommunications data strategy.
- Passive data recovery and viewing strategy.
- Family liaison strategy.
- Use of covert pro-active tactics (eg use/conduct authorities for tasking of covert human intelligence source (CHIS)).
- Use of community advisory/support groups (eg independent advisory groups (IAGs)).
- Publication of a reward.
- Use of an anniversary reconstruction and/or road checks in locality.
- Identifying and prioritizing modus operandi (MO) suspects.

- Making use of National Policing Improvement Agency (NPIA) Crime Ops Support

Witnesses

- Vital to locate any witnesses as quickly as possible.
- Witness capture plan may be necessary where large numbers of people involved, eg use of image recording equipment in crowds or *pro formas* for recording all names/addresses/descriptions.
- Obtain first accounts from witnesses to assess information and apply best evidence rule.
- Determine status of witness, ie vulnerable, intimidated, or significant—must try for interview on video or tape (and conduct risk assessment/welfare/protection).
- Determine interview tactics and method (use of interview adviser or PIP level II trained witness interviewers).
- Witnesses can include: (1) eye witnesses, (2) victims, (3) person who found victim, (4) person who made report to police, (5) last person to see victim alive, (6) background witnesses, (7) identification witnesses, (8) emergency service personnel, (9) first officers at scene.
- Witnesses can be found among passers-by, tradespeople, family/associates of the victim, public transport passengers, taxi drivers, or anyone in attendance at local events at the time.
- Witnesses may also be a 'crime scene' if came into contact with offender (eg trace evidence): avoid cross-contamination and examine tactfully.
- Witnesses may also require a 'TIE strategy' (and may later become suspects).
- Conduct witness assessment—eg may need medical assessment, victim support, or services of an FLO/victim support scheme.
- Select suitable officers to deal with witnesses, ie those who are best at building rapport and winning trust and confidence (ie with good interpersonal skills).
- Consider need for interpreters.
- Consider welfare/protection strategy—resources, suitable officers, temporary accommodation, personal attack alarms, etc.
- Check integrity of witnesses, eg if gave variation of story to someone else, previous conviction for making false allegations, or has revenge or financial motive, etc.

- R v Turnbull rules and mnemonic 'ADVOKATE' re any identification evidence.
- Any media releases should make/reaffirm appeals for witnesses.

Suspects and arrests

- Note that offenders often return to crime scenes.
- Record reasons for declaring any person a suspect.
- All suspects to be treated as potential crime scenes.
- Anyone who has been to scene(s) must not come into contact with suspects (avoid cross-contamination!).
- Multiple suspects must be kept apart at all times and not come into contact with same officers, vehicles, or custody suites.
- Any 'significant statements' made by arrested persons should be recorded and later put to them in a formal interview (check all comments made upon arrest, eg reply to caution).
- Decide what intimate/non-intimate samples required, forensic medical examinations, and photographing (brief/debrief surgeon involved).
- Decide what other samples are quickly required, eg gunshot residue, pollen samples.
- Confirm identities of arrested suspects (eg by finger-prints).
- Check possessions for car/house keys, mobile phones, photographs, etc.
- Consider early initial account interviews with suspects (and 'emergency' interviews).
- Seize and preserve clothing and vehicles belonging to suspects (use different officers if more than one suspect).
- Search any vehicle used to transport suspects to the custody office.
- Check on suitability of facilities at the custody office concerned (eg downstream monitoring facilities).
- Arrange immediate intelligence checks for addresses/associates.
- Check what address details/intimation requests have been provided (option to do intimations by detectives to allow interview of persons nominated).
- Determine/record address search strategy (forensic/PolSA considerations).
- Consider media and FLO strategy re details of arrests made.
- Identify interview team and agree/record strategy.
- Consider early use of trained interview advisor and downstream monitoring.

Community impact and public reassurance

- Community support and gaining trust and confidence are always vital. Liaise with local policing commander to conduct assessment of risks and implement adequate control measures.
- Ensure Community Impact Assessment document completed.
- Conduct profile of the community (can be residential or transient groups that frequent area, includes religious, cultural, historical, political, lifestyle, and ethnicity considerations).
- (If pre-planned operation) check whether there are any other agencies or forces involved in the operation and liaise with them.
- Establish what the risk factors are for community tensions (eg high media attention, revenge attacks, public disorder, or likelihood of further offences).
- Determine what internal consultation is required (eg local commander, media liaison, gold commander, neighbourhood policing officers).
- Determine what external consultation, advice, and assistance are required (eg family/victim, independent advisory group, local authority or any minority support groups).
- Grade potential impact on community tensions (high = possible outbreaks of crime and disorder; low/normal = limited or no issues or raising of tension).
- Check whether there are any additional risk factors.
- Check what other communities will be affected, eg local, force, regional, national, or international.
- Gather 'community intelligence' that will help monitor and assess the attitude, response, and impact on the community.
- Introduce appropriate control measures to reduce community tensions.

Briefings and debriefings

Briefings checklist

- Find suitable venue for holding briefings with adequate equipment.
- Prepare and circulate agenda.
- Allow sufficient time for the briefing.
- Ensure no distractions—all phones/pagers to silent or switched off.
- SIO should positively lead, control, and manage the briefing.

- SIO to set the right standard and tone by speaking confidently, always looking interested, and projecting enthusiasm and energy.
- Content should be kept relevant, avoiding dominating, monotonous, or extraneous contributions.
- Get reports/updates/feedback from staff at random to keep everyone's attention.
- Remember ABC principle—role of SIO is to probe and question everything.
- Do not allow people to dominate on key issues; give everyone a chance to contribute.
- Appropriate humour can be useful and encourages active listening.
- Briefings are a good forum for giving praise and recognition.
- Check levels of understanding of important information and policies.
- Make good use of props such as markerboards, flipcharts, maps, and plans.
- Show images in photos, videos, CCTV, etc wherever possible to make the content more realistic and interesting (consider electronic presentation for key briefings).
- Appoint action manager to allocate/raise new actions during briefing.
- Beware of embellishments from over-zealous staff eager to impress.
- Demand and check *detail, detail, detail.*
- Make accurate record of the content of briefings and all attendees.
- Check staff understand all information and their responsibilities.
- Identify and communicate risks and action required to minimize them.
- Delegate tasks to individuals commensurate with their abilities, training, and experience, and any personal development requirements.
- Identify any welfare needs.
- Invite others to briefings to make them feel part of the team, for example nominated representatives of the Crown Prosecution Service, forensic scientists, pathologist, etc (who can also play an active part by explaining points of law or scientific evidence).

Debriefings checklist

- Hot debriefs are one of the first, most important early functions of the SIO.
- Task *should not be delegated* unless in exceptional circumstances.
- All those involved in the initial response should be required to attend early debrief with no exceptions—*before going off duty*.
- Those attending should have already completed any notes, pocketbooks, etc *before* attending the debrief to avoid collusion of evidence and compromising integrity.
- Designated person to record proceedings and capture all information.
- Can link in the debriefing with requirements of the local commander who may be acting in the capacity of gold command; proceedings will assist in completing a community impact assessment.
- Select a suitable and early time for the debriefing.
- Use suitable venue, large enough to hold all those concerned, with necessary basic equipment available, eg markerboards, plans, and maps.
- All relevant documents and exhibits must be handed in by staff (copies of notebooks, etc) at the end of the session.
- Record details of all those present.
- Obtain details of actions taken and résumé of individual roles at the scene.
- Everything should be recorded for the purposes of disclosure rules (CPIA).

Enquiry parameters

Useful parameters that may be required:

- Boundaries for inner/outer cordons and 'vicinity of the scene'.
- H-2-H enquiry areas—where, what level (2 or 3, etc), and questionnaires.
- Parameters for other search areas (eg escape routes, dustbins, and drains).
- TIE elimination criteria (eg footwear, fingerprints, DNA buccal swabs, etc).
- Action-management policy (how many actions per team, turnaround period for high/low-priority actions).

- Alibi criteria times.
- Personal descriptive form (pdf) completion policy.
- Sequence of events (on HOLMES2).
- Indexes to be maintained on HOLMES2.
- Intelligence research policy.
- Action-management policy, ie frequency of action reviews.

TIE policies

Examples of categories for SIO's consideration and approval:

- TIE persons named as being responsible (normally through intelligence reports, information messages or ongoing work via the enquiry teams, MIR or other sources).
- TIE any persons aged 10 yrs+ at/or who had access to scene (1) between ... (define time parameters).
- TIE all persons aged 10 yrs + within the scene or vicinity of the scene (as defined for HOLMES2 indexing purposes) between ... and ... (define time parameters).
- TIE modus operandi subjects (those who have exhibited similar criminal behaviour to the offence under investigation).
- TIE registered sex offenders.
- TIE recent prison and bail hostel releases (including tagged offenders).
- TIE known associates of or persons linked to the victim.
- TIE relatives of the victim.
- TIE anyone who fits the description of the offender(s).
- TIE lone males residing within half mile of victim last sighting.
- TIE anyone who has committed or attempted suicide or self-referred to a mental institute (stipulated time and area parameters).
- TIE anyone at the SIO's discretion (to ensure sufficient latitude for those who do not fit into any of the other categories but it is decided for stipulated reasons they should be included).

HOLMES2 elimination codes: 1. Forensic (eg blood, DNA); 2. Description; 3. Independent witness; 4. Associate or relative; 5. Spouse/Partner; 6. Not eliminated.

Statement policy

Example [statements will be taken from all persons within the following range]:

- Persons at or near scene (1).

- All relatives/associates of victim and other persons with background information.
- Any person with relevant information for the investigation.
- Alibi witnesses.
- Any others at SIO's discretion.

Action abbreviations

- TIE—trace/interview/eliminate
- TI—trace and interview
- TST—take statement
- TFST—take further statement
- RI—re-interview
- OBT—obtain
- ENQS—make enquiries
- NOMINAL—number used to identify a person (eg N12)
- UF—unidentified female
- UM—unidentified male
- UU— unidentified unknown
- UV—unidentified vehicle
- PDF—personal descriptive form
- AQVF—alibi questionnaire verification form
- M—message form (eg M14).

Pathology considerations

- Strategy meeting should be held with forensic pathologist before anyone goes near the body at the scene or mortuary (record in policy file).
- Once body taken to mortuary, body bag must not be opened without permission of the SIO.
- Identification of deceased always important priority.
- Obtain medical notes (GP/hospital) and any x-rays prior to post-mortem examination.
- Obtain victim's medication and social history.
- Health and safety risk assessment required before examination commences.

Objectives of post mortem

- Establish identity of the deceased.
- Assess the size, physique, and condition of the deceased.

- Determine cause of death (and manner if possible).
- Determine time of death.
- Determine likely survival time after attack.
- Conduct injury analysis (amount of force used, type of weapon used, precise method details, sexual assault indicators, any incapacitation, direction of blows, position of deceased at time of injury, which wound(s) were fatal, whether injuries incurred ante or post mortem, etc).
- Establish whether any indication of self-defence and whether offender likely to be injured.
- Establish/confirm place of death (eg evidence of moving of body post death such as drag marks on feet/ankles).
- Determine lifestyle of victim (eg drug or sexual abuse, health condition).
- Determine whether deceased under influence of drink or drugs at time of death.

Examples of body samples

- DNA swabs of the body from unexposed areas and/or areas not completed while the body was *in situ* at the crime scene (eg swab all biting wounds for saliva traces and any other likely areas for gripping/holding traces).
- Botanical swabs/samples (advice from palynologist).
- Oral, vaginal or penile, and anal swabs.
- Fingernail scrapings and clippings (tip: if victim has long fingernails, photograph them as offender may have scratch marks).
- Head and pubic hair (or other bodily hair) combings and cuttings.
- Blood, urine, and stomach contents.
- Internal swabs of areas such as the oesophagus (eg for sperm heads).

Media handling

- Arrange initial media release/holding statement.
- Initial appeal should be for witnesses or persons with information and any known CCTV cameras or images (eg on mobile phone cameras) that may have been captured.
- Determine consistent incident room number to give out on appeals.

- Make early request for a media liaison officer and get them to monitor all broadcasts relating to the incident.
- Keep the media out of the scene(s).
- Ensure identity of deceased formally confirmed before releasing details to the media.
- Determine if an RV point is required for media away from the scene.
- When speaking to the media, choose words and terminology carefully and avoid speculating.
- General rule—SIO talks to media about investigation and the local police commander deals with local policing issues.
- Prevent media from talking to key witnesses and compromising integrity of evidence.
- Ensure victim's family given protection from media intrusion.
- Decide what information to hold back.
- SIO should fully prepare and rehearse any media interviews (particularly live ones).
- Turn any negative media comments into positives.
- Always use the media to full advantage to assist the investigation.

Media tips—Dos and Donts

The Dos...

- Make full advantage of good advice from a MLO.
- Be clear about the aims and objectives of the interview.
- Retain control of the interview by refocusing on the issues the SIO wants to talk about (and repeat messages as often as possible).
- Ask what type of questions will be asked beforehand so answers can be prepared.
- Prepare and practice thoroughly—identify and remember **3 × key messages.**
- Research any current 'hot topics' in the media. Think what else is current and could have an impact on the line of interviewing.
- Remember the questioner will also use the 5 × WH + H principles – Who? What? When? Where? Why? and How?
- Avoid waffle. Answers will probably be whittled down into 'sound bites' so make sure they're good ones.
- Stay relaxed, confident, and always *positive, positive, positive.*
- Be confident not nervous—treat the interviewer as one individual and ignore how many others may watch or listen.

- Adrenalin is required to produce excitement and stimulation—use it as an advantage.
- Check appearance, hair, tie, etc (if on camera) before the cameras start rolling.
- Check what material is displayed in the background and remove inappropriate or confidential material.
- Ignore noise and/or activity taking place off-camera.
- Look at the person interviewing, not the camera (unless directed otherwise).
- Use straightforward plain language, *not* police-speak or jargon.
- Be clear about the things that cannot be talked about, such as pending or ongoing court cases (or sensitive issues).
- Steer clear of giving personal views on subjects—know your force's media policy and stick to the party line.
- Ensure the victim's family is informed about the contents of any media release or interview *before* it is released.
- Ensure messages are clear and strong, stating exactly what is wanted from the public (ie do not just appeal for 'general information'—be specific).
- Never say 'No comment'—it sounds suspicious. Explain reasons why a question cannot be answered, or information released (useful alternatives are 'It is too early to say . . .', or 'That will be looked into as part of the ongoing investigation . . . ', or simply 'At this stage we are still unsure . . .').
- Avoid comments that imply guilt or innocence—never discuss the evidence.
- Use cognitive prompts wherever possible (eg such as a major sporting event).
- Emphasize the importance of all information, no matter how trivial.
- Remember to state the telephone number of the incident room (write it down!).
- Ensure there is an appropriate answering-machine recorded message and policy for regularly checking the incident room number, if giving out to the public or media.
- Inform the media as soon as possible when a suspect is charged. This helps to prevent the possibility of them inadvertently breaching the Contempt of Court Act and jeopardizing the case. Confirm the name, date of birth, address, full details of charges, and court date.
- Consider giving positive crime prevention advice along with reports of crime and offer public reassurance and help ease the fear of crime.

- Publicize good work, particularly heroics or important court results.
- Use interesting facets of the case to gain extra publicity and interest from the media (eg some useful CCTV footage).
- If being asked a question on behalf of someone else then tell the reporter he/she must speak to that person.
- Do not be afraid to admit when something has gone wrong but always go on to say what is being done to put the situation right—'ah yes, but . . .' (ie turning the negatives into positives).
- Keep full control of the interview and keep turning the subject back to the topics you want to talk about, follow your agenda not the interviewer's.

The Don'ts . . .

- Allow junior staff to provide information or interviews about the incident to members of the public or media without being authorized by the SIO.
- Wear checked or stripy clothing (they look blurred on camera).
- Fidget or sway on or stare at your feet.
- Stare directly at the camera (unless you are doing a 'down-the-lens' interview where the reporter is at a different venue.
- Drop your guard and make 'off the cuff' remarks as the microphone could be still switched on.
- Respond to the reporter's questions with just 'Yes' or 'No' answers. Try to avoid starting responses with 'Yes that's correct, I think . . .'.
- Let the reporter try to put words into your mouth or try to get you to agree to what they are saying. (Instead use phrases such as 'well, that's one point of view but from a force perspective ...').
- Lower your voice or appear disinterested—always look and sound confident, enthusiastic, and in control.
- Ever criticize the criminal justice system or other agencies.

SUDC deaths SIO Actions checklist

- Assume command and control of the investigation.
- Attend the location of the deceased, usually an emergency department.
- Call out sufficient staff to assist. As a rule of thumb, at least a detective sergeant and three detectives will be a minimum team needed undertake the fast-track actions.
- Commence a policy decision log.

- Critically assess the circumstances surrounding the death.
- Keep open minded and be alert to suspicious indicators such as 'staging'.
- Confirm death certified (the cause won't be certified if it is unexplained) and by whom.
- Arrange personal viewing of the body.
- Identify and locate next of kin, if not done already arrange for them to be informed of child's death.
- Deploy FLO where appropriate with an agreed strategy (ideally child abuse/death trained) and consider strategy if it is believed there is a 'suspect in the family'.
- Arrange formal identification of body.
- Develop investigative strategies and deploy staff to explore all reasonable lines of enquiry.
- Ensure all staff engaged on the enquiry are, as far as possible, caring and sensitive to those who are grieving (keep them updated with information and explanations of 'what' and 'why').
- Obtain and review contents of any calls to emergency services (eg copy of 999 call or to any medical emergency helplines).
- Arrange early interviewing of all response staff, call takers, paramedics, medical staff etc. (Note: In the case of the paramedics and A&E doctors, this needs to be done by way of careful and detailed statement taking, ensuring all words used by carers and their actions at the home are accurately recalled and recorded in the statement (eg were they on the mobile phone to anyone during the rescusitation process). It is very important to ensure police investigators speak directly to the individuals involved and not rely solely on their notes. In the case of the A&E doctor this may mean getting them out of bed again!)
- Establish what physical examination has taken place and what if any photographs or written records have been made (eg by hospital staff) and if any suspicious or identifiable marks have been found. (A police photographer should always be deployed if there are any concerning marks on the body—do not rely on hospital photographs.)
- Review rationale for deeming the death suspicious/not suspicious.
- Determine what category and type of investigation is required (ensure there is a proportionate response).
- Establish identification and control of all potential 'scenes' (especially the 'death scene' and child's body if at hospital) and preserve evidence.

- Obtain treatment and medical records of deceased in preparation for post mortem (ie paediatric or joint post mortem).
- Where applicable ensure a pre-transfusion blood sample is obtained.
- Avoid uniform staff attending the home address and using overt cordons.
- Decide whether and when it is necessary to seize any potential exhibits or leave them in place (bedding, clothing, feeding implements, articles used during resuscitation attempts, any evidence of alcohol use in waste bins etc).
- Obtain and record detailed initial separate accounts from parents/carers (may be in conjunction with paediatrician when they obtain medical history).
- Consider obtaining blood samples for alcohol/drugs from parents/carers (by a force medical examiner—FME). (Note: This should be requested in all cases where overlaying is one of the hypotheses, and or drink drugs are believed to be a factor.)
- Ensure other children and members of household are treated as potential witnesses. Check on welfare, conduct risk assessment, and determine if any immediate protection measures or medical examinations are required for them.
- Establish if there are any potential key/significant witnesses (if young in age may be vulnerable) and make appropriate interview arrangements.
- Establish what the sequence of events was leading up to the death.
- Determine what personnel requirements and specialist training/experience is required for resources likely to be required.
- Determine what CSI/CSM and photographers/video required for 'scene' examination and recording (good practice in every case).
- Inform coroner of the death and brief on investigative intentions.
- Assess the risks to staff and the investigation (welfare, investigative barriers, etc).
- Make early contact with the paediatrician and agree parameters for the fast joint response phase (as per 'Working Together' report).
- If required consider arrangements for joint visit to 'death scene' (within first 24 hours) but not to be unduly delayed (potential loss of evidence).
- Assess the circumstances of the death, any unusual facts, behaviour, or responses and develop investigative strategies deploying staff to explore all reasonable lines of enquiry.

- Determine whether forensic or standard post mortem required and co-ordinate paediatric post-mortem examination with a paediatric pathologist or pathologist with some paediatric expertise.
- Liaise with local policing commander to complete community impact assessment.
- Work together in a multi-agency investigation and share information wherever possible.

Appendix B
Action Management System

INCIDENT.. **DATE**.. **Page 1**

No	Source	Action Details	HP Y/N	Officers Allocated	Remarks
1.	**Inc. Log**	**Obtain copy of control room incident log**			
2.	**Log**	**TI (TIE) person making initial report** **(obtain 1st account/decide method of interview)**			
3.	**Log**	**TI (TIE) person finding body** **(1st account/decide method of interview)**			
4.	**Log**	**Identify 1st officer attending** **(obtain notes/debrief/method of interview)**			
5.	**Log**	**Identify 2nd officer attending.** **(obtain notes/debrief/method of interview)**			
6.	**Log**	**Arrange scene (1) security** **(instructions re cordon, scene log/notes/debrief)**			

Page 2

No	Source	Action Details	HP Y/N	Officers Allocated	Remarks
7.	Inc. Log	**TI 1st paramedic attending scene (first account/method of interview/footwear check)**			
8.	Log	**TI 2nd paramedic attending scene (first account/method of interview/footwear check)**			
9.	Log	**Identify crime scene investigator/manager (crime scene strategy)**			
10.	Log	**Inform coroner**			
11.	SIO	**Request forensic pathologist**			
12.	SIO	**Initial H-2-H and witness identification (set parameters/obtain notes/debrief)**			
13.	SIO	**Conduct initial CCTV trawl & seize/secure recordings (parameters/obtain notes/debrief/ check accuracy of date/time)**			

Page 3

No	Source	Action Details	HP Y/N	Officers Allocated	Remarks
14.	**SIO**	**Research background of victim**			
15.	**SIO**	**Conduct research and background checks in relation to location of scene (1)**			
16.	**SIO**	**Search all systems for any linked/relevant incident logs or crime reports (set parameters)**			
17.	**SIO**	**Appoint/deploy Family Liaison Officer(s) (brief/risk assessment)**			
18.	**SIO**	**Debrief all staff engaged in initial response before retiring from duty (obtain notes/documents/exhibits)**			
19.	**SIO**	**Liaise with local BCU/OCU commander and complete community impact assessment**			
20.	**SIO**	**Prepare initial media release/holding statement (contact Media Liaison Officer)**			

Continuation sheet

No	Source	Action Details	HP Y/N	Officers Allocated	Remarks

Appendix C
Missing Person Searches

This is included as a quick reference guide for SIOs who may be faced with high-risk missing person enquiries.

There are three categories of 'missing person' in terms of search considerations:

1. **Lost or injured person:** a person who is temporarily disorientated or incapacitated through injury, who will proactively help those searching for them. This typically relates to small children in urban areas (shopping centres) and adults in remote rural locations (national parks).
2. **Voluntary missing person:** a person who has control over their own actions but has decided on a particular course of action, eg wishes to leave home or commit suicide. These people will not aid any searches for them and may actively conceal their movements and current whereabouts.
3. **Missing person under the influence of a third party:** this relates to someone who has gone missing against their will, eg abduction or murder victim.

Missing person search policy

It is recognized best practice for all physical searches for missing persons to be under the management of a PolSA-trained officer: such searches are in two phases and must be supported by scenario-based searching

Phase one—first responder actions

Here the key resource is likely to be a patrol officer or PCSO who will have perhaps benefited from basic search training. The search scenario here is to be proactive and search in a 'rescue and recovery' mode. If the missing person has been categorized as high risk and there is a time critical element to that risk then first responder resources should be deployed at any premises the person was last seen and conduct an 'initial visual search' by opening all doors accessing all rooms, cupboards, and voids.

If the missing person was undertaking a journey, for example from school to home then a search of the school, the route, and the home address would be required. These searches are most likely to discover someone who is lost, injured, or deceased in a highly visible location. These searches are less likely to discover a person if they have been a victim of crime and have been concealed or if they have gone missing to avoid police contact or to self-harm themselves. In first responder searching it is accepted that they are unlikely to benefit from high levels of resources nor be searches of high assurance. Although record-keeping of these searches may be poor it is as important what was not searched as capturing what was, eg a first responder search for a small child lost in a local park DID NOT search the boating lake and thus generating a possible search action for phase two searching.

Phase two searches

If phase one first responder searches are unsuccessful, conduct a fully managed search, comprising intelligence-led, scenario-based systematic searches of all likely areas based on missing person's background and characteristics using intermediate search trained officers (also known as PST). These searches are suitable for persons that may have been victims of crime or are thought to be concealed in some way.

High-risk missing persons

A high-risk missing person is defined as follows:

The risk posed is immediate and there are substantial grounds for believing that the subject is in danger through their own vulnerability, or may have been a victim of a serious crime, or the risk posed is immediate and there are substantial grounds for believing that the public is in danger.

In any incident involving a high-risk missing person, the following actions should be considered:

1. Immediate deployment of police resources.
2. Initial investigation and assessment should produce some initial lines of enquiry.
3. Should lead to the appointment of an SIO.
4. An FLO should be deployed quickly.
5. There should be an early press/media strategy—this should request where appropriate that people search their own properties and remain on them to provide access for police search

teams, this tactic has the dual benefit of engaging with the local community whilst preventing large numbers of the public gathering to search open areas that would require extensive police marshalling and possible crime scene contamination.

Full 'managed' search for missing persons

This type of search is in-depth and conducted under the direct supervision of PolSA. Close liaison should be maintained between the SIO and PolSA, to develop strategies that are co-ordinated and complementary. The search should take place throughout day and night whilst the missing person is believed to be alive after which only daylight searching should be considered as night searching provides very low search assurance,

A detailed written search scenario should be agreed with clear objectives which may include:

- Person v Body (Rescue v Recovery)
- Evidence—clothing, property, weapons
- Physical clues (struggle, accidental)
- Intelligence—suicide notes, bank details.

The search scenario should be written as a statement of intent, eg 'to search area X for the whole alive or deceased non-concealed presence of . . .'. This enables clarity on what is expected to be detected in any given search area and should the scenario of disappearance change then a new search scenario to re-search an area can be justified, eg 'to search area X for the deceased dismembered sub-surface concealed remains of ...'. The search scenario will also aid in selecting the most appropriate resources to use.

The following information should be considered when setting search parameters:

- Criminal—CATCHEM database
- Lost person behavioural statistics
- Home address details
- Place last seen (PLS) information
- Last known position (LKP)
- Information/intelligence development.

The following is a list of specialist resources that may be available to assist in a full managed search:

- Licensed PolSAs
- Police Search Team PST

- Trackers
- HOSDB (Home Office Scientific Development Branch) geophysical technicians
- Council environment workforce with strimmers and ground clearing machinery
- Height access and confined space search teams
- Dogs—scent trailing, blood, firearm, explosive, drugs
- Air support unit equipped with thermal imaging technology
- Mountain rescue teams under the direction of a PolSA
- Underwater search teams and marine units including coastguard and inshore life boats
- Specialist military search teams from the Royal Engineers 58 Squadron through the MACP protocol.

Appendix D
Communications Data Matrix

Incident ....

Date ....

Number etc	Subject	Attribution	Objective	Type of request	Dates	Comments

Name of person completing ....

Sheet No ....

Appendix E

5 x 5 x 5 Intelligence Form

Revised 1st July 2003
SELECT GPMS MARKER

NATIONAL INTELLIGENCE REPORT

ORGANISATION and OFFICER		DATE/TIME OF REPORT	
INTEL SOURCE or INTEL REF N° (I.S.R.)		REPORT U.R.N.	

SOURCE EVALUATION	A Always Reliable	B Mostly Reliable	C Sometimes Reliable	D Unreliable	E Untested Source
INTELLIGENCE EVALUATION	1 Known to be true without reservation	2 Known personally to the source but not to the officer	3 Not known personally to the source, but corroborated	4 Cannot be judged	5 Suspected to be false

	PERMISSIONS			RESTRICTIONS	
HANDLING CODE To be completed at time of entry into an intelligence system and reviewed on dissemination	1 May be disseminated to other law enforcement and prosecuting agencies, including law enforcement within the EEA, and EU compatible (No Code or Conditions)	2 May be disseminated to UK non prosecuting parties (Code 3.7 conditions apply)	3 May be disseminated to non EEA law enforcement agencies (Code 4.7 and/or conditions apply, specify below)	4 Only disseminate within originating agency/force. Specify internal recipient(s)	5 Disseminated Intelligence Receiving agency to observe conditions as specified below

REPORT

SUBJECT	??? _____ : DoB : NIB				
FLAGGED? ??? : Where Flagged ???		EVALUATION			
OPERATION NAME/NUMBER	NIM Level ???	S	I	H	

PUBLIC INTEREST IMMUNITY SHOULD BE SOUGHT: ???

DISSEMINATION TO:
(Is the handling code correct? If there are conditions on the receiving agency's use of the material, assign the relevant code.)
RISK ASSESSMENT FORM C COMPLETED ? ???
Record location of Form C (When Completed)
Handling Codes 2, 3 or 5? Conditions apply? ???:
???
DETAILED HANDLING CONDITIONS

Time and date conditions agreed between originator and recipient (if applicable).

Appendix F

All Body Diagrams

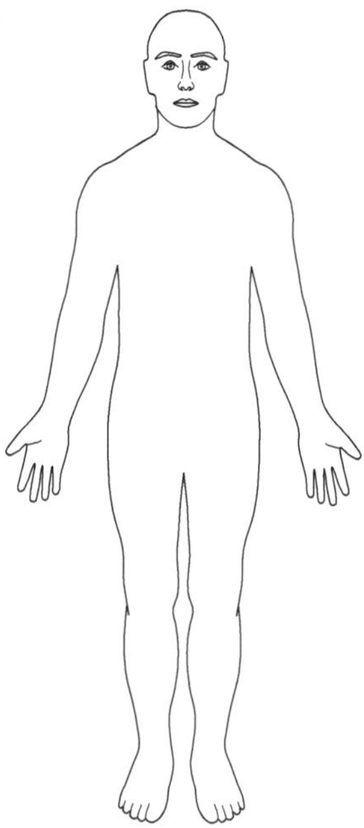

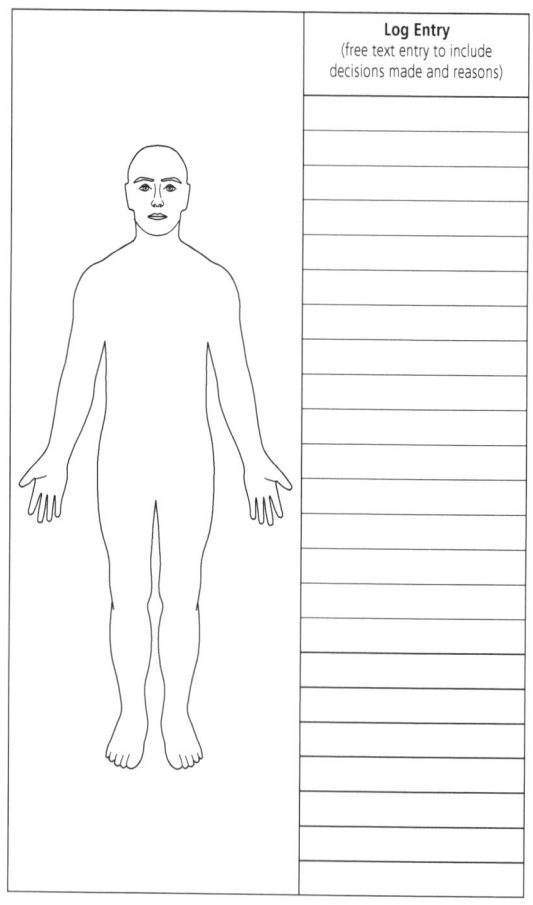

Log Entry
(free text entry to include decisions made and reasons)

Additonal notes:

Notes by: Date:

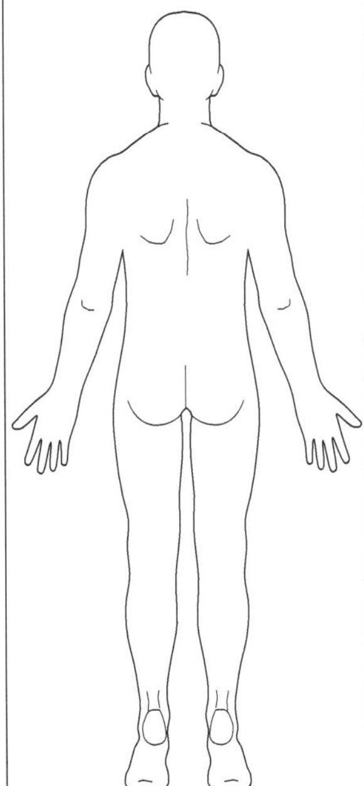

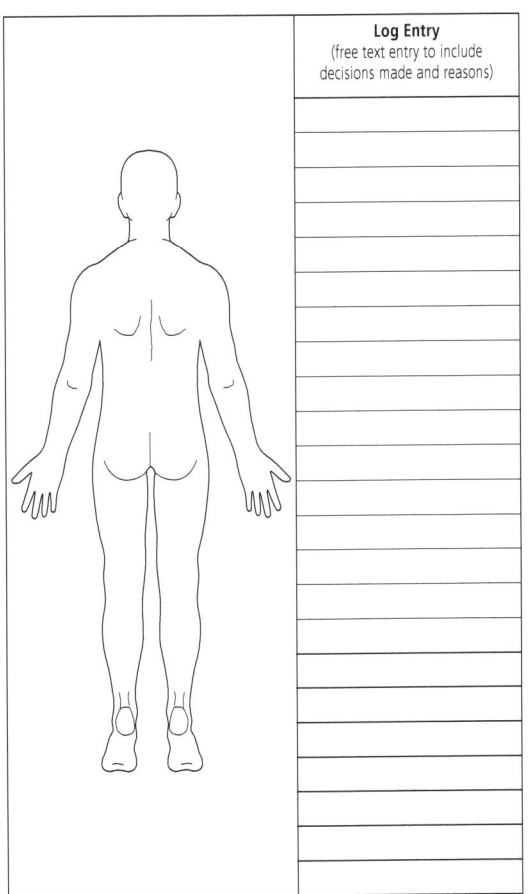

Log Entry (free text entry to include decisions made and reasons)

Additonal notes:

Notes by: Date:

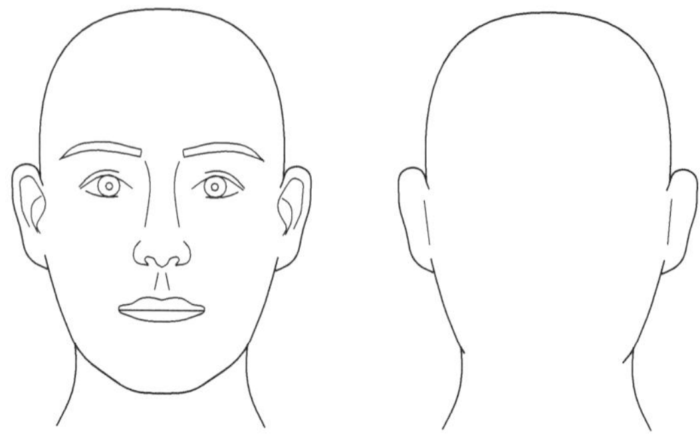

Log entry

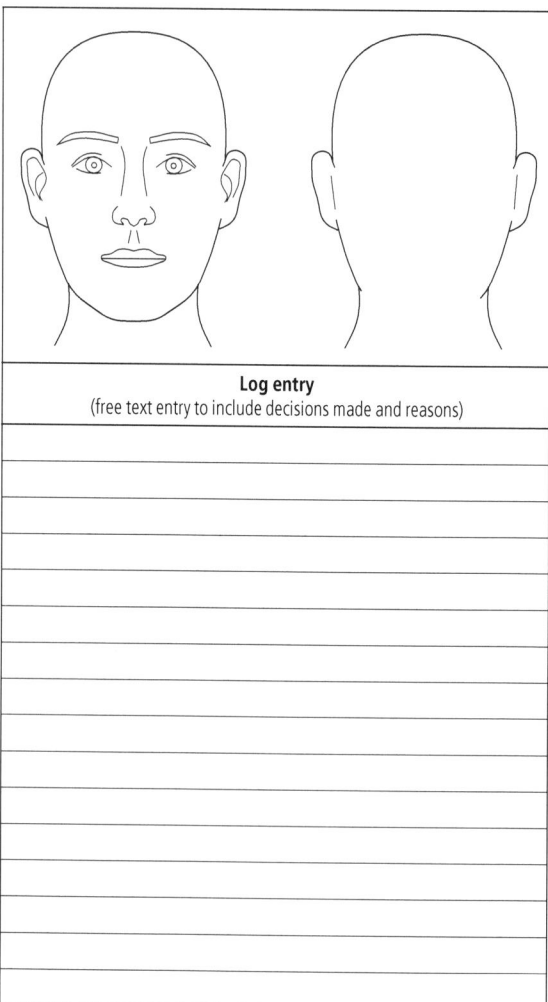

(free text entry to include decisions made and reasons)

Appendix G

Thoracic and Abdominal Organs

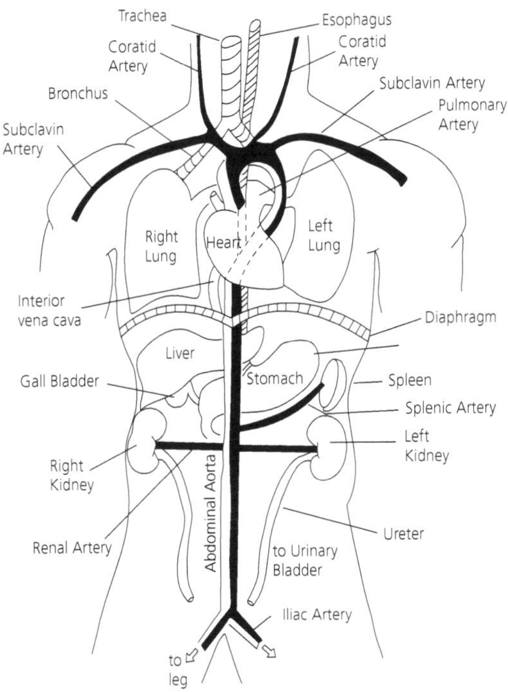

Appendix H

Skeleton Diagram

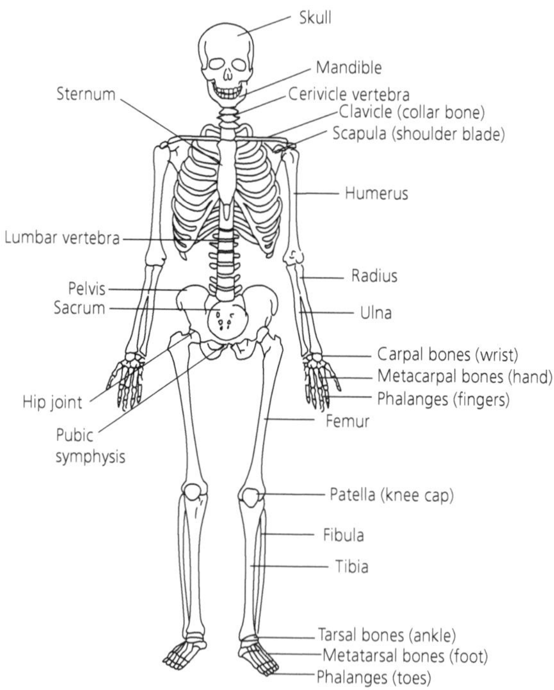

Skull
Mandible
Sternum
Cerivicle vertebra
Clavicle (collar bone)
Scapula (shoulder blade)
Humerus
Lumbar vertebra
Radius
Pelvis
Sacrum
Ulna
Carpal bones (wrist)
Metacarpal bones (hand)
Phalanges (fingers)
Hip joint
Femur
Pubic symphysis
Patella (knee cap)
Fibula
Tibia
Tarsal bones (ankle)
Metatarsal bones (foot)
Phalanges (toes)

Index

3142820R20294

Printed in Great Britain
by Amazon.co.uk, Ltd.,
Marston Gate.